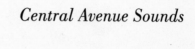

Central Avenue Sounds

ROTH FAMILY FOUNDATION

Music in America Imprint

Michael P. Roth

and Sukey Garcetti

have endowed this

imprint to honor the

memory of their parents,

Julia and Harry Roth,

whose deep love of music

they wish to share

with others.

CENTRAL AVENUE SOUNDS

Jazz in Los Angeles

Edited by

Clora Bryant

Buddy Collette

William Green

Steven Isoardi

Jack Kelson

Horace Tapscott

Gerald Wilson

and

Marl Young

Central Avenue Sounds Editorial Committee

University of California Press   Berkeley   Los Angeles   London

ADA-0100

The publisher gratefully acknowledges
the contribution toward the publication of
this book provided by Sukey and Gil Garcetti,
Michael Roth, and the Roth Family
Foundation.

ML
3508
.8
.L7
C 46
1998

010122 /0

University of California Press
Berkeley and Los Angeles, California

University of California Press, Ltd.
London, England

All oral history interviews in this book are
used with the permission of the UCLA Oral
History Program.

Library of Congress Cataloging-in-Publication
Data,

Central Avenue sounds : jazz in Los Angeles /
    edited by the Central Avenue Sounds
    Editorial Committee, Clora Bryant . . .
    [et al.].
        p.   cm.
        Includes bibliographical references (p.)
    and index.
        ISBN 0-520-21189-8 (cloth : alk. paper)
        1. Jazz—California—Los Angeles—
    History and criticism.   2. Jazz musicians—
    California—Los Angeles—Interviews.
    3. Central Avenue (Los Angeles, Calif.)
    I. Bryant, Clora, 1927– .
    ML3508.8.L7C46   1998
    781.65' 09794' 94—DC21   97-2560

Printed in the United States of America
9 8 7 6 5 4 3 2 1

To all those, in the past, who made
Central Avenue what it was,
and to all the readers, in the future,
who will keep alive the celebration of the
unique glory that Central Avenue is!

Contents

Photographs follow p. 260
Acknowledgments / ix
Foreword by Steven Isoardi / xv
Maps of Central Avenue area / xxv
Introduction: The Formation of
   Los Angeles's Black Community / 1

Part One: The Emergence of Central Avenue / 15

Marshal Royal / 22
Lee Young / 51
Fletcher Smith / 74

Part Two: The Watts Scene / 89

Coney Woodman / 94
William "Brother" Woodman, Jr. / 103
Britt Woodman / 114
Buddy Collette / 134
David Bryant / 164
Cecil "Big Jay" McNeely / 179

Part Three: The Eastside at High Tide / 195

Jack Kelson / 203
William Douglass / 233
Melba Liston / 255
Art Farmer / 261
Horace Tapscott / 282

Part Four: Drawn by Central's Magic — New Faces / 305

Gerald Wiggins / 311
Gerald Wilson / 324
Clora Bryant / 342
William Green / 369
Marl Young / 381
Conclusion / 401

Notes / 407
Bibliography / 415
Index / 421

Acknowledgments

From its inception this project has benefited from the support of a variety of talented people.

The UCLA Oral History Program initiated the project from which this book is drawn and has been a continuing source of inspiration and encouragement. Many thanks to its director, Dale Treleven, and the program's skilled organizer, Alva Moore Stevenson; to editor (and fine percussionist!) Alex Cline, who has labored mightily over the Central Avenue transcripts, and to the many other editors and transcribers in the program for their diligent and vital contributions. The support of Charlotte Brown of the UCLA Library's Department of Special Collections was instrumental in bringing this project to a successful conclusion. Additional thanks to Lucille Ostrow, whose financial support to the Oral History Program was essential to the completion of several key interviews.

Many dedicated and excellent readers reviewed all or parts of the manuscript and helped us create a more readable and accurate book. Our thanks go to Art Davis, Cheryl Keyes, Floyd Levin, Mimi Melnick, Mickey Morgan, Mike O'Daniel, Phil Pastras, Burton Peretti, and Lynn Wiggins.

Valuable research assistance at various stages of this project was provided by the staff at *CODA* magazine, Carolyn Kozo Cole at the Los Angeles Public Library, Steve Fry at UCLA's Music Library, Dan Morgan at Harvard University, Paul Oliverio at Jefferson High School, and Stan Rosen at USC. Jacqueline DjeDje, Eddie Meadows, Michael Bakan, and Ralph Eastman graciously gave us access to the manuscript of *California*

Soul: Music of African Americans in the West (University of California Press, in press).

The staff at the University of California Press has been fantastic. Thanks especially to associate director Lynne Withey, Doris Kretschmer, Suzanne Samuel, Jean McAneny, Amy Einsohn, Nola Burger, Fran Mitchell, Lillian Robyn, and their colleagues for their encouragement, enthusiastic support, and professional skills.

The index was compiled by Mimi Melnick, author and jazz enthusiast, and we offer her our profound thanks.

Our editorial committee originally involved eight people, but during 1996 we lost Bill Green. We miss Bill and honor his memory for his contributions to the history of Central Avenue.

Clora Bryant

My first and biggest thanks and praises go to the creator of us all, God, the almighty, because he gave me the opportunity to continue my life after a major heart operation in April 1996.

I want to thank my father, the late Charles Bryant, for his love, his encouragement, and his free music spirit. These three gifts have seen me through my lifetime. Next, I thank my older brother, Fred Bryant, for his generosity in leaving his trumpet to me, without which I could not have started my "jazz music quest" in 1945 on Central Avenue. My brother, Mel Bryant, is due my thanks because he was the one who chaperoned me on my first stroll down Central Avenue. He really started it all for me.

In 1979, when I returned to UCLA after an absence of thirty-three years, I took a class with a beautiful lady, Dr. Beverly Robinson. She changed my life by making me realize that you can't just play your jazz music, you have to know where it came from, who created it, and whose backs you're walking on. And that has made me aware of the importance of my having been a part of the Central Avenue scene.

A "whole big bunch" of thanks go out to my four children: Charles and April Stone, and Kevin and Darrin Milton. And to my grandchildren— Charles Jr., Sherry, and Gina Stone; Christina Pearson; Jasmine Milton; Marisa Grant, and Darrin Jr. and Selena Milton—and my great-grandson, Vincent Vasquez. Without them my life would have been naught. They've kept my feet on the ground and my head in the realm of the stars.

A great big thank you for Steve, who beckoned me to sit for an interview at a time when I needed that recognition. The interview led to my becoming a part of the editorial committee for this book, and I must say never once did you gentlemen make me feel intimidated by the fact that I was the only female among seven males. This thanks is also expressed to Dale Treleven, the director of us all.

Lastly, I want to thank all of the young and old curious Central Avenue jazz history–seeking readers. You are about to take an enlightening stroll down memory lane and share a few memories with some of the jazz musicians who were on that fantastic avenue. As you read the story of their lives, you'll behold a glorious and swinging world of music history that lived and thrived in the City of Angels on the street called Central Avenue.

Buddy Collette

I would like to thank Steve Isoardi, Dale Treleven, and all of the musician-interviewees who spent so much time in researching and telling their stories for this wonderful project. And a special thanks to Lucille Ostrow and many of the dedicated readers who helped to make this book possible. Here's to the many musicians from Central Avenue and the West Coast who inspired us to tell these stories that belong to all.

Steven Isoardi

I've been very fortunate in receiving unstinting support from many people and want to offer heartfelt thanks.

To the memory of my father, Peter, whose spirit is in much of my interviewing, and the memory of Bill Green, my inspiring saxophone teacher, who first told me of Central Avenue.

To my family—mother Norma, brothers Gary and Rob, sister Diane, brother-in-law Bob Dorricott Jr., niece Carolyn, and nephew Peter—for putting up with my Central Avenue obsession during those all too brief periods we could be together.

To the interviewees and their families for taking me into their homes and confidences, and sharing their lives. To meet my heroes in this manner has been the experience of a lifetime, and I now feel as if I have another extended family of aunts and uncles.

To Dale Treleven for so strongly believing in this project, making it possible, being a friend, and guiding me these many years.

To Mickey Morgan, my friend and colleague at the Oakwood School, for his incredible labors over the manuscript, for sharing his wisdom, and for his friendship.

To the wonderful students at the Oakwood School and Antioch University, especially those in my oral history and history of jazz courses, who have fueled my fires, and, often unawares, reaffirmed for me how important this work is.

Jack Kelson

This wonderful story could not have been told in such a delightful fashion without the literary skills, pure head, and warm heart of Steven Isoardi. To each member of the editorial committee: Thank you for demonstrating, at all of our meetings, what it means to be involved in a labor of love. A special note of gratitude for the friendship of William Green, which began in 1947 in Kansas City. William's life is an example of generosity and commitment to the highest standards of professionalism.

Finally, with an infinitude of gratitude, I acknowledge all of those people who—from the beginning and over the years, just by setting foot on Central Avenue—have made their unique and priceless contributions to the glory that *is* Central Avenue. It took, and takes, contributions from *all* of us in every arena of activity (art, business, communications, education, government, industry, law, medicine, music, religion, science) to make the glory of Central Avenue what it *is*.

Horace Tapscott

Since 1963 the UGMAA (Union of God's Musicians and Artists Ascension) Foundation has strived to contribute and preserve the music and art that comes from African American communities around the nation. Today, because of those efforts, the community is more aware of its culture and of its contribution throughout the world. And because of the

UCLA Oral History project, the Central Avenue scene will be forever accessible and available to readers everywhere.

I wish to thank all those who came to "Every Last Sunday" concerts at Immanuel Church, South Park, Widney High School, Watts Coffee House, and, of course, the "Flatbed truck." Thanks to Mary Lou, Cecilia, Robbie Mae, my children, my lifetime partners, and my many mentors—Dr. Samuel Browne, Gerald Wilson, Red Callender, Art Tatum, John Anderson, Buddy Collette, Lloyd Reese—thank you all for the "magic." To Steven Isoardi—Bright Moments, Keeper of the Flame.

Gerald Wilson

I feel deeply honored being a part of this great project and I thank all of those involved in its production.

A special thanks to Steve Isoardi and Buddy Collette for giving me the opportunity to share my Central Avenue experiences. Thanks to Clora Bryant, Benny Carter, Jack Kelso, Melba Liston, Horace Tapscott, Lee Young, and Marl Young.

Thanks to the owners and managers of the Central Avenue jazz establishments: Curtis Mosby, Sr., Curtis Mosby, Jr., Esvan Mosby, and Gertrude Gibson of the Club Alabam; Elihu "Blackdot" McGhee and Hal Stanley of the Downbeat Club; the kind people of the Lincoln Theatre and the Elks Auditorium; Joe Morris of the Plantation Club, where my band played with Billie Holiday; and, across town, Mr. Shepp and Ben Waller of Shepp's Playhouse.

To those dear friends and colleagues who are not with us, but whose stars still shine bright: Jimmie Lunceford, who first brought me to Los Angeles in 1940 as a member of his band. To Les Hite, Duke Ellington, and Count Basie, among others, who gave me many opportunities to write and play trumpet with their bands, and to Phil Moore and George "Red" Callender.

A very special thanks to all of the members of these bands and to those I may have forgotten to mention in my part of the book.

A warm thanks to former mayor Tom Bradley and the city and county of Los Angeles and the state of California, a place I've chosen to call home for over fifty years.

Last, but certainly not least, a loving thank you to my wife, Josefina, who shared those Central Avenue days, my three daughters—Jeri, Teri, and Nancy Jo—my son Anthony and all of my family, whose love and support have made it possible for me to be a part of this endeavor.

Marl Young

I am proud to be part of the UCLA Oral History Program project and part of this book. To be included in the group of illustrious musicians selected by one of the world's great universities (and my alma mater)—this honor is indeed a high point in my life.

Note: This book is based substantially on a series of interviews conducted by the UCLA Oral History Program. All the Oral History interviews are copyrighted by the Regents of the University of California, on behalf of the UCLA Oral History Program, Department of Special Collections University Research Library, UCLA Library, and are used with permission.

Foreword

Steven Isoardi

"On his good nights Charlie was genial and relaxed. His face was smoothed out, and he looked his twenty-five years. He would welcome young local jazzmen to his dressing room and, when Berg's closed, let them carry him off in their noisy old prewar jalopies to jam at one of the spots along Central Avenue."[1] I put down Ross Russell's biography of Charlie Parker, *Bird Lives!* describing Dizzy Gillespie and Bird's first West Coast appearance at Billy Berg's club in Hollywood in December 1945. Although I'd grown up in the San Francisco area, I had spent most of my adult life in Los Angeles, and I thought I knew something of the history of jazz. But I couldn't recall any discussions of, or references to, "spots along Central Avenue." What was on Central Avenue?

A casual drive down the Avenue merely heightened the mystery. The fires of 1965 had destroyed much of the physical evidence of the past. Aged, decaying buildings and rubble-filled lots, some surrounded with chain-link fencing, seemed to contain few secrets. It appeared a street that people would rather forget than remember, a terribly aged outpost of what had become known as South Central Los Angeles.

From the 1920s through the early 1950s, though, Central Avenue, extending from downtown Los Angeles south through Watts, was the economic and social center of the black population of a segregated Los Angeles. By day it served the community's shopping and business needs. At night it became a social and cultural mecca, attracting thousands of people from throughout southern California to its eateries, theaters, nightclubs, and music venues. This nonstop, vibrant club scene produced some of the major voices in jazz and rhythm and blues, and it was the only integrated setting in Los Angeles. All races and classes gathered in the clubs, from longshoremen and Pullman porters to Humphrey Bogart, Ava Gardner, and Howard Hughes.

Nightlife along Central Avenue meant music, floor shows, dancing, gambling, booze, and drugs. Great talents were uncovered, fortunes won and lost, and all types of stimulants found. In the early morning hours, if you were still on your feet, you could wander from club to club and catch jam sessions with Art Tatum, Lester Young, Nat Cole, Lionel Hampton, Charlie Parker, or younger artists, some still in their teens, like Dexter Gordon, Hampton Hawes, Art Pepper, Wardell Gray, and Charles Mingus. It was a performance center for black music that ranked with New Orleans, Chicago, Harlem, Kansas City, and Fifty-second Street in New York, and during this period some of the most important contributors to black music grew up around Central and in Watts.

During the Avenue's most exciting years, however, little attention was paid to the black community by the media, with the exception of the small black press. Perhaps once every decade an intrepid *Los Angeles Times* reporter would write a feature on the community, sometimes informative, but usually voicing stereotypes and prejudices. Routine stories of misdeeds and illegalities were the norm in the daily news coverage. By the 1980s—except for the dwindling number of people who participated in the Central Avenue scene, and a handful of scholars and black music enthusiasts—Central Avenue was just a downtown Los Angeles exit off the Santa Monica Freeway, a route few had much reason to take.

The appearance in 1986 of Lois Shelton's documentary film *Ernie Andrews: Blues for Central Avenue* called international attention to one of L.A.'s most important and least appreciated cultural contributions. The fifty-minute documentary shows what Los Angeles had, and lost when Central Avenue declined, poignantly illustrated through the career of jazz singer Ernie Andrews. For Shelton the tale did not come easily and possessed an element of mystery. From Andrews, Shelton learned of Central Avenue. If Andrews had been a surprising discovery, Central Avenue's musical history was a revelation, one that involved a great deal of original research. In preparing a review of the film, I interviewed Lois and asked about her source material: "When I started out I thought, well, I'll just go to all the libraries and get the files on Central Avenue and make this film. There *are* no files on Central Avenue." She could find no documentation—no live footage or photographs and few recollections of the Avenue. Back files of two black newspapers, the *California Eagle* and the *Los Angeles Sentinel,* offered information about the period, but Shelton relied primarily on the testimony and personal photos of a dwindling number of eyewitnesses.

The publication in 1990 of Walter Mosley's first novel, *Devil in a Blue Dress,* again called attention to Central Avenue in the late 1940s. Raised in Los Angeles during that time, Mosley offered a view of a vibrant community, but he did not give readers a sense of what was unique about the nightlife of Central Avenue. As a young child, Mosley probably would have been unaware of this activity, and as an adult would have found few resources to help him recreate the milieu.

Similar problems faced Gary Frutkoff, production designer for the 1995 film adaptation of Mosley's book. His search for photographs of Central Avenue exteriors in their prime yielded precious little. He had more success with everyday items, such as clothing and housing, courtesy of the Shades of L.A. photography collection at the Los Angeles Public Library, whose thousands of photographs documenting the city's ethnic communities included an important view of everyday life along Central Avenue. This valuable resource was amassed by Carolyn Kozo Cole and her staff at the Historic Photograph Collection of the Los Angeles Public Library. When Cole had been appointed curator of the collection in 1990, she found appalling gaps: No groups were represented other than the more affluent sections of the white community of the greater Los Angeles area. She inaugurated the Shades of L.A. project to document the city's ethnic diversity, and by the mid-1990s the collection contained photographs from over two dozen different ethnic groups, some of which are reproduced in *Shades of L.A.: Pictures from Ethnic Family Albums.*[2]

Over the last few years a number of books have appeared, supplying pieces of the Avenue's history. Recent memoirs by Lionel Hampton, Red Callender, and Roy Porter and earlier efforts by Charles Mingus, Hampton Hawes, Art Pepper, and Johnny Otis provide a glimpse into the music scene on Central from the mid-1920s through the early 1950s. Two recent books, one by a former music teacher, Bette Cox, and another by media personality and producer Tom Reed, both with roots in the Los Angeles black community, contain collections of photos and memorabilia. Several scholars offer brief studies in the opening chapters of two recent histories of jazz on the West Coast: The work of Ted Gioia and Robert Gordon nicely complements chapters on the earlier part of the century in books by Albert McCarthy and Frank Driggs. A recent collection of essays edited by Jacqueline DjeDje and Eddie Meadows includes a number of important pieces on black music in southern California.[3]

The UCLA Oral History Program's
Central Avenue Sounds Project

When Lois Shelton's film was released, I had just completed a doctorate in political science at UCLA and was studying saxophone in Los Angeles with Central Avenue alumnus Bill Green. As I diligently held long tones, Bill would occasionally offer glimpses into the Avenue's past, stories of memorable performances and late-night jams. With Bill's recollections in one ear and Lois's comments in the other, I decided to investigate Central Avenue's past, and oral history seemed the best approach to explore not only the history but also the motivations, values, worldviews, and insights of the artists and the community.

I sought guidance from the UCLA Oral History Program, one of the leading institutions in the field, which has developed a commitment to documenting the evolution of the black community of Los Angeles. Early in 1989 I met with Dale Treleven, the director of the program. During a lengthy Monday morning conversation, and after many cups of coffee, he proposed that I conduct the interviews through his office. A day later I agreed. The resources UCLA could bring to bear, the quality of its Oral History Program, and the thoroughness and respect with which they treated and preserved each interview—fully reproduced and indexed bound transcripts, as well as preservation of the original tapes— were deciding factors. It was a serious program and Dale was a very serious person. An oral history project of music as a defining cultural characteristic of L.A.'s Central Avenue deserved no less.

Under the rubric Central Avenue Sounds, we set out to document the rich history of secular black music in the Central Avenue community from the 1920s through the early 1950s. The in-depth life-history interviews with the individuals who had contributed to that scene were designed to begin with the interviewee's earliest memories, to move through the early 1950s and the Avenue's decline, and, in many cases, to wind through to the present. In this way we hoped to avoid a narrow thematic focus on clubs, styles, and players, and instead to explore music as an integral aspect of the community. Ernie Andrews is fond of saying there were "many avenues of the Avenue," and we set out to rediscover as many of these as possible. Always in our minds was the awareness of how poorly the history of Los Angeles, and the black community in particular, had been documented. Focusing primarily on music, we also hoped to fill out the life of the community by asking our interviewees to talk about the politics and economics of the black community, labor issues, race relations and racism in southern California, women in jazz, drugs, black artists in Hollywood, and Hollywood artists on Central Avenue.

Thus we did not ask the interviewees to respond to a fixed set of scripted questions. Instead, we worked from Ronald Grele's notion of the oral history interview as a "conversational narrative."

> Given the active participation of the historian-interviewer, even if that participation consists of only a series of gestures or grunts, and given the logical form imposed by all verbal communication, the interview can only be described as a conversational narrative: conversational because of the relationship of interviewer and interviewee, and narrative because of the form of exposition—the telling of a tale.
>
> These narratives, while some may be constructed as chronological tales of personal remembrances of events, are not autobiographies, biographies or memories. The recorded conversations of oral history . . . are joint activities, organized and informed by the historical perspectives of both participants.[4]

We set as our task encouraging the interviewees to share the freest, fullest narratives, told at their own pace and in their particular way of recalling. This approach reminded me of improvisation in jazz, a symmetry I found compelling and satisfying. We also wanted to avoid hearing the canned answers or accounts some of these artists might have given over the years to repetitious queries about their lives. For example, at my first session with Marl Young, he was clearly in journalistic-interview mode, offering quick answers and then sitting back and waiting for the next question. My response was simply to encourage him to keep talking. When I turned the tape recorder off for our first break, Marl sat back, stretched, and said, "Hey, this is great. We're just having a conversation." As a result, his chapter in this book contains an account of the struggle to eliminate segregation in the American Federation of Musicians that is in many ways more revealing than his earlier article on the topic.[5]

My outline of the major topics for the interviews included the political and economic life of the community, various aspects of the question of racism, and the drug scene, as well as a wide range of music-related themes. I gave a copy of the outline to the interviewees before our first taping session to jog their memories and to create a structure for our sessions. My pre-interview preparation centered on the back issues of the *California Eagle,* for years the only publication dedicated to L.A.'s black community. I also read histories, autobiographies, and jazz journals, viewed documentary films, and listened to numerous recordings.

With the assistance of Central Avenue alumni Bill Green and Buddy Collette, our list of potential interviewees grew rapidly, and we proceeded to prioritize our list based upon age, health, status, importance or significance of the individual's contribution, and, finally, current location and availability. As we are now some fifty years removed from Central Avenue's most vital years, there was a sense of urgency. However, despite our best intentions and efforts, there were misses because of deaths or serious illnesses. Samuel Browne, music teacher at Jefferson High School and a key figure throughout this era, died before our interview could take place. Two weeks after receiving a letter from Dexter Gordon's attorney inviting us to interview the saxophonist as soon as he recovered from a bout with pneumonia, I awoke to read in the *Los Angeles Times* of his passing. I still haven't recovered from that disappointment.

UCLA's Oral History Program then sent letters to the prospective interviewees, explaining the program and the Central Avenue Sounds project, and inviting them to participate. A positive response during a follow-up phone call resulted in a pre-interview, face-to-face meeting with each interviewee, Dale Treleven, and myself. The pre-interview meeting allowed us to meet, get acquainted without a tape recorder, and familiarize the interviewees with the project and with the mechanics of an oral history interview. In most cases we would set a date and location for our first taping session, usually at their homes, which would involve just the interviewees and myself.

After each interview the tapes were sent to UCLA to be mastered on archival-quality tape and then turned over to Oral History Program transcribers. Editors checked the draft transcript against the tape for accuracy, added punctuation and paragraphing, and flagged any items that required better identification (for example, full names for all persons mentioned). The transcript draft was then sent to the interviewee for clarification and approval. To each transcript we added a table of contents, index, biographical summary, and other information about the conduct of the interview. The final bound transcripts are available to researchers at the Department of Special Collections in UCLA's University Research Library and at UC Berkeley's Bancroft Library.

Since 1989, over thirty interviews have been recorded. The shortest fills two ninety-minute cassettes and totals about sixty transcript pages; the longest took four months to tape, fills sixteen ninety-minute cassettes, and totals almost eight hundred transcript pages. The initial focus was on black musicians, but over the last few years I have interviewed whites, Latinos, and even the former co-owner of an important independent blues/r&b record company. (For a complete list of interviewees, as of the end of 1996, see the bibliography.) The UCLA Oral History Program is committed to continuing this documentation of the rich history of a vital community.

A Book by Committee

When I first began thinking of the history of music on Central Avenue, I had in mind a rather traditional study of the evolution of jazz and r&b on the Avenue. Conducting the life-history interviews and later working with the editorial committee changed my mind. At a certain point in this project I began having the distinct feeling of being able to "see" Central Avenue on a swinging night—the clubs, the performers, the people became that real to me. Hearing the voices of people who had been part of the sounds of Central Avenue brought the spirit, the emotions, and the passions of the Avenue to life. What these oral histories offer, then, is neither history nor literature in the conventional understanding of those genres; rather, oral history contains elements of both but is essentially a different and unique genre that adds an important dimension for understanding our past.

During casual conversation at the end of my final session with "Brother" Woodman, an early interviewee, he suggested that we should find a way to make this material available to a larger audience. Other interviewees expressed the same sentiment, and I agreed. By 1994 a sufficient number of the transcripts had been completed to contemplate such an effort. With the UCLA library's encouragement, I decided the best way to proceed would be to send a letter to the first twenty or so interviewees asking whether they would like to participate in putting such a book together and if their interview could be used. Only the transcripts of those interviewees who responded positively to my query would be used. Even though copyright is held by the Regents of the University of California, this seemed the ethical approach.

All too often in oral history projects, collaboration between the interviewees and interviewer ends when the tape recorder is turned off. Oral histories that are later published seldom involve the interviewees in the editorial process, much less in the author's credit and royalties. I wanted this book to be different, to be a true reflection of what I had come to appreciate as the spirit of Central Avenue. And so I solicited volunteers from among the interviewees to serve on an editorial committee that would collectively make all decisions about the book.

Every few months the editorial committee gathered at Bill Green's studio or at Buddy Collette's home to review chapters, make editorial decisions, exchange news, and reminisce about days gone by. The editorial committee decided that each edited interview would constitute a chapter, so that each individual voice could be heard, rather than breaking the interviews into pieces and reorganizing the pieces around particular themes. My contribution was to provide this foreword, the introductions, and the conclusion, and to turn the transcripts into chapters, which the editorial committee read, debated, altered, and finally approved. The committee also decided that the interviewer and each interviewee represented in the book would be considered co-authors, among whom any royalties would be divided equally.

The process of making oral history research available to a large audience demands many editorial choices. Converting conversation into a verbatim transcript involves decisions about grammar, punctuation, and paragraph breaks, and converting a transcript into a chapter in a book entails cutting and reorganizing. Since the full transcripts are preserved and available to researchers, we decided to omit my questions, comments, and interjections from the chapters in this book and to restructure the transcripts with as little alteration of the text as possible into a series of prose narratives. .

Since some of the transcripts run hundreds of pages, hard choices had to be made. In narrowing our focus to Central Avenue through the early 1950s, we have put aside the interviewees' comments on subsequent years and the time spent by some outside of Los Angeles. To create a more coherent story, we also elected to reorganize, when appropriate, the flow of the interviews to provide a consistent, sequential written narrative, and we have provided commentary, usually summaries of interview segments, to supply continuity and context.

We decided to organize the book in four parts, based on geographic and generational criteria. Part 1 presents the recollections of musicians who were performing on Central Avenue by the late 1920s and early 1930s, artists who came of age in the pre-Depression United States. Part 2 focuses on musicians who spent their formative years in the Watts area during the 1930s and early 1940s; a distinct working-class community at the time, the area was unique and rich in artistic contributions. Part 3 portrays those artists emerging from the main Central Avenue community, then known as the Eastside, during the 1930s and 1940s. Finally, Part 4 profiles musicians who arrived in Los Angeles during the 1940s as adults, and who for the most part had already established careers in music.

Although the principal focus is music, this book is offered as more than a collection of jazz and r&b reminiscences. It also paints a social history of a community and its interaction with the surrounding dominant white society. While oral history cannot itself be definitive, these accounts represent an indispensable part of the foundation for an exploration of the history of Los Angeles and its black community. As Fletcher Smith told me at the end of our last taping session, "You got it from the horse's mouth." Now, so do you. Dig it.

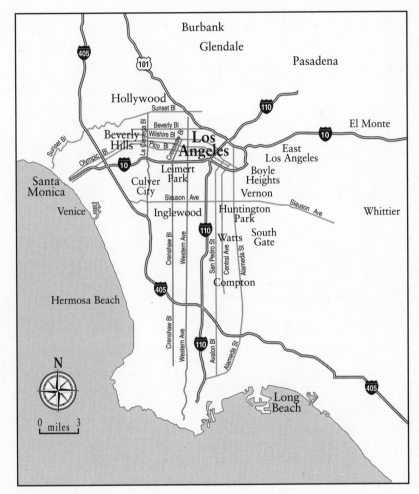

Greater Los Angeles

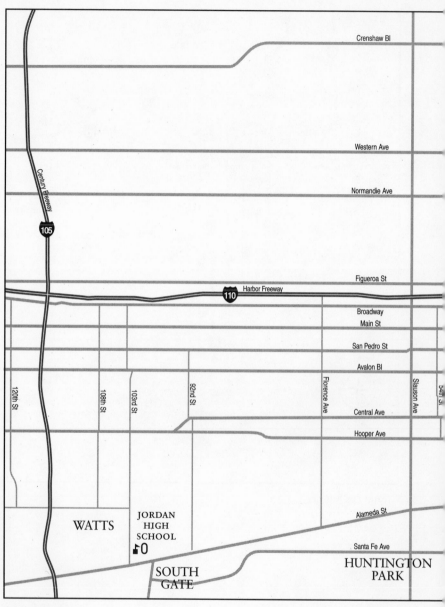

Crenshaw Bl

Western Ave

Normandie Ave

Century Freeway

105

Figueroa St

110 Harbor Freeway

Broadway
Main St

San Pedro St

Avalon Bl

Florence Ave

Slauson Ave

54th St

120th St

108th St

103rd St

92nd St

Central Ave

Hooper Ave

Alameda St

WATTS

JORDAN
HIGH
SCHOOL
↱0

Santa Fe Ave

HUNTINGTON
PARK

SOUTH
GATE

Central Avenue

The Formation of
Los Angeles's
Black Community

Although blacks from Spanish-dominated Mexico had played a prominent role in the settling of Los Angeles in 1781, up through the Civil War their numbers remained small. Sentiment was decidedly pro-Confederacy among the dominant white leadership, and during Reconstruction the California Legislature voted against the Fifteenth Amendment, which gave black males the right to vote. With the land boom of 1887–1890, fueled by railroad promotions during the previous decade, the black population increased to 1,258, or 2.5 percent of Los Angeles's population.[1] By 1900 approximately 2,000 blacks lived in Los Angeles, representing 2 percent of the population.[2]

Despite the pro-Confederacy sentiments during the Civil War and Reconstruction, attitudes on race changed rather dramatically over the next few decades. Los Angeles was one of the first cities in the United States to hire black firefighters and police. A photograph from about 1890 shows black officer Robert W. Stewart posing with other members of the Los Angeles police force.[3] Schools were also desegregated and a civil rights bill passed. "Negroes were welcomed patrons of many of the downtown establishments; they could receive service at any of the downtown restaurants and hotels. Testimonies indicate also that interracial contacts and friendships were the rule rather than the exception."[4] This lessening of racial antagonism was due in part to a change in the composition of white migrants into Los Angeles: "With most of the newcomers to Southern California being Republicans from the East and Middle West, Los Angeles by 1900 had outgrown most of its early hostility toward Negroes."[5] Still identified with Abraham Lincoln and the Emancipation Proclamation, the Republicans represented integration and political equality.

Yet racism flourished against other groups, which may have deflected hostility from the still small black population. "In an era when Chinese were being excluded from jobs and driven from cities, the small and relatively inconspicuous Negro population appears to have enjoyed a lessening of racial tension and a considerable degree of acceptance."[6] (In later years, the Japanese-American and Latino populations became the primary targets. As Arna Bontemps and Jack Conroy observed, "Perhaps the Japanese and the Mexicans are to be thanked. They drew off much of the racial hostility which otherwise might have been concentrated on the Negroes."[7] Hostility against these groups reached a culmination during World War II with the internment of Japanese-Americans and the Zoot Suit riots directed at the Latino population of Los Angeles.)

By 1900 the largest concentration of the black population was downtown, around First and Los Angeles Streets. The center of a small but growing black working class, the area also contained many black-owned businesses. Blacks as a group were emerging politically and economically. "Negroes were poor, they were scattered; there were no restrictions against them. However, as they accumulated property, a definite leadership developed; interest in civic affairs was evinced; and the Negro 'block' began to attract the attention of white politicians."[8]

Although certain areas, such as First and Los Angeles Streets, were developing distinct black neighborhoods, these were usually a matter of a few blocks, and even First Street did not have a uniform aspect. "East First Street had Japanese, Russian-Jewish and Negro businesses side by side, from Los Angeles Street to Central Avenue in what was then a busy workingman's thoroughfare."[9] The majority of the black population seems to have been dispersed throughout town. This is not to say that turn-of-the-century Los Angeles was an integrated city. Rather, blacks lived within the various wards or assembly districts in areas distinctly their own, usually "a single street within the community."[10] Other groups, especially the Japanese-American, American Indian, and substantial Chinese-American populations, were concentrated in fewer and more sharply defined communities.[11]

The Emergence of Central Avenue

Beginning around 1900, Los Angeles entered a period of growth that transformed southern California. During the first decade of the century the city's population increased by over 200 percent to approximately 320,000 people, of whom about 7,600 were black.[12] The growing black community pushed south of First and Los Angeles Streets, but the concentration remained heaviest downtown. "By 1906 the Negroes had established a large colony which was bounded on the south by Ninth Street, on the north by Fourth Street, and on the west by Maple Avenue."[13]

It was generally a prosperous time, and the West's promise of jobs, land, business opportunities, and a mild climate appealed to all sections of the nation's population. The move west was supported nationwide by a variety of publications and organizations, and black newspapers throughout the country extolled the benefits of living in southern California.[14] The growing economy of Los Angeles meant that jobs were to be had, and the availability of relatively cheap land and the possibility of home ownership appealed to many. Workers were also brought in from around the country as scabs whenever local workers went on strike. One such action by Mexican railroad workers in 1903 led Southern Pacific to hire other ethnic workers and import labor from elsewhere to break the strike. The railroad hired "several hundred Japanese employees and brought in 1,400 black employees from other states, particularly Texas, where the Southern Pacific Railway had many employees."[15]

Between 1910 and 1920 L.A.'s growing black population was increasingly confined to the Central Avenue area, and the corridor's southern boundary continued to expand. By the mid-teens the economic and social center of the community had moved from Ninth and Central to Twelfth and Central.[16] "The decision of a real estate dealer to open a hotel at Eleventh and Central seems to have triggered a large-scale exodus of whites after 1912 and a corresponding movement of blacks steadily southward, displacing the Jewish residents, although in most cases not displacing their ownership of businesses on the street."[17] By 1920 the black population of Los Angeles, increasingly confined to the Central Avenue corridor, had doubled again to 15,579, although this still represented under 3 percent of the total population.[18]

The fairly steady expansion of the main area of the black population south along Central Avenue involved numerous confrontations, with whites attempting to contain blacks within existing areas, and set in motion a white exodus. The earlier, more tolerant attitudes of late-nineteenth-century Los Angeles toward the black community gave way as the economy grew, the population expanded, and labor strife increased.

In 1902, for example, a black resident who moved outside the down-town area, south to Thirty-third and Hooper, was met by a hastily assembled mob. Long-time residents later referred to this incident as "the first open conflict between the races."[19] When one black homeowner attempted in 1914 to settle into a house near Eighteenth and Central Avenue, her white neighbors "broke into her home and removed everything she had, throwing her belongings on her front lawn. This act of hostility was reported in the local newspaper, and resulted in some 100 black women forming a brigade to protect the Johnson home during the emergency."[20]

At the same time, restrictive covenants in property deeds, which had been used prior to 1900, were becoming more widespread: "Members of white neighborhoods beyond Seventh Street began to place restrictions in their deeds, stating emphatically that Negroes, Japanese, Mexicans, Indians, and Chinese would be prohibited from buying the land that the deeds covered."[21] These covenants were ruled illegal "or unenforceable by court action" in the courts, but in 1919 the California Supreme Court overturned the lower court rulings and held the restrictive covenants to be legal—a judgment that would stand until after World War II. As a result, "residential exclusion and eviction became much more common and effective than it had been before 1920."[22]

Restrictions were also used at the block level. Homeowners residing on a particular street could form an association based on the principle of not selling their properties to blacks.[23] These associations grew in number during the post–World War I period and into the 1920s. The result was a series of black "islands":

> White exodus and black concentration in the Central Avenue area continued and by 1920 most blacks were living in one physical ghetto stretching approximately thirty blocks down Central Avenue and several blocks east to the railroad tracks, or in a few detached islands, especially on West Jefferson, Temple Street, and just south of the city in Watts. Each of these communities was separated from the Central Avenue ghetto by blocks of solid white resistance.[24]

Jazz Comes to Los Angeles

Nightclubs and jazz came early to Central Avenue—to the dismay of the black professional and business class, which had decidedly conservative musical tastes.[25] A retrospective in the *California Eagle,* then the only black newspaper, detailed some of this emerging nightlife:

> Back in 1908 a cabaret was running at 9th and San Pedro called "Mrs. Dawson's." "The Waldorf," run by a Jap was at 4th and Gladys, the "Triangle" or "Santa Fe" at 3rd and Traction, "The Golden West" was at 3rd street opposite Rev. Hill's church. . . . the Douglas Club, located in the 600 block on Central avenue almost opposite the Union Station was owned by George Henderson.[26]

And it was in 1908 that the new music of New Orleans came to Los Angeles when a group of musicians from that city, led by bassist Bill Johnson, played for a month at the Red Feather Tavern.[27] Over the next few years, several New Orleans musicians settled in Los Angeles, including cornetist Ernest Coycault and drummer Oliver "Dink" Johnson, performing regularly under a variety of names. When needed, more musicians were sent for, including Freddie Keppard and George Baquet. In spring 1914 they organized in Los Angeles as the Original Creole Band and toured the country as a vaudeville act spreading the gospel of New Orleans jazz, the first significant group to do so.[28] In Michael Bakan's assessment, "Over the next four years, the Creole Band was a fixture on the American vaudeville circuit, and introduced the sounds of New Orleans jazz to many parts of the nation even before the advent of jazz recordings in 1917 or the diaspora of New Orleans jazzmen to Chicago and elsewhere in the wake of Storyville's demise."[29]

Pianist and composer Jelly Roll Morton may have visited Los Angeles as early as 1907, but was certainly a fixture from 1917 to 1922.[30] He opened to a full house at the Cadillac Cafe, on Central Avenue between Fifth and Sixth Streets, and soon was the toast of the town, at least by his reckoning: "Then the movie-star trade began, and we didn't have anything but movie stars at the Cadillac Cafe long as I stayed there."[31] Singer Ada "Bricktop" Smith, then twenty-two years old, arrived shortly after Jelly and later performed with him at Murray's, another important venue. Although she'd met him in Chicago, it was in Los Angeles she got to know him: "He was still trying to figure out what to do with his life. He couldn't decide whether to be a pimp or a piano player. I told him to be both."[32] Jelly followed her advice; while continually performing up and down Central Avenue, he apparently "made most of his money from 'the Pacific Coast Line,' a group of girls he pimped for."[33]

Even with this early influx of New Orleans talent, it took Central Avenue musicians a while to master the new approach to playing music, perhaps due to the conservative tastes of much of the community and the emphasis on European music and training. Despite a number of predecessors from New Orleans, Jelly still had to teach local musicians his style.

> The Cadillac was again in bloom. Of course, the musicians couldn't play the tunes we could in New Orleans; they didn't have the ability. So we had to play what we could—"The Russian Rag," "Black and White," "Maple Leaf Rag," "Liza Jane" (a little comedy song, the whole Coast went for that), "Daddy Dear," "I'm Crying for You," "Melancholy Baby"—these were quite prominent in 1917, if I don't get the years mixed up. Then I wrote a tune and called it "Cadillac Rag" that we used to do with a singer.[34]

Other bands soon followed the New Orleans–led aggregations. The Black and Tan Orchestra had arrived in southern California from Texas by December 1915. A few years later, it had turned into a jazz ensemble, led by trombonist Harry Southard and featuring a young Ohio-born saxophonist, Paul Howard, as well as Leon Herriford and Coycault.[35] Within a decade Howard and Herriford became two of the most important black bandleaders in Los Angeles.

When blacks emigrated to California from the South during World War I, musicians followed. With the closing of New Orleans's bawdy redlight district, Storyville, in 1917 and of San Francisco's Barbary Coast by 1921, more jazz musicians made their way to Los Angeles. The sheer number and quality of incoming musicians, some settling, others passing through on tours, transformed the musical landscape of black Los Angeles.[36] Buddy Petit, Frank Dusen, and Wade Whaley arrived from New Orleans to play with Jelly.[37] Kid Ory, one of the most prominent musicians and bandleaders in New Orleans, arrived in 1919, and quickly sent for Papa Mutt Carey to join him in Kid Ory's Original Creole Jazz Band. "They opened at the Cadillac Cafe on Central Avenue with clarinetist Wade Whaley, pianist Manuel Manetta, and drummer Alfred Williams—all from New Orleans. The Cadillac job lasted almost a year."[38] The sound of Papa Mutt's horn, especially, made a tremendous impact on Los Angeles audiences. "Patrons unaccustomed to hearing the pure New Orleans trumpet sounds, were astounded by the range of Mutt's playing and his swinging clarity." [39] Ed "Montudi(e)" Garland, Pops Foster, and later Joe Darensbourg, with strong New Orleans roots, also came west. King Oliver's Creole Jazz Band performed along the West Coast in an extended tour before returning to Chicago in the spring of 1922, and "at one point Oliver reputedly joined Jelly Roll Morton's ten-piece big band at the Grand Hotel in Los Angeles." [40]

Migrations and Segregation in the 1920s

Between 1910 and 1920 L.A.'s black community doubled in size, and Central Avenue had become the center of black social life. Increasing population pressures pushed the boundaries of the community south. "By 1920 the Negroes had advanced as far south as Jefferson Street and had established a business center at Twenty-second Street and Central Avenue." [41] While the expanding white population fanned out through the Los Angeles basin, blacks were forced to move into the existing communities, particularly along Central Avenue.

> If the story of the Los Angeles ghetto before 1920 is one of enterprise and economic opportunities prevailing over racial hostility, segregation, and discrimination, the record of the succeeding decade is in many ways the reverse. . . . While whites built miles of residential tracts along the coast and into rural lands adjacent to the city, blacks were barred from such expansion and had to absorb the influx in their existing community or in older residential areas on its periphery. [42]

In addition to Central Avenue, there were four other major areas of black concentration in Los Angeles by 1920: Boyle Heights in East Los Angeles, the affluent Westside on Jefferson between Normandie and Western, the Temple Street settlement northwest of the downtown area between Alvarado and Hoover, and the Furlong Tract, a few blocks east of Central Avenue between Fifty-first and Fifty-fifth Streets. Each was surrounded by hostile white homeowners determined to contain the black population. For the most part they succeeded until the housing covenants were struck down after World War II. The exception was the Furlong Tract, which was absorbed into the Central Avenue community. [43]

During the 1920s approximately 2 million people migrated to California, and almost 1.3 million of them settled in Los Angeles County. [44] The number of blacks more than doubled to approximately 39,000, or 3.1 percent of L.A.'s population.[45] People of all ethnic and economic backgrounds were drawn by oil strikes and the burgeoning motion picture industry: "What the gold rush had been to Northern California, this real-estate-oil-and-motion-picture boom was to Southern California."[46]

While the black community enjoyed only a small fraction of the millions of dollars pouring into Los Angeles, it was enough, especially when contrasted with opportunities in most other parts of the country, to create an image of California as a land of opportunity. Given the oppressive conditions most had left, California's less overt forms of segregation seemed much more tolerable. "The wage rates of even menial jobs were high by southern standards, a janitor's position returning three or four times what many Negroes made in farming." Perhaps even more crucial was the opportunity for home ownership: "The most important ameliorating factor was the opportunity to buy land and houses at a low price either for personal use or for resale in the boom of urban expansion that prevailed through much of this period."[47]

The steady influx of people intensified the pattern of race relations that had developed after the turn of the century, with attitudes toward minorities, particularly Japanese Americans and blacks, changing for the worse as their populations increased. In addition to restrictive housing covenants and block restrictions, blacks also found themselves excluded from most public beaches and swimming pools, as well as dining areas throughout the county. The fire department, integrated for many years, was segregated during this time; the department now formed black companies to serve predominantly black neighborhoods.[48]

Black renters and homeowners were increasingly met by walls of white resistance. In the more affluent Westside there were attempts to evict longtime residents. The nearby University of Southern California played an important role in trying to restrict black expansion: "When black professionals and celebrities, for instance, began to buy homes in the Adams Boulevard area during the 1920s, USC led efforts to segregate the neighborhood with racially restrictive covenants."[49] Along Central Avenue, the southward movement of blacks was checked by the Ku Klux Klan, which experienced a resurgence in the reactionary, anti-communist, anti-labor atmosphere of the post–World War I period. By the mid-1920s the black community's southern boundary had reached

3

Slauson Avenue. But this was as far as it would go for the next few decades. "Families moving south of that street were driven out with threats of violence and in some cases had their homes raided and wrecked. In contrast to the short-lived efforts at exclusion along Central Avenue in earlier decades, this intimidation, attributed by some to the Ku Klux Klan, maintained Slauson as a racial boundary until the Second World War."[50]

The cumulative effect of the previous decades of legal maneuvering and street confrontations

> was to contain nearly all Negroes in Los Angeles in several isolated communities whose populations were becoming predominantly Negro. Out of fourteen assembly districts, one (the 62nd), running along Central Avenue, had seventy percent of the city's Negroes. In five districts, Negroes were virtually absent. So rigid had the segregation become that the ghetto grew little during the 1930s, even though more blacks came to Los Angeles than in any previous decade.[51]

The growing black population of Los Angeles and its increasing concentration along Central Avenue was also reflected in the Avenue's status as the community's economic and social center. While many businesses remained white-owned, a significant number of black enterprises flourished.[52] Indicative of this growth, as well as the de facto segregation in Los Angeles, was the construction and opening of the Somerville Hotel in 1928 on Central Avenue. Since blacks were not welcome at L.A.'s downtown hotels, John Somerville, a prominent dentist and the first black to graduate from USC, decided to build a four-story, hundred-room hotel. It opened in time to host the national NAACP convention, which was meeting at the nearby Shrine Auditorium, and to welcome among its first guests W. E. B. DuBois, James Weldon Johnson, Lincoln Steffens, and Charles Chestnut.[53] Aside from the guest rooms, the hotel housed "a pharmacy, barber shop, beauty parlor and flower shop. The lobby was decorated with murals, tapestries and exquisite furnishings, while a patio with a fountain and potted palms faced the 41st Street entrance. The dining room, under the management of Fannie Burdette, seated one hundred and included a balcony for an orchestra."[54]

The Somerville was among the finest hotels for blacks in the country and helped fuel the notion that in Los Angeles a black person could find a better living situation than anywhere else in the United States. The stock market crash of 1929 forced Somerville to sell the property to a group, who renamed it the Dunbar Hotel, the name by which the structure is still known. Under its new ownership, the Dunbar Hotel flourished and also came to symbolize the opportunities blacks had in southern California to own property. "In 1930 over one-third of the black families owned their homes, in contrast to 10.5 percent in Chicago, 15 percent in Detroit, and 5.6 percent in New York. Only six cities of 100,000 or more exceeded Los Angeles in black home ownership, and none of these had as large a black population."[55]

Along with day businesses, the expansion of the 1920s also brought a vibrant night scene to Central Avenue. A number of clubs provided night-long entertainment most evenings of the week. One of the most prominent was the Apex Club, next door to the Somerville Hotel and the most lavish establishment on the Avenue; it continued to be so as the Club Alabam within a few years. Usually focusing on violence and crime along Central, the *Los Angeles Times* did run a piece on this scene in 1928, but the description matched Marlow's vision of Africa in Joseph Conrad's *Heart of Darkness:* "Here was the real realm of profane music. To the syncopated staccato of frustration and rebellion, hundreds of couples handled their heels as they have handled the English language, with artistic abandon. . . . Peals of shrill laughter accented with weird rhythms."[56]

The relative prosperity of the twenties gave rise to a great variety of entertainment venues: dance halls—formal and informal, large and small—motion picture houses that alternated films and live performances, cabaret clubs, circus sideshows, speakeasies, social clubs, real estate promotions, and burlesque houses. These and the innumerable parties for Hollywood stars created a growing demand for musicians.

By the 1920s Harry Southard's Black and Tan Jazz Orchestra was still popular, as was the Sunnyland Jazz Orchestra, which boasted at least one native Californian, alto saxophonist Charlie Lawrence.[57] Another early Texas transplant, saxophonist Benjamin "Reb" Spikes finally resettled in Los Angeles in 1919 and within a few years his Majors and Minors Orchestra had joined this elite group of Los Angeles bands. Reb and his brother Johnny became a major force in the black music scene, influencing many dimensions of the music and entertainment industry. He "wrote and produced shows and songs like 'Someday Sweetheart,' operated his own Sunshine Record Company . . . , ran a music store at 12th and Central as a clearinghouse for jazz jobs in the area, and led bands into the mid-1930s."[58] Joe Darensbourg recalled that even in the late twenties, "Every time we did a job we got hooked up with the Spikes Brothers' agency, and they often used to book us on different jobs, like in the movies, where you'd have to have a tuxedo."[59] When Red Callender arrived in 1936, the Spikes brothers' authority was still strong: "One of the great crossroads was at 12th and Central where Reb Spikes and his brother ran a record store that magnetized all the elements. Across the street was the Hummingbird Cafe and Adams Sweet Shop where you could sit and watch everyone pass by."[60]

Perhaps the most important recordings by Sunshine took place in June 1921, when Kid Ory and his band recorded two tunes ("Ory's Creole Trombone" and "Society Blues") under the name of Spikes' Seven Pods of Pepper.[61] As Ory's Sunshinne (*sic*) Orchestra, they also recorded four sides accompanying vocalists Roberta Dudley ("Krooked Blues" and "When You're Alone") and Ruth Lee ("Maybe Some Day" and "That Sweet Something Dear"). Although black blues vocalists had recorded as early as 1920, the two Pods of Pepper sides represent the first known recordings of a black instrumental jazz group.[62]

By the mid-twenties, new bands were emerging.[63] J. M. Henderson's Oak Leaf Jazz Band from Texas, Papa Mutt Carey's bands, and Curtis Mosby's Dixieland Blue Blowers were providing competition to the Black and Tans and the various Spikes brothers' ensembles. Included in Mosby's units was a saxophonist, Les Hite, who would become one of the most prominent bandleaders on the West Coast during the 1930s at Frank Sebastian's Cotton Club in Culver City, then on the western outskirts of Los Angeles. Perhaps the most important band at the time was Paul Howard's Quality Serenaders. Howard had left the Black and Tan Orchestra and "formed his own quartet at the Quality Cafe on 12th and Central Avenue in 1924."[64] The band included a young trombonist from nearby Pasadena, Lawrence Brown, who joined Duke Ellington's band a few years later, and Lionel Hampton, a recent arrival from Chicago and an even more recent defector from Reb Spike's and Curtis Mosby's bands.[65]

Another successful organization of the late twenties was Sonny Clay's band. After leaving the Spikes brothers' orchestra, Clay formed a group that recorded widely and appeared in sixty-five films, by Clay's count.[66] Working with him was trombonist William Woodman, Sr., who left Mississippi and settled in L.A. in 1918, and was in the initial stages of raising a very musical family in Watts.[67] In the 1930s, three of his sons, Coney, William Jr., and Britt, formed the core of the most important band in Watts, and trombonist Britt achieved renown during the 1950s playing in Duke Ellington's orchestra.

To service the needs of this expanding music scene, a black local of the American Federation of Musicians, Local 767, was founded in 1920, and its hall was the meeting place, clearinghouse, and rehearsal space for black musicians denied membership in the white union, Local 47. By the mid-1930s Local 767 was the second largest black local in the country with 330 members, exceeded only by the Chicago local.[68] The booming scene on Central accounted for part of this growth; the rest came from the entertainment industry, which routinely contacted Local 767 for musicians and extras.

Hollywood and Central Avenue

The dramatic rise of the motion picture industry after World War I caused entertainers of every hue to flock to Los Angeles. Many musicians came as part of the great migration from the South, but artists from other parts of the country, most significantly New York's Harlem, also made the move west: "Starting in the 1920s and reaching a watershed during World War II, black New York artists and entertainers made a steady trek to Hollywood. Fame and fortune would be won in Hollywood, and one stood a better chance in Hollywood if he or she had won a reputation elsewhere, especially in New York."[69]

The introduction of radio in the early 1920s and sound motion pictures in 1927 were decisive in opening up more opportunities for musicians in Hollywood, as soundtracks became an integral part of motion picture making. With the success of *The Jazz Singer* in 1927 and the arrival of the talkies, many musicians lost jobs in local theaters and moviehouses throughout the country, where they had been employed to accompany silent films. The talkies, however, meant that Hollywood was more in need of musicians than ever before. "The Harlem Renaissance and Hollywood boomed at the same time in the 1920s. Hollywood for blacks became one of the few outlets—and the most lucrative—and offered the greatest exposure for artists. Harlem artists started going to Hollywood in the 1920s just as New York Broadway stars did in search of fame and fortune."[70]

For black actors and musicians, Hollywood offered employment, but of a very restricted sort. The studios were for the most part a white preserve, and regular staff positions were not offered to black musicians, but there were opportunities to appear and perform in a variety of subordinate roles. Almost from its inception Hollywood provided an additional source of income for black artists in Los Angeles. As Frank Driggs noted, "Jazz has been on the periphery of film making since Wood Wilson's Syncopators, a pioneer Los Angeles black band, appeared in a 1916 short film, Morosco's *Penny Dance*."[71] Indeed, most of the more popular bands, such as those of Sonny Clay, Les Hite, and Curtis Mosby, appeared in dozens of films.[72] Individual musicians and bands were called upon to record tracks as well as appear briefly—sometimes barely a glimpse—in performance scenes. A few individuals, such as Duke Ellington, were given screen credits, but most musicians simply pocketed a day's pay, leaving it to jazz archivists to try to determine who were the members of a band seen in a ten-second pan shot.

During the silent era many black musicians, including Kid Ory, Papa Mutt Carey, and the Black and Tan Jazz Orchestra, were hired to provide mood music for the actors during filming.[73] After the advent of talkies, some black bands recorded soundtracks, which in some cases would then be mimed by white musicians in front of the cameras. Absurdities would occasionally result, such as using white musicians to record a black band number, only to have a black band appear on camera miming the white band's soundtrack! Film work, in any case, was never regular for blacks. The jobs were ad hoc and usually done during the day to supplement earnings from nighttime gigs. Frequently, musicians simply took jobs as walk-on extras.[74]

The story of Central Avenue, from the Great Depression through the Avenue's decline in the early 1950s, will be continued in the introductory essays that precede each of this volume's four parts.

The Emergence of
Central Avenue

With the onset of the Great Depression, many whites along Central Avenue were willing to sell property to blacks and other ethnic groups; thus racism and restrictive covenants at times gave way to mounting economic pressures. By 1933 the southern boundary of the main part of the black community reached Twenty-ninth Street, and the black neighborhoods around the Dunbar Hotel and the Furlong Tract to the east of Central Avenue expanded and soon merged.

Though some blacks were able to afford houses, the Depression hit the black community as a whole especially hard. By 1931 almost 29% of the blacks employed in 1930 had lost their jobs (unemployment among whites did not exceed 20%), and for women the rate was even more dramatic.[1] The competition for living space within the black community was now accompanied by a competition for jobs, the vast majority of which were in the personal and domestic service sector: janitors, porters, servants, and waiters. College-educated blacks, consistently denied the positions their training merited, were forced to become unskilled wage earners to survive.[2] In Chester Himes's first novel, *If He Hollers Let Him Go*, the protagonist, Bob Jones, arrives in Los Angeles and quickly records an unsettling observation on the prospects for decent jobs:

> When I got here practically the only job a Negro could get was service in the white folks' kitchens. But it wasn't that so much. It was the look on the people's faces when you asked them about a job. Most of 'em didn't say right out they wouldn't hire me. They just looked so goddamned startled that I'd even asked. As if some friendly dog had come in through the door and said, "I can talk." It shook me.[3]

17

Job competition among blacks was intensified by some whites' fixation on complexion. An employment agency director, discussing jobs for blacks in domestic service, said that most prospective employers wanted "'workers of a lighter complexion.' Further investigation revealed that one client asked for a worker whose color could not clash with the 'interior decoration of the home.' Another desired a servant whose complexion would match 'their new stucco house.'"[4] Gilmore Millen's partly Los Angeles–based novel of 1930, *Sweet Man,* captured this racist sensibility: "Barbara Pennfield used to tell her friends that she hired John Henry because he matched the upholstery in her Mercedes town car."[5]

Musicians, too, scrambled for work, as many of the bands that had flourished during the 1920s now disbanded. Fewer venues and the collapse of the recording industry forced some musicians, such as Joe Darensbourg, to leave town; others, including Kid Ory and Papa Mutt, returned to farming and railroad jobs.[6]

One venue that seemed unaffected by hard times was Frank Sebastian's Cotton Club, located near the motion picture studios in Culver City. In 1927 Sebastian purchased a "huge barn-like building," formerly the Green Mill Club, and redecorated it "in the swank manner of those days."[7] Like its New York namesake, Sebastian's Cotton Club featured a variety of top-notch black entertainers performing for large affluent white audiences. In the early 1930s Louis Armstrong was the club's featured performer for months at a time. These were productive years for Pops, as he was known to musicians; he launched a career in film and continued to record prolifically, backed by the Cotton Club's house band, often the Les Hite Orchestra. Soon Hite's band was the most famous on the West Coast, attracting the best musicians Central Avenue had to offer and broadcasting nightly. Hite's reign at the Cotton Club lasted from the summer of 1930 until the club closed in 1939. Among the many musicians who worked with him were Lionel Hampton, Lawrence Brown, Lloyd Reese—who became an important teacher and role model to many young Central Avenue musicians—and Marshal Royal.[8]

Along Central Avenue nightlife continued to flourish in many speakeasies, as well as in numerous legit clubs. By the early 1930s the most impressive of the latter was the Club Alabam, located next to the Dunbar Hotel at 4015 (later renumbered as 4215) Central Avenue. During the 1920s the Apex had occupied the site, but it did not survive the onset of the Depression. On September 4, 1931, the Club Alabam opened under new ownership. Saxophonist Leo Davis, later president of Local 767, became the club's music director, leading his "Alabam Mi-Tee Orchestra."[9] New clubs opened in the area, and nightlife on the Avenue seemed to shake off the Depression. *California Eagle* columnist Harry Levette observed:

> With two new cabarets giving the loud hee-haw to old man "Gen'l Depression" and opening up this week in the same block on Central avenue it looks as if the "Furious Forties" of Brown Broadway will take on its old name and aspect. For months with Nite Clubs dark and half the shops closed the famous block where formerly you could stand still and see all the gay fraternity, resembled the "Valley and the Shadows" of gloom. The dizzy white lights are dancing daringly again, lightsome, lilting, laughter, is tinkling from lips curved merrily in happy faces of white, brown, cream, or rich orange as the gay, many-colored gowns of women of all races flutter like so many tropic butterflies.[10]

In the early 1930s the Alabam employed almost one hundred blacks and had a weekly payroll of fifteen hundred dollars.[11] Offering a variety of black entertainment to integrated audiences, the Club Alabam remained the centerpiece of the Avenue's entertainment scene through the early 1950s. During the thirties it featured touring as well as local bands. Among the latter Edythe Turnham and her Dixie Aces, Lorenzo Flennoy's big band, and Leon Herriford's band performed regularly and introduced a new generation of artists, including Don Byas, Oscar Bradley, and Lee Young. Eddie Barefield jumped Cab Calloway's band in Los Angeles in 1936 and formed a big band for the Alabam. In 1936 Floyd Ray's Harlem Dictators arrived and established itself as one of the finest local groups. Ray remained until 1940, and the orchestra disbanded within the year.[12] These bands left behind few recordings, but Flennoy had only superlatives for his band at the Alabam: "We had the best band you ever wanted to hear. I had different musicians from New York wanting to come and join my band. I had a *good* band. Boy, I had some good musicians. I had that basic left hand, a heavy left hand, and everyone knew me. When I took my solo, I rocked the band."[13]

The motion picture industry and the music world surrounding it continued to draw black musicians to Los Angeles. Frequently, musicians on tour would jump ship. Buck Clayton arrived in 1931, as did Eddie Beal during the early 1930s.[14] Among those arriving in town on the show circuit, Nat King Cole appeared in the King Kolax Orchestra and Show in late 1936 and remained on Central Avenue, forming a trio and working in clubs.[15] It was a rare band or show that would pass through Los Angeles without losing at least one or two members to Central Avenue. One of the few exceptions was Duke Ellington's band, which visited regularly and left intact, in some cases picking up an artist or two, such as Lawrence Brown in the 1930s and Britt Woodman in the early 1950s. One of Duke's few misses was alto saxophonist Marshal Royal, who remained L.A.-based until his days with Lionel Hampton and Count Basie.

Perhaps because of the relatively quick rebound of the entertainment scene from the crash of '29, the Avenue continued to offer opportunities to a number of artists, professionals, and entrepreneurs. *Eagle* columnist Levette offered this description of the "Brown Broadway" in 1932:

> Big modern office buildings elbowing tumbledown shacks—Eat shops, in rows—Chicken markets, chicken markets, chicken markets—Missions—Speakeasies, black frocked ministers—Flashily dressed furtive-eyed racketeers'—Ladies of the evening—patrolling in daylight big cars whiz recklessly, cut-outs wide open—colored and white school children arm in arm, no race hatred yet—An "Amos" lunch room—a "Madam Queen" barbecue stand—(Where is Andy?)—Second hand stores, gilded emporiums, colored banks—A wonderful colored life insurance building, colored gas stations—A score of colored drug stores. And dozens of stores run by Jews.[16]

During the 1920s and 1930s many family-centered bands traveled the country, providing serious musical training to the next generation of musicians and also affording the opportunity for women instrumentalists to perform with men on an equal footing. At a time when women had few opportunities to pursue independent artistic careers, the social acceptability of the patriarchal family band gave many women the opportunity to work as professional musicians.

Two important family bands were the Youngs and the Royals. Drummer Lee Young came of age singing, tap dancing, and drumming in a family band led by his father and featuring numerous relatives, including saxophonists cousin Irma and brother Lester. The Royal family, which performed in the Texas and Oklahoma area, featured Marshal Royal's mother on piano. By 1929 both families had settled in Los Angeles and become important contributors to the musical life of the black community.

When pianist Fletcher Smith migrated to Los Angeles from the Midwest in the early thirties, he found the music scene still flourishing, despite the Depression. With enough talent and commitment, musicians found a way to survive. The less fortunate joined the bulk of the community in struggling against the worst economic catastrophe capitalism had yet visited upon the United States.

1

Marshal Royal

Considered one of the foremost lead alto saxophonists of the big band era, Marshal Royal was raised in a musically gifted family. He was concertmaster of his high school orchestra and by his early twenties was playing lead in big bands. Marshal was instrumental in the formation and early success of Lionel Hampton's orchestra in the early 1940s, and repeated the feat in the early 1950s, when Count Basie asked him to join and rebuild his band. For the next twenty years, Marshal was Basie's lead alto, music director, first lieutenant, and straw boss. Recordings of the Basie band from that period carry the unmistakable sound of his Conn alto.

In 1970 Marshal gave up touring, left Basie, and remained in Los Angeles. From then until his death on May 8, 1995, he was a vigorous presence in the local music scene. He took up lead alto duties with the Capp-Pierce Juggernaut Big Band, Bill Berry's L.A. Big Band, and the Ray Anthony Orchestra. He led his own groups, as well as co-leading with trumpeter Snooky Young. The Los Angeles run of Sophisticated Ladies at the Shubert Theater was supported by Marshal's lead alto for the entire nine-month engagement. During most of the 1980s he performed in Doc Severinsen's Tonight Show band. Marshal also recorded with many of these artists, as well as with numerous others such as Dave Frishberg and Warren Vaché. Constantly in demand, Marshal also made frequent visits to jazz venues and festivals throughout the world.

Two years before his death, over two hundred colleagues and friends gathered on the evening of May 5, 1993, to pay tribute to a man critic Leonard Feather called "peerless in his field."

Marshal was born on December 5, 1912, and spent his early years in Sapulpa, Oklahoma, where his family had recently settled. While his father, Marshal Royal, Sr., was from Sherman, Texas, and his mother, Ernestine Walton Royal, was from Denison, Texas, the family's roots are traceable to slave-era Virginia.

David Walton, my grandfather, formed the first school for blacks in Denison, Texas, which was known as the David Walton School. My mother came up through the school, and served as a teacher there. He was married to Mary Alice Walton. My great-grandmother on that side was Carrie Diamond, who came up in the slavery days. My grandmother was conceived through intermarriage. Quite naturally the male part of it was Caucasian. My great-grandmother took her name from the family that she was working for, the Diamond family. They were Germans out of Richmond, Virginia. When they moved into Ohio, it was possibly Columbus, they carried the slaves with them.

My grandmother was very fortunate in that her father, the Caucasian, sent her to school, which was rather unusual at that time. And to my recollection, she was sent to Wilberforce University. But during the time that I was coming up as a child, it wasn't really a big deal to recognize who your family was and who your great-grandparents were, because at that time people were discouraged to even discuss those things, because of the crossing of the races. It wasn't really a popular thing.

On my father's side, I was told that my grandfather was Caucasian. My grandmother was black with a little bit of interbreeding somewhere that I wouldn't know anything about.

My father picked cotton to get enough money to buy a clarinet when he was a kid. To get a musical education, he hired himself out at a girls school in Texas, called Kidd-Key College. He was a cook and a waiter, and at nighttime he received teaching from one of the musical educators there. When he left, he was able to come back to his hometown and teach all of the young fellows in the neighborhood that wanted to be musicians how to play their particular instruments. He was one of the first teachers they had in Sherman, Texas.

My father and mother met when my father came through Texas with his band, and they fell in love and got married. About a year after their marriage I was born. They had a very, very successful marriage. And if I had to be born all over again and be raised by two parents, I'd want exactly the same ones that I had. They were perfect, as far as perfect can be.

I'm very proud of them and the fact that my father always wanted, from the time he was in Oklahoma, to have me taken out of that part of the country so I could come out to California, which at that time was known as the land of the free, where segregation wasn't too tough. And he felt I could get a reasonable education here without pressure. He told me as long as I lived to never go back down South again, which I never did until I was almost thirty years old, when I went there at the end of 1940 with Lionel Hampton's orchestra.

When they moved to Sapulpa, Oklahoma, my father formed a band. That was the first time there'd ever been a band of anything around there, and I eventually became the mascot when I was about four years old. That got me into actually forming a true interest in music, because that's all I knew. I slept on my father's overcoat in back of the piano from the time that I was a few months old. So I don't know anything about anything except music. If I could be anything else, it would be a miscarriage of justice. [laughter]

We came out here when I was five and a half years old, and I had my sixth birthday in Los Angeles in 1918. When I first went to kindergarten at Nevins Avenue Elementary School, they found out that I had perfect pitch. So my father immediately bought me a half-sized violin and started my becoming a violin player. For the first two or three years, he taught me. My mother was a piano teacher and would teach me what an octave was, and how to finger a scale in each hand. And my uncle, Ernest Royal, my father's brother, was a teacher of the reeds. My father had taught him how to play the clarinet and the saxophone during his early age. So, in turn, he became my teacher. In later years, when I graduated from junior high school in 1927, he gave me a clarinet as my present. That's how I got started with my musical education. I never studied any instrument in school.

When I went to kindergarten, I was walked to school by the man that actually turned out to be the first regular music teacher in the Los Angeles [secondary] school system, Sam Browne. He and another fellow by the name of Willie Starks walked me to grammar school, because they were both seniors in grammar school fixing to go to junior high school. We all lived on the same street within five doors of each other. So they walked me to school because I was a little guy.

Sam Browne lived on Thirty-third Street about four doors from me and was a student of a fellow by the name of Professor Wilkins. He had been taught ever since he was a little boy to play the piano and became an accomplished player. Eventually I think he graduated from USC with a musical degree. There was nobody in his family at all that were musicians. He actually lived with his grandmother. I never knew his mother. And he was a very gentle, kind, orderly sort of fellow all of his life. Never raised his voice much above a whisper and was well thought of and respected. But he was the first of our black people to have a musical setup there at Jefferson High School. And he was very successful. He had some good guys come through there. Two of the best were Ernie Royal, my brother, and Dexter Gordon.

"But it was all a mixed neighborhood."

Los Angeles was big compared to where I'd come from. But in looking back from this age, it was very rural. We were called "colored people" at that time, and the localities that we lived in naturally came about through Caucasians moving out. The big spot for blacks at that time was Twelfth Street and Central Avenue, then gradually going south. I was very close to being on the edge of the southern part of where the blacks lived.

After kindergarten I went to the Wadsworth school and it was pretty mixed. All the neighborhoods were practically mixed from like Thirty-eighth Street to Vernon. There were many blacks, many Jewish people. There were several Italian families in that area and a very, very small amount of Orientals. But it was all a mixed neighborhood.

You would find some whites in the neighborhood that had still held onto their homes and had remained there. But usually, if it was a white couple there, if they had females in their family that were graduating from high school, they would move those females to another part of town. And at the same time, if they'd have enough money, they'd have a nose job done on the young Jewish girls to make them look more Caucasian. If their name was Novakoff, it was changed to Nova, and that sort of thing.

But there were no blacks west of South Park or Avalon at all. That was *the* boundary. Covenants were written into the ownership contracts of these homes that would say that they couldn't sell them to anybody unless they sold to another Caucasian. Sometimes they'd burn a little cross in front of the lawn, things of that sort.

Being black was sometimes very rewarding, and it was a laughable thing to know that every day when you woke up you had a challenge, which was the inspiration for many black guys to be more successful. I definitely felt that way.

It was quite a fashionable thing to quit school during those days, because of the financial condition of most of the families around. I would say 20 percent of the guys in the neighborhood never finished high school because they had to quit and go to work. We always had a depression. The generally recognized depression was the crash of '29, but we'd been in a depression long before that. 'Twenty-nine to us was just a carry-on or a little bit worse than before.

"My father would go out to Beverly Hills, and they'd pay him $150 a night or so."

My father had his band, but my family didn't play Central Avenue. The only times he played Central Avenue would be for private parties and private dances for clubs in the area. He concentrated on playing jobs for the rich and the ultra-rich in Hollywood and Beverly Hills. One of his main clients was the president and owner of the Hellman National Bank, Marco Hellman. He took a liking to my dad because they were both big guys. Through him my father would be recommended to other people in Beverly Hills and the Hollywood area for entertainment. And that's what my father did for years and years. He worked private parties and never accepted a regular job. He never worked any of those dance halls or anything like that.

He made good money in those days. We had people on our side of town with four and five kids, and their only income would be maybe $18 a week for the man of the family. It was very tough. But my father would go out to Beverly Hills, and they'd pay him $150 a night or so. And he would split that between my mother, himself, and my uncle. The first time I ever went out on a job to play with my family's orchestra, my father handed me $22.50 as my night's salary. It was a fortune. Most people were making that for the week.

He used to play places like the Breakfast Club and the Beverly Hills Riding Club. I remember one of the first jobs when I was working with my father, we were playing the Breakfast Club, and we accompanied the most well-known trio of that type, the Boswell Sisters. Connee Boswell was very famous as a singer during those days. They were white and they were the greatest of their era, during the twenties. They had established recording contracts and everybody knew them.

During that time, I played a very interesting stag party for Jack Warner in 1926 at the Beverly Hills Riding Club with my father and mother. We were hired to go out there to play by Marco Hellman. They sent a Rolls-Royce to pick up my mother, my father, my uncle, and me. We didn't know it was a stag party, so they had to get another Rolls-Royce to take my mother home, because she couldn't be there. [laughter] I learned practically all there was to know about manhood for the rest of my life at that one party. That was Jack Warner's first trip to Europe. They had a big stage and everything, had it loaded down with great big two- or three-inch-high pillows and with all the ladies. My father went looking for me and didn't know where I was. I was down in the front row. [laughter]

He wanted me to know what was going on. My father would give me a drink of good whiskey and tell me, "I'm going to show you what alcohol is, what it will do to you, so that it will never be strange to you, and you'll probably never be a drunkard." And later on he'd give me another shot, and I started getting tipsy. He said, "Now, that's what I want you to find out about."

So that was a very good starter for me, because after that, during the complete course of my life, I only allowed a drink from alcohol to reach me maybe two or three times. I'd drink a little bit too much, but I was never an alcoholic. I never liked drugs. My uncle and my father explained to me what drugs were about and took me around some people that were into drugs in the business and showed me exactly what was happening.

He wanted me to know everything about the business. He'd been all over the world, and was a worldly man. So he set me up pretty well. And I thank him very much for it, because it panned out just the way he planned it. Same thing with my brother; he never went for any drugs. He drank quite a bit of vodka at times, but no drugs. That wasn't in the scene.

Jefferson High

You brought your own instrument to school. And practically all of the students had outside tutelage. They didn't learn that much in school about their instruments. You had to go to a private instructor to do that, and then you had a chance to work at what they were teaching you in school.

My uncle gave me a clarinet when I graduated from junior high school on June 27, 1927. He told me, "When you go to senior high school in September, you're going to be the first clarinet player in the band." So every morning during the summer vacation, before I could go to the YMCA or anyplace to play a little baseball or whatever, I had a lesson, every day, six days a week. Sunday I got off. That lesson consisted of one hour, two hours, or three hours, or what was necessary, under the tutelage of my Uncle Ernest.

When I went to high school in September, I was the first clarinet player in the band. It wasn't really that hard for me. And I was also a ukulele player in high school. I used to get into a contest on the theater stages where you would win prizes.

I picked up saxophone on my own just after I learned how to play the clarinet. Oh, about a year after I was in high school. Playing the saxophone was the easier way to make a living. My father and my uncle showed me the difference between the two instruments, the fingering and such, and I just started playing. I really never had any outside teachers of saxophone. I did that myself through books and what was available in my house. I progressed very fast, and it became very easy. Although I learned how to play all of the other saxophones equally well, I concentrated on being a good alto player. It was more my size. I was a little guy, and it just fit.

Even in the pre–Samuel Browne era, Jefferson High School had a strong music program. Although not yet offering training in jazz, "Jeff" gave Marshal a solid grounding in harmony and composition.

It seemed that when I went to school it was mandatory that you take some form of music. There seemed to always be open classes for those that wanted to be musically taught. When I was coming up in the twenties, the California school system had one of the highest ratings in the United States. They had a lot of opportunities for people that wanted to learn.

At Jefferson they had started a keyboard harmony class. Then it was harmony one, two, three, and four. It was four semesters. And during that time you had to learn how to write scores, compose. It was a very good system. You could learn if you wanted to learn.

The orchestral part was excellent. I was concertmaster there at one time on the violin. They started calling me "the Concertmaster." I learned how to play leads being a concertmaster. It was completely classically oriented. I was very fortunate to have had as the teacher and music director there a fellow that had a doctorate in music, a fellow by the name of John Davies. He was a very accomplished man so far as legitimate music was concerned. He knew absolutely nothing about jazz and detested it. I was even very fortunate during junior high school. They had an orchestra where I was going, at McKinley Junior High School. There was a lady conductor there that was just a wonderful person. She was very considerate, an excellent teacher, a woman by the name of Mrs. Adler.

My father really had an eye to the future when he brought me out to California, because it gave me an opportunity, and there wasn't a whole lot of variation between the different nationalities. They were all in the same room, and they got along very well. Very mixed. When I went to Jefferson, there were about 20 percent blacks, 5 percent Español, 2 percent Japanese, Italians would be 25 percent, the Jewish people would be 20 percent, and the rest would be just regular Caucasians.

When Marshal graduated from Jefferson High School in 1930, he had already started his professional career.

The best jobs in town during that time were the taxi dances. All downtown. They had bands like Papa Mutt Carey's. He was out here for years and years and years, from the twenties until the time that he died. And Kid Ory and guys of that sort from New Orleans. They used to work in the taxi dances. There were three or four or five of them downtown, and some of them catered entirely to Filipinos.

The first regular job that my parents allowed me to go to—I was still at Jefferson High School—I worked at a place called Danceland, between Second and Third on Main Street. It was one of the best taxi dances and one of the biggest taxi dance jobs. They had about thirty-five girls that went to work every night. Customers would buy a string of tickets and dance with these girls. You would play one and a half choruses, and that was one dime. The girls would tear off one ticket. And sometimes these Filipino guys would have maybe twenty tickets, and they'd go out and dance with this girl until all of the tickets were taken up.

Well, I learned the repertoire, which was maybe a hundred tunes. And if you were slick enough, you could play them backwards and go the other direction. I had a pretty good memory, and I learned the complete book during the time that I was there. I even did my homework for Jefferson High School, my book reports and things of that sort. I'd be reading my book reports during the time that I would be playing in the taxi dance. After a while it's just regulation; you're just going through it. So that's how I got through high school. I would rush through there with what I had read on the bandstand that night.

One of the first arrangements that I ever wrote was for "I Got Rhythm." I think that was 1927 or 1928 maybe. I made an arrangement for the band. We had one alto, one tenor saxophone, one trumpet, and three rhythm. Sometimes we would have four horns. And that was the biggest band of any of the taxi dances.

I was fortunate enough at that time to work in a band that had the best job of any of the taxi dances. It paid fifty-five dollars a week in 1928, and was led by the best violin player in town, a fellow named Atwell Rose. When they called the "Moonlight Waltz," we would play violins together, duets. He was an excellent musician. He died young, but he was the Eddie South* of the West Coast. So that was excellent, just excellent. I was a very fortunate young man.

And on top of that, it was a six-day job. I was off on Sunday. So the drummer in the band, Alton Redd, he could sell cheese to Wisconsin. He would go to the different theaters in town on Sunday and hire out a five- or six-piece band for the stage. Then we'd do things on Sunday

---

*Chicago born and bred, and classically trained as a violinist, Eddie South (1904–62) spent his career performing superb jazz violin throughout the United States and Europe.

afternoon, do two shows or so of musical entertainment. We'd get $15 apiece, anywhere from $10 to $15 apiece. We would make that on top of our $55 from the taxi dances.

Despite the demands of full-time schoolwork, a multi-instrumentalist's practice regimen, and regular, professional work as a musician, Marshal found time to be a teenager.

We always had automobiles. I used to build hot rods starting when I was about sixteen years old. I had grease under my fingernails for years. I had a Ford, a four-cylinder Ford Model T. And the famous block then was the 1925 Model T Ford. They were made into the hot rod racers in town during that time. And everything was predicated on the size of the Model T Ford, which had no gearshift in it. You did everything from your left foot with a hand accelerator. All the guys that knew how to do it would put a Chevrolet transmission into a Ford. Then you had a gearshift and were able to go around a corner. The brakes were so flimsy and bad on the Ford that you would get Dodge brakes and put them on, which had a flat part of maybe three or four inches across, which would stop your car fast. And the connecting rods would burn out in the engine every time that you had a race. So you'd have to have a couple of them to make sure that you had something to run around in. Double Winfield carburetors and multilift for the valves—there was so much new on the Ford block that none of it was actually a Ford. [laughter] But that was the thing. That helped you be very popular with the girls and in the neighborhood, as well as with the men.

We'd go out to Muroc Dry Lake, which is now Edwards Air Force Base. They had the dry flats out there, and that's where you would go out and run them on Sunday mornings. You'd always end up having to tow the damn thing back into town, because you'd burn out your connecting rods. It was fun.

I used to pick up, during Prohibition, illicit whiskey from Canada that would be brought down. There was a big flat part of sand near San Juan Capistrano. These boats would bring up the smaller boats with this liquor on them, and they'd put them on floats and wait for high tide. When they'd put them out, the high tide would bring the floats into the beach. Then you'd pick up the bootleg whiskey, put it in your car, and bring it back to Los Angeles. I did that a few times.

There were these Italian fellows that had the ins and outs of things in those days. Right after that they had this gambling ship off the shore in the early thirties, like 1930, '31. They had the gambling ship, *Rex,* right off of the five-mile limit, with lights, all decorated. And they would have taxis that would run from Long Beach, usually, and some of them from Santa Monica or Venice, that would take you out to the gambling ship. You had all types of gambling out there run by the mob. They even had music out on some of them. But I was never on them, because I was working at Frank Sebastian's Cotton Club around that time.

There weren't too many drugs in those days. As I grew older, in my later teens and into my early twenties, marijuana became popular, because marijuana in the state of California wasn't even declared illegal until later. You could go down alleys, find a plant growing there, pick it, wrap it up in some brown paper and smoke it. Nobody worried about it. It was nothing. Nobody was ever habit-forming when I was there.

After I got into my middle teens, there was quite a bit of marijuana smoking and occasional drinking as an outlet because of a lot of frustration with the musicians, as well as all the other blacks. There wasn't much for them to do to really enjoy themselves, unless they drank or smoked or had sex. You had a hard time competing in athletics and things of that sort, because it was a white man's world. A lot of times many of the habitual drinkers got caught up with the wrong stuff and ended up drinking some wood alcohol, which would turn them blind and turn the stomach the wrong side out. You had to know what you were fooling with to keep halfway straight and survive.

Central Avenue: "That's where the people from Hollywood and Beverly Hills came to go slumming."

In the late twenties they built the Somerville Hotel. And then adjoining that they put up a building that encompassed what was then the Apex nightclub. It was *the* club. That's where the people from Hollywood and Beverly Hills came to go slumming. It was a black-owned place that would have 90 percent white audiences. The blacks didn't have the money to spend. That was during Prohibition, and you had to hide your bottle underneath the table. The Apex would sell food and setups. Periodically the federals would come in, raid the whole joint, and take everybody to the hoosegow.

They always had a very good show at the Apex. It was the top show in town, really. They had singers like Ivie Anderson, who later went with Duke Ellington. I worked there when she was taken by Ellington. I was seventeen years old. I had my eighteenth birthday at the San Francisco Apex, which Curtis Mosby opened as a second club. It was at the corner of Grant and Bush Street, which was the edge of Chinatown. I lived at the Grandview Hotel, which was at the corner of Grant and Pine. I went up there to play in the orchestra.

Curtis Mosby was a businessman. And he called himself a drummer. He wasn't the greatest drummer in the world, but as long as he owned a band, he was the drummer, see. After he got into the real heavy ownership of the Apex, he got another drummer, who was a pretty great drummer, a fellow by the name of Baby Lewis.

At the same time, Curtis Mosby was such a businessman, he had a band at the first black theater ever built on Central Avenue, which was the Lincoln Theatre. In 1926 it opened with a stage show, which was just a terrific thing in that neighborhood, on the corner of Twenty-third and Central Avenue. They had stage shows that were just great, a full line of girls, comedians, people with expertise, tops in their business. Mosby had the band in the pit.

Well, it finally broke him, because in the music business owning a place is the most precarious business there is anywhere. He ended up owing a lot of people and had to file bankruptcy. He finally made a comeback during World War II. He still had an interest in the Club Alabam, which was co-owned by two Italian brothers. Curtis ended up marrying a lady that was pretty well-fixed. She owned a big beauty shop in town and had a few other interests, such as properties. She financed him into a place called the Last Word. I think that was during World War II, around the early forties.

The Lincoln Theatre was a big-time place for the blacks in town, because that was the first theater that was run by blacks in that area. You couldn't get into that place on Saturdays and Sundays. Just loaded. On top of that, they had probably twelve of the most beautiful black girls in town as usherettes at the theater. A lot of the men around the neighborhood just came to look at the usherettes. Oh, yeah. They were out-of-sight, just beautiful girls, all of them. There wasn't a tater among the whole group. [laughter] No, just gorgeous.

The Lincoln imported all of their acts from the East. All the top acts that were black came there. They used to call it the TOBA [Theater Owners Booking Association] circle in the East. The first shows had a beautiful line of chorus girls, and a guy that was actually the funniest comedian I've ever seen in my life. He was part of the team of Bilo and Ashes. Ashes was a straight man, and Bilo was the real, real funny one. The funniest dudes you ever saw in your life. The offshoot from them were people like Moms Mabley and Redd Foxx and all those people. They were cracking the same type of jokes that Bilo was doing in 1926.

There was another cat by the name of Rooster. He would have this rooster in his act. And the man that raised my wife, Noodles Smith, owned three nightclubs in Seattle, and wanted a comedian. I was in San Francisco, and Rooster was working there at the Apex. Noodles sent a wire and told him he had an opening in Seattle. Rooster sent a message back: "I'm sorry, cannot accept engagement. Have eaten my act." [laughter]

Of the many black musicians and entertainers on the Avenue, few were women.

There were very, very few women performing as musicians. My mother performed only because my father was there as a protector. Musicians in that day weren't respected as being great artists or anything. It's like when I was a kid coming up, some of the neighbors that had pretty daughters would tell them, "Don't fool around with that musician, because they're bad people." We didn't have much respect given to us.

Outside of my mother in the popular field, there was only one other woman that I can remember, Mrs. Sturdevant. She was a piano player, and her husband, John Sturdevant, was a saxophone player. They weren't real hot players, but good musicians, good readers. I don't know much about the white side, because there wasn't much mingling going on in those days. All the mingling going on was from the white guys coming over to the black side of town.

By the mid-1930s the Somerville Hotel was known as the Dunbar, the Apex had become the Club Alabam, and new clubs were opening.

A half block or so across the street from the Dunbar Hotel was a place called the Memo. In 1938 the Memo was very popular. It was a very, very nice club, with very, very elegant furniture. As a matter of fact, my wife,

Evelyn Royal, was one of the first vocalists in that particular place. Her accompanist was Harvey Brooks, who was a very good pianist, a very good accompanist, and a very good composer. He had a tune—I think it was "Little Bird" or something like that—that became number one on the hit list.

I was at the Memo one night with Joe Louis and a young lady, Joe's first wife. He wasn't a drinker, but he liked to have fun, drink up all the soft drinks. And if you had any fruit around, he'd eat up all your apples. He liked those great big Washington apples.

They had a couple of smaller places in the area that were pretty good. An ex–California heavyweight boxing champion by the name of Dynamite Jackson had a place out around Fifty-fifth and Central. It was a bar that was very elite. All of the class people went there, the people that were able to pay the tariff. It was very popular. Dynamite Jackson's.

By 1940 a new, reform-minded administration in City Hall had decreed that liquor could not be sold after 2 a.m., giving rise to after-hours clubs.

Then there were a couple of after-hours clubs, hush-hush things. They had a place called Brother's that was popular with entertainment people that wanted someplace to go after-hours. You had to be illegal to sell whiskey at that time of night, after two o'clock. So they would sell drinks, sometimes in a whiskey cup. It was almost like Prohibition. There were several of those places.

The Alabam was going then. Two Italian fellows, the Risatto brothers, bought the Alabam. They had a little push downtown. They also had a place called the Breakfast Club, upstairs over the Alabam. They specialized in fried chicken, hot biscuits with honey, and things of that sort, and had an open bar. And on top of that, for a while they had an open crap game going, because they knew the people downtown. There wasn't anybody bothering anybody. It didn't even open until two o'clock, and they would have clientele there until six, seven o'clock in the morning. You had to pay off. They had some people that were doing business downtown.

Duke Ellington— "He was almost God."

During my last year at Jefferson, Duke Ellington came into town to make his first picture, *Check and Double Check*, with Amos 'n Andy. I was hired by him to work in his band during the making of that picture. It was a real feather in my cap to have been a member of the Duke Ellington orchestra, and was inspirational to me throughout the rest of my life, because, as it turned out, he became my favorite composer and innovator so far as big band jazz was concerned. It made me a pretty popular guy around school to have been a member of his band.

When they came out here to work in the studio, I think it was Louis B. Mayer who said, "Well, you can't afford to have a big band without violins." So they made him, Ellington, add three violins to his orchestra. I was one of the violins. He knew that I played saxophone, because he was living next door to the Apex, where I was working with Curtis Mosby's band. So he hired me as one of the violin players. And during the time that I was there, he did a tour of the Pacific Coast, and I went with his orchestra, up and down as far as Seattle and Vancouver, doing one-nighters.

He came back a couple of years later and did a picture with Mae West. And I worked then as a regular saxophone player in his band and did the West Coast tour with him at that time. It was 1934, I think. I laid off of the job where I was working, Sebastian's Cotton Club with Les Hite. He allowed me to go out with them. It was a lot of fun. They were so well taken and accepted, because they were *the* band. And as long as he lived, they were still *the* band. There were other bands that in variable ways and means were better organized, but it was his looseness that made his band so great.

I always admired them so much that I knew all of his records from memory. I fit right in because I could figure my part as if I was a regular. So he always knew that anytime he had any trouble with the saxophone players, he had a crutch in me. As a matter of fact, when Johnny Hodges left him and formed his own seven-, eight-piece orchestra, he just smiled because he knew he was on his way to Los Angeles at that time, and he knew that I'd be here. But at that time, I'd just left the week before to go with Count Basie. Instead, he hired Willie Smith. I would have gone with him at that time. Yeah, sure. He was almost God. So far as individual musicians go, my admiration would be for my father, my uncle, Jascha Heifetz, and Duke Ellington.

I would have gone with him anytime that it was available. Although he didn't pay as much money as he could have paid at this time. He was a little bit of a tightwad with his pocketbook. Always. During that twenty years I was with Basie, we'd run into each other in airports and so on, and he'd run up and hug me and put his face against mine. He always needed to shave. He'd be scratching my face like it was sandpaper and saying, "Marshal, when are you going to come into my band to make it sound beautiful?" I would say, "The first time you unload your pocketbook and make it happy to me, then I'll come over here, and we'll have a nice little talk."

I did one recording with him out here. I think it was for Victor Records. We recorded Ivie Anderson singing "My Old Flame." That was a long time ago.

I was supposed to go with him as a regular in '35, '36, but my father had a stroke, and I couldn't leave town. I had to be the father of the family. I stayed and helped rear my sister and my brother. I was constantly working, seven nights a week. And I saw that they never wanted for anything. I couldn't get married. I considered my job was to remain at home and be the man of the family. My father never recovered from it. He had high blood pressure and diabetes. My father was a large man, weighed 255 pounds, and at the time that he passed I weighed 155 pounds, and I picked him up in my arms from the front porch and carried him to the bed. He had lost that much weight.

Upon graduation from Jefferson High School in 1930, at the start of the Depression, Marshal found employment opportunities bleak. Forced to leave town for a gig in San Francisco, he returned in a year and established himself as a member of Les Hite's band at Frank Sebastian's Cotton Club in Culver City.

There weren't that many gigs around or that much of a choice. So I left town at the end of my senior year at Jefferson High School and went north with Curtis Mosby's band. That's when I went to San Francisco to work at the Apex. When we came back to Los Angeles, there was a band from the East at Sebastian's Cotton Club, during the time that Les Hite was gone for a month. The band was McKinney's Cotton Pickers. Don Redman was the leader of that group. When they played, there were four saxophones. So when they left and went back East, and Les Hite came back in there, Hite's band wanted four saxophones. So they hired me in 1931.

I ended up playing leads. Les Hite used to play most of the leads himself, but I became the lead saxophone when he would be out announcing. Soon I was recognized as the lead saxophone player in the band.

Frank Sebastian's Cotton Club was probably the largest nightclub of its type in the United States. They could serve twelve hundred people on a Saturday night, and had three dance floors: the main dance floor, where the band was, and off to each side they had curtains covering two smaller dance floors. During the week, the curtains would be closed, and they would only use the main dance floor and the main dining room. But on Friday and Saturday nights, they'd open up the whole thing.

It first opened when I was a little boy, in the early twenties, at least, and was in Culver City, close to Robertson and Washington. The Helms Bakery building was Frank Sebastian's parking lot.

Frank Sebastian was a rather handsome man, and had a lot of old-country charm. To have a bath, he'd have a masseur come in with olive oil and put all different oils over his body, and then take cornmeal and go all over his body and cleanse his body, and then put colognes on. He was a very immaculate man, and you never saw him when he wasn't dressed up. He slept most of the day, but when he came out at night, he came out in class, always.

And the club was very dignified. All of the people that patronized his place were of the newly found rich of Beverly Hills and Hollywood and the motion picture industry. MGM was just half a mile down the road from there, and there were a couple of other studios right within the same area in Culver City. And all of those people would congregate there, especially on weekends when they wouldn't be working.

Leo Carillo used to come in there. His family owned half of the seashore going from Venice to Ventura on the old Spanish land grants. He used to come in, take off his coat, and get back in the kitchen and fix up gorgeous special dinners for people. He was a great cook and a lot of fun.

And I met all of the old stars. I knew all of the old stars of the twenties and thirties by name. One would be dancing in front of you every weekend and waving. There were plenty of ladies that liked to be admired. The men, they liked to flaunt what they had. It was really big-time stuff. And Sebastian only hired first-class people to work in his place. He had Louis Armstrong out there when he was at the top of his career. He kept the place loaded.

I wouldn't know about Sebastian's ties with the mob. He knew them all right, because he knew all the fellows that were with the gambling boat, *Rex,* that was stationed offshore. And behind the curtains at the club, they had open gambling. You'd only see the people come in the front door. They wouldn't come into where we were playing. Big-time gambling. They had to pay off. He was the big man in Culver City. The tops in the police department. The police all came in there and ate for free, you know. They had the run of the place.

Les Hite — "It was the best gig in town."

In the early thirties, Les Hite had the best band in town. We had a saxophone section that was supposed to have been the best. It was Marvin Johnson, who played alto, Charley Jones was the tenor player, and I was the alto player. And Les Hite played alto. There was also at the Apex, when I was there, Leo Davis, who was an excellent alto player. He eventually became the president of Local 767, the black union in town. Then Bumps Myers came into the band. I got him the job when Les Hite got into an automobile accident coming back from Fresno. He was there from like 1937 or so and '38.

We had a wonderful trumpet player by the name of Lloyd Reese. He was going to Whittier College, taking music, and he'd come by my house every night, park his car, and ride to work in my car. He later turned out to be the most successful music teacher in this area. He was born in Venice, California. His parents had property there for years. There was a small grouping of people there that were maybe 50 percent black and white in a particular area, where those little canals were. It was close to the only black beach, where we had to go, which was at the foot of Pico Boulevard at Santa Monica. And that was practically roped off. That was the only place where blacks were allowed to swim.

Lloyd was originally a saxophone player. He turned into a trumpet player during his studies there at Whittier and learned how to play piano there. So he was well lined up to be a good teacher. He knew how to teach, and he always wanted to. He was teaching at the time that he was working with the band. He'd teach during the day and work at night. That's when he started teaching, during the time that he was with Les Hite's band.

Then there was another fellow that played the trumpet, George Oren-dorff. And James Porter. The trombone players were Sonny Graven and Lawrence Brown. He left Les Hite's band to join Ellington. Oh, it was a good band. There's no doubt about it. It was a good band. We backed Louis Armstrong on some things, a couple of recordings.

Most of the band grew up here, with the exception of Joe Bailey, the bass player. He was from somewhere in the East, New York or Chicago. Lionel Hampton went into the Les Hite band in the late twenties, like 1929, '30. He was the drummer. When he first came out here, Lionel worked with a band called Paul Howard's Quality Serenaders. There were only about five or six of them. Lionel was sent for by Reb Spikes, who owned the music store at Twelfth and Central. That was the only black music store there was. That was the hub of the black neighborhood at that time, Twelfth and Central, all through the teens and the early twen-ties. Reb Spikes wasn't too much of a player, but he was a good business-man. He also had a brother by the name of Johnny Spikes.

Les Hite was from the Champaign-Urbana-Chicago area. He came out here and worked, I think, in Curtis Mosby's band at the Lincoln Theatre. Curtis Mosby's Blue Blowers. This was '26, '27. After Les left the Lincoln Theatre, he went to a place called Solomon's Penny Dance, which was the biggest penny dance in town, a ten cents a dance thing. It was some-where around Figueroa, downtown, over on the white side of town, any-way. Les Hite got his band from there, from a guy called Tin Can Henry Allen. I think he died and Les took over his band. I went there one time to hear them. He had a good band, good intonation. In those days they were playing the best jazz that there was around, even though many times it was taken from recordings by Duke Ellington or Claude Hopkins, who had a band back East, or Chick Webb. Out here, we didn't have any competition for playing jazz of that type, because we didn't have that many places open, and the competition wasn't tough.

From Solomon's, Les Hite took his orchestra into Sebastian's Cotton Club, following a band led by Leon Herriford, who was also a saxophone player. Herriford's band backed Louis Armstrong on his first records that he made out here on the coast, and Lionel was the drummer in that band. He was at the Cotton Club for two or three years.

As a matter of fact, Herriford came to my house when I was at Jefferson High School. I was sixteen, seventeen years old. And I can remember, they worked until three o'clock in the morning out there at Sebastian's Cotton Club, from eight o'clock at night until three in the morning. That was the job, seven days a week. He came past my house and begged my parents to let me work in his band. And they wouldn't allow it. They would allow me to work on weekends. But my mother and father absolutely wouldn't allow me to go out there at that young and tender age.

One of my early bands was Leon René's. He and his brother, Otis, wrote that tune "When the Swallows Come Back to Capistrano." Leon's brother was a pharmacist, at Eighteenth and Central, when I was a kid. He wrote lyrics, and Leon sang and played piano. That's the first time I worked with Charley Jones and Marvin Johnson. We had three saxophones. Alton Redd was the drummer in the band. We had some regular places we would play. We used to work out in South Gate at a place called the La Doma Ballroom for some time. It was an all-white dance hall.

Then when Les Hite went into the Cotton Club, I joined the band in '31. It was the best gig in town. You couldn't ask for anything better during the heavy Depression than a fifty-five-dollar-a-week salary with a chance to go out to the studios and be in one of the motion pictures. When you're the best in town, you get first call for a lot of things. We also did a lot of nice things, like going to the hospitals and playing for them and playing for old folks' homes or anything charitable. We tried to contribute as much as possible in those days. We were the first band of that type that actually did charity work around town.

We broadcasted a dance set at least once every night. Sometimes we'd go on two or three times a night. If they'd have an opening, they'd phone up and say, "They want you on." Hell, we'd go out and play half an hour or an hour. I had so many girls calling my house that my mother said I should have a secretary.

We also went on the road. We were out of there for five or six weeks, and went all the way up the coast. And I fronted the band all the way. Hite was sick and had to leave town for a while. This is around '36. Being the leader of the band was fantastic, at twenty-three, twenty-four years old. Everybody in the band was older and grown more, but I knew how to carry myself very well.

I stayed with Les Hite up until '38. Then Frank Sebastian's Cotton Club almost went under. It was no longer a luxury to go out there and be a bad boy. Dancing was getting to be a thing. That was the days of the lindy hop. People were doing a lot of dancing, and they were going to dance places to do some of the new steps. Ballrooms came to be quite popular. So the place didn't have the class that it formerly had. They didn't have enough strong acts to override other things that were going on in town. Finally, Sebastian sold the place and went to Sacramento, California, where he took over the Senator Hotel.

While still with Les Hite, Marshal had the opportunity to record with Art Tatum, during one of the pianist's many trips to the West Coast. On February 26, 1937, as one of Art Tatum's "Swingsters," he played clarinet on a session for Decca Records. The group recorded "Body and Soul," "With Plenty of Money and You," "What Will I Tell My Heart?" and "I've Got My Love To Keep Me Warm."

During that time, I recorded with Art Tatum in 1937 for Decca Records. We did four sides. Lloyd Reese was also on the same date with us. Tatum was the greatest single musician I ever heard in my life. No doubt about it. No doubt. Yeah. He's incomparable.

Union Politics

From his first days as a professional musician, Marshal was a member of the American Federation of Musicians Local 767, the black local in Los Angeles. During the 1930s, he became increasingly active as a progressive member of a new generation of musicians, ultimately becoming vice-president of Local 767 in 1937.

Local 767 was a black union. They were segregated at that time. The musicians local was one of the places where you could go and find your peers. We'd go down there and play pinochle or talk and be friendly. It was not quite a hangout, but it was a good meeting place for a lot of the fellows. And it was located on Central Avenue, at Eighteenth and Central.

My father was president in the late twenties, and then a fellow by the name of Johnson was president. My father didn't really want any part of it. He wanted to get out of there. Johnson tried to run it the best that he could with only a slight knowledge of the music world. He wasn't really a man that had worked many different places, that knew the circumstances of being a president and having other people's livelihoods attached to him. After him, Ed Bailey was president, a pretty good man for what he had to do. He was a good businessman, knew what it was all about, and he was a good musician. But, finally, he had outlived his usefulness.

At that time the union was across the street from Jefferson High School and some of us got together. This was around 1936, '37. We started getting some of the old guard out, so we'd be halfway progressive. I was voted in as a member of the board when I was a teenager, around twenty years old. But in '37 we finally changed over and elected a whole new slate. That's when Leo Davis came in as president and I came in as vice-president.

Marshal's involvement in union politics was curtailed in the postwar period. During the campaign of the early 1950s to unite the black and white locals, he was out of town with Count Basie's band. From a distance he allied with the pro-amalgamation forces.

At that time, all of the hiring for the motion pictures, the recording part of it, was done from the white local, Local 47. So we would get a little dribble every once in a while, when we were called out to do an atmosphere job and they would want black people to play. Other than that, we weren't doing any of the recording. And it remained that way until the turnover of Local 767, when it went into 47, which is now one local.

I wasn't with the real amalgamation that they had. I wasn't even in town. I was with the Basie band. Sure I liked it. My father was the president when I was a little kid in the twenties. And he said segregation in the union was asinine then.

From welcoming touring bands to town, to celebrating the election of the honorary Mayor of Central Avenue, parades were always a staple of Central Avenue social life. One of the most anticipated and celebrated was the annual Labor Day parade. In 1940 during his tenure as vice-president, Marshal turned Local 767's participation into something memorable.

Every Labor Day the city had a parade up and down Broadway for many, many years. And all of the labor unions had their representatives. We used to field a band from Local 767, a walking band. One particular year, when I was vice-president, I helped finagle a different concept to the parade. Jimmie Lunceford's band was in town. Count Basie's band was in town as well. So as a representation of Local 767, we rented three flatbed trucks. We put Basie and his band on one, Jimmie Lunceford with his band on another, and I had a band of all-stars that we picked up from the musicians union on the third one.

My rhythm section was the Nat King Cole Trio. My brother, Ernie, was playing lead trumpet in the band. But I did them one better. I doubled up on all of the people. Instead of having a sixteen-piece band up there, I had about a thirty-piece band up there. I had Red Callender, bass player, with Johnny Miller, the bass player with the King Cole Trio. I had all the better players that I could get. It was quite a thing.

Then after that was over, we always had a big beer bust at the musicians union. We had a barbecue and hot sausages and kegs of beer. Instead of having glasses, each guy would take his own tin can, cut the top off of it, and keep that, because it held the beer cold longer.

On our way back to the musicians union for the beer bust, I had 'em move this flatbed around and stop right in front of Lionel Hampton's house. And we played a couple of tunes. It was right before he left Benny Goodman. It killed him, because he likes that kind of stuff. From me doing that, he formed his band about a month or so later, in October 1940. And from that Labor Day band, he picked a lot of his men.

Lionel Hampton's Band —
"He never took any time off for anything."

In 1939 Les Hite disbanded his Cotton Club Orchestra, and Marshal joined Cee Pee Johnson's band.

After Les Hite I worked with Cee Pee Johnson's band. He was an entertainer, played guitar, sang, and played bongos. He was very popular and a very good entertainer. That's the band that I was playing in when I joined Lionel Hampton in October 1940. He put his band together and anchored it down with a few of the guys off that flatbed in the parade. He tried to get the King Cole Trio for his rhythm section and, thank

God, somebody convinced Nat Cole not to do it and to keep up his trio, because he was just starting to get popular.

I was the lead saxophone player, and my brother was the lead trumpet in the band. My brother, Ernie, had started with Cee Pee Johnson's band. I got him the job in that band so I could sort of tell him what was happening and show him the ins and outs. He was eighteen then, I think. He'd been working around with kid bands, young people's bands. The Woodman brothers had a band, all young fellows. My brother played with them and Buddy Collette and Charlie Mingus. They were all Watts boys. They had a very good kid band, very good.

With Lionel it was full touring, fifty-two weeks a year. He never took any time off for anything. I stayed there two years, practically. We did all of the big cities of the United States and Canada, and most of the small ones, also. It was pretty bad. We toured the South. We'd go down there and stay two or three months at a time. Segregation was rampant, possibly the lowest, just terrible. And when I say terrible, I mean terrible and terrible and all of those other things. L.A. was like heaven. I've only found one place that was any lower than that since I've been a grown man; that was South Africa when I went there in '79.

And the money really wasn't that good. When we first started out with the band, we were making eleven dollars a day, which is what most of the big black bands were paying around that time. After I was there a very short time, I got raised to fourteen dollars a day. But it was a starvation circuit. And money was being made because Gladys, Hampton's wife, was buying a thousand-dollar war bond every week. I know, because I used to go to the bank with her sometimes. So that's how he started to get to be a millionaire. Oh, she was the silent leader of the band. She tended to everything.

My brother and I stayed with the band until 1942, when we both enlisted in the navy together. They were going to draft both of us. I was ducking and dodging, because I was out on the road and I was never in one place. And Ernie was in the prime of life. He was nineteen years old. So we both went in the navy together.

We went in with the promise that we would be taken as musicians, and I was enlisted as a musician. They sent us to a segregated section there at Great Lakes Naval Training Station called Camp Robert Smalls in Illinois. They were going to put black bands together for different stations, like one in Pensacola and one in New Orleans. Then they shipped this complete black band, that I was a part of, to St. Mary's College up north, in Moraga, California. The navy had taken over all of Moraga.

The navy had turned St. Mary's College, a few miles east of the Oakland hills, into a pre-flight school for potential navy aviators.

I was there to stay. I didn't go anywhere. I didn't do anything but entertain, play for dances, play for regimental parades. Of course, you had to learn how to march and such things.

The guys in charge of the cadets were all Annapolis men. But they had quite a few ninety-day wonders in there, because they happened to be fine baseball players or football players. Bill Rigney, who later was one of the professional baseball coaches out here, was a shortstop on our baseball team. We had one of the better football teams. We had the complete Stanford University backfield, the "Vow Boys." They gave them all ensign commissions and put them in there as ninety-day wonders. They didn't know anything about the navy, but they were wearing gold braids.

There were four of us from Los Angeles in there: Jackie Kelso, Buddy Collette, and myself and my brother. I was in charge of the orchestra, and I was second in charge of the whole regimentation there. I was in charge of the number-one band there for three years. That was it from 1942 to '45. I didn't even live on base. I lived in San Francisco and drove in my own car out to Moraga every morning. Six days a week. And they paid me $103 for my room rent off base. It wasn't bad at all.

Postwar Central

When I got out of the service in '45 and returned to L.A., Central was sort of lit up. There was more going on there than before I was in the service. Places like the Downbeat and the Last Word were nonexistent when I went in.

On top of that, at the end of the war there were a couple of after-hours joints, where guys used to go to jam. There was a place called Jack's Basket Room, Thirty-third and Central, with jam sessions every night. It didn't start until everything else was over, at two o'clock. They sold no whiskey in there. Of course, you could see that one of the guys over in the corner would have a half pint you could buy, if you wanted to have one. Then they sold setups, chicken and french fries, called Jack's basket. It wasn't highly decorated or anything, was sort of the barny type, and had some tables in there. It didn't have sawdust on the floor, but it was probably the next thing to that.

The guy that used to be in charge of the hiring of the musicians, as a sort of contractor, was a fellow by the name of Wild Bill Moore. He was a tenor saxophone player. And he tried to always keep a rhythm section there, and then the guys that came in would play according to the way they wanted to play. They'd just jam up there all night having cutting contests. You were liable to have Charlie Parker up there one night, Teddy Edwards, Lucky Thompson, and a lot of good players.

There was another one down around Fifty-sixth and Central. Marvin Johnson and Alton Redd had a group down there that used to play from like a quarter after two until eight o'clock in the morning.

A couple of blocks from the Dunbar Hotel was a place called the Sawdust Inn. It had a piano in there. You'd go by there and jam if you wanted to. I took Art Tatum down there, and he liked to play. We'd go down there and jam sometimes, if the piano wasn't too bad.

There were a lot of out-of-towners. The whole context of black people changed during the war. All those people came out here from the South and went to work in the aircraft factories and the shipyards and made more money than they ever thought existed in their lives. Some of them worked two eight-hour shifts a day, making that dough. And a lot of people were strangers to the city. But almost all of them stayed. So we have a whole different setup of people that are now a part of this area because of the war. A different culture altogether. And the people that lived here were outnumbered two to one by the new people that came in.

But it was pretty good times. The Avenue was in good shape. People had nice places to go and do things. You could go to Billy Berg's out in Hollywood and be accepted as a person there. Segregation was still going on, but that was open.

The end of the full-employment wartime economy brought a sudden reversal of fortune to many workers in the black community, and, consequently, to the economy of Central Avenue. Until he hooked up with Count Basie in 1950,

Marshal survived by taking whatever gigs came his way, including recording dates for all forms of popular black music, then termed "race records," soon to be renamed "rhythm and blues."

The only thing is the money that was coming into Central Avenue wasn't deep enough. When the war was over and they started letting all the people go at the shipyards and the aircraft factories and all of the government-sponsored jobs, the first ones that were let go were the black dudes. Anytime you are last hired and first fired, well, that's the thing. As a matter of fact, it's still that way today. It hit the Avenue hard. It did. It tore them up. Tore them up.

When I got back, the first job I took was at the Downbeat. Lee Young, Lester Young's brother, had a band down there. Our piano player was "the Honeydripper," Joe Liggins. And Lucky Thompson was the tenor saxophone player. And one of the Jacquet brothers, Russell, was the trumpet player. Oh, we had a good band. I stayed there about a week or ten days, and then I went to work out at Billy Berg's on Vine Street.

But it took a long time getting adjusted. I had to start all over when I got out of the service. So I'd work in those recording companies making what they called "race records," and got to the place where I'd probably be doing one or two of them every week, which kept me going. Then, when I left with Basie, I started a different type of life. So from 1945 to the end of '50 I went around making race records and things. And I made it. I was recording for anybody who wanted to pay me, and I made a decent living. I never had to ask anybody for anything, thank God.

When I first came back out of the service, my wife and I were rooming with friends. Then we found an apartment further west that was just having blacks on the street. In a lot of the white neighborhoods, once one or two black people would get in that block, they'd start getting out as fast as they could. We called it "white flight." We stayed there for a couple of years, because at that time the rents were frozen in Los Angeles.

I had a job playing at a white after-hours joint on the edge of Hollywood. My wife was the singer. I can't think of the name of it. Driving home one morning at daybreak, I made a turn on a very nice little street, La Salle Avenue. We looked over, and there was a big sign that said, "For Sale." As soon as we got up that day, we called this real estate man. He said, "I don't know whether I can get by with it or not, but I'll sell you this house if I can."

So in 1950 we became block breakers on that block. When we were moving our stuff in, you'd see curtains moving over on the side, and people peeking out. There was a lovely place right next door to us, twelve units, an apartment. A Jewish lady owned it, and she kept it immaculate. But it was all white. These people were all out there looking. So when they got right to the end of bringing my stuff in, I went to my car, and I took my shotgun out under one arm and my hunting rifle on the other one, took my hunting dog by the tether, and walked in toward the house. And I could see these people all looking to see who in the hell I was. When I got there, I stood on my front porch, and I bowed.

The woman next door saw us moving in, so we introduced each other. She said, "I'm glad to have you in our neighborhood." I told her, "Thank you very much. I'll be a very good neighbor to you. But any of those people that are peeking out of there, if anyone wants to burn a cross on my front lawn, I'm going to kill them." And she started crying. I said, "I'm the only black on this block. If anybody burns a cross or anything on my front lawn, I'm going to give them a double load of my shotgun to start with. And I want you to tell them that." They put signs up: For Sale, For Sale, For Sale.

The next week, I took up my complete lawn by hand. I dug up the whole lawn, turned it over and threw the other lawn away, put in new seeds and new fertilizer, trimmed all the hedges back. Inside of a couple of weeks I had a green lawn in front, and the signs started coming down. Gradually you'd see one of them waving across the street.

I got to know all of them, and they were all friends of mine. As a matter of fact, a man next door tried to sell me a lot that he had in Laguna Beach that I should have bought. I ended up all right. Two doors down were Japanese people, and they turned out to be very dear friends. I met their children and their grandchildren, and I still get cards from them.

By 1950 there wasn't much going on [along Central]. It was just a natural deterioration. It was going to pot, and there was nothing to stop it from going to pot. And there still is nothing to stop it from going to pot. There are no big-time businesses at all on Central Avenue, nothing you can find, except maybe a funeral parlor. And everybody's going to die. But nobody's built anything worthwhile or new. It just faded away. Nothing was happening. It just went kaput.

Now Central Avenue is no longer a black place. And black people are situated in all different parts of the city, from Hollywood to Watts.

They're everywhere. There isn't too much togetherness, because they're all split up.

I'm seven miles now from Central Avenue in a straight shot. When I moved here, I wasn't running from anyplace; I was just trying to find a better place to live. There was no flight. I just tried to better my condition and have a better condition for my wife to live in.

2

Lee Young

Drummer *Lee Young has performed with many of the greats: Count Basie, Benny Carter, Buck Clayton, Duke Ellington, Benny Goodman, Billie Holiday, Oscar Peterson, and, of course, his older brother, Lester Young, with whom he co-led a band in Los Angeles in the early 1940s. Lee was also the first black musician to obtain a regular studio position, and he worked in most of the major Hollywood studios, performing on the sound tracks for such films as* Cocoanut Grove, The Jolson Story, Skirts Ahoy, The Sky's the Limit, *and* Strike Up the Band. *From 1953 to 1962, he was Nat King Cole's musical conductor and toured extensively with him.*

In the mid-1960s Lee became the A & R (artists and repertoire) administrator for Vee-Jay Records and the general manager for United Artists' Sunset Records; from 1969 through 1977 he was the A & R administrator for ABC and Dunhill Records. From the late 1970s through 1983 he served as vice-president of the creative division of Motown Records. In 1971–72 he was president of the National Academy of Recording Arts and Sciences (NARAS).

Lee was born on March 7, 1914, in New Orleans, the son of Willis "Billy" Young and Lizette Jackson Young.

I came from a musical family. They were really musicians and school-teachers on both sides. My mother was a schoolteacher and my father was the principal of a school. I think it was in Bogalusa, Louisiana. And they moved around. I think they taught in Mississippi also, because that's where Lester was born, in Woodville, Mississippi. My sister, Irma, was born in Thibodaux, Louisiana, and I was born in New Orleans. I was the youngest of the three.

My dad played all the instruments. If someone missed the night or couldn't play, he would play the instrument. If the trumpet player didn't show up, he would play trumpet. If the pianist didn't show up, he would play piano. I've heard him play all of them. He played violin, bass, and even mellophone in the street band.

As kids, we were always on shows with him. We'd travel a lot with carnivals. We were on the circuit that most of the other black people were on at the time. It was called the TOBA [Theatre Owners Booking Association]. The show people called it "Tough on Black Actors." So we didn't have a lot of home life, where you would sit and talk normally, like my kid and I would sit around and talk about things. He knows more about our family life than I knew about when I was a kid, because we were always working. That's not a normal life when you're with a carnival and then you work in theaters. And that happened ever since I can remember, since I was four years old.

The three of us all sang and danced before we really got into playing music, but Dad was teaching us music all the time. I had some good teachers. I remember the guy that taught me to dance. He was supposed to be one of the best tap dancers. His name was Jack Wiggins. He used to get me up at eight o'clock in the morning and take me to the theater. And he used to go under the stage to listen to the taps for their clarity. Those people were smart.

My father taught a lot of our great musicians. When we were in Albuquerque, New Mexico, for instance, Ben Webster came to him as a pianist. He had put an ad in the paper for a pianist. That was probably 1927 or '26. But he only played in one key. So my dad said, "You can't play piano in this band. I'm going to teach you to play saxophone." So between my dad and Lester, they taught him.

Lester would practice all day long, when he was a kid. They had to lock me in a room to make me practice, because I wanted to play sports. I did learn to play other instruments because of that. I started off with saxophone. We had a family that played saxophone. My mother played saxophone. I had two cousins, and both of their wives played saxophone. We had ten of us who played saxophone. And I was playing soprano at the time. I think my sister played C melody—that's another of the saxophone family—and alto, and my mother played baritone. And one of the cousins played bass saxophone.

It's a funny thing. When I got into the record business and I worked for Vee-Jay Records, I told Benny Carter I wanted to do an album with him with ten saxophones. He got all the best saxophone players in town. We had Marshal Royal, Buddy Collette, Plas Johnson, Willie Schwartz. And we did an album on Vee-Jay Records. It never did come out, because the company went belly up. It was really interesting. But then it dawned on me why I wanted to do the album; that was because of my childhood. We had done that as kids. But you should have heard this band. Benny made all the arrangements.

But anyway, Dad wanted you to play and he wanted you to play saxophone. After I learned to play saxophone, I told him, "I don't like saxophone. I want to play trumpet." So he got me a trumpet. But I had to stay in the room and practice it. I really didn't like it. I wanted to be out playing ball. So I'd make these excuses. He would make me play it until I understood what the instrument was. Then in five or six months, I told him I wanted to play trombone, and he got me a trombone. I did like the trombone, because that's near the voice. It's really a great instrument. But I would always tell him I was tired of this instrument, and I thought I was putting him in a bind. I thought that he had to buy all these instruments. But he was a music teacher. All he had to do was go down to the music store and tell them that he needed a trombone. They would give him a horn for his pupils. I just didn't realize he wasn't buying them. [laughter] But he was really a great musician.

My dad always had the entire show. He had the comedian, he had the chorus girls—about five or six chorus girls—and he had the straight man, and they had the soubrette. She's a step above chorus girls.

I imagine by the time I was eight years old I had been to about thirty-some states, because we traveled all the time. From New Orleans we moved to Minnesota. And there was another family there, the Pettifords. There was a great bass player who came out of there named Oscar Pettiford. I went to school in Minneapolis until I was in the fourth grade. And then we went on the road again, but we would come in for winter quarters. We didn't work all winter, so we would be home then.

We traveled all around, and went to Albuquerque, New Mexico. I'm jumping to when Ben Webster came. We would play in parks, and we would play these Latino dances up in Albuquerque. And from there we came down to Phoenix, Arizona. We stayed in Arizona about a year and a half. We had a gig there at some park.

Then my dad and I came to Los Angeles, just my dad and I. Lester had run off again. Dad had trouble with Lester. My dad was a hard man. If you spare the rod, spoil the child. He believed in the rod. Lester was a kid that you could not put your hands on, because you could talk to him. And that's what my dad did wrong. Lester was the firstborn. He was crazy about him. They really loved one another. But every time he would say, "I'm going to whip you," he'd whip him, and you'd look in his bed the next morning, he didn't sleep there that night. He had gone out the window. The difference in two kids. He'd tell me he was going to whip me and say, "Get me a switch." I'd go get him a big switch so he could whip me and just beat me up. It didn't matter to me, but it did to Lester. He couldn't handle that. But I'm glad they hit me. Oh, I needed it. I would have been awful. [laughter] It's just like breaking a wild bull. I'm thankful for it, really. But Lester didn't need it. He shouldn't have had it. But they didn't know that at that time.

So my dad and I came to Los Angeles. Lester had gone to Oklahoma to play with a band called the Oklahoma Blue Devils.

"California was different than anyplace else we had been."

Lee landed a job almost immediately upon his arrival in L.A. at the most exclusive club on Central Avenue.

This is like '28. By that time I was really a good dancer and singer. And they had a guest night at the Apex club on Central, which later became the Alabam. And Ivie Anderson was working there when I was there. Eddie "Rochester" Anderson was working there with his brother and another guy called Gus Jones. They had a trio. Lionel Hampton was working in the house band. Anyway, I came at guest night, and I sang, and, like you say, "broke it up." So they hired me. I started working at the Apex. And as a matter of fact, I was closing the show. Well, I closed the show because you couldn't compete with kids. There's a saying in show business: "You don't want to follow dogs and kids on the stage." I worked there several months.

California was different than anyplace else we had been. They found out I was working there—"they" meaning the labor commission—and they came down and said they had to get a permit for me and I couldn't work after ten o'clock at night. California used to be very, very strict. I was thirteen or fourteen. Something like that. I was going to Lafayette Junior High School. Anyway, they made me quit. It seemed to me like I worked there about five or six months before they found out about it.

Most of the clientele at the Apex were white. When most of the black people would come out would be on weekends, because they were working. The Apex used to be packed every night. So I really imagine it was like the same thing that was happening in Harlem with the Cotton Club. Because I know that the white clientele really supported the club, and it was always packed.

But I don't know what else was happening then. Being a kid, I wouldn't know. You don't pay attention to that. By '35 and '36 then I know what started happening. That was a great time, I think, because you didn't have all of this "you couldn't go here and you couldn't go there and be afraid of something." The people that came there were movie stars, directors, and others. You were never bothered by anyone. Well, I will say this: we've really retrogressed as a city and probably as a country. I don't want to become political, but I really believe that, because people were all right with one another. It didn't make any difference if you were white coming to Central Avenue.

My mother and sister came out a few months after we did. Everyone but Lester. My sister started working also when she came here, as a singer and a dancer. She and I started working together as a team. At that time they had a lot of marathons going on in California. Yes, the dance marathons were big things. We'd get our jobs at those places, because they would have entertainment also. I used to call the dancers, asleep on the floor, "sleepwalkers." [laughter] It really was sad, though, to see these people do that. These guys and women, one would be dragging the other one sometimes. He had the strength, and she would want to give up, and he wouldn't let her, and he was just dragging her around the floor. Yes, it was a sad thing. And they did it much longer than two days. I can't tell you how long. Maywood, out near the city of Vernon, is where they had the biggest one that I can remember. It seems rather silly now, but that was the vogue then. They used to have marathons all over.

And the guy that ended up being the walking delegate of the musicians union, he had the band in there. That's when I got to know him. His name was Elmer Fain. When I was a kid, he used to call me "Feis" because I was running all over the place. I was feisty. But it was good to know him, because when I started playing music I used to work with him all the time, because he got all the gigs. One thing I can say about Fain: Fain got all the gigs. [laughter] Because he was the first one there at the union. He stayed at the union. He was there all the time. So when they'd come in for jobs, he would get the band together.

But anyway, my sister and I started working all over town. We worked the Lincoln Theatre together. We'd always stop the shows, because we'd been performing since we were kids. We were good performers, because we were brought up in show business, and we could really dance. We didn't just dance like the kids learn to dance nowadays. It was tap and then I did a little acrobatics. As a matter of fact, that's how I hurt my back. I used to do what they call knee drops. I'd jump from the balcony and do spins. Something like the Nicholas Brothers did. And after you're tap dancing, that's hard. But then you've got to have flair. You've got to have something that will excite the people. So that's why I did that. Then I started playing my drums. I had been playing drums with my dad's band over in Phoenix and Albuquerque. After the trombone, I started playing drums.

When I first moved out here I lived on Newton Street. I lived on the same street that [former Mayor] Tom Bradley lived on. He lived three doors down from us. And everyone on the street was so poor. They really were. The reason Newton Street was so popular, that's the Newton Street Police Station. Most of the kids that lived on that street, they became policemen. All but me. All the rest of them did become cops and sheriffs and marshals. You know Tom was a cop, too.

We lived on Newton Street for quite some time. Our next move was to Twenty-third Street and Naomi. That's just about two blocks from the Lincoln Theatre. At that time my sister and I were no longer working together. She was doing comedy with a guy named Napoleon Whiting. They started working together and I started gigging with different bands as a drummer and vocalist. Singing was my forte. I could get most of the jobs because I did sing, and that was the vogue out here anyway. The vocalist with Les Hite's band was Peppy Prince and he was the drummer. When I replaced Peppy Prince I sang all the things that he was singing.

The person that I worked with first was Papa Mutt Carey. He had a band down on Pico Boulevard. He was from Louisiana. My dad was from

Louisiana. For some reason, the people from Louisiana are very clannish, very, very clannish. So he was holding this audition for a drummer. A guy played, and another guy. Then I played.

He said, "Hey, boy, what is your name?"

"Lee Young."

"Who is your dad?"

"My dad's Billy Young."

"Willis Young?"

"Yes, that's him."

"You got the job." [laughter]

Then Papa Mutt ended up hiring my sister as female vocalist. So we worked on Pico near Georgia Street. I worked quite a little while there. And then Mr. [Paul] Howard, he like adopted me. I was like Mr. Howard's kid. You see I still call him Mr. Howard. I can't get out of it. [laughter] They let you know about that respect thing when I was coming up. So I started working with Mr. Howard out in Glendale with his group, the Quality Serenaders. And Glendale was a very prejudiced place. And I worked two or three gigs with Mrs. [Edythe] Turnham, Floyd Turnham's mother. They had a family band, and I worked with them some.

I'll tell you a funny thing that I did, when I first started. You know they had separate locals here, 767 and 47, so you could bet they had double standards, different rules. The black musicians, they worked for their money. They worked seven days a week when they worked clubs. The white musicians, Local 47, they were not allowed to work but six nights a week, but they got seven nights' pay. That's the way it was. We had to work seven. A lot of the guys that had families wanted to be off a night. I was single and living at home. And I just loved to play so much, I went to different clubs and told the guys that if they wanted a night off, I would play in their place and would never take their jobs. I would always say, "I won't ever take your job." So I got a chance to play all kinds of music, because I used to let these guys off.

Breaking In with the Big Bands

Trumpeter and arranger Buck Clayton earned international recognition as one of Count Basie's leading soloists in the late 1930s. Prior to that he led a big band in Los Angeles and in Shanghai, China.

Buck Clayton's band was the first big band I played with, after he came back from China. As a kid I used to watch his band and sit up and drool over the drummer he had. He was left-handed. His name was Lewis. They called him Baby Lewis. Once they had a battle of the bands at the Apex. It was Les Hite's band and Buck Clayton's band. Buck Clayton's band was called the Fourteen Gentlemen of Harlem, and Les Hite's band was from the Cotton Club. Lionel Hampton was with Les Hite, and Baby Lewis was with Buck's band. But I was crazy about Baby Lewis because he wasn't what I call a contortionist drummer. You can't play drums with the sticks in the air. He was a purist. So that's the way I wanted to pattern myself.

I don't recall what happened to Baby Lewis, but when they came back from China, they were going to a club called the Club Araby. That was up at Fifty-fourth and Central. This guitar player, Frank Pashley, told Buck about me and he hired me. We wore ascot ties and tails, the Four-teen Gentlemen of Harlem. They were all sharp, all of the guys. Caughey Roberts, Bumps Myers, Herschel Evans. So they gave me this music, and we started playing. There was an eighth note or something, and I played it as a quarter note. Frank got up and went crazy. "What's the matter with you? You little S of a B, you can't be in this place." I jumped up with my sticks. "Don't you call me no S of a B! I'll punch you in your mouth!" And the rest of the band said, "You eleven S of a B's, sit down and play that damn music!" [laughter] They called me eleven of them. They said, "Now whip all of us." [laughter] Even when we were playing, I'm jump-ing up and saying, "Don't you call me that!" He said, "Well, sit down and play the music right!" I was the youngest cat in the band, and I had to take a little BS from them. But that guy sat in front of me, and if I dared make a mistake, man, he'd turn around and stare me down and keep playing.

But that's good for you. That's why Ernie Royal turned out to be all right. Oh, Marshal would eat him up when we were with Les Hite's band, and he got him in the band. At the time, Ernie was just a high-note player, and Marshal was trying to make him a well-rounded musician. He didn't want to do anything but whistle [sings high note] on the end of the songs. Marshal wasn't going to have that. He helped so many guys. He got me the job with Les Hite.

But the Fourteen Gentlemen of Harlem, I don't know how long the engagement was. It was not over three months. The Club Araby didn't stay open too long. I think when that club closed, the band broke up. I think that's when Buck and Herschel went back to Kansas City and joined Basie. And then I went with Ethel Waters, because she heard me play with Buck Clayton. That was '37, so the Gentlemen of Harlem may have been '36, something like that.

Ethel Waters came through with her husband. His name was Eddie Mallory. And they wanted a drummer. They'd heard about me playing with Buck Clayton. And Tyree Glenn and I left together. I'll never forget on the front porch my dad told Tyree, "I want you to really look out for my son because he's never been away from home before." So he said, "Yes, Mr. Young. Yes, Mr. Young. I'll really take care of him." I'm saying to myself, "Whoa," because I already knew him. I was a teetotaler. I didn't drink. I didn't smoke. They couldn't get me to smoke a joint or nothing. I just never did. But these guys were wild, and he's turning me over to the wildest bunch of young musicians from New York.

So anyway, I left, and here I'd been going with my future wife [Louise Franklin Young]. She was from Kansas City. Our first stop was Kansas City. She'd call, we'd be talking on the phone, and "Well, I'm supposed to go to New York with them." She came to Kansas City, we got married, I quit the show and came back home. I came back to Los Angeles.

Late in 1936 Nat Cole decided to make Los Angeles his residence. Soon he and Lee struck up a friendship that lasted until Nat's death in 1965. A few years later bassist Jimmy Blanton, then with Duke Ellington, joined the comradeship. At the end of 1941 illness forced Blanton to leave Duke's band. He checked into a southern California sanatorium, where he died of tuberculosis on July 30, 1942, at the age of twenty-three.

Nat, Jimmy Blanton, and myself became really running buddies. And we used to jam all the time. Upstairs at the union. That's when Charlie Christian was here. And Don Byas. I remember the group. We went up to the union and we jammed every day. The people downstairs are trying to work, and we're just tearing the place up. We'd get in there at noon, and when they'd come back from lunch, the building would be shaking. [laughter]

When Blanton got sick with tuberculosis I took him to the City of Hope, out there in Duarte. I took him to General Hospital first and then went and got him and took him out to the City of Hope. You think about those people now, he would have been alive if it had been today.

Then I played with Nat's trio, when Nat had a job at the Swanee Inn. That was when he had Oscar Moore and Wesley Prince. The reason I left was because it had a real small room, and the only thing that I was playing with him was brushes and a sock cymbal and a snare drum. That's all. But I had bought a huge set of drums. And I must play my drums. I can't play brushes all night. It was driving me up the wall. So I left to go with Les Hite.

Les Hite and the Cotton Club Orchestra

Les Hite was a forerunner here. Les Hite and Leon Herriford. These are the guys who were really on the scene. They were adversaries for the gigs with the big bands then. Leon Herriford was a good musician, a good saxophone player. Les Hite played nothing, just the baton. He'd tell everybody, "Are you having a nice time tonight?" That kind of thing. [laughter] Yes, I always thought of them like they were maitre d's. [laughter] But he was a good salesman. He was a really likeable person. And he was a good person. He treated the musicians fairly. He had the personality, and that was popular also. Herriford was very laid back and very businesslike. He was almost elitist and so was opposed over here. He would get certain types of jobs, but Les's band would get the better job. I used to work with Herriford before I worked over at Frank Sebastian's Cotton Club. But that was the ultimate. It was where you tried to get, because Les Hite played the Cotton Club, and then they broadcasted twice a night on KHJ. I used to just sit up and listen and have a ball. And you could listen to Earl Hines from the Grand Terrace in Chicago, and you could listen to everybody from the Meadowbrook Ballroom, like Glenn Miller. The radio was really something.

Frank Sebastian was a guy women said was very handsome. I don't know why I thought he was Italian, but whatever he was, he was salt-and-pepper gray. He was about six feet tall, and he always wore a boutonniere, no matter what he had on. He dressed very well. I think he knew all the movie stars, and he was the greatest host in the world. He met everyone at the door.

Les had it locked up as far as Sebastian's Cotton Club was concerned. He had the band. He had Marshal Royal, Lionel Hampton, Lloyd Reese. Lloyd Reese was probably the best trumpet player in town. And I said in town; I didn't say on Central. Because I had worked with Manny Klein and Raphael Mendez at MGM, and what they thought of Lloyd Reese you would not believe. They thought he was the greatest trumpet player in town. I think he was a natural, really, because he was a good saxophone player, also. George Orendorff was in the band; he was another good trumpet player. Les had a good band. He really did. But then Marshal's never been in a bad band. He always made the band better.

Marshal Royal was a musician who should have been on staff [in the motion picture studios] years ago. He was a great, great musician. And he was legit, too. You should hear him play legitimate clarinet. And he was a violin player. He was very helpful to me. A lot of people don't like arrogance in people, but I do. I like a person that is arrogant and can back it up. He was cocky and he was good. He knew he was good. He walked like he was good. I learned a lot from him that he doesn't even know that I learned from him. I learned preparation from him. The guy was never late. When you're a younger guy coming up, you've got to watch someone that's been successful. Because that's the way you're going to go.

I ended up having a band here. Basie had been here, and they wanted a big band to follow Basie, and I got the band together. One of the first people I got was Marshal Royal playing lead alto and Maxwell Davis, tenor. I got all the best players: John Simmons on bass, Gerald Wiggins on piano. I had everybody you could think of. But Marshal was always the guy to rehearse the band. The best band to me that Basie ever had was when Marshal was there. That's right. That was the best band he had, because they were [snaps fingers] that.

Becoming a Bandleader — "It was a dangerous thing to do."

I had a band at the Alabam at one time. I would say maybe '38, '39. I had Art Pepper in the reed section, Luke Jones, and Jack McVea. I think we had probably ten pieces. It took me a long time before I decided to be a bandleader, because the way musicians were here, once you became a bandleader, and if you didn't have a job, no one else hired you. It was a dangerous thing to do. I knew the moment I became a bandleader I would not be a sideman again, because guys were too afraid that maybe you would take the gig and bring your own band in.

The Club Alabam was run by Curtis Mosby. He was a drummer. A very bad drummer. [laughter] And I can say that because I saw him play when I was a kid. He was what you called a one-hand drummer. Most of those guys ended up on the business end of it. He ended up with a nightclub.

Then in 1940 I organized a good little band with Red Callender on bass, Arthur Twine on piano, Louis Gonzalez on guitar, Bumps Myers on tenor, Paul Campbell on trumpet, and myself on drums. When Lester came out, it became the Lee and Lester Young Band.

Lester had just left Basie. They had a misunderstanding. A lot has been written about it. But we have a family that, as we say, "You don't put your business in the street." Lester told us what happened, but that's not what the writers said happened. So that's why I never even discuss it. Naturally I believe him, because he's anything but a liar. Whatever he told me, that's what I believe happened. But anyway, that's not significant. That was why he came out. So he called me and said, "What's happening out there?" And I said, "Do you want to come out?" He said, "Yes, I want to come out." So I sent for him.

I was working at Billy Berg's then, had been for a long time. We were the house band. It was at Pico and La Cienega, where the Bank of America is now. And with us was the Three Spirits of Rhythm. The guys played tiples. And one was a scat singer. Then Billy Berg built a new club, the Trouville, at Beverly and Fairfax, right across from CBS now. Real plush. Gorgeous place. That's when Billie Holiday worked with us. Jimmy Rowles was in the band now instead of Arthur Twine. We went on at ten, eleven, and one, and we were off. We played three sets a night. And they had Slim and Slam. It was continuous entertainment. We played for Lady Day, and then we would do our numbers in the show.

Billy Berg was just another club owner. He wasn't a musician. He must have been about five foot four. I think he was a New Yorker, because there is a certain aura about the guys from New York. You can just tell. He had that swagger. The first club was Billy Berg's at Pico and La Cienega. He moved from there to the Trouville. Then he went to a place called the Swing Club on Hollywood Boulevard, and then to Billy Berg's on Vine Street.

Jam sessions were always part of the scene, and those held at the Trouville led directly to Norman Granz's productions of Jazz at the Philharmonic concerts.

We used to have jam sessions all the time at Billy Berg's. We had them at the Trouville, some great jam sessions. In all these sessions, Nat [Cole] was the pianist, I was the drummer, and I think by then it was Johnny Miller who was playing bass. Les Paul was playing guitar most of the time. Sometimes Oscar Moore would play. One Sunday I remember we had four tenors: Prez [Lester Young], Ben Webster, Don Byas, and Bumps Myers. And it went on for like three or four hours. Then next week it would be four trumpet players, and the next it would be trombones, and then altos. I remember Johnny Hodges and Willie Smith. Those were really some great things that were happening here.

This is when Norman Granz started doing this. I did them first and I knew Norman. We used to play tennis together. And he said, "If you get the musicians, I'll do them." I haven't told anyone else this before. But that's really the way it happened. I was a musician and I wanted to play. I wasn't a businessman. I was tired of it.

My band sounded like a huge band; it was a seven-piece band, but it sounded like twelve because of the way the band was written for. When Lester came in the band, that's what gave us our bigger sound, because we used two tenors and put the guitar on top. That's electric guitar; that gives you a lot of sound. And the trumpet. So we had four parts, but we had a heavy bottom because of the two tenors. And they would spread the voicing so it really sounded big. That band was very, very unique. We rehearsed six days a week, and we learned one arrangement per day. And we never did read music on the bandstand. And the band always stood up. That was the uniqueness of the band. The only people that sat down were the drummer and the pianist. The guitarist stood up, because he was on the front line with the horns. And musicians would come from all of the studios to hear us. They said, "These guys don't ever read any music."

We had great people doing these arrangements for us. Andy Gibson was one of the real great arrangers at that time. As a matter of fact, he wrote our theme song. He and I were friends, and he called it "The Great Lee." But I was always kind of sensitive to that, so I changed the title to "The Great Lie." Jimmy Mundy made arrangements for us. He wrote a lot of things for Benny Goodman. Billy Strayhorn did arrangements for us. Strayhorn did "Flamingo" for us. We played the same arrangement that Duke played. But Billy made the arrangement. It was really a great band.

We stayed there quite some time. And then we went to New York, to the Cafe Society in 1941. We were at the Cafe Society when we broke up. I left the band because my dad became very ill. I was the youngest, but I was like the one that stayed home all the time and would kind of take care of the folks.

After I came back, I think that was when I started doing and continued to do a lot of studio work and a lot of recording work. Recording is really what kept me going, because I would have five and six dates a day.

A Night with Duke, a Session with Tatum, and a Deal with Mayer

The night that Lester and I were going to open at the Trouville, Duke was opening at the Trianon Ballroom out on Firestone Boulevard. Ben Webster and Jimmy Blanton and I were real good friends. So they called me and told me that Sonny Greer was sick, and "Come on, you've got to play opening night with us." So I called everybody and told them they had to get a drummer, because I was going to play Duke's opening night. They couldn't talk to me. They said, "Well, this is our opening night, and you're the leader!" I said, "I'm not the leader tonight. I may not ever get another chance to play with Duke. I don't care." I went to play with Duke opening night at the Trianon. Biggest thrill of my young life.

Every musician that I knew at the time wanted to play with Duke, because he was the band. And I couldn't wait for them to play the "[Take the] A Train" because in the "A Train" there's a little segment that's like four bars of waltz time. Just that four bars in there that's in three-four, and I wanted the band to know that I knew when the three-four was coming. So when we got to that part, I'm just hamming. [drums with his hands on the table] [laughter] You're crazy, because you just want to show them how much you've really listened to them.

I knew most of their arrangements. They couldn't play anything I hadn't heard, because I was a record collector. And I knew every drummer. Because a lot of people, unless you play, they don't pay that much attention. I found even with pianists, you can tell the difference. All of the great pianists could make the piano sound different from when another guy would play. I remember the time that we had a session over at Gerry Wiggins's house for Oscar Peterson and Art Tatum. All the younger guys wanted Oscar to play, because everybody thought he was going to get Art Tatum. Eddie Beal started off, then came Wiggins. Now, they're warming up the piano. Then Oscar played, and then Tatum. He may have been playing "Liebestraum." Before he finished, about the last four bars, he plays [sings new melody] You know what that is? [sings] "Little Man, You've Had a Busy Day." He was playing that for Oscar, like "I have killed you. I have washed you away." He was unbelievable. He was just an unreal musician.

When Lee left the Ethel Waters show in Kansas City in 1937 and returned to Los Angeles, he soon was hired for what would be the first of many jobs in the motion picture studios. While maintaining his evening gigs and various bands, he spent many days in the recording studios.

When I came back I got a job at Paramount. They were doing a picture with Fred MacMurray and a lady named Harriet Hilliard called *Cocoanut Grove*. And in this picture they had a kid about seven years old; his name was Billy Lee. They wanted him to play drums in the band, because he was supposed to be some type of prodigy. I had to teach him, but I would do the recording. So I did, because he was a dancer, and I could teach a dancer how to do enough to make it where it would be right. I worked on that picture about three months. And I helped get all the family straight. I made quite a nice sum of money.

Two years later Lee was contracted to teach Mickey Rooney enough about drumming to perform his role in MGM's Strike Up the Band. *The gig was soon to turn into a confrontation with MGM and Louis B. Mayer.*

And then MGM did a picture with Paul Whiteman, Judy Garland, and Mickey Rooney called *Strike Up the Band,* where Mickey Rooney had to play drums. They tried everyone before they got me. [laughter] I'll tell you that, they tried. So one of the musical directors over there, his name was Georgie Stoll, he used to come to a club where I worked, and he told them they should try me.

So they called and I went out to MGM. And Louis B. Mayer was there. They wanted to know, "Do you think you can teach him to play drums?" I was young. I was cocky. They didn't frighten me at all. I said, "Oh, yes. I can probably teach him, but I'll tell you in a few minutes if I can teach him."

I said, "Can you dance, Mickey?"

"Yes."

"Do the time step."

He did the time step.

"Okay, now do the time step with your hands."

"What?"

"Do the same thing. Do the same [drums rhythm on legs while singing it in unison]. Do that with your hands."

He said [repeats rhythm].

"Do it again." [drums rhythm twice without singing it] "Now I'm going to put the sticks in your hand, okay?" Now they're looking at this, and I'm a young cat. "I want you to say [repeats rhythm], and that last beat, bop." Because I sang it to him. That's the way dancers sing: "Bob-bob-ba-dop-ba-dop-ba-dop-bop-bop." And you can do that with your feet. [taps rhythm with feet] That's it, right? I said, "Okay, now, I want you to hit the cymbal on the 'bop.'" And he was cocky too; he was a young cat.

He said [taps rhythm]. "Bam!"

I said, "I can teach him."

So I got the job. I worked on that movie forever. And you may want to know this. I had one problem. They said, "What do you charge to do the recording?" I said, "I want $500 to record it." I had been getting $15 an hour for teaching him. Fifteen dollars an hour is a lot of money. And I would work eight and twelve hours a day. I'm rich. So, "Okay, you'll get $500 for recording it." Here the snag came. I recorded it, and they gave me a check for a double session. For a recording session at that time you only got $33 a session. That was for three hours. So the contractor gave me $66. And I said, "Why are you giving me $66? My agreement with you was that I would get $500."

"Oh, Lee, look." He gave me the story, "You've made a good showing, and you're going to get a lot of work at MGM."

"I don't care if I never work for you again in my life if you don't give me my $500." I've always been that way. If you lie to me, that's the end. "Okay, you're not going to pay me my money, right? Okay, well, get someone else to teach him what I did." Then I got lost. I really did. I did it intentionally. I told my mother I was going to play somewhere called Val Verde. And Jimmy Blanton and I went to Val Verde.

So they came by my mother's, and this guy was telling them that "I'm going to lose my job if I can't find the guy." So she told him where I was. They can't move with the picture. Now he's getting the devil. So we saw this big black limo coming up, and we're in the swimming pool, Blanton and I. And the guy said, "Lee, you've got to come back. I'm going to give you your money."

I said, "I don't want to deal with you. I don't even want to talk to you. Nothing you say would I believe."

"Will you believe Louis B. Mayer?"

"Yes, but I won't believe you." They got me up there the next day. I'll never forget going to Louis B. Mayer's office.

He said, "Young man, what's the matter with you?" And I told him that I didn't want to do it because I had been promised something I didn't receive. He said, "Well, I'm going to tell you. I have the rest of your money here. We want you to come on, and we want you to work." He was real nice. He said, "What have you been getting?"

"Fifteen dollars an hour."

He said, "Well, you've got twenty dollars an hour for the rest of the time we're shooting the movie. Does that make up for it?" It did make up for it. I really made a lot of money on that. And that really got me started in the studios. I would have three and four calls a day. I worked Warner Brothers. I worked MGM. And Hal Roach [Studios]. I worked Paramount. I worked Fox. And then eventually I was on the staff at Columbia Studios. But that was later.

Giggin' on the Avenue and in the Studios

By the end of World War II, Lee had put together another great band and taken it into the Downbeat.

After the band with Lester, I worked on the Avenue again. I had Russell Jacquet on trumpet, Lucky Thompson on tenor. The guy that came out here from Chicago was really a great pianist. I'll never remember his name, but he was great. Charles Mingus was the bass player. And Marshal Royal was on alto saxophone. I tell you, I always got the best musicians. So it was a good job. This had to be the mid-forties.

So this was at the Downbeat and they had this big mirror. And we used to tease Lucky and Marshal. They would fight to see who could stand on the bandstand where he could look at himself all night. [laughter] And that's no kidding. Every night they're trying to get—"Now, move over! I've got to—" But that was a good band. We didn't play the same type of things that we did when Lester and I had the band. This was more jam with them. We had just a few charts, and then everybody would solo and solo, and then you'd come back and you'd have the last chorus. They were all great soloists. We used to keep the place packed. This was during the time Stan Kenton came on the Avenue.

Stan Kenton was looking for a drummer. He heard me playing at the Downbeat, and he said, "That's the drummer I want for my band." He hired me, and I took the job, because he's got the money that I wanted. Now I'm supposed to go work with him in two weeks. Then Dave Klein, one of the biggest contractors in town, called and told me that he had a job for me at Columbia Studios.

I said, "What is it?"

And he said, "No, I mean to be on the staff. You know, a year's contract and then a year's contract." He was the guy that was really for progress. All these sessions in the studios I told you about, Dave Klein had gotten me all of them and all of the recording dates. And I was the only black musician doing that. After *Strike Up the Band*, MGM hired a black arranger, who was a great pianist. His name was Calvin Jackson. You should have heard a big bit about him. You just hear a little bit because he was ghostwriting for those people over there. The guy who was doing the hiring was Georgie Stoll at MGM. He was a jazz buff and would go to all the jazz clubs. The other guy that really helped the black musicians enormously in the film business was Ray Heindorf over at Warner Brothers. Ray Heindorf was a Jimmie Lunceford nut. So when they would have anything and Lunceford would be around, he would always get part of Lunceford's band and put it in the studio band at Warner's. But as far as being on the staff, I was the first on staff.

So I said, "Well, I just told Stan that I would go with his band."

Dave said, "Lee, you know how hard it is to break down the barriers, and you have a chance to break down the barriers."

"But I really want to go with Stan because I love this music."

"But someone has to be the pioneer. There's this chance. It's all set for you. All you've got to do is say you want the job."

The hardest thing for me to do was to tell Stan that I wasn't going with him. But I told him face-to-face, and I told him exactly why. And he was one of the nicest people you've ever met, really understanding. He said, "You know, Lee, if you'd asked me which choice you should take, I would tell you to take that one, because you've got to find some way to break the barriers down. And so if they're willing to put you on the staff, you've got to think about the people coming behind you."

Once in the studios at Columbia, Lee's experience was fairly trouble free. Outside the studios it was another story.

You come out of the studios at Sunset and Gower, and down the next block there was a big restaurant. We all went in there to eat, about fifteen of us from the band, and they wouldn't serve me. So all of the band walked out.

I never had any problems in the studios. But you have to produce. There's more than playing the instrument that goes with the recording dates. I was never late for a date. If the date was at one o'clock, I would get there at twelve and set up and then go down to the corner and get a malt or something. Most of those guys would lose those dates from being late. They allowed you to be late once, and if you're late the second time, you didn't get any more calls, because there are guys out there that are never going to be late. They'd always tell you that there was a big clique. "Well, we can't get in there. We can't get in there." There was a reason why they couldn't get in there, because they didn't take care of business, really.

I think I stayed two years. It began to bug me. It's a job more or less for legit musicians. There's not enough creativity there. You do the same thing. You just have to be a sight reader. When they bring it in, they just put it up in front of you, and then you read it. Some of the music is only like four bars long, some of it's just eight bars, just cues. And then maybe you get a chance to play something. But most of it's just spots and spots, and that will drive you up the wall if you want to play. It was getting to me after four months. [laughter] After four months I said, "Jiminy!" Because of the sameness. You never see the music. You come there, you get set up, and they pass the music out. He says, "Go to number one." [sings a couple of bars] "That's all. Number two." And then we go over to two. It was just cue music most of the time. Cues, cues, cues. You have a book full of music, but you don't have three choruses hardly to play. You didn't get a chance to sit there and do nothing like [snapping fingers at medium tempo].

But that was the gig.

When Lee left Columbia studios, he was not succeeded by any black artists.

I've wondered how well I did. [laughter] But nothing seemed to open up. I think the reason for that is the guys I'm telling you about, Heindorf and Georgie Stoll, they were gone. You have to have someone on that side fighting for the guys.

"Mingus was always a character."

By the late 1940s and early 1950s Lee had returned to leading great bands in the evening and occasional studio work during the day.

I came up with another good band that was playing at the Casbah out on Figueroa by either Manchester or Florence. This is with Wiggins, John Simmons, Maxwell Davis, tenor player, with Marshal on alto, a trombone player and a trumpet player called Parr Jones. He was like Harry Edison with that Harmon mute. We played all big-band arrangements, like the "Four Brothers." At that time Dizzy was hot, too. Had a big record and we played that. Les Brown and his band, they used to come in, because they wanted to hear us play. It was really a good band. And June Christy was one of the acts that came in, and Sarah Vaughan. That's when Sarah was singing "Black Coffee." That's the big record she had during that time.

Then I had a smaller band to take into the Oasis, near Rodeo and Western. This is when Nat [King Cole] used to play at the Oasis, Louis Armstrong, Al Hibbler, Sarah Vaughan, Lady Day. We had all the big names coming through there. And now I only had five pieces. I had Wiggins, Mingus, Maxwell Davis, Parr Jones, and myself.

Mingus was always a character. I'll never forget when Billy Eckstine was there, and Billy was singing "Old Man River." He wanted to do this free, with no instruments. The band was supposed to come in when he started singing, "Old man river, that old man river." So Mingus decided he'd help him. Mingus pulls out his bow, and he starts. B is singing, and Mingus is [mimics slow arco bass notes]. B looked back at the man and said, "What's the matter with you?" [laughter] Mingus never stopped. When he started singing again, he said [mimics bass again]. [laughter]

We stayed there quite a while. I'd get off at two o'clock, and then at three o'clock I went to an after-hours place. It was called the Flame over on Jefferson and Raymond. There'd be piano, drums and a singer. It was nice, a cute little place that held maybe fifty people. During that time I got a studio job at MGM. So now I'm working the Oasis, and the Flame from three until six, and then I had a call to work at MGM at nine o'clock. This picture was with Esther Williams called *Skirts Ahoy*. I did that for five weeks.

The Amalgamation of Local 767 and Local 47

Let me tell you about being hired at NBC in 1940. There were separate locals at the time. They called me because the drummers couldn't play a show for them. It was the *Camel Caravan*. That's scraping the bottom of the barrel, because you're in separate locals. This was a Local 47 contractor that called me to work. So I rushed out to Sunset and Gower, set up my drums and I played the show. When it was over, the guys were applauding, and the leader told me that I had the job for thirteen weeks. I was really glad of that, because that's breaking down something.

So I came back the next week. I was setting up my drums, and I saw another guy with his drums already set up. The contractor came over to me and said, "Lee, what are you setting your drums up for? That was just for last week." Because of the separation of the locals, they didn't think I had any rights, because I was from the black local. They figured if a white guy comes to town, he's supposed to take that job. So they told me I didn't have the job. I asked the conductor, "Didn't you tell me I was hired for thirteen weeks?" He said, "Yes, I did tell you that. And you're who I wanted." He wouldn't back down.

I took my drums down, and I went to 767 to file charges. The president, his name was Mr. Bailey, was a gentleman, very good education, but he was from the South. He was a nice man, but wasn't thinking right as far as I was concerned. And so I filed charges with the national organization. I could show you headlines in *Down Beat* [magazine] in red. It says, "Color Loses Lee Young Job at NBC." The musicians told them. I didn't tell them. They didn't like it either.

Anyway, when that story hit, then it was a big thing. Now we had to go to Local 47, before the board. Mr. Bailey, I never will forget him, he had his hat in his hand, and he was telling them, "I really think that Lee is one of our young musicians, and he may have misunderstood exactly what you said." He's got his hat in his hand and he's kowtowing. So I told him, "With all due respect, I've been doing this all the time and I do know when I've been hired. And I'll tell you," and I told him what was said to me and what I asked. So they called the conductor on the phone and he told them, yes, I was right. He was bitterly against it, and he was angry at the manner it was done. When they hung up, they said I won the case. They paid me, but they didn't give me the gig.

So I was for the amalgamation a thousand percent. I lived next door to that union, Local 767, for years. The union was right there; my house was here. So I knew a lot about the union. I didn't think that it should have been separate. I never did think that, and I never did like it. They [Local 767] did function and they did a good job for what they did. But they were never going to be competitive.

"Without Central Avenue there would have been no musicians."

Oh, I think Central Avenue declined because of the war. Because that's when you could see it change. You had different types of people. It's like the freedom that you had out here, and when the guys come from the South, they bring something else with them. I've always noticed that people that come from the South—and this is for white, black, or whatever—when they come from the South, they bring it with them. Such as the neighborhood where you have garages and the lawns are straight. No. In the South they park their cars on the lawn. They come out here, they start parking their cars on the lawn. That may not seem like much to you, but it gets to be a big changeover. And then the people come out here with chips on their shoulders. For instance, like I told you how much the white people used to come to Central Avenue. But now I think that these people frightened them, because they were not used to these people resenting them. Because there wasn't that resentment on Central Avenue years ago. That's a tough question. That's just my opinion of it.

I think it contributed an awful lot. It gave many and most of us the opportunity to earn while you learn, because a lot of guys really started on Central Avenue. Without Central Avenue there would have been no musicians, because really that was the only place you had to work at the time, the only outlet. Where else were you going to play? Especially when you're young and playing music, you don't just come out being great from your first day on the gig. You've got to play a lot of little joints and pay your dues.

I think musically you wouldn't have known a lot of people. A lot of these people wouldn't have known success, either. Central Avenue had to come through for us and it did. There was a lot of work over there. It wasn't a lot of money, but it was enough for you to make a living and be all right and feel all right about yourself. You didn't have to do any things that you did not want to do, because it was clean. You could hold your head up, because you had a decent job.

Fletcher Smith

Pianist Fletcher Smith was one of the mainstays of the Southern California music scene. In the 1950s he played with Earl Bostic and Percy Mayfield. He also performed with Benny Carter, Billy Eckstine, Lionel Hampton, Les Hite, and the Ink Spots, among others. Fletcher recorded extensively as a sideman and toured most of the United States with various organizations. During the early 1970s he was a popular artist in Paris, performing with the Golden Gate Quartet. From 1981 to 1991 he was featured in Las Vegas. Upon his return to Los Angeles, Fletcher continued playing and honing his book of tunes and arrangements until his death on August 15, 1993.

Born in Lincoln, Nebraska, on September 22, 1913, Fletcher was orphaned by the age of eight, and he and his siblings moved in with their grandfather.

My grandfather had a nine-room house. I had two uncles. One of them was working at a grain supply company—he had a little money—and the other one was a railroad porter. He didn't have nothing. They had a bedroom, my sister had a bedroom, and I had a bedroom. My grandfather was downstairs with his master bedroom. But my grandfather was a wonderful fellow. He came out of the Civil War. He fought in the Civil War. His name was Sergeant Pullem. Everybody called him Sergeant.

There was a band that came through Lincoln named the Lloyd Hunter Serenaders, and there was a guitar player there named Finney. I asked Finney if I could get my uncle to buy me a banjo, would he help me learn how to play it. And he said he would. "Before I leave, I'm going to make you out a chart of chords, and when we come back through here, if you know all these chords, we'll go on from there." Man, when he came back, I was so enthused about this, free lessons and everything. And this is 1928. Nobody had any money then. So when he came back through there, he came to the house. Man, I started reciting off those chords and charts and things, and he said, "Man, you're ready!"

So, when one of my uncles got paid, he went down to Dietz Music in Lincoln and paid $12 for a secondhand banjo. It was one of the best, though; it was a Vigon. And, man, you talk about somebody getting busy, boy, rehearsing. When that band came through there again, man, I was playing. I was playing with a band around there. I was sixteen.

And I loved piano, but I was scared to leave the banjo alone and get to the piano, because I knew the piano was going to be a long, drawn-out thing, you know. But the banjo seemed to be kind of easy for me, and I learned a lot of music from that banjo. I learned how to read real good. But I always had my eye on that piano.

My grandfather told me, "If you want to play music, you've got to go where it is, and there ain't nothing here." So I said, "He's got something there."

Hoboing West

I hoboed out here from Lincoln, Nebraska, in '33. It was in wintertime. It was about twenty-two below zero. I think when I left Lincoln I had twenty cents, a sack of crackers, and some water. Now, the water— You see, I had been around hobos, and they'd been telling me all these things, which was very true. When the trains go through the tunnels, if you don't have some water and a wet handkerchief, you get smothered to death. Because the smoke is going to come in that car. See, it was open boxcars then. And a man said, "When you see that train facing to go in that tunnel, you dampen that cloth and put it over your face and lay flat on the car until it comes through there." Because if you sit up there, man, that smoke will kill you. Because those tunnels are long. From Lincoln to Denver it's five hundred miles. There's a lot of tunnels. Where the tunnels come in is from Denver to Las Vegas. The Rockies. That smoke would be this black. You just couldn't see nothing, man. And we tried to shut the door, but the doors were too heavy. You can't move those doors.

I was hoboing with about, oh, two or three guys. And they showed me where the jungles were and all that stuff, and I learned a whole lot from those guys. They were some smart guys. And people say, "They just don't want to do nothing." But those people are very smart. Some of them are lawyers, man, some of them are dentists. I ran into a dentist who was hoboing. He was just trying to get from one town to the next. When I was going to Las Vegas, he transferred on a D&RGW [Denver and Rio Grande Western Railroad] and transferred to go on up to Portland. You see, there are different whistles on trains that will tell you where they're going. Say one long, two shorts, and a long—that's going to Kansas City. Two shorts and two longs—that's going such and such a place. If it was four longs, that's going west. I was listening for the wests, trying to get out of the cold weather.

So I got to Denver, and I got in the jungles. I rode from Lincoln to Denver on a passenger train. See, a lot of guys don't even know how to ride a passenger train. You get behind the coal, and I had an army belt: a great big thick army belt like this. I'd take the army belt and I'd hook it around the ladder of the coal bin. See, because you're liable to fall off of there from the speed and roll. So I hooked it on there—strapped myself to the coal tender—and man, when I woke up, hell, I was in Denver. When I got off in Denver, well, you don't get off at the station. You get off there in the yard, because you'd get killed if you get off at that station. So I got off in the yard, walked and found the jungles and everything. And then guys were telling me what freight train to catch to go west.

When we passed Denver and got over in Provo, Utah, it would start warming up. And man, I started shedding off clothes. When I got to Vegas, I got off right where the Union Plaza is right now, went down in the jungles and washed up, washed my clothes and everything. Man, those clothes dried in about ten minutes. Oh, that town was hot.

On his first day in Las Vegas, Fletcher met a saxophonist, Leonard "Big Boy" Davidson, waiting on a divorce and in need of a piano player for a roadhouse gig.

They didn't have any clubs then. They had what they called roadhouses, out on the highway. So this guy took me to the club where he worked and asked the guy to give me a place to stay. And he said, "I'm going to show you something," and he showed me a tune on the piano, and I went from there on that piano. I was tickled to death. Because the man was interested in me learning how to play the piano, and that's what I wanted to do.

I stayed there the balance of his time, which was four weeks. Then he said, "If you help me drive to Los Angeles, I'll pay your rent for one week and I'll introduce you to some musicians that probably can help you." So I helped him drive to Los Angeles.

Boy, we got closer to Los Angeles, and I started looking at them palm trees, and I said, "Shit, I ain't going to ever leave here." [laughter] Yes. So man, we got there and I never will forget, Fifty-seventh or Fifty-sixth and Central Avenue, South Central Avenue. There was a hotel called the Savoy. And sure enough, he went down and paid my week's rent.

When this guy left, I decided to walk up Central Avenue. So I walked from Fifty-seventh Street down to Eighteenth. Well, Eighteenth was Washington Boulevard. That's the Clark Hotel. And I saw somebody there that I thought I knew. It was a boy I went to school with. He had come out to L.A. a couple of years before me. He wasn't a musician or anything, but he was a good hustler. After you meet one guy from home, then you start meeting other people from Nebraska. So I met a lot of people from Nebraska. And then I settled in and started meeting musicians.

Man, there were so many people on that street. Lincoln was fifty thousand. There were that many people on Central Avenue. [laughter] And the blacks in Lincoln, I bet you there wasn't but twenty-five families of blacks in Lincoln. And, man, that's all I saw walking from Fifty-second Street to Eighteenth. That's all I saw was black people. [laughter] I said, "Damn!"

And Prohibition had just ended in 1933, March 10. I never will forget that. You'd go down there on Central Avenue, down around Twelfth Street where the grocery stores and things were— Man, they were giving away free beer and free wine, you know, in the big barrels and stuff. They were so glad that Prohibition was over. And man, I could go down there and get drunk, man, on that stuff. [laughter] It was free. Yeah. Free! Yeah.

Then I ran into a friend of mine; he was a trumpet player. He was the best friend I ever had. When he heard me play piano, he said, "You're just learning how to play piano? Well, I'll help you all I can." I stayed with that guy—Fred Mason—I stayed at his house about two years. He had a piano in his house. And the way I learned how to play piano was listening to the radio. The band then from California was Les Hite. Les Hite had a band in Culver City at Frank Sebastian's Cotton Club. He'd been out there nine years. But that's where I learned all my tunes, from his band. I'd turn him on at night, and he'd play all the tunes like "Sophisticated Lady," all those kind of tunes. So Fred said, "Well, you're doing all right. Now you've got to get yourself some sheet music and learn how to read the charts right off." And he did that. Man, he helped me. He really helped me.

And there was another guy who came along named Buddy Harper. I never will forget Buddy. Buddy was a hell of an arranger. He went with Duke Ellington. He studied Billy Strayhorn and all those guys. But when he came back to Los Angeles, he had them brilliant ideas. And I used to follow Buddy Harper all night long. Everywhere he went I'd follow him, because I wanted to learn how to write. Everybody who would play my music, they'd say, "You've been around Buddy Harper." I'd say, "That's right, that's right." And he was just an amazing cat, man. And he was a nice guy. That's why I stayed around him, because anything you'd ask him, it didn't disturb him, you know. He was interested. And he was glad to let you know what it was.

I hung around with guys like Leroy "Snake" White, Buddy Harper, Red Callender. Red came here in '36 with the "Brown-Skinned Models." He was standing up in front of the Dunbar, and I was walking down the street, and I ran into him. They'd just got in town. Told me they got stranded in Frisco, and F. E. Miller brought them down here to open the Lincoln Theatre. That's where I met him. We struck up a friendship, and that's the way it was. The whole time, I've never seen Red mad about nothing. He always had that beautiful smile on his face. And Red was a hell of a musician. He was another one of those guys who was glad to tell you something if he knew it.

So I was just lucky, man. I was just lucky to be around those kind of guys. Because, you see, you could have been around guys that wouldn't pay you any attention. But it wasn't like that with the musicians in the thirties. They always wanted to cooperate with you, and they wanted to put their arms around you. If there was something you didn't know, they'd put their arms around you. Even when I was with Benny Carter, it was the same thing. I know a lot of piano players, good piano players, they'd take a lesson— They knew I didn't have any money. So they'd take that lesson and write it down at school, and then they'd bring it to my house and show it to me. So the guys couldn't understand, when I joined the bands, that I could play all this stuff. No, I didn't study with anybody. I guess I could retain things that people told me.

"Man, you could get a job every day."

I was working casuals all the time. Man, you could get a job every day. All you had to do was go down there to the union and tell them you weren't working, and they'd have a job for you that night. The first place that the union was, was the Double V. It was up there on Vernon and Central. Thirty-three, that's where it was, upstairs. The next place was across from Jefferson High School on Hooper Avenue right there by the Cole Dance Studio. That was the second place for the union. The third place was Eighteenth and Central. Yeah, that's the building they sold to join Local 47.

But it's not as much action in 47 as there was in 767, because people then used to congregate every day, not on weekends. Every day they would congregate. And this guy over here, you'd ask this guy, "What are you doing tonight?" He'd say, "I ain't doing nothing." You'd say, "Well, I heard of a job over at such and such place." Contact, you know. I mean, that's why those guys were working. Man, they'd come down to the union, and whatever happened, if you wanted a job, just come on down to the union. Somebody will find you a job. It may not pay a lot of money, but it was still work. And then things weren't as expensive as they are now. See, a loaf of bread used to be fifteen cents. My rent used to be two dollars and fifty cents a week. What the hell! It's a whole lot different now.

I have worked in Los Angeles and gotten fifty cents a night on a job. I worked on jobs where they didn't give you nothing but beer. And where you'd make a dollar and a half a night, you wouldn't tell anybody where you were working. That's the truth. I worked on a job out there on Florence and Central Avenue, and the man gave us a dollar and all the beer we could drink. And I was drinking that beer so fast, the man said, "Man, look here. You leave some beer for somebody else to drink!" [laughter] Oh, we used to have a ball then in town.

I was here in '33; I didn't join the union until '35. Lionel Hampton got me in the union. I did a stint with him in '35. There was a piano player, Ernie Lewis, on his way to join Lionel from Frisco and he got in an automobile accident and broke his arm. So the guitar player in the band knew me and asked me would I sit in until Ernie could get straight. And I said, "Well, man, I ain't never played with no big band before." And naturally, I was scared to death.

So the first job they had was up there in San Jose in the Victoria Theatre. I worked with Lionel about two months. In fact, I came all the way back here and worked at the Cotton Club with Lionel, because that was his first band. See, he'd been with Les Hite all the time. He'd been drumming with Les Hite, the featured drummer. So he pulled out and got his own band, and then he brought me back in the club. But it was too much pressure for me. You know, that's quick. Because they had a big show in the Cotton Club, and you couldn't be faking no music. You had to read some music then, you know. They had the Berry Brothers, the Five Hot Shots, and all these guys—acts. At rehearsals you had to play it down; you couldn't be faking it. So I went and got a buddy of mine to take my place, a boy named Dudley Brooks. He was a friend of mine, too.

The place I would hang out would be mostly the Club Alabam. There was a guy there named Dootsie Williams. He had a little seven-piece band in there. He played trumpet, and three saxophones is four, drums and piano and bass—seven pieces. Let's see. All those guys that did that, all but three—Johnny Miller, the bass player, is still living. Kurt Bradford, alto player, is living. A boy named Fuzzy Gower is still living. Dootsie is still living. The Harlem Dukes was the name of the band. Charlie Evans, the piano player—he's dead. The drummer, Oscar Bradley, was a very good drummer. They always had Lee Young and Oscar Bradley together on a pedestal. But see, I liked Oscar because he was much heavier on drums than Lee. Now, they both could play. They'd cut those charts, I don't care what it was. But Oscar was heavier. He had a heavier foot than Lee. That band—that's where I hung out, at the Alabam, because that was really the only organized band at the time. Let's see, in '33, that was the only organized band that I know of. Lorenzo Flennoy had a big band in the Alabam after that. He had twelve pieces in there.

There was a place called the Breakfast Club. It was up over the Alabam. The Breakfast Club ran for years. I played piano and Betty Treadville sang there. I worked there about fifteen years. It was a gambling joint and after-hours spot. And there was a place called the Last Roundup. That was Forty-first and South Central. It was a joint that had a lot of singers and a piano player, and it was after-hours, too. Yeah, and then there was the Hi-De-Ho club. Now, the Hi-De-Ho club was right across the street from the Alabam. The Big Apple, there's another club I forgot about. It was on Forty-third and Central. There was a place called Leer's Cafe where we used to jam all the time, Forty-second Place, in the back. And the Elks Hall was going then, Thirty-ninth and Central. But the Elks Hall had the worst acoustics in the world. Oh, man, they were terrible.

I worked at a place called Dynamite Jackson's. That was in the '30s, too. That was on Forty-eighth and Central. Black and Gold was a pretty popular club on Twelfth Street and Central. But it wasn't large like the Alabam. The Alabam was the biggest club on the street. All those other clubs I call small clubs. The Hi-De-Ho, the Memo, the Classic, the Downbeat, the Last Word. The Double V was pretty good-sized. Cafe Society was good-sized, up there on Twenty-seventh and San Pedro where the Trenier Twins started out upstairs. And Elihu "Black Dot" McGhee had a club down there on Twenty-third and San Pedro. He was a gambler. He had a lot of clubs. Yeah, Black Dot was quite a hustler.

In 1934 there was a place called the Cabin Inn. That was Twenty-third and Central Avenue across the street from the Lincoln Theatre. Let's see, Lovejoy's was on Vernon and Central. Honey Murphy's was at Ninety-third and South Central. It was an after-hours spot. He had a club, and when they closed it down they made an after-hours spot out of it. Ivie's Chicken Shack. Brother's was on Adams just before you got to Vermont, on the north side of the street. He had a nice place. Yeah, he had an after-hours spot. There wasn't any music. He had a piano in there. Sometimes he'd let you play it. Brothers didn't start jumping till after one o'clock in the morning.

The Watts Scene

The Alabam was the largest club that I know of, with the exception of the Plantation Club. It used to be the Jazzland. It was on 107th Street in Watts. Floyd Turnham's mother had that place. Blainell's. Blainell's was a great big old white building. It looked like an office building, but it was a nightclub. That was before Little Harlem. Little Harlem was a place off of Imperial. Two girls had it, the Brown Sisters. It was just an ordinary nightclub. You could go there and buy some whiskey and dance. That's where T-Bone Walker worked most of the time. In fact, those girls sent for him. They sent for T-Bone from McAlester, Oklahoma. But I worked at Blainell's way before then. The Brown Sisters didn't come into being until '36, I think it was. See, Blainell's was '33 and '34, '35. It was on 118th and Wilmington. A man named Venable had that place. And then there were a couple more clubs out that way. But there weren't any more clubs out that way until the forties.

You'd be surprised at the guys that come from Watts, man. Eddie Davis, a good tenor, he's from Watts. Brother Woodman. He had a whole lot of brothers. And the old man—I worked with him down there on Second and Main Streets at a taxi dance. I worked down there a couple of weeks. It was too much for me. You don't stop playing when you start to working. A guy would take your place, and you go have something to eat, and then you come back, and then he takes another guy's place. I mean, the band is playing three and four hours, man. The old man worked up there for years. He was a trombone player. Good musician. William was his name, William Woodman, Sr. Well, he had all those boys playing that music when they were little babies. The Woodman Brothers is about the oldest bunch of brothers, beside Big Jay McNeely and his brothers, that came out of Watts. And there was a boy named Joe Comfort that went with King Cole—bass player. He was from Watts. And Mingus, Charlie Mingus.

I met Mingus in '43 when I came from New York back out here. I met him at—well, it wasn't the Jazzland then; it was the Plantation when I met him. And he was just a kid then. He was a hell of a bass player, man. He was a hell of a bass player. He was a natural, you know. That cat could play fast as lightning, and play correct. Play nice piano. Played nice classical piano. But he was real belligerent, a real belligerent cat. If you hit a wrong note, it would disturb him. He was liable to jump up and want to fight if he heard a bad note. But those cats in New York fixed him, though. A guy took the bell of his trombone off and had the back of it, and he said, "If you say another word to me I'm going to take it and wrap the rest of this trombone around your head." So he didn't mess with that cat anymore. And this was a white boy.

I never will forget this. Mingus was in a band called Floyd Ray that was working in the T and D Theatre in 1947. We were working for the Will

Mastin Trio. Sammy Davis, Jr.—he was topping the bill. Man, Sammy was on, he was just dancing away. So Mastin, he liked to feature guys in the band. He'd tell them to put the spotlight on me, and we'd start doing some things together. He'd tap something, and I'd do something on the piano trying to do what he was doing. This particular night he put it on me, and I did my little thing, and he threw the light back there on Mingus, and Mingus put his bass up, put it up in the rack, and pointed to the drummer. That was Forest "Chico" Hamilton. He just didn't want to play anything. He said it was too short. It didn't give him enough time to do what he wanted to do.

He was a strange cat, man. He came outside the theater when we were taking intermission, and he jumped on the man's brand new car—jumped on the hood of the stagehand's car. Put a big dent in it. Then jumped on the other side. He'd just do anything. Brother Woodman was in the band. You know, Brother is just like a bull. So, he said something to Brother Woodman, and man, when I looked around, Brother Woodman had that cat up over his head like that. He had Mingus over his head. Buddy Collette was there. He was in the band playing first alto. See, Woodman's been whopping Mingus ever since they were kids in the backyards. He always wanted to jump on Brother Woodman, and Brother Woodman would be laughing and be beating him to death. [laughter]

Fletcher left Los Angeles in 1939 and over the next few years performed with bands throughout the Midwest and on the East Coast.

Around '39 is when they closed the town down. You had a curfew then. Two o'clock. They could have food, but they couldn't serve alcohol. They had to bootleg that. I was with Luke Jones when they closed the town down. I was working at Eighth and Figueroa upstairs, working for Papki. Papki had a lot of brothers, Italian brothers. The cops warned him, though. They called him and told him they were closing him up, closing the town down, and he didn't believe it. See, Papki had some friends on the police force, and they called him and told him that they were going to raid his place, and he didn't believe it. Man, they came up there and chopped up that place. The first time they did it, they told the musicians to get their instruments and get them out, because they were going to tear down the joint. And they did, man. They chopped up those tables.

Those gambling tables. You could gamble in all of the clubs. Everywhere they were gambling. Trying to make a dollar, man.

I don't think there was any mob. Not on Central Avenue. Small time. No big-time stuff. Teddy Lomax had more money than all of them all put together, the one that bought the Alabam. There was a mob out there in Hollywood, though. Different clubs out there like Streets of Paris, Suzie-Q, across the street from Billy Berg's out in there, the Circle Bar— that was all mob joints. You could see them in the back counting their money, man.

I worked with Les Hite in 1939 just before I left. I think it was two or three weeks. I went to Phoenix with him. And I worked a date in Tucson, and we did one night in Albuquerque. Of course, that's the only time I worked with Les, but I worked with him before I left. He was a wonderful guy. You didn't have to worry about anything, you didn't have to buy anything. He had some woman that he was with who bought everything. She bought the music stands, she bought lights, she bought the uniforms for the guys, she bought the music, she bought everything for him.

Then I left here in '39. I was a pallbearer for Herschel Evans in Count Basie's band. I left the next week after that. I left here on the twenty-third of September. Nat Towel sent for me. I stayed with him for a while, and then I joined another band in Omaha named Lloyd Hunter. Then I left Lloyd Hunter and went to McVan's in Buffalo, New York. Then after that I wound up in New York City. I stayed in New York City a whole year. Then I came back to the coast with a group called the Floyd Hunt Quartet. I joined Floyd in Denver, and we worked all the way to the West Coast.

Wartime Hollywood

We came to the Streets of Paris on Hollywood Boulevard. That was in 1943 in the summertime. And they had all kinds of jobs going here then, man, in '43. See, the town was closed but they had so many after-hours spots that you could work, man. You'd work up to twelve o'clock and then you'd be off, and the after-hours would start at maybe one-thirty or something like that, and they'd work till daylight. But you had to have food in the place. If you didn't have food, you couldn't operate. It was just like an all-night cafe. What it really was is they were bootlegging whiskey and had the bands in there. Streets of Paris and Billy Berg's—all those places, man, and I worked every one of them.

In '44 I worked the Lincoln Theatre band, Bardu Ali's, on Central Avenue and then I went with Johnny Otis to the Alabam. I helped Johnny Otis organize a band there in '44, eighteen pieces. I got some guys from back east. We broadcasted twice a night. After I left the Alabam I went up to a place called Shepp's Playhouse. That's on First and Los Angeles Streets. That's the place that during the war they took away from the Japanese, and we were using it. Shepp's Playhouse had two floors. We were on the top floor with the big band. Then they had a cocktail lounge there. Coleman Hawkins was working there. Yeah. It was nice, a nice club.

And then, of course, naturally Hollywood was jumping, man. Hollywood was jumping all over. Billy Berg's on back was jumping then. So it wasn't a problem getting no jobs, you know. I worked with Slim Gaillard. I did 110 sides of Slim Gaillard in one week. That's when they put the ban on the recording. You had to record at night. You couldn't record in the daytime. And Billy wanted us to open up the new Billy Berg's there on Vine Street, Vine and De Longpre. The old Billy Berg's was on Las Palmas and Hollywood Boulevard. See, I'd come from the Circle Bar to Billy Berg's, Streets of Paris, Suzie-Q, all those clubs. This is in the thirties. I wasn't worrying about any jobs. You just went from one to another.

Then I went with a band— The best band I had been with was a band named the Buddy Banks band. Seven pieces. *Bad* band. He was a saxophone player. He played piano for years. They hated to see us coming. The first time I joined Buddy was in '45. And there was another place I didn't even mention, the chicken shack there at Thirty-third and Central—Jack's Basket Room. Boy, that was a jumping place, man. I worked there with Buddy Banks. We'd broadcast twice a night there. That man really had it made. Then he started messing with the government taxes and they put him out of business.

Every musician in the world has worked Jack's Basket Room. I mean, Monday night was a regular session there, you know. Every tenor player in the world has worked there. Boy, I've seen some sessions there. I'll tell you who blew them all out: Paul Gonsalves. Yeah, that guy could blow, boy. Paul and this other guy, Lucky Thompson. I heard Lucky Thompson, Paul Gonsalves, and Wardell Gray. That was another bad cat, Wardell Gray. They were all there one night.

You know that's where Barney Kessel learned how to play? That's right. I worked with Barney Kessel when he couldn't do nothing but play chords. Just strum chords. He couldn't single-string at all. He learned how to single-string down at Jack's Basket Room with the musicians. Because they'd all turn around and look at him. Everybody was looking at him so strange, I guess Barney said, "I'd better learn how to play something." [laughter] Yeah, I've known Barney Kessel for years, man. He's a very nice guy. He learned how to play the blues right down there. And he's got every record that Charlie Christian ever made. He played like Charles Christian.

Norman Granz was a major behind-the-scenes player from the mid-1940s through the 1950s, as impresario, record producer, and label owner, and the originator of the Jazz at the Philharmonic concerts. Fletcher participated in some of Granz's first jam sessions in Los Angeles.

But I worked with Barney Kessel when he could not single-string. The first session we ever had was with Norman Granz on off-nights at the clubs. That's how he got started. Every time the club had a night off, they would put us in there. It must have been around '44. I did the first job for Norman Granz out at the 331 Club where Nat King Cole worked. We worked Billy Berg's off-night. And then we worked Jefferson and Normandie upstairs. They were open to anybody. They were jam sessions. Six pieces. We had Red Callender, we had Oscar Bradley on drums, we had Red Mack on trumpet, we had Barney Kessel on guitar, I was playing piano and Jack McVea, we had him on tenor. And then Corky— What's his name? He was with Stan Kenton, I think. This white boy, tenor player. Well, we started him out at the 331 Club. See, in those days you had to pay six musicians. Now, anybody else could sit in if they wanted to, but you had to pay six men. Some of those jobs we worked down near for nothing. And the job didn't pay but $10, and sometimes he'd come up with $6, $4, $8, and all that kind of shit.

Then I went with Al Killian and Billy Eckstine in '46. In '47 I was with Floyd Ray. Then I went back with Buddy in '48, '49, and '50. Then in '51 I went up to Oakland with Happy Johnson. Oh, I've always worked since I've been here.

"Good times don't roll all the time."

Well, what I've got to say about Central Avenue is that the people that were on Central Avenue closed it up themselves by acting bad. See, we used to have a ball at the Alabam every year, a masquerade ball every year. And people used to—see, movie stars used to come over there all the time. They got to the place where they started messing with the movie stars, especially the women, and all that stuff. See, they did all that stuff themselves. It wasn't the law so much that closed them down. So the people just acted bad, that's all.

I've seen it go from good to bad. They're trying to preserve the Dunbar Hotel— I mean, they need to tear that building down. See, I've been in there. I've seen it, and it's pitiful, man, trying to save something like that. If they're going to save anything, they should have saved the Alabam, where somebody had a chance to work. They tore that down. The black union should have bought that building, then they'd have had somewhere to work. But it's one of those things, man. Good times don't roll all the time; it cuts out sometime.

Central Avenue didn't contribute anything but a whole lot of clubs. But getting on about it, see, I'll tell you something about Central Avenue: the white man owned all the clubs. The black man didn't own nothing. So there was no success for the black man on Central Avenue. You just had a whole lot of clubs, that's all. Selling whiskey, that's all.

But that was one of the swingingest streets in the world, man, when it was jumping. Because I've been to all those places that are supposed to be swinging, like Kansas City, Chicago, and New York, and all those places. But they didn't swing like Central Avenue. No, they didn't. I don't know what it was. It was just— It's more casual out here. See, New York is stiff. People are stiff in New York. People out here swing. They're casual. A man put on a sweater and a pair of pants and some house shoes and would go on out and party. That's a difference. That makes that man comfortable. Where he couldn't do that in New York. He couldn't come in one of those places like that in New York unless he had on a shirt and tie and dressed up in a suit. That was the difference. That's why I say Central Avenue was one of the swingingest streets that I've ever been on.

Next to Central Avenue was Kansas City. Kansas City, the Subway, and where Count Basie was playing and all those places, you know, they jumped real nice, too. That's another one of those casual places. But, those stiff joints, man, they don't go. And I don't care who's playing in there.

Well, everything is lovely. I'm glad you came by and got a few notes so when you hear those guys talking that jive on the air you'll know better. [laughter] Because you got it from the horse's mouth.

The Watts Scene

Major population shifts among the various ethnic communities into the different areas of Los Angeles had virtually ceased by the mid-1920s. "By 1926, the substantial expansion of blacks into adjacent neighborhoods of central Los Angeles had ended; their communities were surrounded by established white areas closed by restrictive covenants."[1] One of these districts was Watts, an area south of Los Angeles, not yet a part of the city. This small working-class community had been populated in the nineteenth century by white workers and their families, with a few blacks, Latinos, and Japanese. Attracted by cheap land, many migrating black families were settling there by the turn of the century with little opposition.[2] One longtime resident offered an explanation during an interview conducted in the 1930s: "To begin with, Watts was sold to Negroes because it is undesirable property. It is low, sandy, and damp. In fact, it is the water basin for Los Angeles; when it rains, the place is inundated by water from the neighborhoods having a much higher level."[3] Watts alumnus and Harlem Renaissance novelist Arna Bontemps depicted life in the black fringe of Watts, which he called Mudtown, in his first novel, *God Sends Sunday:*

> Mudtown was like a tiny section of the deep south literally transplanted. Throughout the warm summer days old toothless men sat in front of the little grocery store on boxes, chewing the stems of cob pipes, recalling the 'Mancipation, the actual beginning of their race. Women cooked over fireplaces in the yards and boiled their clothes in heavy iron kettles. There were songs in the little frail houses and over the steaming pots. Lilacs grew at every doorstep. In every house there was a guitar.[4]

Initially settling on the outskirts, blacks moved into central Watts in the 1910s. The town's white population did not grow as fast, and by the mid-1920s "the town was regarded as likely to have a black mayor."[5] Spurred on by the Ku Klux Klan, the white majority voted in 1926 to merge Watts with the city of Los Angeles.[6] Shortly thereafter Watts was annexed by Los Angeles and "until World War II the blacks in Watts constituted a lonely island in an otherwise white southeast Los Angeles."[7] Central Avenue from Slauson Avenue to Watts remained solidly white until World War II.

Perhaps because Watts was so rural and not part of Los Angeles until the late 1920s, it enjoyed a flourishing social and musical life, exempt from the city's midnight curfew on dance clubs. By the late teens Baron Long's Tavern at 108th and Central (later known as Jazzland and the Plantation Club) was a major gathering place. Reb Spikes's band played for a young exhibition-dancer by the name of Rudolph Valentino and for audiences that regularly included Charlie Chaplin, Lottie Pickford, Jack Pickford, Blanche Reed, and Fatty Arbuckle.[8] During and immediately after World War I venues such as the Appomattox Country Club flourished, and the city's musicians frequently made the trek down Central Avenue to perform for appreciative Watts audiences. In *God Sends Sunday* Bontemps describes how the "shimmy" came to Watts one night at Leak's Lake:

> A flashy pair were showing a new dance that they had picked up in the city, on Central Avenue, in some of the less respectable places, and were attracting considerable attention. It was a dance in which the shoulders and hips twitched rhythmically, but in which the feet made no steps.
>
> Couples, seeing them, exchanged meaning glances. Some of the men said things that made the girls giggle.
>
> "Jelly! A-ah jelly! Jelly on a plate!"
>
> "Slow an' easy."
>
> "Now rock lak a boat."
>
> The denizens of Mudtown were seeing the shimmy for the first time in a public place. In those days it was regarded as a low, unseemly dance, and the young country girls felt a little outraged at seeing it done there so boldly.[9]

When Bricktop arrived in Los Angeles in 1917 one of her first gigs was at the Watts Country Club, owned by George Henderson. "It was in the country, all right—wilderness was more like it. Watts was a woodsy, weedy place, and the club itself was little more than a barn. It consisted of one large room with a bandstand on one side, the bar on the opposite side, and tables set out around the dance floor."[10]

Jelly Roll Morton regularly played in Watts, usually after midnight when the Los Angeles clubs closed, at newly opened Wayside Park, formerly Leak's Lake.[11] Along with his New Orleans cohorts, Buddy Petit, Frankie Dusen, and Wade Whaley, he would teach and then play with local musicians, spreading his style of jazz. "The small combination with which he played was made up partly of neighborhood musicians, including Ben Albans, Jr., a high school boy. Jelly patiently taught the young cornetist, as well as the other musicians he had found in the community, the style of playing he required."[12] Wayside Park was so successful for Jelly he even brought along King Oliver. "Wayside Park is the place King Oliver made much fame in later when I introduced him there in April, 1922." He claimed that his band would earn "$75 a night and the tips doubled the salaries." In fact, "Wayside Park did so well and I made so much money that I came into possession of a gambling club" near Twelfth and Central in Los Angeles.[13]

By the late 1920s and early 1930s Watts still offered a number of musical and dance venues. In 1931 an *Eagle* columnist reported, "The Chateau, and the Villa Venice, both small clubs are still being operated in Watts but old timers say that back in the days of gold headed canes and tall foamy steins there were as many as six and seven night clubs running at once and all doing well. 'Such is life,' sigh the reminiscent ones as they reach to turn on a canned music radio."[14]

It was into this still rural setting that the Woodman, Collette, Bryant, and McNeely families settled.

4

Coney Woodman

The oldest brother in the Woodman Brothers Biggest Little Band in the World, pianist Coney was an influential performer in Watts and along Central Avenue during the 1930s and early 1940s. After Central Avenue declined, he spent the 1950s playing such local venues as Howard Rumsey's Lighthouse in Hermosa Beach and performing with the Jackson Trio and Duke Jones. Coney retired from his professional music career in the early sixties. From 1964 to 1982 he worked at Rockwell International and continued performing in his church.

Coney was born in Jackson, Mississippi, on June 7, 1917. Before he was a year old, the family, including one grandmother, moved to Los Angeles.

My dad was born in Canton, Mississippi; my mother was from Terry, Mississippi. My dad went to a Catholic school, graduated, and he played mostly for the church. After he got to Los Angeles he got a job working at the Follies Theatre and played there twenty-some years. Three shows a day. Every day. He had to be at the first show around noon. We'd eat at lunch all together, come home from school and eat, and then he would leave. We wouldn't see him till the next day. He had to come all the way from Main Street between Third and Fourth. At the booming time in '28, he made as much as a hundred dollars. Things were jumping till it fell, and then he started getting twenty-six dollars at the Depression.

He was great, man. My dad had the opportunity to go with anybody when he was playing. He could have gone with Duke Ellington or anybody. But he didn't want to leave us, because he had four sons. But just three of us [Coney, William Jr., and Britt] were very active in music. The other baby boy, George, had his other ideas.

On my mother's side, everybody could sing. We were musically in-clined. It was mostly related to the church. All of my folks were active in the church. The founder of our denomination was Bishop C. P. Jones. It was the Church of Christ Holiness.

Coney attended the Lafayette Elementary School in Los Angeles until the fam-ily moved to Watts in the mid-twenties and the brothers were enrolled in the Grape Street Elementary School.

We moved to Watts and bought property at 111th and Wilmington, be-tween Grape and Wilmington. We had that property next to the Grape Street Elementary School. Watts was dirt streets, man. It was muddy and everything else when it rained. We saw it just grow. And the main street was 103rd. You had two theaters, the Largo and the Yeager. We'd go on Saturdays to see the cowboys. Yeah, it was the country. There wasn't any-thing out here hardly.

We were all athletic because we'd go to the library and play on the handlebars. All of us liked sports and things. We'd compete to see who could chin the most. We were all strong, and we all liked to fight. [laugh-ter] I always liked it. We'd go where there was boxing, and we'd have fights all the time with different people. You know, this was our territory, and when guys came from Los Angeles down here, we'd roll them back. [laughter] One group was called the Twenty-second Street Gang. And they'd come down here and want to take over, so we'd have to run them back. [laughter] We were called the Tarzans. That's a hell of a name, isn't it? I guess we were in the jungle. No other musicians than us. Everybody liked us, and we socialized with everybody. Most musicians, they weren't in that category, fighting. Charles Mingus, he liked to try to fight all the time. He wanted to fight everybody, man. He challenged all of us. We'd just look at him and laugh, because we knew we could whoop him. Well, he always liked to fight, and always had a reputation. When he got old, he followed his reputation. Any musician will tell you that.

Coney's father encouraged his children to study music.

Well, I didn't know any better. I guess it was just my daddy being a musician. He taught us. He started us all off playing music. Oh, I guess I was about seven. Dad, he inspired us. He knew everything about music.

But he didn't have time to fool with us boys. He'd get after us if we didn't practice. That was his job. [laughter] I had this German lady teacher who came around in a buggy. Just one horse pulling the buggy, man. All of us studied the piano first. See, piano's a good foundation. I studied banjo, and finally I went to the guitar, but I didn't stay on that too long. When we were going to the Grape Street School we were practicing, but weren't doing too much playing. We didn't start really playing till we got up to junior high school. I later took lessons from Professor Gray for technique and everything. Then I left from there and did my thing.

After elementary school Coney attended Jordan, a combined junior and senior high school at that time. Starting in the seventh grade, he made many friends who had a strong interest in music.

David Bryant. Joe Comfort. Big Jay McNeely. Of course Buddy Collette. Little Esther Phillips. Charles Mingus. When I met Mingus he was learning to play music. He was just carrying that cello, walking by the house from school. I guess it got old; he got codgers that would laugh at him carrying that cello. [laughter] But he sure could play. That's how he learned to play so fast. That cello put him in that position to play bass, because cello you execute more than you would on a bass.

We'd walk up to 103rd to Jordan High School, which wasn't too bad, because it was all vacant lots walking through there. We could just take shortcuts and cut over through the wilderness to the high school.

The Woodman Brothers Biggest Little Band in the World

I was the oldest, about fifteen or sixteen, when we started the band. My father wanted us to make that money. At that time we made about two dollars a night. He'd give us a quarter. [laughter] That was a lot of money, though. We were rich. We were the only ones who had a '37 Packard, brand-new, on the street. Yellow. That made us popular. Too popular. [laughter]

We had the Woodman Brothers Studio. That was at 111th and Wilmington. Some Jews had a store, and we bought them out eventually. They sold out. They wanted to leave because there were too many people coming around here. [laughter] And we made a studio out of it. We'd teach piano lessons. I had students. And I was a kid almost. [laughter] Well, I had a good foundation. You only had to teach them the scales. You didn't have to know too much. I didn't teach any theory. But we did know our instruments. And we'd give dances there. T. C. Rucker, he had a printing shop and would make those big placards and put them on posts. We sponsored our own things.

We lived a few doors away. We had all that property. And we had a service station on 112th and Wilmington, my grandma did. Grandma was in business. She's the one that had the brains, boy. We'd have been rich if my father would have listened to her. I hate to say that, but that's the truth. She had a business head. She was smart.

Joe Comfort played bass with us, and he had a brother named Frank Comfort. He played the trumpet. He would sit in sometimes. He was learning. He never did play too much. But Joe Comfort played trumpet, also. He was a pretty good trumpet player. And he didn't take any lessons on that. He had such a good ear, and he could play anything. And Jessie Sailes played the drums. He also played at the Follies. All these guys played down there. Jewell Grant played with us. He came from Texas and he was accomplished. He was a great musician. Maxwell Davis, a great saxophone player. And Maxwell did a lot of writing for us, was a good arranger. You should have heard him play tenor, man. He was great. All those guys could play. But mostly it was just us brothers. See, all the brothers played three instruments. My brothers played saxophone, trumpet. That's what made the novelty, all the instruments we played.

My father managed us. He'd write arrangements for us. We had to play what he'd write. Britt gets mad about it now, but Daddy would write his solo out for him. Nobody would write mine out. [laughter] There's not too much you could write for me. We played everything popular, mostly, all of Tommy Dorsey's music that was popular. We played anything. And we had stocks. We'd play a lot of stock music. We rearranged that. We were known for our reading. That's what made us so great. We'd read anything. And when I would go play for the studios, they'd put the music up there, and they were amazed because I could transpose. They'd go limp. We were pretty gifted.

People began to know about us. We played at the Elks and the Masonic temple, where the colored people had their big formals. The Elks was where all the young kids came and had their formals. We played at the

Follies. My dad got us up there. We played any kind of music. For Mexicans, we played Mexican. We played for movie stars. We played for all the communists. [laughter] A lot of movie stars were communists. They wanted us to join the Communist Party. We never got around to it. It's a good thing I didn't; I probably couldn't have worked at Rockwell. [laughter]

We didn't give politics a thought. We played for this black guy that wanted to take everybody back to Africa—Marcus Garvey. We played for anything, man. We didn't care what it was. [laughter] But we weren't thinking about being active. Everybody wanted us to be active, but we didn't take it seriously. Because we were too young. We weren't even twenty-one, man.

The band's success brought them to the attention of Elmer Fain, the business agent for Local 767.

Old Fain from the union would come down there, from 767, and wanted to make us join the union. I guess we were playing so many places. It was for the best, but we didn't think so, because we had to pay our dues. He got on us. We wanted to kick his butt, though. [laughter] We weren't scared of him. [laughter] The only time they can actually be tough is when you're in the union. But when they're trying to get you, "Hey, man, what are you going to do? Whoop my butt?" [laughter] You know, that attitude. And that would have been fun. [laughter] Us brothers would have ruined him, man. [laughter] We finally joined. Yeah, we joined.

Shotgun Wedding and Wartime Service

I was around twenty years old when I had to leave town. [laughter] I had to kiss the wagon, man. [laughter] Shit. [laughter] The girl laid it on me, let's put it that way. She wanted to have a wedding in Los Angeles. Not that I thought I was too good, but I didn't want to marry like that. Shotgun wedding: that's what you called them. I caught the train and left.

I messed up the band, man. It broke up shortly after I left. They all went their separate ways. It was great while it lasted and I kind of made a name. You wouldn't be out here doing this if it didn't pay at all some kind of way. I'm making history, aren't I? [laughter]

Coney headed for Chicago, where he stayed with an aunt.

I worked there playing the piano down in the dugouts, basement clubs, gangsters' places. I made two dollars a night and tips. I played on Michigan Avenue, that main street downtown in the Loop almost.

I boxed while I was there. I got my papers and everything. I fought where Joe Louis trained, fought lightweight. I was called the California Kid. I ran with [boxer] Tony Zale a lot. And he helped me a whole lot. We were courting the same girl in Chicago.

You made three dollars when you fought amateur fights. I needed the three dollars, man. I didn't worry about my hands. Hell no. I worried about going down, man! [laughter] I never gave that a thought. Well, I finally got whooped. You know who I fought? Sugar Ray [Robinson]. He wasn't popular then. He was an amateur, too. Shit. He was just starting off himself. [laughter] He was more talented than me. He had more fights than me. And, boy, he hit me in my stomach and it sure did hurt. After that, I quit.

But I took the fights to make that money. You didn't have to be all that good to fight amateurs. They'd need somebody, they'd give you three dollars for three rounds. I never got knocked out, though I got hit a lot.

About a year later, in 1939, Coney returned to Los Angeles to face a paternity suit brought by his girlfriend's family. When she didn't show, the case was dismissed. He took a gig that landed him in Seattle, until he got a call to tour with Les Hite's band.

I went with Les Hite in '41. I was in Seattle when they sent for me. There was this rich lady with Les Hite. She owned the band and we had the best of everything. We may not have been the best band, but we made more money than the rest of them. I got ninety dollars a week, man. That was a lot of money then. She liked Les Hite. [laughter] Yeah. We lived good. I left the band in New York. Gerald Wiggins took my place when I got drafted.

I got inducted in '42. I should have been inducted right when I joined Les Hite. I started getting those papers. But we moved so much. Finally, they caught up with us. We came home to Los Angeles and went down to Fort MacArthur, this camp down here in San Pedro.

They put me in a car company in the Presidio, in San Francisco, the guys that drive the officers around. And I drove a chaplain—he was a colonel with the Fifty-fourth Coast Artillery, the 155-millimeter batteries all down the coast. And he had me playing for the church services.

Then they took the coast artillery from us and changed us over to combat engineers. That's what we did, build bridges. Pontoon bridges and all that. They sent us to Louisiana, out of Alexander. We got in trouble there. I was the first one that got put in jail down there. We had a bus driver and he was talking to a white woman. I walked up to him, and he kicked me. I guess I shouldn't have interrupted. And I tried to catch him, boy. He ran. I couldn't catch that guy. He was a big, tall guy. And the MPs [military police] were coming, saying they were going to hit me with those billy clubs. I told them, "You hit me, man, I'll kill you. You'd better kill me." They put me in jail, and my commanding officer came and got me out. And he told them, if they do anything like that again, he's going to give us some ammunition and we're going to come up there and tear up the town. He had but one arm. He'd been in combat. He was a great colonel.

So we went to Bastrop, Texas, and then they sent us overseas in '43. I went to the Philippines, to Tangas, seventy-five miles from Manila. I was stationed there for a while. Then we went to Yokohama, and then Tokyo. So we were stationed in Tokyo till I could come home, in April '46. I was in for three years and ten months.

Los Angeles in the Late Forties

When Coney returned from Japan, he moved in with his parents, on Forty-ninth Street between Main and Broadway, closer to Central Avenue's center.

That's when I sent for the girl I married, Emily [Riley Woodman], from Louisiana. We met when I was stationed there. I was playing the piano at the USO, just fiddling around, that's all. I passed by her and said, "I'm going to marry you." [laughter] I found out where she lived, got a jeep, and came on by the house and met the folks. I was over there eating every Sunday. Married to her forty-three years. I almost started to get married before then. But I was scared. I heard a guy talking about Shorty George. He's the guy that, when you're married and you leave your wife, he takes over.

But four years later I married my wife. I met her when she was eighteen or nineteen. She was twenty-two when I married her. I wish I had married her then. It would have put me ahead, way ahead. Because she was a good girl. She's a Christian girl and everything. But I was just scared, man. I'm still scared. [laughter]

She stayed right in my mother's house on Forty-ninth Street, and we got married in the house. I stayed there about a year, and then I went and lived over on Ninth off of Jefferson.

In 1947 we started working at the Title House in Culver City. Scatman Crothers was there with Slim Gaillard and then our group, Connie Jordan and the Jordanaires. George Mason played the bass. Louis Gonzalez, Mexican guy, played the guitar, and Connie Jordan played the drums and sang. We rehearsed at Connie's house practically every day for about six months till we built up a repertoire, and then we were ready to go. We got an agent who got us the jobs and we stayed busy.

We were also at Cafe Society on San Pedro. We'd come and play after-hours. We worked at the Title House from eight till twelve, and then we came there and played from one till four. We did that for quite a while and made good money till the police started harassing us so much that we had to close that down. So many white people were coming over that way, man, I guess they didn't appreciate it. And then, I guess, the people started messing up with dope, and things started changing. But I didn't pay attention, because I was still playing. I wasn't doing any of that. But all those places started folding down.

Most of the cops Chief Parker would hire, he would get from down South. All the cops in Watts come from down South. There was discrimination everywhere; there wasn't supposed to be, but there was in some parts of Los Angeles. You couldn't go to Compton. Well, we'd go over there shopping. It's just that you couldn't live there.

And we played at Billy Berg's during '48, '49. We were the house band. We would play for intermissions, when the featured attraction would take their breaks. Then we played all around. The Brass Rail in Glendale. Just a club. Very prejudiced during that time. Glendale has always been prejudiced. Cops harassed us all the time. They wanted to look at my cigarettes to see if I had any dope in them. I never gave that a thought, because I didn't have no marijuana. I smoked some, but I didn't smoke any around like that. I wouldn't dare do anything like that. They harassed us on the streets, not in the clubs. When we were getting out or something like that. But we were used to that. We'd had a taste of that, because they started doing that on Central Avenue.

During the struggle in the late forties and early fifties to unite the black and white locals of the musicians union, Coney strongly supported amalgamation.

Well, it was all right. To me it was a better location. It seemed like I was going to a building. This was a house on Central Avenue. That was nothing but a big, old raggedy house, man. It wasn't anything. Over there, it's like a union, a big building. You had offices, and they had a recreation place; you could play pool in the basement and things. It seemed like you're in something. To me, it was great.

So I supported it. Sure. I had no doubts about following them. Because there wasn't anything happening in that black union. And anyway, they got all the work, it looked like. When you get over there, you get some jobs. So I'm a life member from '39 to '69.

My experience playing music was real great. I didn't accomplish all I should have and could have if some things had been another way. But I don't regret it. I enjoy it and appreciate all the experience I've had with my music. I'm going to tell you, it was something that I will never forget.

5

William "Brother"
Woodman, Jr.

Tenor saxophonist Brother Woodman has spent his life in Los Angeles and *has performed with, among others, Fletcher Henderson, Maxwell Davis, Joe Liggins, Bumps Myers, and Jake Porter. As a teenager he was one of the most promising performers in southern California, with a sound likened to tenor sax great Chu Berry, and he was a founding member of the Woodman Brothers Biggest Little Band in the World. His health forced him to give up playing professionally in 1967, after two decades of consistent freelancing with the finest bands in Los Angeles, but he continues to perform in his church orchestra.*

Brother's mother and father grew up in Mississippi, the children of sharecroppers, and moved to Los Angeles along with many family members during the 1910s to escape the Jim Crow South. Brother received his nickname from his parents.

I was born in Los Angeles, April 22, 1919, and I was raised in Watts. My family consists of three brothers: Coney, Britt, and George. I went to Grape Elementary School, which was right next door to where I lived, which was 111th Street.

The environment there was almost all races, and we all got along very well. There were whites, Mexicans, Orientals, Jewish people. That's why, at that time, I didn't really understand about prejudice. I said, "How could that happen? Right here, we get along so beautifully, all of us together." Everything was beautiful. The environment was great.

My father, being a trombone player and a musician, he gave all of us brothers music. He worked at the Follies Burlesque Theatre, which was one of the main burlesque houses on Main Street. He worked there for about seven years, and he did well there. As a matter of fact, he provided for all of the family, a very, very wonderful provider. He was never out of work. He played with various bands, but the latest band that he played with was the Teddy Buckner Dixieland Band. He was with him for quite some time.

I was about seven years old when I started playing piano. I took from this German teacher. I don't know her name. We wanted to play. My father asked each of us which instrument we'd love to play. I said, "I want to play trumpet." Britt said, "I want to play trombone." So he said, "Well, I'm going to give all of you piano lessons first. Then that will be the fundamentals, the foundation." I played piano for two years. Then he gave me trumpet lessons, which I took from Lloyd Reese for two years. Lloyd Reese taught you out of the book. Intervals and scales, chords. And I learned to read well. All these things helped. Then he decided that he wanted me to play clarinet, so I took clarinet from Marshal Royal's uncle [Ernest Royal] for two years. Then, after two years, I took up saxophone.

My early influences were Chu Berry and Coleman Hawkins and Don Byas and big bands like Benny Goodman and Roy Eldridge. Those were my idol musicians, each one of these. Chu Berry was my idol on the saxophone. I loved his style, and I loved his tone. And everybody that heard Chu Berry said, "Man, hey, Brother"—they called me Brother—"You know who you sound like?" "Yeah, Chu Berry." "Yeah, you sound just like Chu Berry."

My brother Coney played piano and banjo. There weren't any guitars around at that time. Banjo was the main string instrument. Coney stayed with the piano. Britt took piano lessons for two years, and my dad gave him trombone lessons for two years. Then he took clarinet lessons, and the saxophone self-taught.

I graduated from Jordan High School in 1936. Jordan was mostly Mexicans and blacks, because Watts consisted of more blacks and mixed, and we were all integrated there. We all got along wonderfully together, though. It was all right. Of course, my best friends at that time were Joe Comfort, Charles Mingus, Buddy Collette, Big Jay McNeely, and Bumps Myers. All of us were brought up in Watts.

Charles Mingus used to play cello. He took lessons. He carried that cello right on his arms to school. And we used to rehearse over at a little apartment I had. We just had a lot of fun. He and I were the best of friends, because we went around together to different places, went to shows together and all that. The only thing about Charles Mingus, he thought himself above other musicians, which was a very bad attitude that he had taken. He had a very mean temper. I really don't know what brought his attitude. Nobody really knows.

We had the Woodman Brothers Biggest Little Band in the World at that time. In Watts there were two bands before us. Dootsie Williams, a trumpet player, had a band. And the Irving Brothers had a band. They were very popular at one time in Watts. They had, I think it was, three brothers and the rhythm section. I think it was about seven pieces. When we started getting pretty popular, they were still going, too. Just local. Nothing great. But we were the most popular of anyone who had a band, period. [laughter] Those are the only two I can think of who were before us.

We started playing together around about 1934. Britt was about fourteen, and I was fifteen. Coney was seventeen. We started playing professionally. My father did all our arrangements and he was like our manager, and did all the bookings. We were recognized because we were the only musicians who doubled on three instruments. You didn't hear of anybody doubling on brass. Everybody was amazed to see us. All the musicians said, "How do you do it, man? How can your embouchure change from a brass to a reed?" I said, "Well, you just practice and get used to it." [laughter]

With our little orchestra we had Jessie Sailes. He was a drummer. He played with Teddy Buckner out at Disneyland for about fifteen years. And Joe Comfort was our bass player. Now, you talk about something unique, he played trumpet, and he could play every one of Roy Eldridge's solos. He could pick up the trumpet and play all those high notes. He had a terrific ear, and he had a good embouchure on trumpet. He just picked up the trumpet and started playing it. Amazing, isn't it? Because bass was his instrument. Of course, he was a great bass player. And then Ernie Royal, Marshal Royal's brother, played trumpet with us. So we really had a terrific band.

My father arranged standard tunes at that time for us. Like he'd arrange for the trombone and the trumpet to play maybe a chorus of "Sophisticated Lady" or whatever. Then we'd set our instruments down, pick up our clarinets, and we'd play our clarinets together. Then we'd put down our clarinets and pick up our saxophones and play them. We really were something. Britt and I were what you call sight readers. Anything put up in front of us we could read.

And we kept working. At that time three dollars a night was good money. We would play at least three dances a week. There's three of us, so that's nine dollars a week that we would bring in. And we didn't value money. My daddy would give us an allowance. Every Monday night, he'd put a quarter on the dresser. Monday, we'd be looking for that quarter. That was our allowance. He'd made nine dollars, and he'd give us a quarter. [laughter] But we were so happy to get it.

We played everywhere. The Lincoln Theatre, and that was really something, too. That's when the Lincoln Theatre was pretty outstanding and big bands played there. We played for clubs, dances all over the region of Los Angeles. We played at the Elks Hall on Central Avenue, the Masonic temple on Fifty-fourth and Central. There's a place called Leak's Lake Ballroom. That was a big ballroom, out there about 116th, right off Central. Somewhere out there in Watts. It was a real huge place, and that's all they did was just ballroom dancing. We played in Bakersfield. We played in Arizona and San Diego.

We also played at this little club in Watts run by the Brown Sisters, three of them. That was very unusual for three women to have a club. But they did very good business. It was, I would say, about 116th Street. It was just a small club. But it was very popular, packed all the time. Once Elmer Fain, the business agent of Local 767, happened to come out. He was very strict. Man, he would pull musicians off the job if they didn't have their card or weren't paid up. He was going to pull us off that job, but my father talked him out of it. We weren't in the union. My daddy said, "Well, just let them play and I'll make sure they're all put in the union." So he went down, and he put us all into the union. We've all become life members.

Then, on 111th Street and Wilmington we had the Woodman Brothers Studio. It was really something else. We could play there every Saturday night, and it cost, I think, fifteen cents admission, and people from downtown used to come down there. Every Saturday night, that would be reserved for a dance. My daddy put that on and made this into a little dance hall. Every now and then, you know, some of the fellows, they'd get in fights. At that time the fights were clean—no knives, no guns. The best man wins, shake hands, that was it. [laughter] Every Saturday we'd expect a fight. But they didn't tear up anything. They went outside like gentlemen, and they fought. [laughter]

Recently arrived in Los Angeles was Maxwell Davis, a young musician who became a leading saxophonist, bandleader, arranger, and orchestrator, and later, in the 1950s, one of the major creative forces in the burgeoning Los Angeles rhythm and blues scene.

Maxwell Davis came out here when we had the studio. I can't recall what year. It was in the thirties. He was maybe about twenty-two and a very homely looking fellow. He was trying to get in contact with musicians because he didn't know anyone, and, of course, everybody had heard of the Woodman Brothers. His saxophone looked raggedy. It was painted all different colors. He played tenor, and I was playing tenor. At that time, we didn't have two tenor parts in our arrangements. Three altos and tenor. He said, "Well, give me the alto part." We looked and said, "Man, you're going to have to transpose. How are you going to play that?" He transposed that like it wasn't nothing. [laughter] I could do the same thing. But, like I say, he looked so homely, we looked at him saying, "He can't play, man, the way he looks—" Judging him, you know. [laughter] Yeah, he taught me a lesson. After he played with us when we were rehearsing, we were glad to meet him. We were all admiring his playing, how great he was. We said, "See that, man? From now on, we'd better not judge people because of how they look and if their instrument is all beat up." Later on, I started playing with him. He knew I could play.

We had that studio for about three years, and it did very good business. My grandmother [Henrietta Jones] owned the property around there. She owned about four or five homes within that block, and the Woodman Brothers Studio was within that block, also.

Then our band broke up. I'm the one who caused the breakup. Like a fool, I got married. Then I started playing with various groups, and Britt started venturing out with different bands and with different orchestras. I started playing with Maxwell Davis, Cee Pee Johnson.

**"People wanted to go places, and
Central Avenue was the place to go."**

Central Avenue before the war was almost like Broadway in New York. It
was just great. People from all over would come down on Central Avenue.
The entertainment was great, and they even had after-hours spots. The
Memo Club was one of the main hangouts for musicians on Central
Avenue. And the Ritz Club, which was an after-hours spot, musicians
from all over the world would come there. And Honey Murphy's on
Central Avenue. That was another after-hours spot where all the musi-
cians came, musicians like Art Tatum, Illinois Jacquet, Lester Young, Ben
Webster. We'd come up there and jam. Another place called Brother's,
that was another after-hours spot on Adams Boulevard.

The most important club was the Club Alabam. Hollywood used to
come down there all the time. Most of the clientele were white people
from Hollywood. It was a place where you had all kinds of big bands and
entertainers. I worked there with Happy Johnson. Curtis Mosby owned
the Alabam at that time. And some of these guys who owned these clubs,
they'd forget to pay the musicians. [laughter] They took him to the musicians union because so many musicians had complained about his owing them. So, you know, he had to pay. I got a part of that money. Another club that was doing very well was the Downbeat. I played there
with Lee Young, Lester Young's brother.

When the war came, Brother was drafted.

I was in the service for about eleven weeks. I had narcolepsy. It's a sleeping
sickness. When I was about fourteen years old, I used to do quite a bit of
exercise on the bars, and I fell off the bars and fell on my head. I began
to sleep a lot, and that's how I got out of school, because I slept through
school. I couldn't do any work.

That's how I got out of the service. When I was inducted, I told them
I had sleeping sickness, but they didn't listen to me because there were so
many soldiers at that time who tried to get out and talked about how
crazy they were. They thought I was goldbricking, but I was telling the
truth. They took me. While I was in there, I would be standing up in
the middle of the road and fall asleep. So I got an honorable discharge.
[laughter]

During the war, that's when Central Avenue was jumping. People wanted to go places, and Central Avenue was the place to go. That was it. All kinds of people from Hollywood, stars would come out there. They're what kept the Alabam open, really. The Plantation Club in Watts was where all the big bands played. Jimmie Lunceford. Basie. All those big bands came through there because it was the place. It was like a big, big barn. It had sawdust all over the floor. Oh, yeah, it was fine at that time. Everybody loved the Plantation.

After the war, that's when things began to change. People from the South, blacks from the South, I mean, they came down there, and the environment just changed. And then a lot of the Mexicans began to what you call migrate. Right now there's nothing but Mexicans down there, more than blacks, I believe.

When I came out of the service, I started working with the various bands. I worked with Cee Pee Johnson, Maxwell Davis, and Jake Porter. We played at different places. I worked with Jessie Price in several places. He was an outstanding drummer. He had a good beat, but he was loud. He played with any and everybody around here. He always worked. I once worked with him at the Melody Club on Slauson. That's when we played with Sammy Davis, Jr. He and his father and uncle, they always worked together. The Will Mastin Trio. He was just a young kid, but we all said someday he's going to be great. He finally ventured out. His talent exceeded them so much. All they were doing was this old-time dancing, which was real good at that time.

The Melody Club on Slauson. I'll tell you what happened there. Well, as I said before, I wasn't used to prejudice. I just didn't see how it even existed. I was born in Watts, and at Jordan High there was a mixture of various races: white, Mexican, Oriental. We all got along wonderful together. At the Melody Club people were coming in, the place began to pack, and they had "reserved" signs on almost all the tables. I wondered about that within myself. White people would come in. It was packed every night. Then the blacks would be coming in, and they'd turn them away. And that really got to me.

So I went to Jessie Price. I said, "Man, did you see those colored people?"

"Yeah, man. I don't like it, either, but there ain't nothing you can do about it."

"Well, man, why don't you talk to the man and ask him what's happening?"

"No, man. I can't do that. That's just the way it is."

"Well, I'll talk to him." So I spoke to him. I forget his name. He was a Jewish fellow. I asked him, "Why is it that the colored people come in here, and you're turning them down, and these reserved signs on the table surely aren't reserved for everybody? But the reason why you've got them reserved is because it seems like you just want to make the colored people think that all these tables are reserved."

"Well, I'll tell you, Mr. Woodman, that's just the way it is. That's the way it is, and there's nothing I can do about it."

I said, "You can do something about it."

He didn't like it when I said it to him. He told Jessie Price to fire me. So he let me go. I wanted to hit him in the mouth, but I couldn't do that. They wouldn't allow any blacks in there, no colored people. That wasn't the only place. There were many places like that.

Glendale — "If they caught a black man on the street after midnight, they'd throw him in jail."

I was touring with Joe Liggins and the Honeydrippers for about two years in the fifties. As a matter of fact, I kept working. I never was out of work. Yeah, I made my living playing music, and I did very well. I never did want to travel. I could have gone with various bands. Lionel Hampton wanted me to go with him. He wanted me to play trumpet with him. That's when I was playing trumpet and playing trumpet real good. As a matter of fact, I loved Roy Eldridge, and that's who I more or less was playing like, copying Roy Eldridge. I loved his playing and Chu Berry on tenor. Those were my favorites. Yeah. It was something else.

Now, the place that I enjoyed playing most was the Melody Club in Glendale. This was around '53 to '58. There was Bumps Myers, Poison Gardner, the piano player, Bob Harvey was the drummer. And I think Ralph Hamilton, a good bass player. He played with Teddy Buckner for a long time. Monday night was jam session night, and it was packed. That place was packed every night. It was open every night except Sunday. All we did was jam every night. We didn't have no music. We just jammed, period.

I was an entertainer myself when I played. It was in me to be pretty lively all the time as a saxophone player. I was always moving and— I don't know. It just happened. "Flying Home" was my featured number and I would go out and lay on my back and I'd be playing. [sings melody] Just blowing, you know. Blowing. I used to get up on the bar and lay on my back. [laughter] When I was playing the Melody Club in Glendale, everybody would come out to see us. And I would go outside and start playing. Big Jay McNeely used to get up on the bar, lay on his back. He'd walk outside, and people would follow him. He'd walk down the street, they would come on back. I never taught Big Jay. But he was inspired by me, most likely.

Speaking of the Melody Club, Clora Bryant would come out there every Monday night and even through the week. It was amazing just to hear a woman play like she played. At that time, you didn't find too many woman trumpet players. You don't find too many now. We just couldn't believe that a woman could play that well. She surprised all of us. You know, she was good. Everybody accepted her.

At that time, prejudice was existing then in Glendale. If they caught a black man on the street after midnight, they'd throw him in jail when nobody was doing nothing. But the police knew us. After we got out, we just went on home. But the other clubs around there were jealous of Mr. Perry, the owner. We had all the business. Even the fire department gave him trouble and tried to put in an exit over here and an exit over there, where it really wasn't necessary. He finally closed up because of them giving him a hard time. He was Italian, too, and they didn't care particularly about the Italians, either. [laughter]

Last Gig—
"But I enjoyed myself when I was out there."

The last place I played was with Jake Porter at the Largo on the [Sunset] Strip. It was one of the most outstanding burlesque places on the Strip. I worked there for five years. Then the owner, Mr. Stern, came up to me and said, "Brother, I've got some bad news for you. I'm going to have to let you go. The girls"—which were the stripteasers—"they got together and said I'm going to have to get rid of you." The girls conspired against me, and they wanted to get a white man in there. That's what it was. That was the last place I played. After that I worked for Sears Roebuck.

See, after that, my memory began to fade, because the narcolepsy had affected my memory. I wasn't able to comprehend tunes. I wasn't able to remember well. I couldn't have stayed out there and played music because to be a great musician, you've got to comprehend tunes, be able to have a good ear and grasp tunes, remember tunes, which at one time I could do. I had perfect pitch. I was born with it. Hear any note, any sound, I could tell that's C, B, G, that's a C chord, an F chord, whatever. And I knew that I was going to be one of the greatest saxophone players, which I would have been, when this happened to me—

I believe that it was only God's will. I look at it in this way. Because I believe that if I had not had this sleeping sickness, and if I had been in the service, I wouldn't have gotten out, period. At that time, I was very bitter against prejudice. I know I probably would have gotten hurt, because I heard that down South the blacks couldn't eat in the restaurants. I said, "Why?" I heard that even the prisoners, German prisoners, could go eat anywhere they wanted. Here I'm fighting for my country, and I couldn't go in there. Well, all this really registered on me, and I said, "Lordy, I couldn't take this. I wouldn't be able to take it." So it just happened that because I had this narcolepsy I got out.

And then I also believe that if I had kept on and not had this narcolepsy and was playing in different clubs all over, I might have gotten myself in trouble in the sense of not being thoughtful and not taking care of myself. I might have gotten into dope, I might have gotten into anything, you know. But I got out of it, and I believe that it was only God's will that it happened this way. But I was pretty cool while I was in there. I didn't do too much drinking, I didn't dissipate, I didn't run after women, and that's why I feel as well as I do now. Thank God for that.

But I prayed. I'd just say, "God, give it back to me. Just give me what I had. I'll take care of everything. I'm not going to do anything wrong." [laughter] Anyway, I guess God doesn't work like that. But I enjoyed myself when I was out there.

Fighting Segregation in the Union

I wasn't involved in the amalgamation, but the personalities who were involved in that were Buddy Collette and Marl Young and Bill Douglass. Those were the three main persons who got this thing rolling. The amalgamation came, really, through them, because they were something. Finally we amalgamated, which was a good thing. All of us felt that segregation was a terrible thing. We're all here as human beings and musicians. And particularly musicians, we're supposed to be like brothers and sisters. They say music is the greatest language in the world, so why are we separated? It doesn't make sense. We knew white musicians, and they used to say the same thing. And it came about.

Some opposed it. There's always some stupid person who says, "We're doing all right," like even Elmer Fain did once. You know why he opposed it? See, movie studios would call the musicians union for different ones to come out there. We'd usually pose, you know; it wasn't really playing. They would call 767 and say, "Send three or four musicians out to the studio." He would go out on all those gigs himself. So naturally, he was doing great, man. He'd get all the studio gigs. So naturally, he opposed it. [laughter]

"A showcase for talent . . . a melting pot for all races."

A change of environment, the crime rate rose, and that's what really stopped the people from supporting the clubs. And clubs had to close down because of this. That's what really stopped the people from coming out and supporting the Alabam and other clubs.

Central was a showcase for talent. That's really what it was. It was just that great. A place of entertainment, a melting pot, that's what it was, a melting pot for all races. And it had very much to offer the young kids coming up. Things were really nice, and no violence and no crimes. It was just a wonderful place to come and even to see, just like Watts itself was a great place to live. Everybody was getting along wonderfully. There wasn't any crime. There wasn't any shooting and killing and all that.

Watts was a great place at one time. Central Avenue was a great place. It was really a wonderful place to behold. It really was.

6

Britt Woodman

rombonist Britt Woodman left Los Angeles in 1951 to join Duke Ellington's band, where he remained until 1960. He then settled in New York and performed in various jazz combinations and Broadway show bands, including The Sound of Music, A Raisin in the Sun, The Wiz, Pal Joey, Sophisticated Ladies, Ain't Misbehavin', *and* Jelly's Last Jam.

Britt returned to Los Angeles in 1970 and remained until 1979. He freelanced, worked on various TV shows, and played with Bill Berry's L.A. Big Band and the Toshiko Akiyoshi–Lew Tabackin Big Band. In 1979 Britt returned to New York, where he continues to perform.

During his long career Britt has recorded with many jazz musicians and ensembles, including Miles Davis, Mercer Ellington, Chico Hamilton, Jimmy Hamilton, Johnny Hodges, and Charles Mingus, and he has performed with Benny Carter, John Coltrane, Dizzy Gillespie, Benny Goodman, the Capp/Pierce Juggernaut, Nelson Riddle, and Jimmy Smith.

I was born June 4, 1920, in Los Angeles on Fourteenth Street, I think it was off of Hooper, and I had at that time two older brothers: William, who was one year older than me, and my older brother, Coney, was three years older. I'm quite sure that my parents moved out here in 1918. I don't know for sure, but from what my dad [William B. Woodman, Sr.] was saying to other people, he was a musician, and there wasn't any work there in Mississippi for him. Grandma, my father's mother, had sent him to college, Alcorn College, Mississippi. He studied music, because he could arrange, and he could read music very well.

When Britt was six the family moved to Watts.

We moved to 111th Street, right next to the grade school that we attended. The name of the school was Grape Street [Elementary] School. We were the only house on a dirt road. And my dad dug a cesspool in the back, because at that time Los Angeles County didn't have any toilets or anything. Sometimes it would flood. You'd see it come up. [laughter] We also had a well back there. Fresh water. We had all kinds of trees in the backyard: peach trees and plum trees and grapes. Oh, we had a big grapevine there. Then we had chickens and geese.

I can remember my mother taking us to church—all three of us to church—every Sunday. I played trombone in church. I'm so glad that I was raised up in church, man, because I had the chance to hear the truth, and that's why I've been free all my life. See, certain things in the Bible, you know, it's true. The truth will make you free. So I learned part of the truth when I was young. Because the main thing is don't hate. Hate is one of the worst things in the world. And I learned that people are people. There are ugly people in every race. All those things I learned.

In Watts you didn't run into racial problems. But we knew the outside: Inglewood, Bell, South Gate. We knew they were prejudiced. We knew Long Beach was prejudiced, we knew Compton was prejudiced, we knew San Diego was prejudiced, all those places, Burbank, Pasadena. But Watts was beautiful. There were no slums in Watts. And we had friends. Most of my friends never were real popular—they were just being successful as a family person, but not in a musical way. Joe Adams became very popular, being a disc jockey, one of the first black disc jockeys in Los Angeles. Eleven o'clock, everybody tuned in to hear him playing the Ink Spots, and different groups that were very popular at that time. His studio was in Santa Monica. KGFJ. Also, now he's managing Ray Charles's band— did it for years. But a lot of my friends were just good friends that I visited: Teaque Johnson, Alfred Daniel, Joe Adams, William Luke.

People got along, and everybody was beautiful. Now, the Mexicans were beautiful. Mexicans were like us in a sense—minority. They couldn't go into certain sections over there because that was the white neighborhood. Now, the whites went to our school, but we couldn't mingle over there. One day when we were rehearsing in our home, some of the white fellows asked if they could come and listen. We said sure. So one of them made a statement—I never forgot it—"Britt and Coney," he said, "I sure wish you could meet my mother and father, but the neighbors, they'd resent it, you coming over there."

The white neighborhood was on about 96th to 101st Street right off of Wilmington Avenue. Just like the Japanese. The Japanese lived off of Compton Avenue. And the Chinamen, they had a little community where they lived. It was all divided. You know, the Japanese had the grocery stores in the neighborhood where the blacks would go. But they all were going to our school.

There wasn't much of a shopping area. On 103rd Street you had a shoe store there and a little store where you could buy little things. The market's there and a theater—the Largo. The Largo had the main pictures: cowboys, Tim Tyler, Buck Jones—all those cowboys. Mickey Mouse was the main comedy then.

I can't remember the section, but around 118 Parmelee was a club— T-Bone Walker was the main star there. The Little Harlem. That's it. I think the club was owned by the Brown Sisters, and it was one of the popular clubs where people from Los Angeles would come down there to see him and other artists. Scatman Crothers. He played there. Played the ukulele, you know. And the trumpet player that was with him—James Howard—he was in the service with me. So that's how I happened to go down there to see him and Scatman. Scat was very popular, too, at that time—an entertainer.

Now, the reason why my dad wanted us to be musicians I don't know, but I know that he would say that musicians would have a better life, a better chance to make money during that time. He noticed that kids that were able to go to college, black kids, whatever they majored in, they never got any jobs, so they had to refer back to the post office. So he figured that being a musician—if you're on top, you have a better chance to make a better living. So we all started on piano. I was seven years old. It was my dad's idea. I'll tell you what, I didn't want to practice on the piano, but I had to. [laughter]

We had piano teachers. First was a white German teacher. And from there we went up to Los Angeles to another teacher called Professor Gray, a great black teacher who not only taught piano, but he taught harmony and theory. And you know, all during that time I didn't want to play piano, I didn't want to take theory, but I did remember all the things that

I was taught. In later years it sure helped me a lot, especially when I went up to Westlake College of Music to study arranging and other forms of music.

When I was seven years old, going on eight, my dad gave me a trombone, the instrument that he played, and William, next to me, a trumpet. Coney stayed on piano, and he gave him a banjo. My dad taught me trombone, and one of the teachers at the Follies Theatre taught my brother the trumpet, and one of the teachers at the Follies Theatre taught Coney on the banjo. When we moved to Watts, that's when dad started working at the burlesque theater. We called that the Follies Theatre. On Main Street. Around Sixth and Seventh on Main. That was one of the popular theaters. And I'll tell you, after playing the Follies Theatre— They talk about how the black musicians couldn't read— All those musicians were superb. I don't know where they got their training. Just like my dad could read very well.

So after three years—I was ten—on trombone, he gave me a sax, a tenor sax, and my other brother, William, alto sax, and Coney, guitar. I was eleven years old when I got the sax. I can't remember: sometimes I think my dad taught us the sax. I can't remember anyone else teaching us on the saxophone. When I was thirteen, he gave us the clarinet—me the clarinet and William the clarinet—and Coney just stayed on the guitar and banjo and piano. Now, our first lesson on the clarinet was with Marshal Royal's uncle, Ernie Royal. That's when I met Marshal and Ernie [Marshal's brother]. And he was a terrific teacher. Now, he taught us about eight months or six months or seven months, like that. Then my dad went to another teacher, a German teacher, that played in one of the symphony orchestras here in Los Angeles, and so he taught us the remaining year or so.

After school we'd do our practice first, then we'd go play. And you know, during all that time, Coney would be on the piano practicing, my brother in the other room—the screened porch—and I'd be in the bedroom, and we'd be practicing all together. We didn't think about that until we got older, how our mother could stand all that noise. [laughter]

I went to high school when I was fifteen. That's when we started playing professional, at fifteen. We were very apt on the instruments; we were learning so fast. I played music in the high school band and orchestra, and sometimes I would play the clarinet part when the clarinet player wasn't there. And the teacher was so amazed. And my other brother played clarinet. I decided not to take my trombone, so I learned to play the baritone, because I didn't want to take my trombone. It's too much trouble carrying it. [laughter] But I would carry my mouthpiece. Anything that some other trombone player couldn't play, then I would take it and play it on the trombone. All my solos that I would play or perform were Arthur Price's. He was first trombonist with John Philip Sousa's band. So my daddy taught me how to double tongue and triple tongue and all that, and I was very fast on the trombone.

In fact, Mr. [Joseph Louis] Lippi was the musical director. So he told my dad, "Britt could be a virtuoso on the trombone, and I can recommend him to one of our noted teachers here that plays with the symphony orchestra." And so my dad, which I regret today— I wish my dad had accepted that suggestion. But he told him, "Well, there's no future for Britt to play that type of music. He can't get into the symphony orchestra." But, you see, it was wrong thinking. I stayed in the book more so than I did jazz, playing exercises and playing the trumpet part and all that. I could play from an exercise book practically everything in there. In fact, I could play "Flight of the Bumble Bee" on the horn. I could play that fast. And I didn't double tongue; I single tongued. Most of the trombone players, when they play that they double tongue. He taught me how to transpose from the trumpet part and the tenor part and the clarinet part, because my range was very high, so I didn't have any trouble playing high.

I was gifted. My dad had never told me how to form my lips or anything. When I picked up the trombone, I played a note. First time, just played the note. And pretty soon I was playing just higher, altissimo B-flats and all that, just so easy. In fact, there's a B-flat above the staff on the trombone, then there's another B-flat way up above that. Well, that B-flat I could make. At that time, it sounded so big and round that you wouldn't think that it was an altissimo B-flat. It was just natural. I wasn't told how to play it. I was just gifted. In fact, we were all gifted.

Turning Pro

When I was fifteen, that's when we started playing professionally. Initially it was three of us. Our dad arranged the numbers. He would use some of the stock arrangements up in front, the melody, but then he would arrange different things so that we would change—be able to show the flash. In two bars we'd change and play the saxophone. I'm on the sax, then I'll jump on the trombone, and William—we called him Brother—on the trumpet, then change to sax. Coney was improvising. My dad wrote most of my solos out, because at the time I couldn't improvise at all. Now, William had a very good ear, so he started improvising and playing things. So I didn't do much. Most of mine was reading.

Our first drummer, Martin Hurd, played in the school band. He didn't stay with us too long. Then there was another drummer named George Reed. Now, he played with us for quite a while until he graduated. Then he left us and went with Horace Henderson, Fletcher Henderson's brother. In fact, he married his daughter. Then the other drummer we had was Jessie Sailes. He didn't have a drum. My dad bought a drum set for him. Then Joe Comfort, bass and trumpet. All that happened around '36, '37 with Jessie Sailes when the band was really tight.

So we played in weddings, dances, and homes. Doctors would have house parties for their kids, and we'd play for the kids. The doctor's the only one who can afford to pay us, you know. [laughter] And we played down at the Elks. But there we enlarged our band. Ernie Royal was with us for a while. And there's a fellow by the name of Terry Cruise who played just clarinet; he was a star with George Brown. George Brown had one of the big bands very popular in Los Angeles, from Pasadena.

I can remember so well that we played the Dunbar Hotel, and there was a room called the Golding Room, where they had dances. So we were playing, and I remember so well when Illinois Jacquet and Dexter Gordon were standing in front of us, looking at us. Well, everywhere we played, at the Elks, people would stand in front of us amazed because we were switching horns as we played, which we didn't think anything of. Sometimes we had one bar. [mimics frantic switching of instruments] [laughter] And we played up in the hills for actors. I remember once Joe E. Brown was there at the time and John Wayne. And we played for the Dandridge Sisters [Dorothy and Vivian] before Dorothy Dandridge became an actor.

So every weekend we were working. We played so many dances for the Mexicans—Montebello and places, and weddings and things. We knew this: when we played for a Mexican dance, we knew they were going to fight. Every time. Sometimes it got so bad we'd have to stop playing and pack up because they couldn't stop them from fighting. A lot of times, when they'd start fighting, they'd break it up, as they'd be fighting their cousins and friends. They'd get juiced and they'd just start fighting, throwing chairs. So we'd know: We'd say, "Well, we've got this gig, we know that in an hour and a half they're going to start fighting." [laughter]

Most of those gigs I'd get $1.50 or $2. Coney would get more, being the leader. My dad put the price, whatever it was that we charged. At the Follies Theatre, during all those years my dad raised us, he was getting $21 and something a week. And I went there to play—that's when I found out what he was getting. Twenty-one dollars. But my father got it all. No, he gave me a dollar. Well, see, actually I didn't need the money for anything. At the time, he bought all my clothes and stuff, and I was still going to school. We weren't doing anything as individuals to be somewhere or to show something. Because playing for dances, house parties, etc., we didn't hardly go anywhere. We went to a show on Saturdays, matinee, and went to church every Sunday.

I was seventeen or eighteen when we joined the musicians union. I think it cost us seven dollars each to join. Ernie Royal and I got the cards at almost the same time. He was playing with us and rehearsing with us. Now, during that time he got a chance to play with Duke Ellington overseas. He left us just for that gig. And then, when he came back, he went with Lionel Hampton, when he formed his band in 1940. When he came in our band, he wasn't a good reader. But I'll tell you, in no time, in no time he caught on, man. That's when he began to read fairly well, playing with us. And that's when he really first started playing jazz, see, with us.

We had what we called a studio on Wilmington. We lived on 111th, but the studio was on the corner of 111th and Wilmington. In the back it had some rooms where we could teach, and also in the front a small, very small place for dancing, and a platform. The Woodman Brothers Studio. I think we charged fifteen cents to come in. Well, that place would be packed. Once a week we played. I can remember us playing Tommy Dorsey's "Indian Love Call." [sings melody] Because sometimes they would ask for that. So we had that going. That's why if you ever mention the Woodman Brothers to Illinois Jacquet, "Yeah, Watts! The Woodman Brothers in Watts!" He came down to catch us playing down there. [laughter]

Charles Mingus —
"Mingus was so natural: what he heard he could write."

One of Britt's early teammates and a fellow student at Jordan High School was Charles Mingus.

I love sports. I specialized on the rings and bars and ping-pong and basketball. In fact, that's where I taught Charlie Mingus all that. Ping-pong and basketball and horseshoes. In fact, we had a little basketball team. There was two of us. We'd go to different playgrounds. We called it twenty-one. Whoever gets twenty-one first wins the game. The only trouble we had was the tall fellows. [laughter] We had to work like the devil to beat them.

Mingus was about two grades below me and playing cello at the time. In the senior orchestra they didn't have any cellos. He was playing in the junior orchestra, so Mr. Lippi the next semester arranged it so he could play with the senior orchestra. That's when I first met him. And, boy, he was bowlegged and shy. The kids used to make fun of him. They used to take his lunch from him; they used to tease him. But anyway, that's when we became friends. When he was playing there, I just started talking with him. So he asked me to come over to the house and so I went with him to his home, met his mother. And he had two sisters, Vivian and Grace, that were older than I. One played the piano; one played the violin.

His parents were beautiful. Their father was pretty strict, though. They attended the Baptist church, which was right on the corner, and I belonged to Christ Temple. But I went to their church a couple of times. And I had eaten over at his house, and I took him to my house to eat. Now, I'm trying to pinpoint this. I think by '37, I guess.

So in the meantime, there was a fellow that was teaching my other two brothers and I how to fight. So we put up a big bag in our garage, punching bag, one of those big bags. When Charles was over one time for dinner with me, I said, "Charles, come on over to the garage. I'm going to show you something that I was taught." And I showed him the one-two-three punch. Little combination. He liked it. So off and on he'd come into the garage and punch the bag. Meantime, he was kind of getting out of the shyness thing. Now, all this was happening before he met Buddy Collette. We were like brothers.

My father made an arrangement with the principal for me to go to school half the day so I could play at the Follies Theatre. He wanted me to get the experience of playing all types of music. So the principal said as long as I do my lesson and have my lesson ready for the exams to graduate, it was okay. Well, during that time at the Follies Theatre, I found out that the main comedian was Joe Rooney, Mickey Rooney's father. He was a great comedian. The jokes he would tell. I would learn them, and I would teach them to Charles Mingus. So during recess, boy the kids would gather around and we'd tell them these jokes. [laughter]

One day Charles said, "I should like to play trombone."

I said, "Okay, I'll bring my trombone to school, and I'll go by your pad, and we'll see," which I did; I went by his pad. And he'd always take his cello with him every day. So I said, "Oh, let's play out of the cello book for a while."

We started playing in unison. We got to one note, B-double-flat. I said, "Charles, why did you miss that note? That's B-double-flat."

"Yeah, okay, B-double-flat." He'd miss it.

"Charles, you know what key you're in, don't you?"

"No."

"You know what the note is?"

"No, you said B-double-flat."

"Do you know your line space?"

"No."

Now, this is unbelievable. I said, "Come on, Charles."

"No, the teacher said—"

"Well, how do you read the music?"

"Well, the first note, when it says go up like that, I hear it, I just play it."

So I told his mother, "Mrs. Mingus, I don't know, this teacher that's teaching Charles, he's not teaching him correctly." Charles said, "Man, I don't want to play no cello, anyway; I want to play bass."

I told Mrs. Mingus, "Well, Mrs. Mingus, he has a good ear. He'll be a very good bass player." And Mrs. Mingus said, "We ain't got no money to buy no bass." His father was never in most of the time. I guess he was at work in the post office. But I talked with his mother, and in two weeks, Charles called me, "Britt, I got a bass." Somehow or another his mother arranged that he could get a bass and convinced her husband to buy him a bass. Now, this is when he made contact with Buddy Collette.

Britt left Los Angeles in November 1940 with Les Hite's band. When he returned home in 1942 to be inducted into the military, he found Mingus to be a much improved bass player.

When I came back, this fellow was playing so much bass! [laughter] Oh! First, Red Callender taught him. Then he went to another teacher—I don't know who he was, the other teacher. But man, he had it correctly. Yeah, man. [mimics facility on the bass] Oh, man. But I can say this: about three months after he got his bass, he started fooling on the piano. Listening to Duke's playing, he could hear some of those chords. He could play it on the piano. So I said, "With his ears, he's going to be one of your great musicians," which he came to be, because with that kind of ear and liking Duke— That's why his writing was similar. He had Duke in mind. See, the thing was, Mingus was so natural: what he heard he could write.

Returning on furlough from the army to Los Angeles in 1944, Britt found Mingus developing as a writer.

I heard one tune that he wrote that was called "Kiss of Death." He wrote the lyrics, and he wrote the background music for it, and he made a home recording of that.

However, one constant was his temper, a Mingus characteristic until the day he died.

If someone disagreed with him, the first thing, he'd want to strike. But most of the time, when he'd strike a person, it had a background to it. The person to him was prejudiced, or the person, one of the musicians, claimed to be great but didn't play his music right. So the person would say something to make him angry, then he'd want to hit him. He'd say, "You're a jive musician. I thought you were supposed to play anything." And if a person was prejudiced, then he'd want to fight. People think that he hated white persons. They called him the angry man. But if you'd go to his pad, that's all he had surrounding him, white people. The blacks were the ones that couldn't understand him. He never had too many black friends, just his musicians that were with him: Eric Dolphy and

Ted Curson and his drummer, Dannie Richmond. But lots of the other outside black musicians, they didn't really know him, his heart, how beautiful a person he was. So he didn't hate white people, he hated prejudice. And that's when he'd get angry.

But I didn't like his kind of showmanship. When people came to see him, he'd be playing, and he'd stop the band. "Look, you keep quiet and you'll get an education about what music is like! Quit that talking! I don't want to hear all that talking!" [laughter] And a man might say something, and then there would be an argument between him and the man in the audience. Well, a lot of people would come just to see that.

In the sixties, there was a club called the Five Spot in New York, a very popular club where well-known musicians would play. So he said, "Britt, I'm opening there. I'm the house band there." I made an excuse. Oh, no. That kind of stuff, no. Within three weeks, the word got out: Charles Mingus broke the piano. [laughter] Broke the piano at the Five Spot. He got into an argument with the manager or somebody. Smashed the piano. Doing that barred him from playing in New York for over a year. He couldn't work anywhere.

"If you don't improvise, well, you're not a jazz musician."

When I quit my family band, my first big band was with a fellow by the name of Dootsie Williams, a trumpet player. He was very popular around that time. He had like a rehearsal band at his home on Central, at Ninety-seventh and Central. I met one great alto player there, Kurt Bradford. He had just quit Jimmie Lunceford's band. He sounded like Marshal Royal. He had that kind of leading sound, that leading tone. And that's where I met Fletcher Smith, the piano player. Floyd Turnham. And a trumpet player by the name of Snake White. A trumpet player by the name of Red Mack. But the main thing, that was my first experience playing with great musicians that could improvise. My reading was equal to them or maybe better than some of them, but jazz-wise, if you don't improvise, well, you're not a jazz musician. [laughter]

A fellow by the name of Phil Moore had a band. He taught Lena Horne dramatics and coached her. He became a very big man at coaching, well known all over the United States. I remember playing with his band. I think he played at the Masonic. It was off Central Avenue, a Masonic hall that was a very popular place there. A lot of musicians were

Masons, you know. I know my dad was a Mason at one time. And we played there, too.

Then my first club job was at the Alabam with Baron Moorehead, a trombone player. He was one of the delegates at Local 767 at the time. He was the leader of the band. And I can remember the dancers well—the Hi Hats, and Pot, Pan and Skillet. [laughter] They were from New York. They were very popular, so they settled out here. And the Hi Hats were a dancing team. Now, I can't remember who the comedian was, but they had the whole bit there: the comedian, the chorus line, chorus girls, and everything. And during the period I was playing there, Stepin Fetchit came by with Mae West in his Rolls-Royce. It was such excitement, and at the time we weren't playing, so everybody went out to the front door to see what was going on. [laughter] And that's when I first saw this car—a yellow car, too. At that time, a lot of movie stars would come to the Dunbar. Central Avenue was like 125th Street in Manhattan. It was a little expensive. An ordinary person, working person, really couldn't afford it because it catered to people with money and the movie stars. It drew that kind of clientele.

We had the Lincoln Theatre. They had shows there. It was very popular. Ordinary people could go there, because the prices were lower, for pictures and things. And then the Elks. A lot of bands would play there. For instance, when Floyd Ray came out and played the Elks, man, he upset Los Angeles. He had with him three sisters called the Brown Sisters. They were singers. And he was [sings fast two-beat riff] with his derby. [resumes singing] "Three o'clock in the morning—" That was his theme song. Oh, man, it was an upset, man. He had a flashy band. He's a little old short fellow out there in front. The Elks was big. Fit at least five or six hundred people. They had three floors. The second floor could hold dancers and different things; another floor had smaller rooms. Yeah, the Elks was a very big thing.

Then we had another hotel called the Clark Hotel down further, not too far from the Lincoln Theatre. Pullman porters used to stay there when they came to town. It was a little cheaper than staying at the Dunbar, but it was a very popular hotel.

And we had eating places there. A place called Finley's, on Central, must have been about Forty-third Street. Hot dogs, tamales, malted milks, and sandwiches and things of that sort. Down by the Elks they had a chili place, Coney Island Chili Parlor. Spaghetti and chili, chili and rice. And musicians, everybody, would hang out and eat there. And then, where the musicians really would hang out was a place called the Fifty-fourth Street Drugstore on Fifty-fourth Street and Central. It served sandwiches and malts and stuff. But it was just where musicians would hang out and meet after the gigs. No whiskey sold there; they maybe brought their own whiskey. But in the back room they had a couple of slot machines, one-armed bandits.

But I'll tell you what. The Downbeat was owned by a gangster called Mickey Cohen. Our payroll checks were signed by him. This was in '46. I was saying that because we think that the Drugstore was owned by mafia. See, they could get away with that. Well, during that time the mob owned practically all the clubs the musicians played in. That's why we were treated so well, because they wouldn't let anything happen. Nobody would bother us or anything. But see, there weren't any other clubs in the forties that I can remember until the war broke out. Then a lot of clubs came in there, small clubs. Jack's Basket Room. There were quite a few clubs that opened up during the war. But in the late thirties, before the war, the Dunbar was the biggest thing there and the Lincoln Theatre and those eating places.

Food and nightlife weren't the only attractions, and visiting musicians often abandoned the tour and stayed in town.

When Cab Calloway came out here around '39, Al Morgan quit the band. Eddie Barefield left Jimmie Lunceford. But I can recall people were saying that with every name band that came out here, they'd always lose one or two musicians—which was true. All except Duke Ellington. When Duke came out here, he didn't lose any. When Floyd Ray's band came out here, quite a few of them stayed. Because of the slow pace, the climate, different things.

Most of the fellows came from the South, too, you know, so out here it's what you'd call a big country town. It was a better chance for them to make a living than the hometown that they were from.

On Tour with Les Hite

Les Hite's band was playing in Culver City at Frank Sebastian's Cotton Club. He was the only black band that was broadcasting in L.A. And they heard him back east. Across the country. Just like Benny Goodman and Paul Whiteman and those other bands that were playing in those hotels, well, they could hear him all over the country.

He had a leader personality. His alto was on the stand but I don't think he ever did play it. I'll never forget how he knocked off his numbers stomping with his two feet. He had a nice personality out in front of the band. There were some beautiful fellows in the band. A very good experience of brotherhood we had.

But anyway, in 1940 he met this rich lady, Mrs. Vera Crofton. She's the one who said, "Les, I'll manage the band. Let's go back east." In the winter months in Chicago, that was our first stay. We were supposed to do some one-nighters, but the weather was so bad. So for four weeks she paid our room rent and went to a boarding place where they gave us some food. She also gave us twenty-five dollars a week. Well, she was liking Les Hite, after her husband died. She was a white lady, and had an interest in ABC and property in South America. Every three months, she would get a check around about eighteen thousand dollars. When they found out, everybody wanted to join our band. Oh, we were living like kings.

But at first none of the fellows wanted to go. Marshal Royal didn't want to go. Bumps Myers and all the other fellows didn't want to leave. So he got Floyd Turnham, and the other musicians, including me, playing with Floyd's band.

Around December, we were in Middlewell, Texas. Ernie Royal sent a telegram to me: "Britt, come back. Lionel [Hampton] has organized a band." So he called all the names, all the cats that I knew: Jack McVea, Ernie Royal, Marshal Royal, Dexter Gordon, and Illinois Jacquet, and some of the other fellows—popular cats around Los Angeles. But I couldn't leave Les Hite. I was playing first trombone and in an isolated place it was very hard for him to get a first trombonist. I just couldn't jump like that and leave the band out there in the cold.

Wartime Duty and Postwar Central Avenue

I got drafted in New York. Yeah, both of us, my brother Coney and I, they sent our greetings. So we both came back to Los Angeles. April '42. Then I was shipped to Camp Walters, Middlewell, Texas. When I finished basic training they transferred me to the band. So I was there in the band for about a year and a half. Then I was transferred to Fort Bragg,

North Carolina, and I remained there until I was discharged. In fact, until the end of the war I was playing in the band, so I didn't have to go overseas.

Yeah, man. I had a good time. [laughter] Well, you know how in a band chicks look at musicians. At that time, see, musicians were looked up to like rock and roll musicians. Chicks were waiting for them. Now, like in Middlewell, Texas, we'd go to Fort Worth or Dallas. If you went to the Fort Worth bus depot, it would be the same as the Dallas depot. There would be about twenty chicks waiting for you to unload—black chicks I'm talking about. So at the window you'd look and see, "Oh, I see what I want." So you'd kind of scoot by these to get to that one down there. And they'd take you to their homes.

I almost got married to a chick I met in the service. In fact, I built a little house for her in back of my mother's house. But things were shaky, man. So I wrote this chick a letter: "I'm sorry, but will you please send me back my engagement ring? I haven't received a letter from you in eight months, and it seems like there must be someone you're interested in." She was a schoolteacher. She had graduated, and I was trying to get connections for her to teach out here. But I found out that she was going with some other cats there.

Stationed in the South, Britt witnessed numerous racial incidents. Perhaps the most galling involved German prisoners of war in North Carolina.

In Fayetteville we could go downtown, but there was no place for you to eat. At that time, they had German prisoners. They were marching them somewhere. They wanted to go into a restaurant for something, and they let them go in. We couldn't. You saw that we had the uniform on, still fighting for this country, especially the ones overseas dying, and then we're still segregated. That was the hardest, one of the hardest things you had to swallow. So many things that you had to swallow in the forties. It was worse in the thirties, when your parents would tell you about things. I don't want to go into that to tell you how bad it was.

One thing I realized that the people with the money— That's the way they had the blacks in control, because they let the poor white man use their justice on us. So they felt grand and proud, and they didn't realize that the millionaires were keeping them down. They couldn't make any money, but it kept them being so proud that they were white to keep us down. So a lot of them didn't know that until they went into the service. Poor people then realized that. It helped to make them kind of free to realize what was going on. But that's one thing, though. You take a prejudiced white person, and he finds out the truth, that all blacks are not the same and this and that, he's one of your best friends after he realizes. He's one of your best friends.

So getting back now, I had a ball. Outside of all those little incidents I was talking about in the service, I was in a band playing for the dances. All these beautiful chicks, it's hard to pick who you want, man. [laughter] Playing in the band, we could stay out late and come in just before curfew and things. We had a lot of privileges that the regular soldiers didn't have.

After being discharged in March 1946, Britt returned to Los Angeles and hooked up with friends from his Watts days, Buddy Collette and Charles Mingus.

So in April of '46, Charles Mingus was still in town. I got with him. We were doing little things with Buddy Collette. I guess it was Buddy Collette's or Charles Mingus's idea to organize the group, which we did. The Stars of Swing. We started rehearsing. Lucky Thompson was with us. John Anderson was the trumpet player. He was an arranger, too. Charles Mingus, Oscar Bradley—the drummer that was with Les Hite with me—and Spaulding Givens, piano player. Now his charts— You'd have to really play his charts about four or five times, really, to get in it. Something was deep about them. You'd play it once and you'd say, "Oh, man, this is nothing." But we saw something. So we played it till we could really feel it. And it made the band sound all together in a different sense than the other charts that we had, even with Charles Mingus's charts and Buddy Collette's charts and Lucky Thompson's charts. I had one number that I wrote, but it was mostly Charles Mingus and Buddy Collette.

So we rehearsed about five weeks. Elihu "Black Dot" McGhee was managing the Downbeat. We approached him and said that we had an orchestra. So we set a date, and we came in there and played. We had a band that we didn't realize how good it was ourselves because we didn't even record it. Didn't make a home disc or anything. But, man, people would come to hear this and were so killed by it that years after when I went to New York, musicians that were coming in and out of town in different bands and heard us, said, "Man, you cats, boy, you cats had a group there. Man, that was something else." Although we knew we had a good group, we didn't realize how good it was.

At one point Lucky Thompson quit, and Teddy Edwards took his place. And he gave it another flavor because of his style and things. Lucky Thompson— I have to start back at the beginning. We had a sign, The Stars of Swing, featuring the names all right there. So opening night, we came out and saw, "Lucky Thompson, featuring—" the cats in the band. We took the sign down and put our original sign up there. Lucky Thompson, well, he started losing interest then.

So somehow or another we had to take him to the union. Mr. Leo Davis was president of Local 767 at the time. And during the conversation, you know what Lucky Thompson said to Mr. Davis? "Well, I changed the sign because I have more prestige here in Los Angeles." And Mr. Davis said, "You have what? I've known the Woodman Brothers since the thirties. And Charles Mingus and Buddy Collette, everybody knows them. You mean to say you've got more prestige? What?" So he said, "Well, fellows, what do you want to do?" We said, "Well, the best thing is to let him go." And that's when we got Teddy Edwards.

When we were getting to the end of our contract, Eddie Heywood came by the club and left word he wanted to see me. He wanted me to join his band in San Francisco. In the meantime, some lady approached us—she had a club in Culver City—and said, "I've been here two or three nights to listen to you. You have a terrific band. Now, if you would get a vocalist, I'd like for you to come to my place indefinitely." Charles Mingus said, "That's it! Every time we get a band or something they want to have a vocalist in there!" I said, "Well, Charles, man, there isn't anything wrong with having a vocalist." "Oh, no, no." Nobody else said anything. Charles was going out there, "No, we'll just keep this band; the band will get a chance to blow." So I said, "Well, look, man, I have a chance to go with Eddie Heywood's band. Now, if you don't have anything before we close here, man, that's it." And I went with Eddie Heywood's band.

In September 1946 Britt signed on to tour with Lionel Hampton.

It was a good deal with him. Actually, nothing was happening. There wasn't any work for me to blow my horn there, so I took that. I signed a contract for two years. And being in the band, I had a ball with those cats. But things got so bad. Hamp, the way he ran the band— We had white gloves and things. We'd have to clap our hands. So, when somebody didn't clap their hands, he'd see who it was. And he made this statement one time, and I'm not lying: "Look, I want you all to know, my band is three-fourths Tom and one-fourth play. Whoever don't like it can get out right now." That's what he said. "My band is such that you're supposed to act like I tell you to act and grin and smile." So after a while, man, I said this is supposed to be the top band? I said no. I put in my notice. First part of '48.

So then in '48 and '49 I played in Gardena, California, for about a year. The Bal Tabrin in Gardena. They had name stars there: Butterbeans and Susie, and Oscar Bradley was in the band. Floyd Turnham was the leader.

In 1949 Britt enrolled at the Westlake College of Music in Los Angeles, under the G.I. Bill.

I was focusing more on solfeggio, ear training. I needed a much better ear for jazz. My brother William—he's the one that had the ear. A person who plays music, especially jazz, you're supposed to have an ear. The chords are not important. Hearing them is what creates the melodies or a song or a tune. You hear that sound, so you're going to say [sings phrase] because of what you hear. And that's what creates some of a person's style. Because if you use your mind, well, then you'll be technical. But hearing, you're playing from the heart, the soul, in other words. That's what I know about playing jazz.

So I had two classes of solfeggio and arranging, and two classes of concert band—playing my baritone horn—and the jazz band. We had some great cats come out of Westlake College. Some of them were in Stan Kenton's band, did the arranging for his band. Bill Holman, he was one from Westlake College. I was there until Duke called me in '51.

By the late forties the younger members of Local 767—Charles Mingus, in particular—were expressing their dissatisfaction with the segregated locals.

Charles Mingus said, "You don't let us join because you're just prejudiced, that's all. You don't want any blacks to join the union." We started getting together with some of the musicians from Local 47. They were the ones that hipped us: "Well, do you know that in our clubs, we get more money than you when you play the same club?" We found all that out. After we told them about the scales on other jobs, and they found out that there were lots of good musicians in 767, then they were for it, to amalgamate the two unions.

We were invited to some of the musicians' homes and just talked about music, about the conditions. The first time I went fishing was with some musicians from Local 47. Now, that's how we discussed scales and different things. Buddy and them would be saying that blacks don't get any calls for studio work, so the white musicians said, "Yeah, I know that the contractors say they figure that none of the blacks can read. They don't know." So that's why it seemed like the unions should be one.

So we got together playing in this symphony orchestra. That was in '49. I was the librarian. I went to the library and got the music. Now, the time they started getting some of the white musicians, well, Duke called me. That's when I left them. I left in '51. It took a little while before they got together. I heard about it when I was on the road.

Closing Central Down

What happened, as far as I saw, the policemen started harassing the people standing out in front of the clubs. The police would start getting people off the street, going in and arresting people and things, maybe because they found people were selling dope and all that stuff. At times they would stop a car, look in and see who's driving, and stop the car and search the car to see if there was any dope. Pick out a car, a nice-looking car, to see if there were blacks driving it. They were doing a lot of things during that time. There wasn't crime or anything going, but the dope was getting kind of big. I guess maybe that was it, trying to clean up the dope. This is starting around '47, '48. In '46, the street was booming. It's still jumping.

Around about '49, the last part of '49, clubs started folding on Central Avenue. Things started moving. Clubs started moving onto Western Avenue. Like a club called the Oasis. Oscar Bradley and John Anderson and Buddy Collette, we were all in the band. And other clubs like the Waikiki, where Oscar Moore, a guitar player, had a trio. That was on Western. I think on Avalon Boulevard there were some clubs. So things were leaving Central Avenue.

There are things during my career that were all connected with Central Avenue. Being part of Central Avenue, playing, hearing Paul Robeson speak at Wrigley Field, being connected with the symphony orchestra, all these experiences. Well, all that was really a treasure, an experience of things that I'll always treasure in my life.

I think musically it was one of the greatest eras in jazz. Because for about seven years, all the musicians, the great musicians that came out there, Central Avenue was the place for them to be. Central Avenue was like 125th Street in Harlem. So when it declined, it was a very depressing sort of a thing not only for musicians, but the people themselves that loved music. It was really pitiful.

There are so many things I wish I had been aware of in that environment when I was young—to listen, man—because I was with some very important musicians at the time, great musicians. We had some great Los Angeles musicians here. They stayed right here to play. And they were qualified to play with any band if they wanted to go. Yeah, it was a great scene during that time.

7

Buddy Collette

Multi-instrumentalist *Buddy Collette, a lifelong resident of Los Angeles, became widely known to jazz fans as a member of the Chico Hamilton Quintet in the mid-1950s. In 1956 he formed his own band, which at one time included Red Callender, Earl Palmer, Al Viola, and Gerald Wilson. Buddy has also worked for and with various artists and bands, from jazz festivals to the Los Angeles Neophonic Orchestra. Since his days with the Groucho Marx Show band in the early 1950s, he has been a prominent studio musician.*

Buddy has a substantial number of recordings to his credit as a bandleader. Many of his original jazz tunes are collected in the Buddy Collette Songbooks, *published in the Netherlands; he has also composed for films and documentaries, and written classical pieces, such as "Suite for Harp and Flute," several fugues, and pieces for the Philharmonic Orchestra of Chile.*

Since 1946 Buddy has given private lessons, taught in secondary schools and universities, and conducted clinics. His students have included Eric Dolphy, Frank Morgan, Sonny Criss, Big Jay McNeely, and James Newton.

Buddy continues to be busy and in demand. He tours and performs frequently, in small groups and orchestras, and organizes the occasional Central Avenue Jam Session at Catalina's Bar & Grill in Hollywood.

January 23, 1990, was declared Buddy Collette Day in Los Angeles.

Buddy Collette was born in Los Angeles in 1921. His parents, Goldie and Willie, met when her family, just arrived from Kansas City, rented a house owned by Buddy's father's parents, who had moved to L.A. from Knoxville, Tennessee, a few years earlier.

We grew up in Watts, and there were all kinds of people there, all races: whites, blacks, Mexicans, Chinese, Japanese. Part of the reason was because it was a reasonable area, cheap, plenty of land. For maybe one or two thousand dollars, you had a home. Houses were built mainly by the people who lived in them. My dad built our house, and he did a good job.

We lived in the Central Gardens area, which was Ninety-second Street south to about One Hundredth Street. And I went to the Ninety-sixth Street school. There were other schools in that area, but they were for whites only, like South Gate Junior High School, which was near Firestone Boulevard and Alameda. But there was a borderline there. You could walk past Alameda, but you'd feel like a stranger, and you sure couldn't go to school over there.

Nobody seemed to have a lot of money then, but we had food on the table. But the greatest thing about Watts was the people together. I don't know whether they thought, "Well, the kids growing up together would be great," but it was. The kids really got a bonus, too, because all those kids that grew up that way, wherever they are, these kids and their kids to follow will be free of the racial problems. So that's what we found. And even with my mom, she didn't seem to have a bone of prejudice. I could bring home Japanese, white kids, for lunch and she'd say, "Well, you brought all your friends. Let's fix food for them!" It was sort of like a melting pot of everybody being there.

I didn't have any problems with people. For example, later Jerry Fielding hired me for the Groucho Marx show *You Bet Your Life*. I'm thrown in with fifteen white guys and a couple asked me, "Well, do you feel a little strange? You're the only one in this band." I said, "No, it's great!" I was happy to get a good job. I wasn't worried about that. I was just trying to be the best musician.

And we drew from the school, Jordan High School, studying with Louis Lippi and Verne Martin. That's definitely where I started music. Actually, the teachers weren't as integrated. There weren't many black teachers then. Maybe there weren't any. But the teachers that wanted to come to that area had to be special people. So we got beautiful human beings. They didn't just come for the money, and they knew they had to really teach. Both music teachers would say, "Hey, do you want to stay after? I'll teach you this, I'll show you that." And it paid off.

So I think the area was very conducive to creativity. When we were living and going to school, we saw Simon Rodia working on the Watts Towers. Charles Mingus lived on 108th Street and the McNeely brothers on 111th, and the Towers are on 107th. So when I would be going to Mingus's house, we'd walk right by and see Rodia. Of course, then it was only maybe a four- or five-foot wall. No towers yet. It was a great period and very productive. It seemed to be very rich in producing all kinds of talented people.

My grandmother started me on piano at ten. When I went to junior high school, they had an instrument class and I took the saxophone. After a while—it took me about six months—I began to play. I learned pretty fast and my ears were good. And with all the music that my parents played, I began to get into it. My parents loved the Louis Armstrong band and all the good records. We loved Fletcher Henderson. We loved Duke Ellington together. A piano was always in the house. My Uncle Jimmy could play enough piano.

One night, when I was twelve, my parents went to a party at Dootsie Williams's house. He was a fine trumpeter who had a band. When I woke up the next morning, there was big trunk full of music that Dootsie's band didn't need. I figured, "I've got to hear this stuff. The only way I'm going to hear it is if I've got a band." So I got some friends—Vernon Slater on saxophone, Minor Robinson, a drummer, Charlie Martin on piano, and Crosby Lewis, trumpet—and we started rehearsing the music. A little while later, when I was thirteen, we formed a band with Ralph and Raleigh Bledsoe, who were sons of one of the top doctors in the area, Ralph Bledsoe, Sr. We didn't have any bookings except maybe a party every now and then, which our parents or some people would hire us for on a Saturday night and give us three or four dollars. And fifty cents apiece wasn't bad payment at that time. But the doctor was a tough task-master, a disciplinarian. Big guy and never smiled. He'd come to rehearsal, and we felt that pressure on us. We didn't like it.

Charles Mingus —
"All he could really do was play the bass and write music."

Sometime before I'm fourteen, we break up and I start my own band again. But now I don't have a bass. Then I hear about Charles Mingus. He wasn't a bass player; he played cello. I kept hearing about this kid that

lives on 108th Street. News traveled fast then. Somebody in town that
was different, you would hear about it. They said, "Well, you'll know
him when you see him; he's bowlegged and he's always doing something
different than anybody else." One day I'm walking on Ninety-eighth and
Compton and I see this bowlegged kid. His hair's kind of shaved and he
had a shoeshine box on his shoulder, but it was a most unusual shoeshine
box—about three feet tall. So I said, "You've got to be Mingus, right?"

"How did you know?" He was so surprised.

"Well, I knew how you would look. Your legs—" He didn't like that.
"But they also said you'd be doing something different. I shine shoes,
and I know that my box would never be like that. What is that for?"

"I have my people sit up on the hood of a car, so I need a higher box."
He was like that. He would look at something and figure, well, heck, it
could be different.

Then I said, "Look, I know you play cello, right?"

"Yeah, why?" He was not too happy to talk to me at that point.

"Well, if you've got a cello, I've got a band. I'm thinking about getting a bass player in there. If you can get rid of the cello and get a bass,
you got a job." And that's the first time I sparked him. He got so excited
about it.

"Well, I'll ask my dad," and he took off. He found me after about two
weeks and said that his dad had gone to the music store and traded it and
got a bass. I said, "Well, I got a job on Saturday. You with me?" And I
didn't know whether he could play or not. It's amazing to hear somebody
with musical talent. His notes that first gig were not right—not that he
didn't have good ears. It's just that he didn't know where they were and
maybe his tuning may not have been perfect then. But his time was good,
if you could believe that. And he was plucking at the bass. Then he got
pretty serious. He hung around me a lot and he was always in my band.

He wrote about this period in his book *Beneath the Underdog.* We
weren't quite as wild as he portrays. I think he was probably 50 percent
accurate. Mingus was a very creative, very inventive guy who loved a lot
of fanfare. As a young man he would always be doing something to sort
of attract the crowd or have people look at him. He shaved his head. He
was into his own thing when it was very strange. And he wasn't a shy
person at all; he could do things like that without feeling self-conscious.
Then every now and then he would pick fights with guys that he couldn't
win just to keep some activity going. We were active young guys, but,

heck, we were kind of nice young guys, meaning no drinking and dope at that time for us. We were lucky sometimes; we would have young ladies come by. But at that time there was no way to pull any fancy stuff or get real serious with them, because at that period I don't think we were aware of any kind of protection, maybe condoms a little bit, but it was almost hush-hush. And if you had anything to do with any young ladies at, say, age fifteen or sixteen, you knew good and well that it would be marriage, almost like shotgun-type from the father.

Mingus was always a disaster to have around. I loved him, but he was worse than a child. He didn't know how to clean up behind himself. He could cook, but there would be eggs on the floor and ceiling. Couldn't find his shoes when he had to go to work, didn't have a white shirt, couldn't write a check. All he could really do was play the bass and write music.

And his music was always interesting. It wasn't always the same. Tomorrow night he would start somewhere different and try something completely different. Even as a kid. That was his personality. He didn't come from any mold. Of course, he didn't like studio work very much. And in a way he was right. He believed in creativity, in expressing his own side of everything. He knew music didn't have to be the same. You just never knew what he was going to do. Mingus was so unpredictable. Once, he rehearsed one way, and when we got on the stage, he did nothing he rehearsed. It was all, "Watch me." And he started playing and then looked at me, "Do something." So I picked up the flute, walked to the front, and we just started talking to each other [mimics flute and bass interaction]. Everything was just so impromptu; we were on the edge of the chair. The spontaneity was just amazing. It was almost like those amazing moments of life. You could not rehearse that to get it to where we had it. And when we did it, Al McKibbon, a fine bass player, walked up to us and said, "I don't know what you all did, but you did it."

He finally studied with Red Callender, who was his first teacher. And then he went to Herman Rheinshagen, one of the finest classical bass teachers. And Mingus worked. He worked with rubber balls for about a year, just those rubber balls in the hand, because Rheinshagen's technique required powerful hands. He had strength. When he would start playing the bass, you'd hear something.

I don't exactly know why, but we were closer than brothers in a way. He was a problem guy in a sense, but when I was around he was peaceful.

He just had all the faith in the world in me. We only fell out one time, at the time of the Town Hall Concert in New York around 1962. It was a marvelous concert, which he spoiled because he was fighting with George Wein. George Wein wanted a concert; Mingus wanted an open recording session, where you could play a tune, then you could stop it if you didn't like it and do it again. I said, "I want a concert; I don't want that." So when the concert began, we all had tuxedos on and Mingus walked out in his blue jeans, short-sleeved shirt, a sort of leather vest and sandals with no socks. We got 50 percent of him with me being there; if I hadn't been there, he could have killed that whole thing.

That was also the time he hit Jimmy Knepper in the mouth. I got there a little after it happened at his apartment. When I walked in the lamp was broken and music was all over the floor. And the first rehearsal was at midnight. He said, "Man, Jimmy Knepper called me a name and I had to hit him." They were so tight that no matter what Jimmy called him, it wouldn't have done it. He might have been under pressure. The music wasn't ready. So I throw off the topcoat, get down on the floor, and start writing to fill in the parts. At the rehearsal Jimmy Knepper came, missing one tooth, and they were again like lovers, man they were so close. He couldn't play the trombone, but he still brought his music in. He was dedicated to him.

Then we'd go to breakfast and Mingus would say, "I don't want to do the concert." And I'd say, "Man, don't blow the concert. Do it." He said, "Well, okay then." He could hear my voice. I don't know why. But that was the way it happened. We did the concert, and with me being there we might have done a little better, although he still blew it. We played a piece and he stopped it in the middle. And everybody was uptight because we didn't know what was going on, because you never know what he's going to do. He walks to the mike and says, "I wouldn't like that, would you?" So he goes back to the orchestra and calls another number. And this is a marvelous band, the best jazz players in New York. Trombones: Eddie Bert and Urbie Green. Reeds: Eric Dolphy, Pepper Adams, Jerome Richardson, Phil Woods, and Seldon Powell. Bass players: George Duvivier, Milt Hinton. Snooky Young, Ernie Royal, Clark Terry in the trumpets. For the first set he didn't play anything complete. We were so frustrated. He had played games with all of us. And he had marvelous music.

We got on stage again; he was into the same mood. So now it's getting pretty close to eleven o'clock, and he still hadn't played anything. He's just stalling and doing nothing, and all the people are sitting there. Then he walked offstage and as the stagehands began to slowly pull the curtain, Clark Terry went into "In a Mellow Tone" and the band started jamming like you've never heard a band jam. Everybody was so hungry and pent up with emotions that we jumped on it. And the crowd ran out and pulled the curtains back. You know, it's New York, man!

I could do a whole book on him. People know certain stories about him, like maybe that Jimmy Knepper story. Those are the things that get around. But there was another side to him, a very quiet and a very nice side that he didn't show very much unless he was in a comfortable setting. And I would help him find that. Nothing that I did particularly. I was some person that he could be comfortable with and he believed what I said.

Local Heroes

An important inspiration for all of us in the Watts area was the Woodman Brothers—Coney, William, Jr., and Britt Woodman, and a little brother named George, who'd do the tap dance thing. "The Woodman Brothers Biggest Little Band in the World." They were one to four years ahead of me, but they were playing jobs when they were fourteen and fifteen, really on a professional level at that age. They worked three or four nights a week and were making pretty good money. Maybe they'd make ten dollars a night. That was a lot of money in the mid-1930s even for a whole band. Their father, William Woodman, Sr., trained them all early and then sent them to very good teachers. And he was a good trombone player, once offered the job with Duke Ellington to play lead before Lawrence Brown. But he turned it down because he wanted to stay with his kids. Britt got the job that his father turned down thirty years later. His dad knew. "They'll take my son, because he'll be good enough."

William played trumpet, alto, and clarinet. Britt played trombone, clarinet, and tenor sax. They could get any combination of sound. Then Coney played piano, guitar, and banjo. Joe Comfort was also in the band, playing bass and cornet. And he was amazing. He never practiced, but he'd pick up the trumpet and play. They also had George Reed and then Jessie Sailes on drums. I joined them later, when I was about fifteen.

It was such a good band, man! Although nobody says what happened in Watts, except the riots and maybe the Watts Towers, and maybe Mingus and I came from Watts, but they're the strong points. They're the inspiration of even all of Central Avenue. Because even if it wasn't heard right from the Woodman Brothers, the thing for me, for Mingus, through others, from Sonny Criss, the McNeely brothers— All of this is the Watts part of what we brought to Central Avenue. The real credit goes to the Woodman Brothers, who were doing it. We were all attempting to do it, and were fortunate, the ones who lived in the Watts area, to hear them and be their friends and exchange ideas with them. In the Los Angeles part of Central Avenue people like Chico Hamilton, Jackie Kelson, Ernie Royal, Dexter Gordon—their big influence was Sam Browne, a great teacher at Jefferson High School. But our big influence was the Woodman Brothers, because they not only could play it individually, we would hear them in a band with arrangements. So the Woodman Brothers kicked it all off, and some of us picked it up from Watts and took it wherever.

Still a few years shy of high school graduation, Buddy had already begun venturing into Los Angeles, making contacts with some of the Jefferson High School musicians, and embarking on a professional career.

I was also getting occasional gigs at the Follies Theatre downtown on Main Street. Mickey Rooney's father, Joe Yule, was one of the top comedians there. That was a tough job. Plus, the ladies up on the stage— Tempest Storm, Lili St. Cyr—you could not believe. You're trying to read the part and— Yeah, well, I was about fifteen years old. I wasn't even out of school.

Then I really met some of the Jefferson guys in a battle of the bands at the Million Dollar Theatre in downtown L.A. This was for a job in an all-black show with Lawrence Criner and Nina Mae McKinney. I had my band with Mingus and Crosby Lewis and the whole gang. The other band had Chico Hamilton, Jackie Kelson, and Al Adams on bass. Our band lost, which we were kind of ill about. We were about eighteen and upset at losing a good job. Somehow we wanted to get out of Watts to play. Then their leader, a Mr. Myart, came over to me and asked me to join their band. So I got a chance to do my first big show. We were making twenty-one dollars a week, a lot of money for a kid at the time.

After we left the Million Dollar Theatre, Al Adams organized his band with Chico, Jackie, and me. Then we finally got Mingus on bass, and Al stood out in front. He was a bass player, but he was no bass player like Mingus. We did a lot of things at the Elks Hall, which was on Fortieth Street and Central. The Elks held all the big dances, the big club affairs. We played there quite a bit. And you'd hear people there like T-Bone Walker or Lowell Fulson. We once had a battle of bands with George Brown's band at the Elks. We also had Illinois Jacquet with us, and that night was the first time he ever played tenor sax. We lost our tenor player and asked him if he would go get a tenor.

We had some contact with Dexter Gordon then, but not much because he was like a fun guy, seemed to be just all tongue in cheek. Everything was just laughter. He was a player and he knew where he wanted to go, I guess. Later, he finally got to be real serious. I heard that Sam Browne at Jefferson High School used to keep him after school and tried to make him play scales. He was not an easy guy to teach. But we all kind of laughed at him. He could play, but he was a big, tall guy and he wore Li'l Abner–type shoes. Sometimes he'd take his horn out in the street, just on the sidewalk there, and start playing and kicking his legs out. He was kind of a character. But he made it with style.

About 1940 I started studying with Lloyd Reese, who had played with the Les Hite band. A lot of us did. He was a marvelous teacher and everybody went to him—Eric Dolphy, Dexter Gordon, Bill Douglass, me, Mingus, Bob Farlice, the McNeely brothers, Bob Cooper, Lamar Wright—I could go on and on. Even Ben Webster would come over and take lessons.

The ones who went to Lloyd Reese all did very well, because they could go anywhere. It wasn't just that they could play the instrument well. They had to be able to meet with people, conduct themselves properly. They knew how to make time. They were concerned about the whole orchestra. It wasn't just "Well, I played mine" but "Yeah, guys, could we all get an A? Could we all tune up again? Could we all maybe play a little easier?" That was a Lloyd Reese–type student. Everybody had to play piano. Most of us could write, most could conduct. You were getting all that other knowledge. He was opening our minds.

He also had a workshop or rehearsal band once a week. All of his students were in it. It was the most marvelous experience we've ever been through. It was not so much how much you played, it was how you played it. And we were aware of it. He was into reality and calling it like it is. And when you do that, you can really get in. This guy was preparing you to be a giant.

Central Avenue Before the War

In 1938, 1939, we were old enough to hang out and stay out until three, four in the morning on Central Avenue and it was a fun place. There was the excitement of the after-hours spots and the drugstores and things that had the malts and food late at night, where people could meet after whatever job they had. The Fifty-fourth Street Drugstore was probably the prime place after-hours. It was a big spot. They had all kinds of food there. In the Drugstore and places like that, they had the jukeboxes and we could hear things like "Jack the Bear" by Duke Ellington and featuring Jimmy Blanton on bass. Jimmy Blanton inspired Mingus. We just played that over and over again. And all the celebrities were out at night, anybody you wanted to see would be there. If the Ellington or Basie bands or a big fighter like Jack Johnson, who was heavyweight champion of the world, were around on a Friday or Saturday night, they'd probably be hanging in there. It was great, because you could mingle with them. You knew they were real people, which was always great as a young player. We heard people on records and they're standing there!

There was a place called Finley's, which was much smaller. But Fifty-fourth had the space and had the atmosphere for just hanging out. There was also a place called the Brooks Bathhouse, if you wanted to go have a steam bath, get doused by buckets of water. And places like the Club Alabam on Central and the Bal Tabrin in Gardena, that used a lot of chorus girls. And they were all very flashy women, all so beautiful and probably only about twenty years old then.

The barbershops were there and the guys were conking their hair. You'd spend a lot of time there. Might have cost you a couple of bucks and you had to spend an hour or so to do that. But that was all part of getting ready for the night stuff, being sharp. There was getting your clothes to the cleaners, even if it was your last two dollars, so you'd look sharp for the evening. The emphasis was on a little flash or even a new car. Maybe your house wasn't in great shape, but you had to hit the Avenue with your hat on and your new pinstripe suit. There were these great dancers, the Three Rockets, and they were the sharpest three guys you've ever seen—tall and handsome. Most of the time they didn't have any money, but you'd never see it in the way they looked. They knew sharp was it. Somehow that was much better than being ragged with a lot of money in your pocket. [laughter]

The Avenue was a fun place. There was a lot of variety. There were a lot of people who were sort of playing pimp roles. Guys would be walking the street and chasing the ladies down and trying to get into that kind of activity. The pool halls were jumping, and there was a little gambling.

Most people worked and could have one or two nights on the town and pay the rent. Maybe twenty-five bucks a week was one of the top salaries then. My dad was working with the garbage department as a truck driver, and twenty-five dollars was pretty good money at that time. Most of the black people at that time didn't have good jobs. There was no post office stuff then. There were few doctors to speak of. Dexter Gordon's father, Dr. Ralph Bledsoe, Sr. My mom would take occasional jobs like cleaning house or keeping the kids of some family out in Glendale or Beverly Hills. And that wasn't much money. You might work all day for three or five dollars. My grandmother used to tell stories about Booker T. Washington and a few greats. You'd hear about this one person; you would try to relate to that. But it would be difficult when you saw your friends and all the people in your neighborhood. The guy next door to our house was a junk man, Mr. Craig. He would go out, get junk and sell it. That didn't appeal to me, but he did all right. I mean, he fed his family. He had about six or eight kids. But it was tough stuff: the little junk truck, and he was dirty, and he was really working.

So when we started seeing the other world, meeting musicians that was what was interesting. They were dressed nicely, and it seemed they were enjoying themselves. There was a whole other magical thing going on.

When I started working in the bands on the Avenue, I was about eighteen and it was fabulous. I was with Cee Pee Johnson. We played in Hollywood quite a bit. We played the Rhumboogie, which was at Highland Avenue and Melrose. I played the Club Alabam and a few spots on Central. We were coming from high school into this big world where we were making a little money, maybe about $30 or $40 a week, when my dad was only making about $25. And I bought a new car when I was about eighteen. The car cost $1,200, but payments were about $50 a month. I mean, I could do it, you know? At first I was living at home, but then I even moved away. It was a very exciting period for a young man. The only thing was that we didn't know how long we would work. It wasn't like having a real steady job.

The War Years

We began to worry. A lot of our friends were being drafted. Then we heard that a chief from the navy had come into the musicians union, Local 767 on Central at Seventeenth Street, to recruit musicians for an all-black navy reserve band to be stationed near San Francisco, St. Mary's Pre-Flight School in Moraga. Charles Mingus, Bill Douglass, and me grabbed a Greyhound bus a week later to go to San Francisco for a physical and also a musical test. When we got there, Mingus had changed his mind and tried to destroy everything, saying he had a bad heart and couldn't walk. He did everything to get them to throw him out, which they did. Bill also changed his mind.

I was sent to Great Lakes in Illinois for training. And there must have been hundreds of musicians from all over the country. A number of people from the West Coast were there—Marshal and Ernie Royal, Jerome Richardson, Wilbur Baranco, Andy Anderson, Quedellis Martyn, and many others. Two nights later they had the big jam session. Clark Terry kind of ran things. You had twenty saxophones, sixteen trumpets, and about fifteen trombones, all in this big hall waiting to introduce themselves musically. And if you played well, you were sort of like a hero. People would like to know you based on how you sounded.

From Great Lakes we were sent to St. Mary's Pre-flight School. Eventually we all got our own apartments in the area. And we were able to play a lot of clubs around the Bay Area, even though we weren't supposed to. We spent the duration there, from 1942 until December 5, 1945.

Buddy was one of the many artists who traveled to Billy Berg's club in Hollywood for Charlie Parker and Dizzy Gillespie's opening night in December 1945.

Actually, before we got out of the service, Ernie Royal and I came down to see Dizzy Gillespie and Charlie Parker, when they opened at Billy

Berg's, and that band: Ray Brown and Milt Jackson and Al Haig and Stan
Levey, and, then, a little later, Lucky Thompson. We had been impressed
by the records we'd heard and we had to drive down. Opening night was
really fabulous. The place was packed with people. It must have attracted
most of the L.A. musicians. This was for real. The stuff that you heard
on the records that you didn't believe, you almost had to believe because
you saw people standing playing it. You couldn't believe it on the record
at first. We'd put the record on and everybody would stand around and
say, "What are they doing?"

It was kind of scary to hear, because they were playing so fast, a lot of
notes, that we didn't understand what they were really playing. And the
flat nine and the flat five. Then, nobody was trying those things. They
were using notes that we didn't even dare to use before because it would
be considered wrong. And those stops and gos between Dizzy and Bird.
And it would be so rhythmic. You know, you'd look at everybody and
say, "Can you believe what we just heard?" That was the way it was. And
they were just doing it like there was nothing to it. And then Bird would
come out with his solo, and he was masterful. His time was just flawless.
You could see he was like a force. That's the way he played.

Postwar Central

I wanted to come back to L.A. to see if I could make a living as a musi-
cian. I had been away for almost four years. I had one child at the time,
Zan, born in 1944, and my wife, Louise, who I married up north in 1943.
We figured it was our home and both our families were here.

When I came back from the service, which was about 1946, there was
a big change. The war years had brought a booming economy and also
an awareness that people could do more than just what they were doing
before. They began to expand and venture out. There were schools opening up then and many of them music schools. The Central Avenue players, even before, were not into a lot of schooling. We had Lloyd Reese,
some of us, and some of the ones who came from Jefferson High School
had Sam Browne as a teacher. But a lot of the club players on the Avenue
couldn't read. There was nothing wrong with it, because you didn't have
to read at that time. The world hadn't changes as much into studio work,
where everybody must read, and you wondered about minorities in the

symphony orchestra. The main thing then was if you had a little gig and it was paying the right amount of money and the group was swinging, you were in.

When we came back we had the G.I. Bill. I got four years of study for free, as well as books, metronomes, reeds, and all of that. I attended the L.A. Conservatory of Music and Art, where I met Bill Green, and I had three private teachers. I started studying with Merle Johnston, who had a studio at 4992 Melrose, near Western Avenue—the junkiest shop you've ever seen. I was told that "the big guy from New York is out here teaching, Merle Johnston." He was kind of a nut, a brilliant guy, but I'm saying he had you blowing six or eight hours a day, full volume, with the metronome and everything. If nothing more, you got a hell of a sound and got your fingers going. It was the only thing you should have been doing. You'd say, "Yeah, but my wife and—" He says, "Well, look now, are you going to be a musician or not?" At one point he had some microphones out in front of his studio. So when you were at the bus stand, he could hear you talking. If you'd say, "That Merle is full of shit," he'd say, "I heard you talking about me when you were at the bus stop." Wild. His studio was about eight by twelve feet and just full of the biggest speakers, record player, horns, books, and the place was trashy, too. But you were in there, and he would close the door. You felt like you were in a death chamber or something. But he did wonders for everyone that studied with him. Me, Teddy Edwards, Eric Dolphy, Frank Morgan, Jewell Grant.

Things were changing and there were more new musicians in town, like Bill Green from Kansas City, and many had the G.I. Bill for studying. That was the period, too, I took up flute. Bill and I took it up about the same time.

One thing that didn't change was that there was still a lot of musical variety on the Avenue. The tenor players, even the great tenor players, were all sounding so different. You heard Lester Young, that was one world. And Coleman Hawkins was a whole other. And even Ben Webster was somewhere in between. He wasn't either of them. They would all meet up, you'd listen and you knew exactly who was playing. There were almost as many styles around as people. Dexter Gordon was around. Wardell Gray was different. Teddy Edwards. Gene Montgomery was different from them. I was playing. Bill Green was around and we were different. Jackie Kelson was different than me. We all hung together, but we never had the same sound or the same approach to it. When Frank Morgan came, he was quite different. Sonny Criss. Nobody had the same tone or the same approach. And it was very enjoyable to hear that. It was exciting. Just like when you pick up the phone and somebody says, "Hi, Steve," and right away you know instantly, the first word, who it is.

It was very enjoyable, because we knew the importance of having your own thing. You were respected for having your own thing. The conviction of saying "I'm going to play me" was something very special. And we didn't have the categories as much as they do now. T-Bone Walker and Pee Wee Crayton, all of them played at the Last Word and the Downbeat. It was all a pretty good mixture. You'd find a jazz tenor player sitting in with T-Bone.

The clubs were flourishing. People were out living it up a little bit, dressing great. The Club Alabam had chorus girls and big bands. About this time Johnny Otis opened his big band there. Sounded a lot like Basie's band. Across the street Big Jay had a band—he was Cecil McNeely then. Big Jay was a very hot jazz player, a very fine jazz player. He can still play it, but he knows where the money is and he's got a show business thing. But he was one of the hottest. When Bird and Diz came to town in '46, he and Sonny Criss had this band and, shoot, man, they were doing all the stuff they were doing. A hot group with Hampton Hawes on piano, Buddy Woodson on bass, and Leon Moore, the drummer. Later on, he got with Johnny Otis and they began to do some rhythm and blues and moved away from bop. Then Lorenzo Flennoy might have been in a little club. There were so many clubs down the Avenue. And the after-hours spots were going. Jack's Basket Room, where the tenor players would go. The Jungle Room was across from the Lincoln Theatre on Twenty-third and Central. The Lincoln Theatre had big shows: the Will Mastin Trio with Sammy Davis, Jr., Pigmeat Markham, the stand-up comedian. And we were at the Downbeat with the Stars of Swing.

I think the only trouble was with the cops. The law enforcement people didn't like seeing too much mingling, especially with all the white women who would come down. The cops would give them a bad time: "Stay out of here. If you're caught in here, we'll run you in for something." They tried to make it illegal for doing it. And it seemed after the war it was happening even more.

In 1946 some of the finest players in Los Angeles joined forces as the Stars of Swing.

Shortly after I got back to L.A., got my feet on the ground and started studying a little bit, I got with Mingus, because we'd always get together anyway. And Lucky Thompson was there. He was in town. He had done that gig at Billy Berg's with Bird and Dizzy, and he was working with Boyd Raeburn's band. And we got John Anderson on trumpet. Britt Woodman was here, Oscar Bradley on drums, Spaulding Givens on piano. A perfect group of players, because everybody could really hold their own and most of us could write.

We started rehearsing at Mingus's house, every day for about three or four weeks with dynamics. We'd go have a sandwich for lunch together, come back and blow another two or three hours. Just every day. Nobody was going anywhere. Maybe you'd have a lesson somewhere. "I've got my lesson at three, but I'll be back." We got so good—we really did. Then we invited guys from the Downbeat: Black Dot McGhee, the manager, and Harold Stanley, the owner. It was scary; it really was. They listened and they just—"What is this we're hearing?" We knew it was great, but we didn't know what the people were going to say. That guy said, "You're hired! When do you want to open up? Next week?" The Downbeat was the hot spot on the Avenue. Man, it was jumping in 1946.

We decided to put a sign up in front of the club. We had to figure on a name. No one was the leader, so with a corporate idea in mind, we settled on the Stars of Swing. "We're all stars and we swing." A couple of us went to the sign painter and said, "Here are the names of seven people. Make us a sign that says 'Stars of Swing' and just put these stars anywhere with a name in it." That was a Monday night. Our opening was on Tuesday. We arrived that night, all happy, walked up and saw that the sign had been changed. It said, "Lucky Thompson and the All Stars." Mingus wanted to kill him, of course. "What are you doing, man?" He said, "Man, I'm the one with the biggest name, and I'm the best player." We were just outdone. The people are waiting; we're in the back arguing. It took all the fight out of us. The band still played its can off. Lucky still played his can off that night, but he wasn't a team player anymore, and now he knew he had blown it. But Lucky was like that. Lucky was for Lucky. He was very good on his instrument, but I knew that along the line you cannot make it by yourself.

The next night we put the original sign up. When he came to work that night he was less of a player. He wasn't going to play the real Lucky. · And the third night, I think, he didn't show up at all. We called in Teddy Edwards at the last minute, who was a very good player, but he hadn't been with the group and this was a team effort. We had some shading and stuff he could never catch. So we faded away. Just that one gig for a few weeks. We recorded Spaulding Givens's arrangement of "Laura." But we never got anything out. We did it just for our own benefit. It was never released as a record.

But there it is. Bird used to come every night when he was in town to hear us. We had a marvelous group, probably heads and shoulders above anything that had been on Central Avenue as far as an organized group and dynamics and the best musicianship, and I think that set the pace for a lot of things in the L.A. area.

Eric Dolphy—"He was just a joy."

One of those listening nightly to the Stars of Swing at the Downbeat was Eric Dolphy, a teenage student of Lloyd Reese's from Dorsey High School. Like Mingus, Dolphy developed a special relationship with Buddy.

I didn't know Eric until I came back in town in 1946. He might have been nineteen, and I might have been twenty-four or twenty-five. He used to come around the Last Word, Downbeat, clubs like that where we'd be playing. He used to come by the Downbeat all the time to hear the Stars of Swing. He said he knew of me through Lloyd Reese. Eric at the time was working at Lloyd's. He was the cleanup guy and errand guy and everything, doing that for his lessons. He was around when everybody was coming for their lessons. Eric was just learning his craft then at Lloyd Reese's, with piano, with clarinet, with saxophone, and hearing everybody.

Eric was a young man with a lot of energy, a lot of ideas, very creative. Music was very important to him his whole life, of course. When Eric was around nine he was practicing and trying ways to approach something, very creative, on the piano. Hearing one thing and saying, "Yes, but I could do this with it." Also drawing from many, many different people in his life, and not just music people. He was a very good listener.

The thing I liked about him, too, he had a high level of appreciation. Most people would say, "Well, I like this one better than that." Eric liked everybody. And that's a rare talent in itself when you're appreciating a lot, because then you're picking up things. You're not filtering; you're not editing. Eric liked it all, and he used what he wanted out of it.

He loved the outside notes. He loved being different, altering chords. I'd give him a couple of melodies, and he would alter everything. He loved it, to use the notes, even with a lot of his flute stuff. He used to get some interesting density in a few things that would be far out. He wasn't just a one-three-five kind of person. He loved all those strange notes to the point of being out there even when the tune didn't call for it. But he'd also had a background in classical music. He loved to practice it. He'd spend more time practicing classical than jazz, so he had the fingers and he had the difficult things always behind him.

He was a joy to teach. You didn't have to teach him that much. He just loved it. Whatever you gave him, he'd approach it like you had given him a toy or a bowl of ice cream. It was fun, and the fun was always there. He was just a joy. There's not too many that you meet that have the magic within their makeup. He would smile when he played or practiced, just enjoying it. Yeah, he had the right attitude, had a great family. Mr. and Mrs. Dolphy believed in the kid. He had good manners and upbringing. All good qualities.

Eric studied with me for a while, and he used to come and practice with me all the time. And I loved him. Eventually, I got busy with a lot of work and I couldn't spend the time with him. So I sent him and Frank Morgan, who was also studying with me, to Merle Johnston. I had them both for a while, but it was on a level where all I had to do was kind of shape them, give them a few ideas. I finally said, why not just send them both to Merle. And I knew he would help them both. They both needed that little kick in the butt that you get from a teacher like Merle.

I told Eric to study with him, but don't study any more than a year—that was my advice. And Eric took that as golden. Because after a year with him, you're going to lose identity and everything. Because he's got you blowing and he's got you on those books, and you get faster and you get to the point where you can read everything. But Merle was going on like this was the only thing that's going on. You know what I mean? He wasn't a jazz player at all. So Eric had a lot of rough edges, but he had the ideas. The tone would not be too good, intonation was not too good. I'd say, "You don't need but a year. He'll straighten your tone out, teach you how to blow." One year later Eric waved good-bye. And it was just right.

In L.A. Eric was practicing hard, he sounded good, making a gig one day a week. They'd have jam sessions in the early '50s at places like Normandie Hall, at Normandie and Jefferson, every weekend, with Eric and Ornette Coleman. Ornette didn't seem to have his horn together very much. He had a beard all over his face, and his hair sort of looked like a dog. I heard he had gone to one teacher, who said, "We'll have to do something with your tone." And Ornette said, "No, I don't want to change that. I don't want to sound like every other saxophone player. I've got my own thing." He knew where he was going all the time. A little later, around here, when the group got together with Don Cherry and a few people, the tunes were first so strange, and even the intonation was weird. But they began to even make some of us believe that they knew where they were going.

But Eric was almost going crazy practicing. And nothing was happening to him. He was getting known, but just locally. He was staying at home, so he didn't need a lot of money. His whole life was one horn to the other. So when Chico Hamilton called around 1957 and wanted me to come to New York, I said, "I've got a guy for you." I knew it would do wonders for him. "Get out of here! Out of L.A." Very few could make it here, very few have. They've all left. Chico said a couple of years ago that I was the only one who probably made it here. When he went with Chico, he took his bass clarinet and he started utilizing everything. After a month or two Eric called me back. "Man, why do you stay there? You can get anything you want here. This is where they want you. They're looking for you." I would have liked to, but I was raising my daughters then and really couldn't leave.

While I was in New York in 1963, Eric and I used to get together every day. We'd have breakfast, a little cereal, and then we'd duet for about three hours, and then we'd go to lunch, although he wasn't eating any lunch then. He told me he and John Coltrane were on health food pills and honey, two or three tablespoons of honey. I didn't think that sounded too good, but they felt it made them much stronger when they played. It must have been all that sugar giving them great energy. A year later in Germany he passed out on stage, went into a coma and died. The autopsy revealed that he was a diabetic, which he didn't know. The parents weren't aware of that either. Maybe those eating habits really did him in. He was riding on top of the world, and for it to happen kind of like that. It was a tough one.

Teaching, Jamming, and Recording

Frank Morgan was just fourteen years old around 1948 when he came out here and he was playing marvelous. His dad was Stanley Morgan, played guitar with the Ink Spots. He also used to own clubs. One was called the Casablanca.

Bill Green and I had started these regular jams at the Crystal Tea Room, Forty-eighth Street and Avalon Boulevard, in 1948. The idea was to have jam sessions to have people hear each other and to learn and to exchange ideas. And we had a lot of people over there: Eric Dolphy, Walter Benton, Ernest Crawford, Kenneth Metlock, Sweet Pea Robinson. All these kids came over. When Stanley heard about the Tea Room, he brought Frank over. Frank was a beautiful young man. And he broke it up. He was a young, green kid, but he could really play. Soon he was out playing the jam sessions with the older guys like Dexter Gordon and Wardell Gray. Soon he began to meet with people and go to parties. How will you hold up through that? He went along with a lot of that. And there was dope going on.

Buddy and Mingus made some of their first recordings for a small independent black label, Dolphin's of Hollywood, in the late 1940s.

Mingus and I did some stuff for Dolphin's of Hollywood in maybe '48, '49. Dolphin's was one of the few outlets for the Central Avenue and black musicians at the time. John Dolphin was a guy who had a record store on Central Avenue for a while. He also had a radio station. He recorded everybody, did business with everybody musically, but he was a hard-pay guy. He wouldn't pay anybody. I know Mingus and I did records for him about '49. You'd come by to get your money and he'd say, "I gave you a chance to record, didn't I? So you should be happy."

I did two pieces for the Dolphin's of Hollywood label: "It's April" and "Collette." It was a two-sided 78. I think I used Jimmy Bunn on piano,

Harper Cosby on bass and probably Chuck Thompson on drums. I have
the tape now, and it's still pretty good. It holds up well. "It's April" was
later recorded on Prestige by Wardell Gray and Art Farmer, and they
called it "April Skies." Mingus also did a lot of things in that period, and
we did some of the tunes from him. He had "Baby, Take a Chance on
Me," and they did a tune of mine called "Bedspread." There were a lot
of tunes that we were experimenting with, and we were writing a lot.

The Amalgamation of Local 767 and Local 47

*With gigs in Hollywood, jams on Central Avenue, and classes at schools such
as the Los Angeles Conservatory of Music, Buddy started meeting more musicians from Local 47, the white union, who were also unhappy with segregated
locals.*

We thought about it, especially a bunch of the guys who had been in the
service, and Mingus, who hadn't been in the military. We kept thinking,
"Man, we'll never make it with two unions, because we're getting the
leftovers." All the calls came to 47. Maybe now and then they might want
a black band for a sideline call, where the music had been recorded and
they wanted to show the black group. You'd wind up making a hundred
dollars, maybe. That was a lot of money, but that may not happen for
another year or two, while at Local 47 that was happening all the time. I
knew it was because I was around those guys. I'd go to *The Jack Smith
Show* with Barney Kessel and some other guys at other shows. A bunch
of those guys would be doing this all the time, working those radio shows
and things. They'd be pulling down maybe two or three hundred dollars
a week. But it wasn't going to get better, I felt, with the two unions. That
was a real shaft.

The actual beginning of the amalgamation, I'll give Mingus credit for
that. He was always fighting the battle of the racial thing. He got a job
with Billy Eckstine at the Million Dollar Theatre on Broadway. Mingus
was the only nonwhite or black in the band. Since Billy Eckstine was a
black leader, he figured, "Why couldn't there be a few blacks in there?"
Mingus was the only one, and he let them know that he didn't like it.
And he could be tough on you. Everybody in the band had to hear it
every day: "You guys are prejudiced! You should have some more blacks.

You could hire Buddy Collette there." So my name was being tossed around every day until the guys even hated me without knowing me!

I was finally invited down and I was curious about the band. We wanted to meet people that understood what we were talking about: the unions getting together, people getting together, stopping all this. I met their flutist, Julie Kinsler, who supported the idea and drummer Milt Holland. Milt said, "Man, we've been wanting to do this, too. I know about six or eight people that think just the way you guys do. We can get together and start meetings or something." Mingus and I lit up, because that was the first time we heard anybody who was really excited about it. The next day Mingus and I met with a few of the guys who felt the same way. They wanted to call a big meeting. I said, "Well, I don't think we should call a meeting, because the guys that I know, they don't like meetings too much." Instead, most of us had been studying for a few years and I said that we need a thing where we can learn the music, possibly like a symphony rehearsal orchestra together. Milt said, "If that's what you want, that's easy. I know all the people from that world." That was the beginning of the Community Symphony Orchestra.

We also wanted to make sure more blacks were placed in different circuits, because at that time we had only worked clubs. If we did play the Orpheum Theatre or the Million Dollar, it was in a black band or when an all-black show would be there. But the other shows, if they'd need twenty musicians, then blacks wouldn't get the call at all, no matter how good you were. It just didn't happen. So that was the idea: can we show that it can work? So Milt said, "Okay, get as many people as you can, then we'll fill in." Milt was beautiful, is still beautiful. So I got Bill Green, me, Britt Woodman, Jimmy Cheatham, John Ewing, Red Callender, and another little kid named James McCullough. That wasn't a big number, but those were the only people that we could say were in the right direction, who had probably enough behind them to take advantage of this thing and who were also interested in playing this kind of music. Mingus wasn't there. Didn't want to do symphony music. He always wanted to do his own stuff. He was with us in a way, but it wasn't his world.

So we scheduled a rehearsal and the excitement started mounting. People were on the phones trying to get people who just wanted to be there. "Interracial symphony? Let's do that." We got the top clarinetists and flutists. Later on we got Arthur Cleghorn, who was one of the finest flutists at that time. Joe Eger was a great French horn player. John Graas was classical, and into jazz with the French horn. A lot of enthusiasm. Some would approach our rehearsal like it was one they were getting paid for downtown. We had something like five flutists, when you only needed three. They just wanted to be there. The orchestra had about sixty-five pieces. The orchestra was at Humanist Hall, Twenty-third and Union, and then we moved every now and then to Hollywood, Le Conte Junior High School, near Sunset and Gower. This was just rehearsals, but people could come.

The first night we had a conductor who was world renowned, Eisler Solomon. And he was excited, he really was. That got us in the papers. The press was there snapping pictures like crazy. People were really buzzing. That first night we also had a black bass player named Henry Lewis. He was playing so good he sounded like three basses. Later on he got to be a conductor. He even conducted here for a while. A very fine talent. He was only about nineteen years old then. Later he married an opera singer, Marilyn Horne. We had other great conductors, too. Peter Cohen, Dr. Al Sendry, Dr. Walker.

The orchestra kept getting better, and we began to publicize what we were doing. We had a board to set policy. We had meetings, and we wanted to let people know what the orchestra was about. The main aims were to bring about one union in L.A., black and white under the same roof.

Then somebody said, "We're doing okay on the classical. Why don't we concentrate on a jam session for the jazz, and we can also get more of the people who aren't in tune with jazz to also understand that part." So we had Monday night for classical, and then we got Sunday afternoon for jazz, and we'd invite the classical people. The Sunday built up really great. We had great jam sessions.

We then got ahold of "Sweets" Edison, who was working with Josephine Baker. We wanted to get her and some other names to appear on one of the Sunday afternoon things. She didn't have to perform, but come out publicly. So she was playing the RKO or one of the theaters downtown, and she agreed to come between shows. And that place, Humanist Hall, you could not believe it; we really exceeded the limit. The place could hold about two hundred people; we had about five hundred in there. When she got on stage, she said, "I wonder why you have two unions," something to that effect. "Well, I think it should be one, and I don't know why you people are wasting time. You've got all these beautiful people here." She just kept talking about how there was coming a time when people could work together. Bang! Zing! So finally she looks down in the audience, and there were two little girls, one black and one white, and they're about five years old. She knew when you've got something to work, right? So she said, "You and you, come up here." And they both dance up on the stage, and she whispers. And they grabbed each other and they hugged like that and they wouldn't let go. And she winked. "These kids will show you how to do it" and walked out. And the crowd was [freezes in astonishment] great!

Later on we got to Nat King Cole. He was great and did the same thing for us. We got the Club Alabam and just had all the people in the world. Sinatra didn't do a thing for us, but he sent a statement saying, "Well, there should be one union."

We were building an organization of sorts. We'd get money for mailings and notified people. We got Marl Young and Benny Carter into it. But we had a few years of hard work before a lot of the guys came in. Part of it was rehearsals and the jam sessions, and there were meetings.

Then I ran for president of Local 767. You see, we had all the publicity and people were doing fine, but we didn't know how to pull it off. So the next thing would be, "Maybe we'll have to be officers so we can move it from that standpoint." Because our officers at the black local didn't want it. Our place was not a great union. The building was kind of tearing down and the pianos were terrible. We really didn't have that much. But, the way they thought, at least it was still ours. So we set up a whole slate and we ran. The incumbent guy beat me by about twenty votes out of about four hundred. We did win a couple of seats on the board of directors. Marl Young, Bill Douglass, and John Anderson were running also, I think. But we still didn't have enough power.

Elections were every year in our local. So the next year we tried again. We ran Benny Carter for president and he lost to the same guy by the same number of votes I did. But this time I ran for the board and got in. Marl got in. Bill Douglass won the vice-president's spot. Now we got a little power underneath the president, who was Leo Davis, who was a nice man.

So we were able to move through resolutions and proposals toward a meeting with Local 47. And finally we got negotiations going. We pretty much had to drag 47 into it, because it finally got to the point where if we wanted it and they didn't, why didn't they want it? They were getting more members into the thing; we could work better together. But they stalled. James Petrillo, president of the American Federation of Musicians, stalled. A lot of people at 47 stalled. But the more it kept coming out that "Is it a racial thing or what is it?" they had to say, "Well, no, it's not that. We just don't know what to call it or how to do it or we can't because it's never been done before and . . ." So the big stall goes. In the meantime we're checking out information, too—how it could be done. Finally, they had no excuse.

It took about three years, but we brought the unions together in 1953. Looking back, the amalgamation helped a lot of musicians, gave them a better focus or a better picture of what they had to do to be on a more broad scope of understanding, not just the Central Avenue–type jobs. The ones who really benefited were the ones who wanted to have a successful career in music rather than just being a leader or somebody who has a record out. It began to make better players out of the good players, and the ones who weren't doing it had to decide to either back away or get serious. If somebody was just doing nightclubs, they were probably doing basically the same. But anybody who wanted to meet with people and experiment with different kinds of music and do studios and records and be like a top craftsperson, then I think they benefited a lot.

Plus there's better health and welfare, and pension benefits. It wasn't that we weren't doing it well with 767; it's just that it wasn't a big business thing over there. It was just kind of an afterthought. And it did allow some periods to be very lucrative for a lot of black musicians who were doing recording and shows through the years, shows like *The Carol Burnett Show, The Danny Kaye Show, The Flip Wilson Show*. Those shows began to hire people because they were all in the same union, and the word got around who could play, who couldn't. The other way we were isolated.

It was a step in the right direction. It wasn't designed to solve everything. It was trying to get people together. And maybe that's the hard thing, because thirty-five years later, people still have trouble getting together. It was a great historical step, the first time there was an amalgamation in musicians unions. Since then, there were thirty or forty of the locals that followed our method of amalgamating. I think what we found in playing music and being in an artistic thing is that color is not very important; it's what the people can share with each other. And I can look back and say that if there were still black and white at these times, we'd have a lot of problems.

The Jackie Robinson of the Networks

One evening, Jerry Fielding dropped by during a rehearsal of the Community Symphony Orchestra. He was the music director of Groucho Marx's show You Bet Your Life, *as well as* The Life of Riley, *among others.*

Jerry Fielding was in the audience one night, when I took a flute solo during a rehearsal of Bizet's *Carmen.* After he learned I could also play clarinet and saxophone, he hired me on the spot for the Groucho show. The first time I played the show I wasn't nervous or anything. I just knew that it was something I had been working for and looking forward to, not just musically. Even meeting the guys and sitting with them. Some of the guys, Milt Kestenbaum and Seymour Sheklow, were part of the Community Symphony and that made it great.

When I saw Groucho the first time, he looked glad. He said, "Wow, we got a new guy in the band!" And he starts screaming, "Hey, how are you doing?" It got to be a good thing. And most of the stuff didn't bother me. It was hard, though. I was like a fighter in top shape; I was ready for a challenge. And I knew everything was based on me doing a great job. I couldn't let down. Everything we had been doing over the two years or so was based on me or somebody getting an opportunity and pulling it off. I always thought this was kind of a little bit like Jackie Robinson felt.

During breaks we'd all go to dinner, five or six of the band guys. We'd go to restaurants that I could never go alone, but they accepted it somehow. Then, later on, sometimes I'd come there with someone else, and especially if it was someone white, just two of us, then you'd get the "you can't do this" treatment.

Sometimes we used to go to Nickodell's on Melrose right behind NBC in Hollywood. A very classy place. Once I went in with this white lady, Nan Evert, who was a good friend of mine. I had gone with my players in the band, but not on my own. I was kind of afraid to go in, but she said, "Oh, Nickodell's. Great!" She had no idea. We go to the door, and the maitre d' just about lost his teeth. I said, "Two," because I was trying to just outdo him. Stammering, he points to the back of the room. As we walked through this crowded restaurant the audience reacted. They couldn't believe this. Spoons fell off the table, and it got so noisy for a while, I really got frightened. And he put us in a place in the back where everyone could see us. It was good they had big menus. The noises lasted throughout dinner.

It happened once when we went to see Mingus with Red Norvo and Tal Farlow. They were working on La Cienega Boulevard in a little spot, and Jerry Fielding wanted to hear some sounds. And we had Milt Kestenbaum, the bass player, Thelma Walker, a black woman, and Nan Evert. We go to the restaurant and we sit down and we're trying to order, and all of a sudden the waiter comes and says, "We can't serve this table." So all of a sudden Fielding says, "What do you mean you can't serve this table?" "Well, it's mixed company." So right away, I'm knowing that the band is too. They probably don't know that Mingus, with his light complexion and wavy hair, is black. I didn't want to blow the whistle. But it was weird. We got angry.

Red, a very nice man, came to the table and kind of looked like "don't do that." I guess it was their thing and they were trying to protect it. I don't know if I could ever be that way. I've given up stuff, man, even when it means I had to lose, too. I'd probably get up and walk off. But even Mingus went along this time. It was a good gig. And they kind of said, "We can understand them suing and being mad, but why don't they also sue some of the other places that are doing it?" That's where we were hurt. So I was surprised at Mingus. But I guess they needed money. They just took that way out. So we backed off on that one.

But anyway, in this period I was getting to know the Hollywood area. And it was very lonely, because most of the time there were no other blacks out there.

I also began to look further than just the union fights. I looked at the fights that the ACLU and people like that were doing. It was a great move on my part. It started me thinking in a way different than just reading the papers and thinking this is the only thing that's going on. During this time I was probably more with the Democrats. But there were times when I was viewing some of the socialist views, not that I was going along with it. I'd read the *People's World* paper and get a different view. And it was okay for me. I think a lot of people would think you were communist if you were reading it, but I got a view of things that I had never gotten before. It sort of opened up the mind. It's like when you're searching for answers, you need to have more than one sign. Well, I'm that way about my music, too. There's more than one way to play a song. I think versatility is the thing. But I didn't see myself as that political.

And the House Un-American Activities Committee, I got a lot on that, too. I saw them topple Jerry Fielding from the Groucho Marx show. After I was hired, Jerry then hired Red Callender on *The Life of Riley* show. He began to integrate all of these orchestras. He had another TV jazz band with Red Callender, Gerry Wiggins, and myself. And we got a lot of exposure. The camera's panning us all the time. He got so much hate mail you would not believe it. But he kept on. And it got him into trouble. One night while we're doing the Groucho show, two big guys from the committee come in to serve a subpoena on Jerry Feldman, his real name. This could have been 1952. So Jerry was nervous. Leading up to this, he was getting phone calls every night from somebody. It would be two or three in the morning, the phone would ring, and they would say, "Feldman, we're going to get you." So he wasn't getting much sleep.

Before he appeared at the hearings, he got all of his band together and said, "Guys, here's the scene: I'm not a communist. They're after people. If I talk, then I've got to say that I spent time with Buddy. The only way, the lawyers say, is to just take the Fifth Amendment. Otherwise, they'll just keep this thing going. They'll call another fifty people or so. I'm going to take the Fifth, so you'll understand." Then one of the guys who had served him the subpoena came over and said, "If you've got $200,000, we'll get you out of this." He said, "If I had $200,000, I wouldn't give a shit who you guys were."

For a long time we helped him, because they dropped him, Groucho and the director, Bob Dwan, and the producer, John Guedel. We were all making about $130 a week then. I think the guys chipped in about $20 a week for four or five months, because he was cut off completely. They wouldn't play his records. So he went through a period of about four or five years where he did very little work. He only started writing when Betty Hutton insisted that Jerry write a picture she was in. She was very powerful and got her way. He got back in, but he was never the same after that. He was the most angry man because he had been so hurt by all of that.

It was an experience where I could see he was the kind of fighter that we don't have too often. We got to be good friends, not just because of the musical thing, but we had a lot in common in the battles we fought.

As you can see, that period was very frightening for us. Like I said, many teachers, many people, lost jobs, because if you did stick your neck out, you'd lose your gig.

I was also making all kinds of friends. I was living in sort of two worlds. And I began to do a lot of things. I wasn't just Buddy Collette the saxophone, flute, and clarinet player. It led to formal teaching, to being invited to do classical programs, and to doing some concerts, flute and string quartet, with Paul Robeson and with a woman named Frances Williams, who had her own theater. I was around Robeson during this time. He had his side to tell, which was great: it was a whole different side. At times at Frances's house he'd talk about the attacks on him because of his statements on his trip to Russia. "All I said was that I got treated better there. They treated me like a king. And when I go home, they discriminate against my people." So he was a truthful man, and I was in awe of him. He was one of the first to speak out in that way, and that really did a lot for me to see that. And he wasn't afraid. Being around him, it was a turning period for me. I loved it, I really did. I was with these string players and playing my heart out, and there was this big man.

At the first concert, he spoke at the end. But it was a period where they didn't really want him to speak because too many people would hear him. So he came back in another few months to do it again. This time the powers-that-be had put signs up: "There will be no public speaking." So if he speaks, they could go in during the concert and cart him off to jail. Now, we're all there; we've got this group and the place is packed. But he was a giant of a man, and you don't stop him much until he dies, right? Guess what he did? He sang his message! He really did. [sings] "They can't stop us." And he smiled—his shoulders were about that broad— and he put his hat on and just walked out.

A lot of people don't realize the inspiration he was for a lot of the black people who were leaders, who were able to stand up. Because it can be costly if you stand up and say "I believe in this." He was the kind of person who was true. Without him, things would have been a lot worse, more difficult to achieve, even what we had achieved with the union. And these kinds of stories are so the youth can say, "There were people who were doing it. It didn't just start right here."

Central Avenue —
"There was something wonderful there."

Central Avenue was a place where you could bring your own ideas to the stage, to the audience, whatever they sounded like. You were not being judged because you didn't sound like this or that. I think now there's more of that. There's a certain way that you should play or a certain horn or mouthpiece that you should have. Then you're kind of "in." On Central, if somebody had a different approach, it was well accepted. So I think the creativity was at its highest level. Your concern was, "Can I think of something different, a different way to approach this? Then when I go into the session on the weekend, I'll really wow them."

There were not too many rules to be broken in music at that time. I think it was easier to just be you. You were playing for you. We all respected each other, and we didn't all want to play like each other. The charm of it was that you came in with your own little sound. Every night there was stuff to hear. There was interplay. Dexter Gordon and Teddy Edwards and Wardell Gray and Gene Montgomery and Big Jay McNeely—close your eyes and you could tell who was playing. Alto players, the same thing. Sweet Pea Robinson and Sonny Criss and Eric Dolphy and Frank Morgan. No way could you miss it. You know, four bars or whatever, you could hear it. There was something wonderful there.

8

David Bryant

Bassist David Bryant has been a mainstay of the Los Angeles jazz scene since the late 1940s. He has performed with Clora Bryant, Benny Carter, John Carter, Nat Cole, Buddy Collette, Sonny Criss, the Delta Rhythm Boys, Dexter Gordon, Wardell Gray, Chico Hamilton, B. B. King, Percy Mayfield, Johnny Otis, Joe Turner, and Gerald Wiggins. Television band credits include the Tonight Show (with Steve Allen) and Run for Your Life. His extensive recording experience includes sessions with Nellie Lutcher, Horace Tapscott, and Gerald Wilson. He was in Gerald Wilson's band in the late '40s and early '50s and toured extensively with pianist-singer Nellie Lutcher. In the early '60s David joined with Horace Tapscott and a few other musicians to create what became the Pan-Afrikan Peoples Arkestra, and he remains a committed member of the "Ark."

David's mother, Indiana Herrington Bryant, and father, Joseph Bryant, met and married in Chicago, where David was born in 1921. Two years later, he moved with his mother and brother to Los Angeles.

My mother came, but my father never showed up. To this day I don't know what happened. There were three of us with my brother, Roscoe. A lot of our family was out here. My mother's brother, Hixie Herrington, and sister, Ida Herrington Sturgis. They were raising families, and I guess they were doing all right. Of course, that was before the Depression. My aunt Ida had a big house on Fifteenth Street, so we moved in with her and stayed a couple of years. I don't remember much. I remember the fire station. [laughter] The one on Fourteenth and Central was a black company. And the police station, because we lived around the corner from it.

Then my mother bought some property on 115th Street in 1926, and she built a house on the lot. It's the place where I'm at now. Up until the Depression it was great, but when the Depression hit, wow. You know, a single woman raising two kids and buying a home, it was rough. She worked for some of the movie stars and directors. Housework, that kind of work. During the Depression she was also sewing for the WPA [Works Progress Administration]. But we survived with a big garden out in back. We had chickens, turkeys, you know, fowl. Pigeons. We used to sell squab. You say squab, that's a delicacy, right? We used to take it to school every day for lunch. [laughter] Yeah. If we didn't have any bread, then on a biscuit. And we used to sell eggs and vegetables. We only had to buy a few staples. She even went to night school to learn about chickens. Built a neat chicken house with a cement floor. She was really serious about it. It was tough. But we did all right.

Watts was no problem. You could leave your door open. And the kids knew they had to walk a straight line, because the neighbors could kick their behinds, too. So everybody helped. You were raised by the neighbors. It's not like it is now. If you go to a parent now, they might say, "Mind your own business" or "My boy is a good boy." And we respected the older people. Everybody was "mister."

I went to the 111th Street School. I guess they had a few black teachers. That's where I first learned about black history, because this teacher in fifth and sixth grades, Miss Robinson, was really something. She would talk to us. She knew one of the first black aviators. She used to talk about him and Mary Bethune, who was an educator and had built a college down in Florida. And even the white teachers were really interested in you.

There were mostly black and Mexican families in our area. And through grammar school, I think there might have been a couple of white kids. Then it was junior high and senior together at Jordan High School. That was before they built Markham Junior High. At Jordan it was multiracial: white, Mexican, black, Asian. They had some Arabs. I remember one guy was from somewhere in Syria. His name was Davis. Well, they changed his name. So it was like a multicultural school. As a matter of fact, one of the guys that was on the Atomic Energy Commission was a scientist who went to Jordan. He was white.

David and his friends were early observers of Simon Rodia's work in progress, the Watts Towers.

I remember playing in that when I was growing up. That's not too far from where I lived. We used to run over there and be playing in there while he was building it. We used to take his fruit. As a matter of fact that's one of the reasons why I went in the yard, because he had fruit trees. We didn't realize then what was happening and where he was coming from. But a little later, we really had a lot of respect for him, even before it became what it is now. We realized what was happening.

And we'd go crawfishing at a place on the canal. It's like 108th and Central and then further south. They had Japanese gardens farther out. Japanese people had their farms. But this canal had crawfish in it. We'd get a big bag of crawfish and get some potatoes and stuff, and we'd have a feast. Big gunnysacks full of them. And we used to go swimming, because it was a swimming hole, too.

Yes, I watched Los Angeles and Watts grow. Because when we moved to Watts, there were cows right in back of us. And a guy down the street had a smokehouse. I think he was raising hogs and had a smokehouse. He used to make the best barbecue. His name was Elam and, as a matter of fact, one of his sons became a musician.

There were a few black police out there. I remember two offhand at the Watts station. I'll tell you, I got a bad impression of the police when I was a little kid. Once my brother and I went down to the cleaners, which was on the corner. As we were coming out, these policemen—they were plainclothes—got out of their cars and stopped us. They scared us to death. They probably asked us what we were doing and where we were going. So that gave me a bad impression, because it scared me to death. They were white. There were some good police, like there probably are now. Probably harder to find now. But the attitude was us against them. I've always known the police to be rough.

"I was surrounded by musicians."

When I was growing up you could hear music everywhere. On the street, coming out of the houses, you could hear Louis Armstrong and maybe Bessie Smith or some of the blues singers. There was a guy who lived next door named Peter Kennard, who played tenor saxophone and used to bring me sheet music. When I finally went out and learned to play bass, I'd go over to his house and we'd sit and play. And there was a guy across the street, Mr. Switcher, who worked for the city, but he played trumpet. He'd always be in his garage practicing. And later on there was a really good trumpet player who lived down the street from me. Fletcher Galloway. He was a professional, and he'd be practicing all the time. Later on Floyd Turnham lived down the street for years. So, yeah, that's why I wanted to play. I heard it all around me. I was surrounded by musicians. So I was already hooked. I knew what I wanted to be when I was about five or six. I knew that I wanted to be a musician.

One-hundred-and-third Street was the business district. That's where all the stores were. There was a little neighborhood theater called the Largo on 103rd. They had stage shows on weekends. They had mostly local bands, I guess. The Irving Brothers I think was one. There was the Little Harlem club on 118th between Wilmington and Central. That was almost like a cow patch at that time. [laughter] There was nothing out there but this nightclub. They had a lot of blues singers like T-Bone Walker. Also people like Stuff Smith later.

The Woodman Brothers had a studio over on Wilmington Avenue, called the Woodman Brothers Studio. Coney, William, Britt. George, the youngest one, didn't really play. On Fridays and Saturdays they'd have dances. So I used to sneak out of the house and go and listen to them. Because I was too young, I'd stand outside and listen. They were swinging. Joe Comfort was playing bass with them. Then he'd pick up his trumpet and play. Joe Comfort lived right around the corner from me. His father was a barber and used to cut my hair. The drummer was named Jessie Sailes. They had a good band.

We used to go downtown to see stage shows at the theaters like the Orpheum and the Paramount. Once Duke Ellington was at the Orpheum, and my mother had given us some money or we might have gone and cut lawns or whatever. They had two pictures in between the shows, so we stayed all day. We'd just keep seeing the pictures over and over. Finally, my mother came and said, "Roscoe! David!" and took us out of the theater. We were in there all day and part of the night, because Duke Ellington had two basses at the time. That really knocked me out. Duke Ellington turned me on. When other kids were going down the street whistling or something, I would have the whole orchestra in my head. I'd think, "This is the reed section," and I'd have the thing in my head. And I'd be going down the street just directing the orchestra.

I didn't start playing music until junior high school. In elementary school, I wanted to play, but we never could get enough money together to get an instrument. But I could sing and that was one of my favorite subjects, music. In junior high I started playing the violin. My mother was able to go to the pawnshop and bought a violin. I wanted to play trumpet, but we couldn't afford it. So me and my brother both used it.

My brother was very talented. I think he had more on the ball than me. He had a beautiful voice. But we had a music teacher who would embarrass you in front of the class. In fact, that's what happened to my brother. He made him feel so bad and embarrassed him so that he just stopped playing. It must have been pretty rough on him, because he came home and he was just destroyed. He was playing by ear, when he was supposed to be reading. And I did the same thing, and the teacher did the same thing to me. But I was maybe a little tougher. My brother was so sensitive, it really got to him. So he just stopped playing. The teacher was [Joseph Louis] Lippi. He was there for many years.

The guy that got me started was another teacher, who came in later, and his name was [Verne] Martin. He played reeds. He played everything, I guess, because he started me on bass. During lunchtime all the guys would get together and play, like Charles Mingus, Buddy Collette, Eddie Davis. So I'd go and sneak in with my violin and I'd put it up like it was the bass. At that time, if a cat was playing violin he was considered a sissy. [laughter] So I started playing bass. And Mr. Martin told me, "Come to school maybe half an hour before school, and I'll show you how to play it." So he started me in on it, showed me the positions and how to hold it. I got in the senior orchestra. I didn't have a bass. What I would do was on weekends I'd take the school bass home. Do you know how far that was? It was a mile and a half to school. That's how much I wanted to play, man. I'd take the bass on my back and bring it back Monday.

Charles Mingus was playing cello at that time, and then he started playing bass. But he wasn't in the orchestra, because he couldn't get along with the teacher, Mr. Lippi. Lippi clashed with a lot of people. They couldn't get along. Another guy—Joe Adams—played drums, and he couldn't get along with him either. In fact, they wanted to expel him. Somehow he got out of that. I guess his father had a little push. He was a manager for Ray Charles for years and was the first black disc jockey here in L.A.

So Charles Mingus used to bring his bass to school, even though he wasn't in the orchestra, and played at lunchtime. I first met Mingus in about the fifth grade at the elementary school. He lived on 108th between Compton Avenue and Grandee. He was nasty at first. Once in class Charles Mingus called me a "black motherfucker." [laughter] At that time, "black" wasn't cool. We were "colored" then. So I swung and hit him; I took one punch and hit him in the stomach, and it knocked him out. He just went over, whoosh. [laughter] And I was scared. But Mingus was always fat. He would go through periods where he'd slim down and he'd get fat. Most of the time he was fat. He loved to eat, man. But he slimmed down, because he was into sports. He played basketball and football. We were on the football team together. But anyway, after that incident at the 111th Street School, we became friends. I got his respect.

They had a band at Jordan called the Hep Cats. We'd go to different schools to play. We played stock arrangements, but we had a pretty good band. It wasn't as good as Jeff's [Jefferson High School]. But I guess it compared pretty well, because we had Coney, William and Britt Woodman, Buddy Collette, Eddie Davis. Charles Mingus wasn't playing in the band. There was a bass player by the name of Perry Lee. I can't think of her last name. She could play, man, and was in the Hep Cats playing bass. I think she also played piano. I can think of a couple of girl singers, but no other girl instrumentalists that continued.

In high school I came up under the tag "nice boy." "Oh, he's a nice boy." Shit. [laughter] You realize how many ladies that I didn't get because of that? Damn, I hated that. It took me a long time to live that down. I just hated it. I was kind of laid-back. I guess you could almost say shy.

David graduated from Jordan in January 1941. Still engaged in music studies, he wasn't ready to play professionally, and his mother did not encourage him.

My mother used to say, "Music is fine, but—" At that time the post office was a big thing. "At least learn enough so you can work at the post office. That's a secure job." Now, I'd say there is no such thing as security. Later on I found out she was right, because I found out how tough it was in the music business. But I was fortunate, because I did all right. It was just the fact that I knew what I wanted to play. I wanted to play straight-ahead jazz. The blues thing, I got tired of that. I just wanted to play jazz. So I turned down other gigs, unless I really needed a gig.

My first job was at a foundry on Alameda. [laughter] Finklestein's, I believe it was. I was digging a ditch; that's what I was making. [laughter] And that lasted a week. I wasn't used to the work and I quit. I got one paycheck. [laughter] Then I got a job at an auction gallery for some people that my mother worked with. Bringing up furniture, antiques, and stuff when they wanted to auction them off. That was in Hollywood. I stayed there for about six or seven months. Then I got a job for the State Board of Education washing dishes at Fairfax High School. I also worked at a drugstore for maybe a couple of months. And I traveled to them on the red car. They had rapid transit then. But they got rid of it. Politics, you know.

David continued to study music and to practice with Charles Mingus and other friends.

I didn't get a bass until I got out of high school. I used to go over to Charles's house, and we used to practice together. He was taking lessons before I was, while he was in school. I couldn't afford a teacher until I got out. But when I got out, through Mingus, Red Callender became my first teacher. I had seen him, because during the Depression they had the WPA, and they used to send orchestras and groups out to all the schools. That's where I first saw Red. He came with some group to Jordan. So through Mingus we got together. Good teacher.

Red was working with Lee and Lester Young at the time. They had a group. So he took me out to his gig, and I met Lester Young. I'd just gotten out of high school. I think I was about nineteen. That was a gas. It was just so beautiful. I'll never forget how he was very encouraging. What did he say? Whippersnapper? Some kind of name. And they were outside getting high. I didn't know at that time, but they were smoking a joint. I was really square. In fact, I didn't start smoking or drinking until I was twenty-one, when I was in the army. But anyway, he was so nice, man. He really made a great impression on me.

I had another teacher before I went to the army. He was a fantastic teacher. Schull Lipschultz. I went to this cat for about two or three lessons. He told me that every time Jimmy Blanton came in town with Duke, he would come out to see him.

David also joined Lloyd Reese's rehearsal band, which met Sundays at the musicians union on Central Avenue.

Lloyd Reese had this band made up of his students and some other youngsters. Like Buddy Collette, Jackie Kelso, James Nelson, Jack Trainor, Jake Porter, Charles Mingus. Charles was in the band so he got me on the band, and we had two basses. We played charts that Lloyd Reese had, and learned how to play. And they used to laugh at Dexter Gordon because I remember he couldn't read as well as some of the other people. But that's what it was all about: learn how to play in a band.

Lloyd Reese was a legendary teacher, along with Mr. Browne. Eric Dolphy and Buddy and all the cats went to him. But I didn't go because I didn't have the money. He was very philosophical and a good teacher. Good musician, good player. When Ben Webster would come to town with Duke, he'd go to Lloyd.

Then I got my first job as a musician—I mean a steady job, because I had worked with people like George Brown, Al Adams, and John Moulder's band. I had a chance to work on the WPA band, just before they phased it out. That was the same organization where I first saw Red Callender. The only guy I remember from there is Elmer Fain. He played baritone saxophone. Then I got this steady job in Long Beach with a guy named Johnny Shackleford. He had four pieces: a rhythm section and a saxophone player. I don't remember the name of the club, but I worked there for about six months.

I'd also go to places like Lovejoy's. That was an after-hours place in 1942. And Art Tatum used to play there. He'd have a big case of beer. I'd see all the cats like Lester Young. All the guys that were in town used to go by Lovejoy's and a couple of other places, like Brother's. One time, when I was in the army, I went by Brother's, and Art Tatum was working there with Joe Comfort. Joe persuaded me to come up and play. I said, "Play with Art Tatum? Are you kidding, man?" But I went up and played. Whew! I didn't know what was happening. That's how much nerve I had.

See, I grew up with Charles Mingus. So I guess that's why I had that much nerve. And I played. Yeah, I played with Art Tatum. I got a chance to spread my wings, so to speak.

And that's where you got work, because you go to a jam session and a guy would hear you and say, "Hey, are you working, man? Yeah, okay. I've got a gig for you." In fact, that still happens, to a lesser degree, but it still happens. That's the name of the game, visibility and people knowing you. I still have to do it. I should do it. I don't do it as much. Even though I've been doing it all my life, they still say, "Damn, I thought you were out of town, man." So if you don't get out and let people know you're still into it, well, they don't call you.

Military Service

I was 1-A, and the army was organizing this band for the Tenth Cavalry, stationed at Camp Lockett, which was just about sixty miles outside of San Diego. So they came to the union and recruited all these Los Angeles guys that were 1-A. So I enlisted and went to the army band. They also got Elmer Fain, Lloyd Reese, Jake Porter and Bill Douglass, James Nelson and Herb Mullins, John Randolph and Bill Hadnott, who was my first sergeant, but he was already in. He's a legendary bass player around here. He wasn't originally from L.A., but when he got into the army he stayed here. Being stationed outside of San Diego, we came home almost every weekend.

It was nice. But I hated it. I hated the army, man. It was segregated then. I'll tell you something: being from here, if I didn't enlist, they would have sent me to the South. That's what they were doing. They were sending the guys from here and New York to the South. And that would have been a drag. I know some guys who went through some things. They had never been South, and they had to go down there. So I avoided that.

I was at Camp Lockett for a couple of years. Then we went to North Africa—Algiers, Casablanca, Oran—and stayed there for about three months. Bill Hadnott, Fain, and Lloyd Reese didn't go overseas. They got discharged. Well, I guess I can spill the beans now. Bill Hadnott told me he just played crazy, and the rest got out because of their age. I even tried. I took almost a whole bottle of aspirin trying to get out, but it didn't work. I hated the army.

Then we went to Italy. We went up the southern part of Italy, through Naples, and straight up to Rome. When Rome fell, there was a big ceremony and our band played for that. We stayed in Rome for about three months and lived in a hotel. Rome was just beautiful, like it is now. I had a ball. We just played for parades, retreats, and dances. That was good duty.

I enjoyed it more overseas than I did here. We experienced the segregation less. I'll tell you what. Now, this is pretty chickenshit. They tried to program the people over there that we were less than human. The U.S. did, because they didn't want us socializing. Anyway, it didn't work, because first we wound up in North Africa. It's a Muslim country, and women wore robes and veils when they went in public. Consequently, some of the soldiers that didn't know what was happening, especially some of the white soldiers, were found castrated with their testicles stuffed in their mouths because they messed with these women. But they were a little lighter on the black soldiers. Sometimes I'd go to the Casbah, and I'd spend the weekend with a lady, but nobody bothered me.

Then in Italy—now, this actually happened—someone walked up to me to see if the color would rub off. I'm talking about grown people. Several guys had processed hair, and they'd pull it to see if it was their real hair. And they'd raise your coattail to see if you had a tail. That actually happened. But when they found out that they were a bunch of lies, bullshit, they fell in love with the black soldiers.

I was going to stay and go to school in Italy. We were stationed most of the time near Naples, and I used to go to the opera once a week, because I liked the orchestra. I went to the San Carlo opera house, which is very famous. So I got turned onto opera. I met the bass player, bought some books. I bought a bow and stuff. I had really planned on staying over there, getting a discharge over there, and going to school. But I got sick with tuberculosis after the war was over and I had to come back on a hospital ship. I wanted to stay over there. I didn't get back until years and years later. Actually it was '87, when I went back with Horace [Tapscott] to Italy.

Postwar L.A.

Oh, it was really happening during the war. L.A. was a boomtown, because they had the defense industry here and soldiers. So L.A. was jumping twenty-four hours a day. But by the time I got out, it was all over. I got out in '46, came back, and I was out at the VA [Veterans Administration] hospital in Van Nuys. I was finally discharged about the middle of '47. I'd come home on passes. But, like I said, it was all over. There were some clubs. One was called the Downbeat, where they had jam sessions every, I think, Monday night. Different places. Like Jack's Basket, that was an after-hours place with jam sessions. On 103rd Street in Watts they had a club called the Savoy. That was a jazz club, restaurant and club, with an upstairs and downstairs. Billie Holiday sang there in the late forties, maybe '48, '49. It didn't last much longer than that.

But it had changed. It was still happening, but not like it was during the war. There were a few jobs left, and then eventually everything just dried up when the economy got bad. When we got back into the peacetime thing, it began to get worse, steadily worse, just straight downhill. Musicians that played jazz also played other kinds of music. I mean, to live they had to. All the commercial, top forty and all that shit. They were good musicians. That's why they used to have after-hours places, so they could come after they got off from their gig. They had to get the shit out of their systems, so they'd go to sessions and play until morning. Really, that's the value of sessions. Plus making contacts for gigs. But, yeah, it was to blow off your frustrations.

When David was released from the VA hospital in 1947, he moved back home and resumed his musical studies.

I figured that I'd stay home so my mother could take care of me. The tuberculosis was arrested in 1947. Since then, I just got progressively better. And I never had medicine. All I had was bed rest and vitamins. I was very fortunate, because they were dying all around me. A lot of people split with tuberculosis. It was a dangerous disease.

I also went to school. I started at the L.A. Conservatory [of Music and Art]. I went there for about a semester or so. It was mostly classical. I left because I wanted to play, and the teachers that I wanted weren't there. I wasn't interested in getting a degree. Consequently, I went to Westlake College of Music, where a lot of name musicians out of the bands went. There was Chet Baker and Bud Shank, a lot of Tommy Dorsey's, Duke Ellington's sidemen. Britt Woodman and John Anderson, Bill Green and

Buddy Collette went there. A lot of the guys. One of my teachers was Paul Villapeg, who taught harmony and orchestration. As a matter of fact, he got me a gig with Sarah Vaughan and Lucky Thompson. And I got a better bass teacher. I stayed there about four years.

I used to run into Mingus all the time. He didn't go to New York until later. One night I was practicing at home late at night. I heard a knock on the door. "Who is it?" "Charles Mingus." He came in and he was crying. "They won't hire me. They won't give me any work." And we sat down and talked. They wouldn't hire him because Charles Mingus felt like the bass should be able to solo too. He wanted to be on the front line. They just didn't like Charles Mingus. But I understood him, because I was raised with him. People like Buddy Collette and the Woodman Brothers, they understood him, too. So he had to go to New York to make it. That's really sad, because a lot of people had to go to New York to make it, because of the attitudes out here.

He was playing a lot more bass than before. [laughter] He was studying with a guy named [Herman] Rheinshagen. I had a chance to study with him, to get about three lessons, before he stopped teaching. Rheinshagen used to tell me that Charles Mingus would argue with him. He would say, "You're supposed to do it this way." And Mingus would say, "Well, man, you can do it this way, too." Yeah, he'd argue with the teacher. That's why he was what he was. He took what you told him, but then he expanded on that. But that's what you're supposed to do.

While in Europe during the war, David had heard the new sounds of bebop on records. Not long after returning to Watts he had an opportunity to play with Charlie Parker.

I first heard bop when I was overseas. I heard those early records. I liked it. Remember I was turned on by Duke Ellington. Now, he was way ahead of his time. So when I heard bop, it wasn't a big thing for me. The guys could play. When I came back, Bird was spending some time here. One particular time, just before he returned to New York, this artist gave him a going-away party. She had a ranch up in Pasadena, up in the hills. Let's see, who was there? Frank Morgan, Larance Marable, a piano player named Amos Trice. A couple of more people. Anyway, we were burning, man. You know Bird. We were playing. So Bird had a tie, had a suit. He was all dressed up. Then he took off his coat first, then he took off his tie, then he took off his shirt. He did a striptease, down to his birthday suit. You hear me? [laughter] His birthday suit, man. He said, "Okay, everybody get like me or split." [laughter] Now, more people got like him than split. And I was hiding behind my bass. And we were burning, man, burning!

After we got through playing, we all went out and jumped in the swimming pool. When I got out, I saw these two big cars from the sheriff's department. Whoever the lady artist was, she had pull or something, because she said something to them and they split. You'd think that there would be all kinds of shit going, and there was, but it was discreet, very discreet. I didn't see anything ever. But they had rooms. I guess a lot of things were going on. But I didn't see anything. I used to smoke a little weed, but other things were going on, too. But it was so discreet. I guess you could say it was a wild party, but it wasn't like the average person would think. That's how cool that party was. It was quite an experience.

But Bird was a beautiful cat, man, a beautiful cat. He was just strung out on dope. And he used to tell the cats not to do that shit, but they wouldn't listen. They'd think "If he could play like that, well maybe I can." That's bullshit. That isn't what made him play. It's like if he made mistakes, then they played his mistakes, too, thinking that that was it. He was beautiful and very, very intelligent, very sharp. I never had another chance to work with him, per se, but I did sit in.

David was an early supporter of the movement to eliminate segregation in the musicians union. He played in the integrated Community Symphony Orchestra and participated in the political struggles within Local 767.

There was an orchestra called the Humanist orchestra, which was about having first-chair studio musicians teach the cats in each section. We were training for the studio jobs. Sometimes my teacher at the time, Nat Gangursky, a Russian Jew, came out and worked with the bass section. There were a whole lot of cats. Buddy Collette. Britt Woodman. He brought Horace Tapscott along, I think, who was playing trombone then. Of course, later he got proficient on the piano. I'm just watching him grow after all those years. Wow. Shit. He's been a monster for a long time. But he's only now just beginning to get a little recognition.

The amalgamation. That's why they call me the invisible man. [laughter] I was part of it, but I'm never mentioned. I was involved, because I wanted to improve things. One way we had to do it was to run some young musicians for union office. So I ran on a ticket. I think Benny Carter ran for president. I ran for treasurer against Paul Howard. I got a lot of votes. I didn't lose by much.

After the amalgamation Local 767 merged its assets, property, and funds with Local 47.

They made some mistakes. They should have perhaps kept the property. But they just let everything go. When we became amalgamated, the fellowship and all was gone. You'd see different cats, but then you never saw anybody.

The Decline of Central Avenue

Actually, what closed down Central Avenue in the fifties was the powers that be and the police, because of the mixing. All the stars and all the people would come over to Central Avenue and listen to the music. They didn't like that mixing, so they rousted people. Stopping you and patting you down. Going into the clubs and messing with people. They did that for a long time. And that's how they closed it up. White ladies would come down, and they didn't like that. So people got tired of being messed around by the police, because they weren't doing anything. Mixed couples or even white people they'd stop, "What are you doing over on this side of town?" It was about racism. That's what it was. It was rampant then. That's why they hassled people. So people got tired of that shit and stopped going over there. Central Avenue shut down, and things moved west.

Of course, they had a little dope problem. Heroin and cocaine, those were the drugs then. Heroin was the hip drug. But how could this shit have gone on if they don't sit back a little bit? They go through the pretense of cracking down, but they don't. They crack down on the people that use, but they don't crack down on the people that put it in the damn community. I mean, it's the big shots, like even the government, I believe, that had something to do with some of it getting in the country. But the cats that are making the money, they don't get them. Consequently, the shit is still here. The only way that it's going to be better is for the people to wake up to the fact that they're putting it in the community. It's a damn shame, but that's the way it is.

And people started leaving, moved west. When I was a kid, that was when professional people were living in the ghetto. There was a doctor down the street, Dr. King. There was a lawyer over here. And there was Dr. Bledsoe, who had two sons who were musicians, living on Wilmington Avenue. All that was in the neighborhood. Later on they moved to Beverly Hills or Baldwin Hills. But at that time they couldn't live anyplace else, so everybody was in the community. We had so-called role models. Doctors, lawyers, teachers, living right down the street. A lot of musicians out of Jeff and Jordan. It's a matter of having somebody to show you the way.

But the scene changed. Everybody split. The only reason I didn't split was because this was my mother's pad, and I said I wasn't going to sell it. So when she passed, I just moved back here. I've tried to work with kids since then, to be involved. Because that's what it's all about, man: passing it on and trying to encourage the youngsters.

9

Cecil "Big Jay" McNeely

One of the original honking saxophonists, Jay McNeely was an early
exponent of rhythm and blues. A versatile musician with roots in the early
bebop movement, Jay played with a wide variety of performers including Cab
Calloway, Nat King Cole, Lionel Hampton, the Ink Spots, Johnny Otis, Little
Richard, and the Modern Jazz Quartet.

Jay spent most of the 1950s recording, touring, and performing rhythm and
blues. In 1959 he enjoyed national success with "Something on Your Mind," a
tune he penned which was subsequently covered by many artists. By the mid-
1960s, Jay had left the music business. He entered the Jehovah's Witness minis-
try, took a full-time job at the post office, and raised a family.

Twenty years later, in the early 1980s, a number of r&b reunions brought
Big Jay back to the stage. Since then he has returned to full-time performing,
recording, and touring.

I was born in Watts in 1927. There were three boys in the family: my
brother Robert, who played saxophone with me, and Dillard, who later
came in and played bass. We traveled together on the road for many years.
We were born on 110th Street. It was a mixed community, all nationalities
were there. It was complete peace at that time. Spanish kids, Orientals,
and whites. We all went to school together, no problems.

We used to go down all the time and watch Simon Rodia building the
Watts Towers. Watts was a beautiful place. They used to deliver the milk
in a little horse-and-buggy. We had the ice man—we had to buy ice. We
had a lot of chickens and ducks and things in our place. We had a hundred feet by a hundred, and had a well on it, and grew all types of vege-

179

tables. See, my father [Dillard McNeely] was from the South, and, like a farmer, he knew how to grow all the vegetables. We had to take a bath in a number-two tub. We had a pump. The water was fresh. We had a little windmill there. I think we were about the only ones who had a well, though. It was strictly all rural country out there at that time, because everything was downtown. There was no Orange County. So it was real country and very wholesome.

That was quite the thing to go downtown. Get on the Watts local, go downtown and shop. We only had one freeway, the Pasadena Freeway. See, they had the "big red" [red cars] that would go out to Pasadena, big red to San Pedro, big red to Long Beach. They ran fast, so it didn't take you any time to get there. Transportation all through the city was electric; no bus, see. A great system, just like in Europe. Good transportation, and no smog, because you had no cars. If we had the rail in now, it would be much better, you could move around. If you could move in this city, it would be much better, but it's so hard. [laughter] Yes, that's the problem. So then it was very wholesome, a very good time.

Parents were concerned about the other parents' children. You'd get one whipping down the street, you'd get another whipping when you'd get home. The teachers had the authority to teach and punish, so there was a lot of respect for parents and for one another's property and for one another. No crime. We had all nationalities, Spanish, Chinese, Japanese, white, all living together, no problem.

It was a beautiful community, self-contained. Two shows, two drug-stores, and a bus. We had two shows there, the Largo and the Barrel-house. That's where Little Esther Phillips got discovered. Johnny Otis had the Barrelhouse there on 108th by the Santa Ana track. And a lot of acts: Little Esther, the Robbins. And they had a lot of comedian acts. A lot of movie stars used to come out to catch the show. At that time, it was real great and no problems. We had little stores in all the communities. So it was very peaceful. The farthest thing from one's mind would be crime. Rape or drugs or anything, that wasn't there. So it was a good, wholesome way to grow up.

"A lot of tenor players came from Watts."

Well, we had the Woodman Brothers, and my brother, Bobby, played saxophone, and we had Eddie Davis. Buddy Collette and the Woodman

Brothers and Charles Mingus, they all went to school with my brother, who was older. A lot of tenor players came from Watts. Like Walter Benton. He was a great saxophonist, man. He could play. Then you had Walter Henry. He used to live in Central Gardens there, and we used to have a little band together, with Ralph Bakeman on piano. Walter, well, he was bad. Clifford Solomon. See, I used to go out and study, and then I'd come back and teach them. They wanted to learn, but they didn't have any money. So we had Walter Henry, Walter Benton, and then we had Clifford Solomon, and Paul Madison—that guy can play, man. He's in Hawaii now. He used to work with Trummy Young there in Hawaii all the time. Boogie Daniels. They all used to come over to the house, and I'd give them instructions, lessons and things.

There was a Spanish kid—Anthony Ortega. He worked with Lionel Hampton. We had this Japanese guy who was— I forgot his name, but he was a bad cat. He could play. And then you had a Spanish kid who could sing and play—Gil Bernal. He came out of Watts. Bad. Big following. He went out with Hamp [Lionel Hampton] for a while. Then, you had James Jackson, who played with the Honeydrippers. Joe Liggins, he's out of Watts. So, like I say, you had a lot of good players out of there.

And I used to go down to the black musicians union, Local 767. They used to have Dexter Gordon and all the guys down there rehearsing on Central Avenue. So I used to go down and listen to the guys. My brother was playing in the band. I wasn't even playing then, but I'd go down and listen to them play. That was the Lloyd Reese rehearsal band. He was a great teacher. All the guys studied from him. Even Eric Dolphy studied from him. A lot of good musicians: Ernie Royal. I studied from him.

At school, I'd pick up a horn, play a little bit. I'd have my brother write something out for me, and I'd play it in school or something like that, but I didn't really get interested in it until I was around sixteen. I was working at the Firestone Rubber Company. I said, "Hey, there has to be a better way to make a living than working eight hours." So I picked up the saxophone. My brothers had both gone into the army. I knew he had left his horn with a guy named Buddy Harper, who was a great arranger at the time. So I went up there and got the saxophone. I studied from Miss Alma Hightower. That was Vi Redd's aunt. And Sonny Criss. We all went up there and studied together for like fifty cents a lesson.

I played tenor one day, and I liked it—because I started on alto. Then I wrote my brother, and he sent me his tenor. In fact, I'm still playing it today, the same horn. In school I wanted to play in the band, and they wouldn't let me, so I formed my own group. We were called the Earls of '44.

I went to Jordan High School. Then I left and went to Poly [Polytechnic High School], were I met Hampton Hawes, an incredible pianist. Then I went to Jefferson for a year and graduated under Samuel Browne. He was the one who started teaching about the different types of scales and how to play tonal. You got where you could play in any key. Great arranger. We learned lots from him. All the guys studied under him: Arthur Farmer, a lot of the jazz musicians came out of there, and he was a tremendous teacher. Sonny Criss and I went from Poly and Jeff. This was around '46 when we got out.

I hit Central Avenue when I was a kid, man, because that was the thing in the forties, '44, '45. The Avenue was popping then. You had the Club Alabam—Johnny Otis playing there—and they had a full chorus line, just like the Cotton Club in New York. And you had the Downbeat. You had the Last Word. Then, you had Shepp's Playhouse. You had all the clubs. So I started going there, because when I was going to school I was playing Central Avenue, playing there and other clubs besides that in Watts.

I remember Duke Ellington came over to my party. I was born April 29, and he was born April 29. I was with Harold Oxley. He used to book T-Bone Walker and all the guys—Fats Domino, Jimmie Lunceford. So he brought Duke over; he knew Duke. We sat down and talked with Duke and all that.

I was always on Central sneaking in. Young cats were getting in there to see what was going on. The clubs were grooving, because money was popping; people had plenty of money. You didn't have this big racial thing going. Oh, man, Humphrey Bogart, all the big stars would come down there and were what they called slumming. They'd just like going down and seeing some black entertainment. So all the big acts were coming out playing and cooking in the clubs and having just a ball. It was just incredible. Even the Beacon Theatre, that was a big thing. And the Elks Hall. They had Lionel Hampton, all the big acts. I played there. Roy Brown played there. So the Avenue was just on fire. You know what I mean?

Like I said, I played the Elks, a lot of times, many, many times. The

Last Word many times. The Downbeat. Go by Jack's Basket with Jack McVea and the other guys. Scatman Crothers would be down there. Scatman Crothers played great drums, man. He really did. I know he got into movies and was real big. But, yeah, he used to play drums, incredible drummer. You could just go from one end of Central Avenue to the other end and it was just cooking. Oh, yeah. After-hours. Like at Jack's Basket they'd have after-hours. The Nightcap was after-hours. All the bands came out and jammed. It was grooving down on Fifth Street and Sixth Street close to Central, downtown.

"I wanted to be a comedian, but that didn't work . . ."

At the Lincoln Theatre on Twenty-third and Central they used to have the amateur hour. Pigmeat Markham was there, and they had a whole, full theater, chorus line. But on Wednesday night they had the amateur hour. They strictly wanted guys who really could perform, where they could shoot them off the stage. [sings fanfare] And then they'd take a gun and shoot them off the stage. The first time I went up there, I went up as a comedian, and I got shot off the stage.

At that time I wanted to be a comedian. I used to clean up all the shows downtown when I was young. They had the burlesque right across the street, and I used to go down and listen to the cats and take a lot of their points. At one time I had two girls who worked with me. I'd blow my horn and their skirts would come off, and they would dance while I was playing. I knew Skillet. Pan, Pot, and Skillet: that was a comedian act that used to work with Jimmie Lunceford and all the guys then. Skillet's right here now working with another guy, Leroy Daniels. So what happened is that I used to work with him; he used to give me a lot of ideas. I wanted to be a comedian, but that didn't work, so I came back the next week and won second prize playing my horn. I was sixteen then, about seventeen.

Then I went to San Diego and worked. I was still in school. I went to San Diego, and that's when we had all the guys in the navy. So they were playing a lot of standards. They weren't really getting into a lot of soulful things. I stayed there a while, and then I came back home, and that's when I got really interested in playing the music. I played all up and down Central Avenue. We used to go out to the Plantation to catch Billy Eckstine, Gene Ammons, and all the guys out there, Basie and all that. That was right out by my house in Watts. It was right on Central Avenue. You had all the clubs, the Hole in the Wall on Central Avenue, the Last Word, the Downbeat, and Jack's Basket. We used to go jam all night.

One of the first bebop bands on the Avenue featured Jay with Sonny Criss and Hampton Hawes, all still in high school.

I was playing with Sonny Criss, Hampton Hawes—a great jazz pianist. We were still in school, but we formed a band out of school. We had Buddy Woodson on bass, William Streetser on drums, various guys. It was a groovy band. Hamp developed into a tremendous piano player, but at that time he used to sound like Nat King Cole. He used to love Nat. But we were very progressive. That was the only thing we did. We followed Bird very closely. Howard McGhee, Diz, Miles Davis. See, they were all down on First Street. Teddy Edwards was playing alto with Roy Milton; then he went to tenor with Howard McGhee, and Roy Porter on drums. So we stayed very close. We were very progressive. We listened to the records, were taking things off the records. When the stuff was hot, we were right on top of it. When we first heard this stuff, man, it was just incredible and we really enjoyed it and we got right into it.

Sonny had such a great ear that he could hear something once and play it. I didn't have the ability or the ear like he did to hear something and to play it as fast. I'm kind of glad, because I was able to develop and create my own style. But then everybody had their style. You could tell who's who. Now it's money and getting into a certain bag or certain groove.

And then, when we got out of school, that's when each one began to go his own direction. Fortunately, I found where I belonged in this stream of music, and Sonny had his thing, and Hamp did. So they stayed in the progressive thing. But periodically we would cross paths. We'd laugh, we'd talk, and we'd have a good time. So they respected me, because they knew what I could do, what I was capable of doing, and what I felt about music. The showmanship was one thing, playing is another thing, and sincerity is— It doesn't matter how many notes you play.

And I used to go and listen to Mingus and Lucky Thompson, the Farmer brothers, Ernie Andrews was around then. But Sonny Criss and I used to have a good band together, and we used to jam after-hours together. He really was a lovable person. He'd give you the coat off his back. Just a great guy. He never got the recognition, I think, that he should have gotten. We were always together until we parted, until I went to start studying. Very close, like brothers. We'd eat together, sleep together, practice together; we were together all day every day, because we both were living in Watts. He never felt that he was superior, although he always had nice clothes, a nice car. But he was a down-to-earth country boy. He was from Tennessee, you know. And could play, man. Great guy.

Postwar Central

That's when Central Avenue was really grooving. I played the Downbeat and played the Basket Room, played down on First Street. That's when they had Shepp's Playhouse and all the guys used to play down in the music room. We used to play in an after-hours spot there. That's when I met Teddy Edwards, who was playing with Roy Milton at that time. He came out here with Ernie Fields out of Oklahoma.

I was very close to Charlie Parker, very close to Howard McGhee, and also, like Roy Porter and Miles Davis, because they were all playing in the band then in Los Angeles. That's when Los Angeles was really groovy. We jammed with Bird and Miles and Howard and all the guys. We used to do that all the time. Bird used to go down to First Street, and we used to follow him around to the different clubs and play wherever we could play.

Bird was a great guy. I'd take his clothes home, and my mother would wash his clothes. Wasn't ever high style, never thought "I'm the great Bird" or "I'm the great this" or anything. Just a down-to-earth guy. You'd ask him, "Bird, what's this?" and he'd show you this, show you that. And McGhee, the same way. He taught us how to write changes, progressions, in numbers rather than chord structure. That way you could transpose.

A lot of people, if they see me, the style I play now, the one note and the showmanship, they never know that I started off playing jazz and wouldn't play anything else but jazz, because that's what I love. I still love it. I love to hear it, and I'd love to play it anytime, because I think it's very creative, and you can express yourself.

Sonny Criss and I played together quite a while until I went to study with Joseph Cadaly. That's when Sonny and I split up. He continued on into the progressive jazz, and I went and studied. When we split, he started going all up and down the Coast playing and going to Europe. But I don't know, it just didn't happen. He'd get records. People said he was great. They played his stuff. But it just didn't happen for him, and I think that kind of disturbed him. Especially when you put your whole soul and your whole life and just wrap up everything into something and it doesn't happen. He was pioneering and when you're pioneering, it's kind of more difficult to get recognition. And, I'm sad to say, the white musicians come along— And they can play, now, but they come in, and they get all this recognition, see. They get into places and they can do things. You have to suffer when you're a pioneer. So that's what happened, really, I think, with Sonny. He was just early.

Mr. Green, who was the teacher at Poly, was the one who put me in touch with Joseph Cadaly. He played first chair at RKO studios. He taught us harmony, solfège. We had ear training and the whole bit for about a year. I learned how to play very legit, learned how to read. I was playing saxophone, clarinet, and studying solfège.

By studying for a year, I lost a lot of— I don't know. I didn't lose the soul, but you get very technical. But now I'm able to use all of this. I even studied from Buddy Collette on the flute. See, there are certain things that you learn from a teacher that you can't learn on your own. I don't care how talented you are. These things don't come natural.

Jay had recorded with the Johnny Otis band. He debuted as a band leader in fall 1948. During his second recording session in December he cut "Deacon's Hop," which became one of the r&b hits of 1949.

And then, after I studied for a year, I had my big hit, "Deacon's Hop," in '49, and I went just strictly solo. One kid [Ralph Bass] came by. He said he wanted me to record. I said yeah. I didn't know what to do, so I went to a little record store in Watts, a guy named Pete Canard, and he gave me an old record ["Nothing But Soul"] of Glenn Miller when the drum went [mimics cymbal sound] with just the cymbal. I took "Deacon's Hop" from listening to that. I took my horn, and I created and then recorded it. It was a big thing. I just forgot about everything I learned and just went in and played soul, so to speak. Soul. One note. Don't try to play a lot of notes; just play some soul. And it worked.

I think there was a dynamic at the time, because I went from one stage to another stage altogether. It wasn't like I was doing it all the time. It was such a drastic change, because I listened to some of my old things that I did at that time, and they were very soulful, very simple. I look back at some of my old things like "Deacon's Hop," and there was so much honesty there. It was straight-out soul. And people could tell it on the records.

I went into the studio, and I said, "I'm going to forget everything I've learned," because I learned a lot of things, but then you had to apply them as time went along. But this time I just said, "Let's just drop every-thing and just blow," and that's what happened. Like a light turning on and off, it was that much drastic change. Because what I was doing they never would have recorded. [laughter] Just let everything down and play.

It's like playing a tune for the first time. You're so brilliant because the feelings are different the first time. It was like going out of one world and into another. Because I'd gotten very legit, sounded like a cello on the tenor, four vibratos to a hundred, and very "e" sound, singing. It blended very well, but no soul, because there wasn't room for soul, because you can't study those things and play soul. Like you study Bach from a teacher, you play just like Bach played. Same as with Chopin. You have no self. If you're going to blend in a section, you can't be too self-stylish. When you come out of playing legit and then you just drop everything behind you, it's a whole new world. I think it was a real fresh approach. Because it was like I'd been in a shell for a whole year, and then I came out of that shell. So it's brand-new. Like night and day. Pow!

Herman Lubinsky of Savoy Records flew out here to my house in Watts, and we signed a contract. In fact, he's the one who gave me my name. He asked me, "What's your name?" "Cecil." "Well, no. Do you have a nickname?" "Yeah, Jay." He said, "Big Jay." I was small then, so that's how I got the name. When I was recording, he said, "Blow as long as you want to." We had Britt Woodman. John Anderson was on trum-pet. I forget who was on bass. Let's see, who else? I had a piano, bass, and drums. [sings some of "Deacon's Hop"] That was the thing.

I think I was the one who cut the new ground. I think the style that I was creating was more backbeat and drive, more or less like Hamp [Lio-nel Hampton] was doing, a little swing, hard swing type of thing. And then, the showmanship just came into the fold. That was really what we were trying to do then. When the whites came along, they just took what we did and put the guitars and voice on top of it. They called it rock and roll, because they could market it in the white market.

"I got on my knees; nothing happened. I lay on the floor and that did it."

One thing just led to another as far as showmanship, creating excitement, finding my place in the music world. I must have been about twenty years old. When I got the hit, bam, I went out on the road. I formed a band. I had so many different guys over a period of years. "Tight" was with me. He was a drummer out of Fort Worth, Texas. Leonard Hardiman. He was with me for a long time. My brother, Bobby, and various piano players, guitar players. The band was constantly changing during that time. I had so much trouble with bass players, I told my brother, Dillard, he had to play bass. I threw him on bass, and that's when everything got to moving.

We traveled quite a bit all over the United States. We had big hits. I played at the Shrine Auditorium. I had *Life, Ebony, Point, Quick,* all the big magazines run big stories on me with the kids from Los Angeles. I was drawing five or six thousand kids every week.

I started walking, I guess, after I had my first hit record in '49. Like I say, I was trying to find my place in music, and that's when I started to put on a little showmanship, walking. I had a great band then, but nobody was responding. I got Carl Perkins, a great jazz pianist. I brought him out. I was in Clarksville, Tennessee. So I said, "I don't know what I'm going to do." I got on my knees; nothing happened. I lay on the floor and that did it. I got to Texas and I tried it. So, when I got to Los Angeles, I tried it and Spanish kids and white kids began to eat it up. And that's how come I started lying on the floor.

I did a thing with Lionel Hampton one time. We did it at Wrigley Field. Once a year they used to have the big Cavalcade of Jazz where they'd start the march downtown, and they would march all the way down Central Avenue, round to Avalon, back up to Wrigley Field. And then we had what was called a Cavalcade of Jazz, have all the bands set right out on the field. Jesse Belvin was working with me, because I was the first one who carried Jesse out on the road. He was very young.

Hamp's wife, Gladys, was very protective of Hamp. Nobody stole the show from Hampton. When she looked up and saw me—she had evidently heard about me before—she let Jesse sing one number and [snaps fingers] pulls us off, because we were the opening act. But then Hamp called me up to do "Flying Home." I got on the stage, and we started doing "Flying Home." And then my brother and I jumped off the stage, and we walked up into the arena, walked all around. Hamp couldn't do anything. I didn't have a wireless, so nobody could hear me, but all the people were screaming and hollering. He wouldn't stop his band; he kept on playing. When I came back to the stage, then Hamp took his whole band off the stage. We got all the way down to home plate, see. So then I lay down on the grass and started crawling on my back, and everybody started putting their attention towards me, so Hamp brought his whole band with him. [laughter] So we all ended up in the dugout. Then, after that, they wrote up "Young Boy Breaks up the Cavalcade of Jazz." [laughter] Gladys didn't like it, but there wasn't too much she could do about it.

And I broke up a Johnnie Ray session, about '55. We outdrew him. He had Ray Anthony, Kay Starr, in San Diego. That's when I got locked up and put in jail. I was outside blowing my horn, and a guy came by off duty. It was right downtown in San Diego, and there was no reason for him to do it. It was a black cop off duty, and he said I was disturbing the peace. And the other guys who were working there, they were grooving, having a good time. [laughter] So, anyway, they locked me up. Another guy was trying to help me, and they locked him up. And then, when the people found out about it, they wanted to come down, but Hunter Hancock, a KFVD disc jockey, said, "Oh, don't go down there, man. They won't never let him out." So I went back to report the next day before the judge, and he said, "Fifty-dollar fine, suspended."

Then guys started copying me, different artists and saxophonists started copying me. And then I had my horn put into color, and it changed colors when I played. I did that because everybody was copying my act. So I said, "Hey, I've got to do something else." I went to the Nightcap. The Nightcap was an after-hours spot where all the guys went and jammed at that time, groovy sessions. I saw this girl dance. They turned out all the lights, and she was fluorescent. I said, "Ah, that's it." So I went down and had the music store do my horn up for me. Of course, now I use two horns. I keep one, the fluorescent, and change it just before I get ready to do my act.

Then I used to have a light act. Little lightbulbs used to light up. But now I don't do that, because, hey, you've got to have all these bulbs and all that stuff, and then they get broken and all that. So I don't bother with that. But I still do my light act, and I have a wireless now, an SPX 90, floor stuff, a lot of electronic things that I use as I play now.

Banned in L.A.

At that time Hunter Hancock was the only disc jockey that played black artists. None of the stations would play what they called rhythm and blues records, so he was the only jock, see. But I would go to schools and play, and then I'd play afterwards. So I developed a tremendous white audience. And they didn't understand, because I was acting so wild. They didn't know if I was using stuff or not, because they'd never seen the white kids act this way, the Spanish, you know. I know one guy wrote up— I played at Huntington Beach, and he said it looked like a thousand Watusi dancers! [laughter] Because, man, they were just baffled. They'd have guys coming around taking pictures.

So, eventually, they just barred me out of the whole city. I couldn't play at all. Los Angeles County. Nowhere. They barred me from Los Angeles, Long Beach— See, all these kids would give these dances, and I couldn't get a permit. They wouldn't give me a permit to play. I even tried to hire a special police department. I said, "I'm going to pay you guys so much money." But, nevertheless, Johnny Otis and Hal Singer came right in and did the same thing I did. So I think it was mostly a racial thing. If you're white, no problem. You see that? But I was black, and I was young, and they were seeing these kids acting, so they just couldn't figure everything out.

Like many other musicians, Jay received a flat fee—but no royalties—for his recordings.

Well, all the record companies, to be frank with you, they just exploit all the black musicians—probably white musicians, too. Because they give you a penny a side, and they'd charge the whole session against you, and you never got any money, never got any money, because you were always in debt when you got your statement. You were always in the hole.

And they'd always tell you, "Hey, you make your money on the road. There's no money in publishing, no money in recording. You make your money out there." Well, we don't know. And a lot of kids want to get on a record, are so glad to record, you understand? They were willing to do it. I was getting like $1,000 a session, maybe $2,000, but that was all. I never got any royalties on Savoy Records. Like "Deacon Rides Again." EMI put it out there in New York, and they don't pay me. I'm on all these records. I've got two or three out. And I never got any money from King Records. They've got my three albums out now, and Charle Records put it out in Sweden. You walk in the store and you see two different colors, same album, and I'm still not getting any money now. I've got no money on my album in Europe.

So the record scene was that they recorded you and then paid nobody anything. Now the record companies are putting all this stuff out in Europe. They pay the record company, and the record company still doesn't pay you. So it was a bad scene. We didn't know about the whole thing. We weren't smart enough then to get our own record company and do our own producing. Dootsie Williams—from the neighborhood, right there at Central Gardens—got in there, got "Earth Angel," made a fortune. But we didn't know about it. We were playing. We didn't get into going in the studio and recording, put out your own label and try to get a distributor. We didn't have that business mind.

Then, if you start asking questions, they try to blackball you. They wouldn't record you or tell other guys not to record you. I asked one guy, and he just came out and told me what was happening. So that was the scene. And you were so glad to get on a record.

The Musicians Union: Merger or Takeover?

Well, I really wasn't for it [the amalgamation of Locals 47 and 767]. I was out of town. A lot of them would have voted against it. When they got the quorum to vote, people voted, they merged, gave up the property, all the money, everything. They came over here [to Local 47], they kept a few blacks here to find out everything that was going on. They hired a couple of blacks, and that's it. And when a job would come in, you're not going to get it, man. Let's face facts. A job comes in, a black musician is not going to get it. They're going to call in one of their boys. It's all politics. It's the same thing as the politics that we have today in the country.

I remember when I was working for the post office, I went down to this crippled children's hospital. We had to pitch in for it, that type of thing. I asked the lady, "Would you like a band to come and play?" She said, "Yeah, okay." So I called the union. We went down there and played, and the kids liked it so much. Then, the next thing I know, the union turned it over to some white guy to book the place.

I've had a lot of bad experiences. So I'm with the local, but, hey, you've got to belong to the local. I'm a lifetime member. I come up here, I pay my dues, and that's it. I don't bother with them. I don't ask for no job.

Yeah, with 767 you had an organization that at least looked out for you. It was great. We had our own local, we had our own money, we owned the building. If I was on the road traveling and got into trouble, they sent me money. They realized the problems that we had. I talked to the guy in Cleveland, and he said, "Man, there's so much prejudice even in the international. Keep your local." But they eventually merged, too.

But there was no benefit to be over there. None whatsoever. Because, right now, I don't need Local 47 to work, man. I'm not getting gigs out of 47. If we had our own local over there, we'd be going to work. We'd probably be better off now with that local, you see. But the thing is that some of the musicians say, "Well, you can never work in the studios unless you belong to 47." So then, when they come over here, they still don't use them. It's just one of those things.

At that time, the union was much stronger that it is now, even as far as local jobs are concerned. The union has nothing now, unless you're in the studio maybe, which they've got all tied up. The conductors, they hire who they want. You can even see this trumpet player, the black guy, Quincy Jones, you may see one black musician out of that whole ninety pieces. So, still, it's there. I don't care how good you are. Of course, you've got guys like Buddy Collette, qualified musicians who should be in there. But they've got everything sewn up. So you're over there, so what?

Central's Decline

Well, right after the war, that was devastating, because money just, pow, seemed to cease. And things just began to slow down after a while because people didn't have the money. Clubs started closing. They weren't doing the business. Then I started going out on the road. So, basically, that's what it was: a change of conditions, times. Then, I think they got kind of hot on the after-hours spots and started closing them up. They must have gotten some kind of heat behind them, because, like Jack's Basket and different places were going out.

As long as the blacks had the money, it was popping, and you had the movie stars and other people coming in. But times change. So it just starts going down and down and down. They cut out the Alabam and the chorus-line stuff. The Last Word was down, the Downbeat went down, and then the music scene began to change. Then the Avenue just ceased because of economics, I think. That was the really big thing.

The Eastside
at High Tide

During the late 1930s and early 1940s the black community along the Central Avenue corridor continued to experience growing pains: there were more businesses but also increased competition for jobs and fierce competition for housing. For artists like Jack Kelson, Bill Douglass, Melba Liston, Art Farmer, and Horace Tapscott—all of whom came of age during the 1930s and 1940s—Central offered a vital music scene and the everyday presence of inspirational teachers and gifted players. With segregation forcing blacks of all socioeconomic strata to live in one neighborhood, black role models were plentiful, and professionals in all fields were an integral part of the life of the community. When leading black political figures or artists visited Los Angeles, they had to stay in the few hotels along Central Avenue, such as the Dunbar. These visitors were also, then, to be seen on the streets, in the stores, and in the diners, eateries, and clubs, which allowed for personal contact and conversation. Teenagers and young adults in search of an alternative to street life could also look to the 120 social clubs—including fraternal orders, musical societies, and church groups—along Central Avenue.[1]

One of the most visible signs of racism and segregation in Los Angeles was the small number of blacks employed in the businesses along Central. The majority of businesses servicing the black community were owned by whites, and of these only about one-quarter employed blacks.[2] In the early 1930s Floyd Covington of the Urban League began a campaign to improve the employment situation under the slogan, "Don't spend where you can't work." This effort was later supported by Leon Washington, newly arrived in Los Angeles and the founder of the *Los Angeles Sentinel* newspaper, who vigorously campaigned against racist hiring practices.[3]

Discrimination in employment was also practiced by the Los Angeles public secondary schools. The high schools along the Central Avenue corridor were integrated—blacks, Latinos, Japanese-American, Chinese-American, and white students sat in the same classrooms—but the faculties were not. Although many college-educated blacks lived in the community, the first black high school teacher in the district was Samuel R. Browne, hired in the mid-1930s to teach music at Jefferson High School, a few blocks east of Central Avenue at 41st and Hooper. Educated in Central Avenue schools and a graduate of Jeff, Browne had attended the University of Southern California and earned master's degrees in music and education. Years later Browne recalled that after being hired he was "called into the office of an assistant district superintendent who cautioned him: 'Remember, Brownie, now that you've got the job, you're going to have to do the work of three white men.'"[4] Browne remained at Jeff for over two decades, where he created a model program in jazz education. Many of his students later became major artists. Dexter Gordon fondly remembered, "In high school we had a very good teacher named Sam Browne—very dedicated. He had all these wild young dudes. We used to call him Count Browne."[5]

The Main Stem in 1940

By 1940 blacks constituted 4.3 percent of the population of Los Angeles,[6] and the main hub of the Central Avenue community had become the blocks around the Dunbar Hotel at Forty-second and Central. From the downtown area, past Forty-second to Vernon Avenue, Central was full of businesses, clubs, and meeting places. It had truly become the geographic, economic, and social center of the black community. "A common thought among old-timers was that 'if you wanted to meet any of the people you went to school with or had ever known, you could walk up and down Central Avenue and you would run into them.' . . . One long-time resident of the area expressed the importance of the street this way: 'You didn't want to hit the Avenue with dirty shoes.'"[7]

While the L.A. night scene never had quite the underworld push of Chicago in the 1920s or Kansas City in the 1930s, the tide of reform that curtailed the entertainment scenes in those cities came to Los Angeles in May 1940, when Mayor Fletcher Bowron prohibited public establishments from serving alcohol after 2 a.m. In Fletcher Smith's words, City Hall "closed the town down." *Eagle* writer Harry Levette described the immediate effect of the new regulation:

> "Swing Street?" There ain't no sich [*sic*] animal. . . . No it's just plain Central avenue now. . . . Long ago I named it "Brown Broadway," "Whoopee Highway" and similar monikers, designating the 40 to 50 hundred blocks as the "Frivolous Forties" and the habitues of the principal blocks as "Wisecracker's Row," "the Curb-Stone Cowboys," etc. But that's all "Gone with the breeze" now and last Sunday night where all was once laughter, lights, gayety and color, with swarms of white visitors making the rounds, the old Avenue was the personification of a country graveyard.[8]

The funereal mood did not continue for long, however. After-hours spots proliferated, providing music, food, setups, and surreptitiously serving alcohol to those who knew where to look. After dealing with Prohibition for years, resourceful entrepreneurs had little difficulty circumventing the 2 a.m. restriction. Spots such as the Ritz Club, Lovejoy's, and Honey Murphy's regularly featured great jazz between 2 a.m. and sunup, and the music continued to flourish in the regular clubs—the Alabam, the Club Memo, the Little Harlem, the Lincoln Theatre, and the Elks Hall. The whites-only Cotton Club in Culver City had folded, but it was replaced by the Casa Mañana, which opened its doors to an interracial dance audience in 1945.[9] The Capri, near the Beverly Hills district, featured Lee and Lester Young's band—broadcast on radio station KHJ— as well as after-hours jam sessions. One memorable Wednesday evening in June 1941 found members of the Lunceford and Ellington orchestras joining the house band in an after-hours session.[10] Owner Billy Berg also ran several other clubs; his Swing Club in Hollywood was one of the first clubs outside the Central corridor to have an interracial admittance policy, which Berg initiated in 1942.[11] And occasionally there was great music during the day. Saxophonist Illinois Jacquet remembers the Labor Day parades and bands that Local 767 would put together for the celebration.

> Every Labor Day, they'd have a big parade down Central Avenue, winding up with a jam session at the Union. I was lucky; at that first session I played with the greatest rhythm section imaginable—Nat King Cole on

piano, Charlie Christian on guitar, Jimmy Blanton on bass, and Big Sid Catlett on drums. Incredible! Then, through Nat, I met Lionel Hampton, switched from alto sax to tenor and joined his band.[12]

Wartime Transformations

In 1941, black communities in the United States were still suffering from the Depression, even as the defense industry was gearing up for war. A. Philip Randolph, founder and president of the Brotherhood of Sleeping Car Porters, called for a march on Washington to protest the exclusion of blacks from defense industry jobs. On the eve of the march President Franklin Roosevelt promised Randolph that he would strike down discrimination in those industries. Shortly thereafter, Roosevelt issued Executive Order 8802, which prohibited defense employers from discriminating on the basis of race, creed, color, or national origin, and Randolph called off the march.

By mid-1943 California was receiving almost 10 percent of the war contracts issued nationally, and much of this work was in southern California. "Between 1940 and 1944, more than $800,000,000 was invested in over 5,000 new industrial plants in the region."[13] The change in government policy, the expansion of the defense industry, and the general increase in demand for labor brought on by the war resulted in a job boom for blacks in southern California, and the black population of Los Angeles increased by some 100,000 people.[14] "This was a period of a fast developing black working class whose economy was girded in factories making coolers for B-17s, pouring moats of liquified rubber for tires, portering, mechanics, cab drivers, secretaries, post office workers, and the like."[15]

Despite the job boom and the dramatic growth in population, for the most part the restrictive housing covenants held firm, creating serious housing shortages. "Some members of the National Housing Authority, feeling the situation had reached catastrophic proportions, suggested limiting entrance into the city."[16] As Chester Himes observes in his second novel, *Lonely Crusade*, "Migrants poured into the city from the East, North, and South, each group bringing the culture of its section. Racial tensions rose and racial prejudices ran rampant."[17] But when "blacks tried to jump over the 'white wall' to buy shelter in outlying suburban or rural fringes, they were met by a new wave of homeowner hostility." [18] In *If He Hollers* Himes's protagonist, Bob Jones, captures some of the racial tension in the days after Pearl Harbor:

> It was the look in the white people's faces when I walked down the streets. It was that crazy, wild-eyed, unleashed hatred that the first Jap bomb on Pearl Harbor let loose in a flood. All that tight, crazy feeling of race as thick in the street as gas fumes. Every time I stepped outside I saw a challenge I had to accept or ignore. Every day I had to make one decision a thousand times: *Is it now? Is now the time?*
>
> I was the same color as the Japanese and I couldn't tell the difference. "A yeller bellied Jap" coulda meant me too. I could always feel race trouble, serious trouble, never more than two feet off. Nobody bothered me. Nobody said a word. But I was tensed every moment to spring.[19]

The one area that opened up to the black community was the Little Tokyo section of downtown Los Angeles. As Japanese-Americans were sent off to internment camps in the deserts and other sparsely populated areas, the black population moved in. Several important entertainment venues opened here as well.[20] Throughout the rest of the city, however, with the exception of Billy Berg's Swing Club, blacks were refused admission. When trumpeters Snooky Young and Harry "Sweets" Edison, in town with Count Basie's band, went on an off-night to see Jimmie Lunceford's orchestra at the Trianon and were denied entrance, Lunceford threatened to pull his band out of the club.[21]

Wartime Music Scene

Many members of Local 767 enlisted or were drafted into the military. Marshal Royal, Coney and Britt Woodman, Buddy Collette, Jack Kelson, and Bill Douglass were among the musicians who served. Back on the Avenue, the employment boom and the scarcity of consumer durables fueled a thriving entertainment scene, and new clubs, such as the Downbeat Room and the Last Word Cafe, opened. During the spring of 1942, Joe Morris took over a large space at 108th Street and Central in Watts, formerly known as Baron Long's Tavern and then as Jazzland, and reopened it as the Plantation Club. Soon he was hosting the country's leading bands, confirming one local journalist's prediction that the club would become "the 'spot' where the 'jive' is really going to be on the 'solid side.'"[22]

Club owners now turned to hiring Rosie the Trumpeter, Rosie the Trombonist, and Rosie the Drummer to perform for all the Rosie the Riveters who kicked back in the clubs after long, arduous shifts in the plants. Although several all-women bands had performed regularly around the country,[23] and a few bands featured female singers, women rarely had the opportunity to play in the big bands. Lil Hardin, originally with King Oliver's Creole Jazz Band, and Mary Lou Williams, the pianist, composer, and arranger for Andy Kirk's Twelve Clouds of Joy, were two names on a very short list. And women who did break into the professional scene were overwhelmingly pianists—not one drummer, brass, reed, or bass player had any professional visibility. Mary Lou Williams was almost the sole woman to play a role other than that of pianist-singer with a major band. As the main writer and arranger with Andy Kirk's Kansas City–bred band, she was responsible for many of their most successful charts, including "Walkin' and Singin'," and the band acknowledged her contribution in its 1936 recording "The Lady Who Swings the Band."

World War II gave women the opportunity to pursue professional musical careers on an unprecedented scale. They were hired to fill chairs in bands, and women's combos and orchestras emerged as national acts. One of the most important of these groups was the International Sweethearts of Rhythm, who performed at the Alabam and the Plantation. Led by Anna Mae Wilburn, the Sweethearts' summer of '44 stay on the Avenue was a roaring success, "the hottest attraction to hit the coast since the Frisco fire," columnist J. T. Gipson wrote: "Speaking purely from a serious point of view, the girls, without a doubt, have one of the finest musical aggregations to come out of the swing kingdom in many a moon. And that goes for the Basie crew, the Lunceford lads, and the Goodman guys."[24] Local artists such as Melba Liston, Clora Bryant, Vi Redd, and Ginger Smock launched their careers during this period on Central Avenue.

10

Jack Kelson

Multi-reed artist Jack Kelson (aka Jackie Kelso) has been a lifelong Los Angeles resident, performing in a number of different fields. He has played with Bill Berry, the Capp-Pierce Juggernaut, Benny Carter, Buddy Collette, Benny Goodman, Lionel Hampton, Roy Milton, Kid Ory, Johnny Otis, and Nelson Riddle. He has also recorded with various artists, including the Capp-Pierce Juggernaut, Sam Cook, Dave Frishberg, Lionel Hampton, Jan & Dean, and Jake Porter.

From the mid-1950s until his recent semi-retirement Jack was much in demand in the film studios, rock 'n' roll and pop settings, as well as r&b and jazz. In 1956 he joined Johnny Otis for two years, playing in Johnny's band and performing on his weekly TV show as featured saxophone soloist. He was also the artist and repertoire (A&R) representative for Otis's DIG Records. By the late 1950s, he had formed his own band and was performing around Los Angeles. During the 1960s Jack taught himself guitar and played on many rock 'n' roll and pop recordings, including Helen Reddy's gold single, "I Am Woman." A complete list of his TV and film performances would fill several pages.

Jack continues to live in Los Angeles, reading voraciously, freely dispensing his accumulated wisdom, and performing as he chooses.

Jack was born in 1922 in Los Angeles on East Twenty-third Street. His parents had moved to southern California from Mississippi, where they had been raised.

Both my mother and father were born in the southern part of the United States: Mississippi. Both of them were issued from illegitimate couplings—in those days, I guess you would say colored women and white men—and marriage was not even in the picture. So my father took his illegitimate name. My mother did, too.

My mother came to Los Angeles in 1911. She had family friends and relatives already out here. My dad came out about the same time, because he got a good job. He told me one of the first things in life that he realized that was important for him would be to get on the payroll of some big company. So the company turned out to be the Southern Pacific Railroad. He got a job as a waiter, and I think he was involved in a steady run between New Orleans and Los Angeles.

Just off Central, west of Central on Twelfth Street, less than halfway down the block, was the cooks and waiters union. Clarence Johnson was the real driving force behind that. In the old days, before there was a union, when the men had a day off, they had to report to the commissary on Alameda to see if there was a job that needed filling. In other words, a man was booked to go out, but in case he didn't go out, you had to go down there on your day off to cover for this man.

So there were many, many things about working conditions on the railroad that I was aware of, because I'd heard my father talking about it. When he got a job, he was paid $25 a month, minus $2.50 for breakage, whether you broke anything or not. So you see there was some motivation for establishing the cooks and waiters union. My father had an interest in that, and he was involved in helping to set it up.

My father also maintained his job all the way through the Depression. So we, personally, did not feel the pinch of the Depression, but we were aware of the fact that all over the neighborhood there were people who were very much hurt by the Depression. And there were places in the neighborhood where food was distributed.

Before Jack was a year old his parents purchased a house for two or three thousand dollars and moved to East Twenty-sixth Street. At the age of eight Jack received his first instrument, a clarinet.

I took music lessons from the time I was eight until twelve and, fortunately, had a great music teacher, Caughey Roberts, who started me at the beginning of one of these highly organized classical methods. At twelve he stopped teaching me because he got a job in Buck Clayton's band to go to Shanghai, China.

Early Images of Central Avenue

One of my first memories of Central Avenue was being in the Elks Auditorium on the second floor. I was there with my mother and sister, maybe some church gathering or something, because there were auditoriums on both floors. The first floor was a very large auditorium, beautiful stage, and on the second floor was another, smaller auditorium, and that was where they held the Sunday afternoon dances or Saturday afternoon dances, the matinees. I couldn't dance, so I never went. But that was where the Woodman Brothers orchestra played for the matinees.

But the second floor of this building had this facility for meetings. I just remember being in that building with my mother, and it was at night. And I remember looking out a window that looked south on Central Avenue, and I could see all of these neon lights. I thought I saw the sign that said Apex Club. It was a nightclub that was on the west side of the street somewhere down in the forties. And I remember, as a kid, looking south through this window and seeing all of those lights. I was so impressed. That's my first impression of Central Avenue. It was probably before I was playing music.

Another important event in my life was attending an event in the Elks Auditorium, in the big hall downstairs on the big stage, with my parents. There was a minstrel show with Mr. Interlocutor in the middle—white man—and Mr. Bones on one end and— I don't remember the other comedian. Blackface, you know, with the big lips and the funny things, the guys who would jump up and down and really act the clown. Well, that was one of my first memories of what show business was about. It was a legitimate, bona fide minstrel show.

One of the most important people on Central Avenue was Leon Washington, the founder and publisher of the *Los Angeles Sentinel.* The most important thing that I remember about him was the fact that he was the publisher, and he had a very, very important campaign movement on Central Avenue. It was defined by the phrase "Don't spend where you can't work." That is something that ran for many, many, many years. There was a lot of money being spent on Central Avenue in these stores that were not black-owned, and very, very few blacks worked as employees in the stores. So the campaign worked, and very gradually some of the money that was spent in the stores found its way into the pockets of black employees.

During his grammar school years Jack met drummer Chico Hamilton, who became a lifelong friend.

We met at Nevin Grammar School, when we were, I don't know, seven or eight, nine, ten years old. Chico taught himself to play drums, and I was just the opposite. You know, I had all this formal training. So very early in life, I had that sense of discipline and rigidity and sense of propriety and structure. And Chico was just the opposite: a creative artist from the word go.

That distinction between the two of us, I guess, has remained all of our lives. I've gone on to be an extremely efficient producer of any kind of music. Because my idea was "I am a professional musician. I'm like a first-class plumber. I will fix any problem you have with your plumbing and do it better than anybody." So my attitude about music was "I don't care what it calls for, I can do it. I'll play any style, do anything you want done."

It's a matter of being determined to be a survivor in the marketplace. You know, whatever's required or whatever's demanded, you certainly want to be familiar enough with it to say, "Oh, is that what you want? Fine. Here it is." Yeah, well, that attitude certainly pays off, all of your life if you're concerned with being a commercial artist—if people can stand seeing those two words side by side. But it has to do also, I guess, with almost the Zen Buddhist approach. Whatever you're doing, you become one with it. If you're sweeping the sidewalk, if you're taking out the garbage, if you're playing the blues, or if you're playing bebop, just be authentically at one with it without feeling— It doesn't have to be the idea "I am now being insincere." No. "I'm being sincerely all of these things."

When I played with Lionel Hampton, I played one way; when I played with Roy Milton, a totally different way. Both of them equally authentic, both of them equally real. If I can offer this: humanity is bigger than style. I refuse to limit myself to only one mode of expression when I know that my humanity is as big as those twelve tones. There's no limitation to what you can do with those twelve tones.

Consequently, I've never considered myself unemployed. I've never been without a job, because, if I didn't have one, I was just hustling or trying to get a job. For me—this was just personally with me—to sign up for an unemployment check was a waste of time. I would prefer spending that time polishing my craft, becoming better at what I do. And, as a result, never in my life have I drawn one unemployment check. And I've never thought of myself as being unemployed. I am simply between jobs. [laughter] I'm getting ready for the next one.

Every year, as part of the education of the students at Nevin Grammar School, there would be an assembly—it was called an aud call, auditorium call—and the orchestra would play. And each instrument in the orchestra would be introduced by the conductor, a woman named Mrs. Gertrude Smith, a violinist. She would introduce each member in the orchestra and have the orchestra member play a little something by themselves so the entire student body could hear what the instrument sounded like.

Well, every semester this was done, Chico would break it up every time! [laughter] You know, the piano player would say [mimics simple piano solo], the violin would say [mimics simple violin solo], trumpet [mimics simple trumpet fanfare], clarinet [mimics simple clarinet solo]. "Now, children, this is what the drums sound like." [mimics wildly swinging drum solo] [laughter] Pandemonium! Chaos! Every semester! Chico loved that. One of the highlights: Chico's drum solo.

He was my leader in so many, many ways. He took me on my first gig. He took me out shoeshining, where you build a little box and you walk around town anywhere, hopping trucks, stealing rides, jumping on streetcars, not having to pay. A shoeshine boy can have untold marvelous adventures, can go in and out of everywhere. It's almost like down South. Put a white coat on a black man, he can go anywhere, because that white coat indicates "He's a good one. He's got a job. He can be trusted." It's like [Ralph Ellison's] *The Invisible Man.* You put a white coat on a black man, you know, you just don't see him.

We loved the same music. We were really together. We can remember the orchestras and the styles and the hit records in those days. Yeah, we were exactly of the same mind when it came to music. And the first orchestra that we both loved was Jimmie Lunceford, with that precision and quality arrangements. We didn't like Duke Ellington because he was out of tune and ragged, we thought. And it took a little time before I saw the light. It wasn't that Duke changed; it was just that I grew.

Chico, to me, is, in a sense, like Duke Ellington in this respect: Chico plays his music using any player, any group of instruments. He doesn't care what it is. He puts his stamp on it. You know, Duke Ellington, whenever a new man would come in the band, as Bill Berry says, Duke Ellington made sure he used all of the material available. No matter what material comes into the band, what stylistic offering the man has, Ellington would create a setting that would show off that man's uniqueness in a way that— Like a jeweler: a fine stone being put into just the right setting in a ring. Chico, same way. Pure creative artist.

My father took me to see Duke Ellington when I was eight or nine years old. I fell under the spell of Duke Ellington. It was at a theater, either the Orpheum Theatre or the Paramount. And it wasn't the music that grabbed me. It was the Ellington presence. I remember very clearly, they wore black tuxedo pants, a cummerbund, and an Eton jacket. Man . . . every man a picture of sartorial elegance. Well, it reflected Ellington: race pride, black pride and all of that, before it was invented.

But my father took me to the theater to see that, and I remember Duke Ellington walking up to the microphone. The command, the confidence. That smile, that raise of the eyebrow. Without saying a word, here's a man who was in total control of everything. I sensed this at eight years old. It wasn't the music. It was this man's stance. And it wasn't what he said, it was how he said it. He could have been speaking a foreign language. He could have walked to the microphone and impressed me the same way if he had said, [adopting debonair speaking voice] "Buenos costa para mandeguse. Mande rolla ganze. No sé?" That was his kind of magic for me.

Jack and Chico both attended Lafayette Junior High School and soon organized their first band.

There was a Mexican piano player in junior high school at the same time, Jesus Reyes. He turned out to be "Chuey" Reyes, a great bandleader. Well, Jesus Reyes and Chico—they must have been thirteen, fourteen years old—went to the Burbank Burlesque Theatre on Main Street to appear on an amateur contest. Junior high school kids. Drums and piano. Took first prize.

So, somebody in Jesus Reyes's family gets married, so Chico, Jesus, and I provide the music. I play the clarinet. House party, you know. At night, too. Twelve, thirteen years old. And we made the agreement, the three of us: "Wow, we're so good. Chuey, we played free for you, so, Chuey, you're going to play free for a Hamilton party and a Kelson party." I don't think we made any money. We were just happy to be playing together.

Several local music teachers made a strong impression on Jack, among them a new teacher at Jefferson High School, Samuel Browne.

My music teacher, Caughey Roberts, went to Jefferson High School. Marshal Royal went to Jefferson. Sam Browne came to Jefferson just shortly before I did. He was very supportive and very inspirational at the beginning, and he got even more influential as time went on. One of the things he did while I was there, he transcribed or rearranged some music by William Grant Still, and we played for the student body. He was a very highly respected and very devoted person, but very, very relaxed. Very low-key, soft spoken, tall, looked like he never overate, because he remained quite slim and always quite impressive in his appearance. Impressive, not that he was pretentious in any of his gestures, but he was just withdrawn, supremely self-confident, a man who knew what he was about and cared enough to try and share with the kids what he knew. He had the same image of many, many black men that I knew as a kid.

Another man who fit that bill was a professor—they called him "Professor"—John A. Gray. His name was simply Mr. Gray, my godfather, who set up the Gray Conservatory of Music, who had studied in Paris. He had a music school located on the southeast corner, on Forty-first Street, of Forty-first and Central. Catty-corner from that was a building that's now still standing. It was called the Western School of Music.

Mr. Gray would have monthly recitals at a building just around the corner, on Central Avenue. Bach piano duets, violin— There was even a woman named Mrs. Gross who taught artistic whistling. Violin teaching. And all of these kids were getting just incredibly marvelous educations. But the main thing, they had these public recitals every Sunday, and Professor Gray always had words to say that were inspiring and things that would remind parents that— I'll never forget this phrase—"We have got to get behind the kids and push." The importance of the parental influence was always very, very clear, and he always pushed that.

There was another professor called Wilkins. A very dark man. He let his hair grow long, and he looked like Oscar Wilde in the way he dressed.

You know the Little Lord Fauntleroy collar and the fluffy black tie? And he wore capes. Professor Wilkins was a piano teacher in Los Angeles, too.

But, in any event, there were many black men— In fact, there was a particular image that is still in my mind, and whenever I mention it, other people seem to remember it, too. Before World War II, almost all the black men that I knew who were not ditch-diggers, all of them wore three-piece suits, shirts, and ties. This relaxed thing happened after World War II. I have a very, very clear image in my mind of black men as having the appearance of almost automatically demanding respect, because they simply looked like cultured gentlemen.

Jefferson High

As I think back now, so much has developed at Jefferson High School since then that when you say Jefferson High School, just this beautiful haze comes over my mind. I can't really separate those wonderful things that have happened after I was there, because when I got to Jefferson, Sam Browne had only been there a short time. I think the bulk of his contribution happened after I'd left, because I understand that some of the programs he set up were just mind-boggling. How he would have almost special classes before school began. Some of the musicians were so enthused and wrapped up in the opportunities that he had created that they would come to school and have rehearsals or confabs actually before school began. And they would stay after school, and I imagine they did many things far outside of school hours.

Ernie Royal, Marshal Royal's brother, was ahead of me, and he was always just one of the finest trumpet players who ever lived. He could play all of the trumpet solos off the Count Basie records. There wasn't anything he couldn't do.

Dexter Gordon was a year or two behind me, but my impression was not unlike many others', I guess. As you know, Dexter was quite tall, and he talked slowly, moved slowly, always had a big, beautiful smile on his face. Due to the fact that he was a little younger than me and his musical training started undoubtedly a little later in his life than some of the rest of us— He had all of the soul and dedication and feeling and total commitment to jazz that a person could have, but his training was a little late, so he was what we might call second-string. But when it came to sincerity, he was totally committed. And his playing always reflected his bodily actions in a sense. Even today, when you listen to his records, it's always laid-back just a little bit, as though, "Look, I'm not in a hurry. I'm going to say what I want to say, how I want to say it, and nobody can rush me."

But, you know, Dexter loved this thing so much that it was his life. If you love anything, you just live it, sleep it, and eat it. And it seems to me that I've heard Marshal say that Dexter told him once, as a very young man—Marshal said that Dexter's ambition was to become a junkie. He was so committed to music—well, jazz music—and he felt that the epitome of being what he wanted was to be a junkie musician. In other words, I guess he felt that the dope was going to help him be a more completely formed musician. And Dexter apparently experimented a little too much with narcotics.

No matter how strong you are as a human being, if you tamper with the poisons too long it will get the best of you. I had enough silly, pioneering, adventuresome spirit about myself that I managed to make sure that I didn't miss anything. So I have experimented with just about everything. There were a certain couple of things I drew the line on because I didn't think I needed to make those experiments. But I've experimented widely enough to feel that, yeah, fine. Like some people say, "Don't knock it if you haven't tried it." Well, I've tried almost everything, so I am in a position to knock it.

Emma "Ginger" Smock. She was a couple of grades ahead of me in high school, and she was the main violinist in the orchestra, concertmistress. She apparently started at a very, very early age, so by high school, she just played any and everything that needed to be played with great finesse and quality of performance. She continued playing the violin all of her life. She worked in Las Vegas for many years. And I think she even played the violin on the boat that went to and from Catalina Island at one time.

Oh, Lamar Wright is somebody who should be mentioned. Lamar Wright, a little trumpet player, son of a trumpet player. Lamar Wright was, I guess, about Dexter's age, because Lamar Wright was a semester or two behind me. And somewhere I have seen a photograph taken in the backyard of Dexter Gordon, a family snapshot with Dexter and his tenor saxophone and Lamar Wright with his trumpet. It was almost like a Mutt and Jeff comedy routine in that they were, in a sense, almost inseparable buddies. They just loved each other. And Dexter Gordon is over six feet tall, and Lamar Wright is quite short. We played in bands together around Los Angeles. He was in the big band, the Al Adams big band with Buddy Collette, Charles Mingus, Joe Comfort. Eventually Lamar Wright went to New York. One of the first big things he did was play with Dizzy Gillespie's first big band. So Lamar Wright followed in his father's footsteps and became a well-known, fine, trumpet-playing, big band musician.

Jack and his friends followed the big bands whenever they appeared in Los Angeles.

The Shrine Auditorium, the Vogue Ballroom. There was a ballroom out at— Selig Zoo out near Lincoln Park. Now, the Vogue Ballroom downtown; many, many bands played there. [laughter] Let's see. Buddy Collette, Dexter Gordon, me, Chico Hamilton, James Nelson. So this group, we would go down to the Vogue Ballroom. It was a ballroom, but for us it was a chance to stand right there at the bandstand, right up close, you know, look at those uniforms. You're so close you could pick up their music. One of the marvelous bands that we used to love to see was Floyd Ray's orchestra. He never got to be a super band, but he was a very short fellow, very classy. He could direct an orchestra and look like ten million dollars.

Shortly after beginning Jefferson High School, Jack started playing alto saxophone and soon joined a band that included some of the finest young players in Los Angeles and Watts: Chico Hamilton, Buddy Collette, and Charles Mingus.

When I got to be fifteen, I got an alto saxophone. I don't know what prompted me to do it. I guess Chico must have been partially responsible, because Chico was making money from the very beginning, a very practical person. "Hey, man, you can't make no money playing the clarinet. Get yourself a saxophone." "Okay, boss!" So I got an alto and took lessons for, I guess, five, six months from a guy named Mr. Wilbert Sturdevant, who was a saxophone teacher at the Gray Conservatory of Music.

The first steady job I had, I guess, was a job that paid $2.50 every Saturday night, a Mexican dance in Garden Grove. There were other steady jobs in those days. [laughter] In high school we would work in the beer joints up and down Main Street, from First down to Sixth Street, it was just one right after the other. They would have what they called B-girls, because they would sit at the bar, and they drink beer, and the women would induce men to drink probably more than they would have had the females not been there. My goodness, they would be holes-in-the-walls. You could almost touch either wall of the place, and it would be long and narrow. In the back, there would be a little stage where the band would play, and in front of it would be a little area where the girls would take turns doing little shake-and-grind dances. We would make $1.50 a night plus tips. Those were considered good steady jobs.

I started immediately making money at fifteen, and I've been a profes-sional musician since, because that's when we did a scab job at the Million Dollar Theatre. One of the high points at that time was the black motion picture produced by Harry L. Popkin called *Bargain with Bullets,* starring Nina Mae McKinney, Lawrence Criner, and Mantan Moreland. It was given the world premiere, I guess, at the Million Dollar Theatre at Third and Broadway. And with the motion picture was produced a stage show, an all-black stage show. The stars of the motion picture appeared on stage. And there was a line of chorus girls, and there was a singer— Well, in any event, there was a stage show, and stage show means an orches-tra is necessary. To keep the budget down, they wanted to hire a non-union band.

So word got out that at the Million Dollar Theatre there was going to be work for a black band, and we heard about it. Mr. Jerome Myart, the guy that Chico and I were gigging with, I guess he heard about it. So we made an audition at the theater. There were any number of bands, and one of the bands that made the audition was from Watts, which included Charlie Mingus and Buddy Collette. To make a long story short, we amalgamated the Watts band and the Los Angeles band, and we kind of wanted to eliminate the leader, Mr. Myart, because he was an older man. They didn't want him on the stage. So, we had our band, the Al Adams Band. The guy's name was Al Adams and he played bass, and he was the oldest guy in the band, so we made him the leader. Working day and night for all of the shows, twenty-one dollars and fifty cents. Never had so much money in my life.

And after the theater job was over—man that band was so good, we just knew that we were going to conquer the world. So we stayed together. Buddy Collette used to write arrangements. He would take it off the record. He would take off arrangements of the Jimmie Lunceford Orchestra. Things like "A Ship at Sea," anything that had those elaborate reed choruses in it, you know, where you would show your technical prowess [mimics fast, complex woodwind solos]. And Chico would get up sometimes and would sing things like "I'm Walking Through Heaven with You." That was one of the big Jimmie Lunceford things. And Chico could get up from those drums and walk to that microphone in such an all-powerful, commanding way—like Ellington—pick that microphone up, and sometimes he wouldn't know the words to the song! [laughter] But he knew enough words! I loved this guy's genius. He's— Well, enough of that. I'll break into tears if I get too involved about how I feel about Chico. [laughter]

All the work that we were doing in those days was nonunion for us, because we were kids and hadn't joined the union. We started playing dances at the Elks Auditorium on Central Avenue, and the musicians union began to picket the hall whenever we played, because we were nonunion musicians. I remember one of the pickets was Elmer Fain. No-nonsense, and he scared everybody to death. Just his appearance: he was very soft-spoken, gentle, calm at all times, but it was just that it was like the Rock of Gibraltar moving in. You weren't afraid of physical violence, but this man just exuded competence and power. He had the bylaws memorized. He knew what was right, and he knew what the scales were.

I've played on jobs out in Hollywood. It was with Eugene and Freddy Jackson, and Dorothy Dandridge's sister, Vivian Dandridge, was the vocalist. And we had a trumpet player. I've forgotten his name now, but he was a union musician. Nice little gig out in Hollywood. And we got word that Fain had just parked his car outside, and very quickly the trumpet player jumped up off the stand, took his chair and—you don't leave an empty chair because it would be obvious: "Well, who was sitting here?" [laughter] And, sure enough, Fain walked in, and he gave us that look, you know, looking to see if there was some mixing of the musicians.

Well, the motive behind it was, of course, laudatory and proper. Here's a bunch of high school kids taking work away from adult musicians who needed to earn money to take care of their families. So I imagine the motive, fundamentally, was to make union musicians out of us. And that's how we decided to join the union. We had no fight with the union, and they made the offer so attractive that we all joined the union at the same time. They gave us an opportunity to join the union at a great dispensation. I think all we had to pay as a joining fee was twenty-five dollars, and we were able to handle that. In fact, my life membership card, on the back, has the date January 7, 1970, which means I became a life member— I had been a member of the union for thirty years as of January 7, 1970. And Buddy Collette's date is the same thing. I was still in high school, because I graduated from high school either later that month or in February; I'm not sure which.

Prewar Central— "An aura of mysterious wonderfulness."

One factor that is very clear in mind was the pride of ownership of property that seemed to be reflected in prewar Central. Nowhere in my memory are there dirty streets, graffiti, a lack of sense of pride in physical property, whether it's automobiles, dress, or the appearance of buildings.

Jack summed up his memories of prewar Central in one word.

Glamorous. You were only aware of it, the intensity of it, by viewing it at this distance, because it was simply there, and you had nothing to compare it with because it was just there. You know, some parents, in a sense, felt like they didn't want their children on Central Avenue, because that's where the night people hung out. That's where crime and vice and all of the so-called unholy things were. That was really the street where glamour and color was.

One picture has come to my mind countless times. It's that block in which resides the Club Alabam and the Dunbar Hotel. And it was just a marvelous thing that that hotel was constructed on the west side of the street. I've thought of this so many times. About the way the shade would start. Central Avenue ran north and south. In the morning, the sidewalk in front of the Dunbar Hotel was bathed in bright sunlight. About noon, the shadow of the hotel started to shade the sidewalk, making it a perfect stage on which to perform, to see and to be seen, to teach and to be taught: for the rest of the day, it was cool and comfortable.

It's like putting makeup on. When the sun goes down, all of the flaws and imperfections, whatever you might perceive them to be— Suddenly,

there's an aura of mysterious wonderfulness. It wasn't nighttime as spooky and scary. No. There's a new, special magic that comes, a type of paint-brush that paints all of the flaws. New glamour comes to life. It's almost as if special spirits of joy and abundance bring special gifts at night that are not available in the sunshine.

That's my favorite spot on Central Avenue, that spot in front of the Dunbar Hotel, because that to me was the hippest, most intimate, key spot of all of the activity. That's where all of the night people hung out: the sportsmen, the businessmen, the dancers, everybody in show business, people who were somebody who stayed at the hotel.

There was another spot like that—similar, but not. At the corner of Washington Boulevard and Central, there was the Clark Hotel on one corner, and across the street there was the Clark Annex. But by far that block, that Dunbar Hotel, for me was it. And it was it for, it seemed to me, everybody else. Sooner or later, you walked in front of that hotel, and that's where everybody congregated.

From corner to corner there were stores. The Dunbar was on the northwest corner, and the next corner would be the Downbeat nightclub, and across the street would be the Last Word. There were three main buildings, as far as I was concerned, three main entrances. One was the Dunbar Hotel, the other was the Alabam, and the other, on the northern corner, on the west side of the street, was the Downbeat. That was the heart of Central Avenue for me.

That's where you would go to look and go to be seen and go to talk and exchange the joy of being alive and having the privilege of being part of the audience and being on stage. The sharpies would take turns holding forth and being in charge. And the physical appearance of these men— I don't see women in the picture. It's always extremely well-dressed, sharp, sophisticated, worldly men. Show business people. Not businessmen. But these were, in a sense, maybe the night people or the sportsmen or the people who had time to talk and have fun and be seen and look good and establish camaraderie and sort of that secret bonding that sportsmen have among themselves.

I've never seen more glamour anywhere in the world than in that one spot. Because, even if you weren't working and if you were just part of the group, it was almost mandatory that you were sharp. Beautiful clothes, tailor-made clothes, beautiful suits and socks. And that was the day when men had their hair gassed or processed, whatever word you

want to use. Everybody was just immaculately, you might say, splendif-
erous in their appearance, and they took great pride with everything
about their appearance. The way they walked, you know: proud. And
they could tell stories, and the body language, and all this.

And the economy of language, sometimes there would be just maybe
one verbal sound or a word or a syllable that could be used that would be
more eloquent than a paragraph. A shrug of the shoulder or a gesture
from the hand or an elbow or a turning of the head. And the storytelling.
Wow! Those are the people who could sit here and hold you spellbound
for years. You know, there's not enough tape in the world to record all of
that glory.

There was a group called the Three Rockets; another trio, the Top
Hatters, a dance team, supremely meticulous and synchronized in their
dancing. This picture of Andy of the Three Rockets comes to mind, because he was keen featured, a beautiful color of brown, slim. The other
two fellows in the Rockets were a little heavier. It looked like maybe these
guys went to the barbershop every day. They were just impeccable. But,
in any event, suits, clothing, posture, carriage— It was just spellbinding
to be in that block. I was just dazzled by the show.

I have come to realize, later in life, that the appearance of the clothing
was very, very important, but also their posture. It was almost like everybody realized that they were part of a certain type of royalty because they
had discovered who and what they were about. It was a sense of not only
black pride, but just pride in being. "I have weathered the storm of growing up as a kid. I've got some good clothes. I'm happy and proud of
myself. I take good care of myself."

There was Stepin Fetchit with his long white Auburn-Cord or Packard
or whatever it was, with a lion sitting in the back. That wasn't far-fetched.
That was just one of the things that you were lucky enough to see if you
happened to be on the street when he decided to drive down the street.

But, yeah, it's really amazing to have been on that street, not realizing
at that time what it was going to mean. You never thought that this thing
could disappear, because this is reality and the glamour and all.

And Central Avenue was quite the focal point of many people in the
film industry. The movie stars would come over there, because there was
more glamour, in a sense, on Central Avenue. There was a magnetism
about it that was at a much more personal level than the magnetism that
drew people's interest to Hollywood Boulevard.

An especially vivid musical memory of Jack's is of blues guitarist T-Bone Walker performing on Central Avenue during the 1930s.

One of the biggest and lasting and most indelible influences in my life happened at the Lincoln Theatre at Twenty-third and Central. They had stage shows on Sunday, and I went as a kid. I can remember many times seeing T-Bone Walker on the stage: blues singer, wore those lovely bright-colored suits, sharp as could be. You know, the business of putting the guitar behind his head, picking it, and doing the splits.

One of the first and certainly the most lasting impressions was T-Bone Walker singing the blues and the way he played the guitar. It was the most authentic, fine classical blues guitar I had ever heard in my life. As far as I'm concerned, everybody who plays good guitar, in a sense, has been influenced by T-Bone Walker. Because, right now, I find myself, fifty years later, on the saxophone or clarinet sometimes playing a typical T-Bone Walker blues lick. I later learned how to play guitar when I was a bandleader. You know, the Beatles came in. And I found myself, when I would play little blues guitar solos, playing this T-Bone Walker lick. It's like on the fifth of the tonality. If you're in C, it's going to be, like G-natural with F-sharp, and it's a double-string thing. [sings guitar lick] I heard that when I was what: eight, nine, ten, eleven years old? That is one of the cornerstones of my style. And I heard it on Central Avenue.

But T-Bone Walker was one of the big sounds. Yes, he played at a night-club out in Watts called the Little Harlem, run by these sisters. An almost 100 percent black club. We're talking about 1930, '31, '32, '33. A little later on there was Big Joe Turner and Wynonie Harris and many, many others. And the blues singers would have cutting contests at the clubs.

Jack's father would not let him join a professional band immediately after high school graduation. Instead, at his father's urging, Jack attended Los Angeles City College.

By the time I was ready to graduate from high school, I was already a proficient, professional musician making great money with Chico Hamilton, Charles Mingus, Buddy Collette. And Buddy Collette had just started working with a band called Cee Pee Johnson. I wanted more than anything else in the world to join Buddy Collette in this band. And the opening came up because Lionel Hampton had just left Benny Goodman, and Lionel Hampton was forming his big band. Marshal Royal had been playing with Cee Pee Johnson, and Marshal Royal was responsible for putting together Lionel Hampton's band. Also leaving Cee Pee Johnson's band at that time was Jack McVea, whose father was one of the pioneer musicians in Los Angeles. There was a listing in the Yellow Pages called Satchell McVea's Howdy Entertainers. Well, his son was named Jack McVea, who recently just retired from playing at Disneyland on a regular basis. But, in any event, there were two openings in Cee Pee Johnson's band. Now, this is right at the pinnacle. This is the top of the heap. Marshal Royal and Jack McVea left to go with Lionel Hampton's big band. Well, Buddy Collette joined Cee Pee Johnson's band, and it was just understood that I was going to be in that band, too, with Buddy.

When I told my dad about it, foot went down. "Absolutely not. You will continue going to school, and you will get yourself an education." I'm going to City College now, junior college. And high school? Academic preparation? Me? Oh, no. Nothing like that. By the time I was twelve years old, I knew who I was. I had that competence.

Well, let me put it this way. Human life to me—it seems to me—consists of being a specialist in order to earn a living and a generalist to be a well-rounded human being. Well, at twelve years old, my future was secure. Fortunately, because of Caughey Roberts and my parents, my future was secure.

But my father was smart enough in those days to realize that the future for a colored, Negro, black musician was not very secure, and he wanted his son to have something more going, no matter how well he played. Because my father just loved to hear me play the clarinet. But that was why he put his foot down about becoming a full-time, seven-nights-a-week musician right at the top of the heap in Hollywood. Greatest job in town. But he wanted something more for me.

So I went to City College. I had nothing to do with music. It was a mishmash of business, accounting, three different law courses—contracts, negotiable instruments, and real estate law—business methods, learned how to type, work an adding machine, business management—You get the feel for what that was about.

Wartime Service

I did enlist. I was not drafted. And I'll tell you why, but the draft-card story should come first. Somehow I knew where I was supposed to go in order to fill out my draft card, and it was at the Bank of America on the corner of Twenty-third and Central Avenue. It was a very simple thing to do. I filled out whatever they asked me to fill out, I handed the card back, and they made some additions. What they filled out was my race and my complexion. I hadn't even left the bank. I was so proud of my card, you know. "I'm an adult. I'm a man. I've got a draft card. Wow, look at me!" I'm looking at it with great pride. And I turn it over and I look at both sides, and before I got out of the bank, I see that they have checked me off as being white.

I took it back to them, and I said, "I'm not white. I'm colored." I think that was the term that was used in those days. It might have been Negro. But, in any event, I gave it back to them and we had to make out a new card. They corrected "white," but at the same time, without any discussion, they changed my complexion. This is one of my favorite all-time stories. Because they had checked off the symbol "B" for complexion, which was "ruddy," "light brown," or whatever it might have been. In other words, a white person who has this color skin, that kind of complexion, would be labeled "B." But suddenly, if that same person with the same complexion is suddenly checked off as "Negro" or "colored," the complexion label changes. To me, that was one of the milestones in my life. I didn't say anything about it. I just thought, "Well, gee whiz, isn't that strange? My color has changed because my race has changed." [laughter] And that to me is one of my favorite, warmest stories about the patheticness of the human race as it struggles on toward enlightenment and wholeness.

The navy had taken steps to arrange it so that—I'm more comfortable using the term "black," and I like it because it's so clean—that blacks could now enter the navy with options of choosing something other than being members of the mess, of being a cook or a waiter or a valet for commissioned officers, because, fundamentally, that's all that blacks did in the navy in those days. So they had decided that they wanted a black band at St. Mary's Pre-flight School in Moraga Valley, just east of Oakland and Berkeley. The navy had taken over St. Mary's College, which was a Catholic college, and it was going to be used primarily as part of the training of naval flyers.

Well, they put the call out in the Bay Area, and they weren't able to recruit a sufficient number of qualified black musicians to make up a forty-five piece military band. So what to do? Hey, they just simply call down to the black musicians union in Los Angeles. So those of us in Los Angeles who were about to be sooner or later drafted into the army, suddenly we have a chance. "We can join the navy and be musicians, and we're going to be stationed at St. Mary's Pre-flight School? Let me in it right now!" Never questioned. "We'll guarantee that for the duration you will be stationed to do this very definite function." It sounded too good to be true, so I jumped at it. There was no doubt about it. Let's see, it was Buddy Collette, Quedellis Martyn, Marshal Royal, Ernie Royal, Andy Anderson, tenor saxophone player, just a whole gang of us from Los Angeles. The other saxophone players were from the Bay Area: Curtis Lowe, Jerome Richardson.

While serving in the navy band at St. Mary's, Jack had his first experience with bebop, courtesy of trumpeter Ernie Royal.

Ernie had been to New York with Lionel Hampton's first band and had heard all of the modern sounds, the bebop idiom. And when I heard Ernie play for the first time, when the navy band got together, I recognized that Ernie was the best bebop trumpet player I had ever heard. Ernie had been exposed to Dizzy Gillespie's style. As far as I was concerned, I liked Ernie's playing better than I did Dizzy's, simply because Ernie had a polish and a finesse that every note he played was a gem and a jewel. It sounded certainly like spontaneous, improvised jazz, but his mastery of the instrument in the classical fashion was such that I thought he was, again, the greatest trumpet player I'd ever heard.

What did I think of bebop? My god, it's like, "How am I ever going to learn to play like that?" [laughter] And that was the marvelous thing about being in the navy. We were full-time musicians, and we had free time to just get better and better and better.

Postwar L.A.: "Hey, Mingus, have you lost your mind?"

Jack was discharged on December 7, 1945, and returned to southern California from the Bay Area. During the war he had not visited Los Angeles.

I returned to Los Angeles after I was in the service, came down from San Francisco as fast as I could, and one of the first things I heard on the radio at night was broadcast from the Jungle Room, which was the old Gaiety

Theatre, almost directly across the street from the Lincoln Theatre. It was now a nightclub. And it was a live broadcast. I heard some of the greatest alto saxophone playing in— Never heard any alto saxophone playing— I said, "My God, Bird is in town! They didn't tell me Bird was in town!" Well, to make a long story short, it wasn't Bird. It was Sonny Criss. That guy was playing beautiful, brilliant tone, just cascades of notes. Wow! As far as I was concerned, he never got any better than that. He was so great in 1945.

Jack also reestablished contact with Charles Mingus.

Charlie Mingus was part of Al Adams's band. You know, the band that got together after the Million Dollar Theatre gig. Yeah, Charlie Mingus was part of the family before World War II, and he was a marvelous, wild human being even then. Highly emotional, loved to play bass, and he admired, as you know, Red Callender and Joe Comfort.

He wasn't involved in the service. So all during the war, Charlie Mingus was just developing himself as a jazz bass player. And he'd gotten involved in some Oriental religions, some sort of religious monk studies. That's very clear to me, because after I got out of the service, I remember very clearly Charlie Mingus and I had a heart-to-heart, loving, brother-to-brother talk one afternoon at Pershing Square, downtown. We were talking about the things that were most important to us at that time. He was talking about the big questions of life—religion, God, philosophy, and all of that sort of thing—and somehow it just seemed to me that all during my life I felt like I had all of the answers. [laughter]

Now Charlie is telling me about psychic experiences, religious experiences, things that he's had and all. And immediately I knew exactly the book I wanted to recommend to Charlie Mingus, because he was still searching and looking, desperately looking. "Well, Charlie, let me tell you. I've got a book for you. I found it extremely valuable. And I love you like a brother, you know that. This is what I want to suggest. If you don't read anything else, read *The Varieties of Religious Experience* by William James." I said, "I've just read this within the past couple of years, and that is one of the great treasures of the human race. And I think you're really ready for that." That was one of the milestones in our relationship.

By then he was heavily involved into composition, and he had learned how to play marvelous piano, harmonically speaking. I remember, after the service, he had taken me over to his house. He was living somewhere in the Forties, it seems to me. But, in any event, he was living in a little house and had a piano there, and he wanted me to hear some of his material. Man, I got scared. This guy was playing all of this marvelous Duke Ellington harmony, you know, rubato style, and singing all of these way-out lyrics, something about a woman, the power of a woman and all of this. This guy was so involved poetically and had such incredible images going. "Hey, Mingus, have you lost your mind?" This guy had just— While everybody was fighting the war, this guy was just developing himself artistically and compositionally and in every way.

I remember him telling me in Pershing Square about an experience he had during the time we hadn't seen each other. He said he'd been working on the bass and just practicing and wild, just growing, becoming. He said, "One night, I had an experience. I was playing better than I've ever played, and I kind of went off somewhere else, and I felt like I had become the bass. The bass and I were one." And that, to me, is what happens to a real artist. I mean, you just become. Now, that's the ideal situation. That's what the Zen Buddhists are talking about. You become one with that which is.

That's what jazz is. It's exploration in public. That's what you do. Jazz solos, real jazz solos, are that, because if you're really attending to your business, you are not at all concerned with whether or not your offering is being consumed by those people out there. Fundamentally, it's a private event between performing musicians. And if the public can come in and listen and observe and participate in the joy that's being experienced by the musicians, well and good. But a jazz performance, a pure jazz performance, in a sense, totally ignores the audience. Oh, you get the energy from the audience, but I'm prone to believe that if you are as committed and as totally given over to the process yourself, a factor in your brain is not gathering signals to see what effect you're having on that audience so as to stay with this idea or that idea.

Well, we know what jazz is. It's getting up to play a solo not knowing what your first note is going to be. You know, I've tried it many, many times. Other musicians, too, have maybe had a preconceived idea of what the shape of the solo is going to be like. I've never had an experience talking with a jazz musician where he has told me that he has conceived the shape beforehand and executed that plan successfully. Now, maybe some of the jazz greats do. I certainly don't consider myself a jazz great. I simply have had great fun improvising music ever since I was a kid. And I know that my experience has been that I can have a beautiful plan, and I can even decide what the first note is going to be and what register and whether it's going to be a descending line or an ascending line, but before I get out of the first four bars, spontaneity has taken over.

The New Orleans Revival

I came right back and started playing gigs. It was just a matter of play any kind of music with anybody. Jobs don't grow on trees, but I guess I was proficient enough so that I was not the bottom man on anybody's list. But there wasn't enough work for me or for anybody I knew, unless you got one of the so-called real good jobs. So I just played it by ear and took anything that came along—this, that, and the other, change, go, yes, yes, no, stay and milk anything dry.

Lucky Thompson was still here in town, and he had formed a large big band, and I played in Lucky Thompson's big band. I played alto. We did some rehearsals, and I only played one gig. It was at the Elks auditorium. Buddy DeFranco had done some writing. And it seemed to me his entire brass section was white. There might have been a couple of black players in it. But Lucky Thompson's band was primarily made up of white players. That might have been due to the fact that Lucky Thompson got a lot of recording with white bands in Hollywood.

Before the war Jack had played in clarinetist Barney Bigard's first band. After the war Jack rejoined the band, then under Kid Ory's leadership.

Barney Bigard pulled Kid Ory out of retirement. He was the trombone player, and Red Mack played trumpet. I played alto with him. Henry Green played drums. Now, that was before the war. By 1945 the big man was Kid Ory, and the clarinet player in his band was Barney Bigard. And I think this was brought about because of Orson Welles's interest in Dix-. ieland music. During the war, Orson Welles had been instrumental in popularizing or exposing that music to a larger audience.

I think it was more in the white community. I don't think I heard any clear-cut Dixieland music on Central Avenue at any time. Dixieland was never, as I recall, a part of the everyday diet on Central Avenue. It simply

wasn't harmonically satisfying enough for the tastes on the Avenue, because you couldn't get any hipper than being on Central Avenue. Well,
the Avenue represented the contemporary scene.

In any event, before the war, Kid Ory and I played in Barney Bigard's
band. After the war, I was the clarinet player in Kid Ory's band shortly
after Barney Bigard had left the band. But Albert Nicholas had played
clarinet, as well.

This, again, illustrates the fact that I'm out of the service, I'm married.
"Music, Los Angeles, here I am! Where's my job?" Any job that comes
along, "Yes, I'll take it." Kid Ory was one of them. We worked at the Jade
Supper Club on Hollywood Boulevard, Larry Potter's Jade Supper Club,
one of the focal points of interest in jazz. Movie stars used to come in
every night, music lovers. It was one of the big events. That was shortly
after the war, and Hollywood Boulevard still had a residual Hollywood
glamour about it. So I was working there with Bud Scott on guitar,
Minor "Ram" Hall on drums, L. C. Cooper, piano, Papa "Mutt" Carey
playing trumpet. And there I was, man.

The black people that I saw in the audience at Larry Potter's Supper
Club, I get this feeling that they were not, in a sense, just the regular part
of the black population that had come all the way out to Hollywood just
to hear Kid Ory's band. Many, many, many black musicians came out
just to pay homage, and they realized what this band represented. Now
that I look back, of course, that was just an incredible moment to consider that on that bandstand was Papa "Mutt" Carey playing trumpet.
[laughter]

And they go back to, in a sense, pre–Louis Armstrong days. Kid Ory
was a marvelous specimen. Still playing that same marvelous trombone
style. He could say more with one or two notes than any other trombone
player I know. And what he would do, he would growl on it, bend it, and
play it, and smear it. [laughter] He got more music out of the smallest
amount of material than I've ever heard anybody. And while I was playing with him, I was so delighted to be, in a sense, involved with the real
live guys. You know, I was born at the right time. I'm sort of right in
the middle of everything, and here they are, still in the flesh, playing this
stuff.

But after working with the band and enjoying all of that thoroughly,
just very, very happy times playing with them at that one job, I decided
that somehow I didn't want to stay for the rest of my life playing that kind

of music. It was less than a year that I worked with him, but, somehow, I was torn between appreciation for the job and the tradition and the music and the feeling that, really, I don't want to get locked into this thing, because it looked like it could have been a lifetime career. It really could have. Because my teacher, Caughey Roberts, got in on that stream. He started playing clarinet in Teddy Buckner's Dixieland band. Caughey Roberts stayed there out at Disneyland with Teddy Buckner for fifteen years, twenty years, I don't know how long. So, somehow, I sensed that I didn't want to spend the rest of my life playing Dixieland. So I quit that job to go to another job. I just didn't know what it was.

Moving On

But one of the big things that happened right after the war was I got a chance to play with Lionel Hampton, playing just clarinet. Let's see, it was 1946; Lionel Hampton was out here playing theaters and ballrooms. Paul Howard, the treasurer of the black musicians union, told Hamp, "You ought to hear this guy play clarinet." When Hamp first came to Los Angeles, he played drums in Paul Howard's band, the Quality Serenaders. And on one of those gigs is where Lionel Hampton met his future wife, because Paul Howard's Quality Serenaders was, at that time, playing almost all of the dances and affairs by black society. And, in any event, Paul Howard knew Lionel Hampton. Paul Howard knew that I could play clarinet quite good.

So one night Joe Adams, I think the first black disc jockey in Los Angeles, and now Ray Charles's manager, picked me up on the corner of Long Beach Boulevard and Twenty-fifth Street with a car full of musicians—Gladys Hampton was there—and took me out to the Trianon Ballroom. No uniform. I just sat in and played a couple of clarinet solos. And Hampton was impressed. "Hey, Gates, when you going to join the band?" I said, "Well, fine." Lionel Hampton had five saxophones. So he hired me to play just clarinet. I loved that, because that meant I didn't have to carry a saxophone, too.

He called everybody Gates. In his autobiography he tells you why. Because when he first played with Louis Armstrong, Louis Armstrong said [imitating Armstrong], "Hey, kid, you sure swing. You swing so good like a gate!" And Hamp said, "I started calling everybody Gates then."

So I got the job with Lionel Hampton, stayed with him for almost two years. I started in 1946, working one-nighters, making twenty-two dollars a night. After I'd been there for, I don't know, a year and a half, something like that, I asked for a raise of one dollar a night to twenty-three. So we talked. And the guys in the band were quite amused by it because, you know, guys who have been there for a long time, they know how the game works. When a new man gets in the band, he gets a lot of solos and, wow, everything is wonderful. You see very soon that guys in that band [snaps fingers] come and go just like that.

It's a marvelous training ground, and Hampton has done just a priceless good deed for music, because more young guys have gotten that break, that experience to see the big time. And one thing you learn in that band is how to put on a good show. That is the best place you can go to learn how to really be in the, quote unquote, "entertainment" business. Lionel Hampton can turn a group of people into a mob. He takes it as a personal challenge, because that is his thing. He feels all of this enthusiasm in himself. And right now he is just as enthused and as on fire with this as he was when I used to see him as a kid. I used to see him at the Lincoln Theatre, Twenty-third and Central. If he is able to really get that out of him into the crowd, and the crowd responds in such a way that he knows that he has shared it—that's his challenge, to share that ecstasy and that joy.

So I worked with him, tried to get a dollar raise. Couldn't. I felt, just on principle, "If I don't rate a raise after this period, I should move on."

I did some recording with Benny Goodman. Benny Goodman didn't have a band then. He was just sort of semi-retired. I was working with Jake Porter at the Downbeat at Forty-third and Central, and Benny came in once to hear us play and sat there with his hat on all the time. Esvan Mosby, the "mayor" of Central Avenue, who was managing the club at the time, asked Benny to take his hat off, and Benny said, "No, there's a draft in here and my head will get cold."

I went to Benny's house a couple of times, met Fletcher Henderson. Jake Porter and me. We sat up there and chatted. We played a little bit, and Benny asked me some questions about my clarinet embouchure. You know, that man is totally dedicated to the clarinet. He didn't care who I was.

I made some records with Benny. He had a record date which included Bumps Myers, a black tenor saxophone player, Jake, me—I played alto—I think Red Callender played bass. Vido Musso was in the band, too. I was playing third alto. Somehow Benny just wanted to see what I sounded like playing lead alto. So without saying anything, Benny just took the lead alto part from this topflight studio guy: suit on, bow tie, brown suit. I'll never forget it. You know, Benny had a reputation then, and he said, "Let's try this again." Lead alto, well, yeah. You know, I'm black, I'm supposed to add some little something special, and Benny wanted to see what that special might be. In any event, the lead alto player, man, you could just sense it. He just bristled. Under his voice, loud enough for me to hear, "I don't have to take this shit." [laughter]

But, in any event, Benny was going to reorganize his band, and I was going to be in the band. So I thought, "Wow! Wow, that's my next band. Wow! Okay, I'll wait, wait, wait." Weeks went by. No call for rehearsal. Weeks went by. Weeks turned into months. "Damn, Benny. When are you going to form your band?" I just decided, "Gee whiz, I just can't hold myself open just waiting for Benny." So an opportunity came along to join Roy Milton's rhythm and blues band, and I said, "Bye-bye, Benny."

Jack stayed with Roy Milton's rhythm and blues band until the mid-1950s. Although based in Los Angeles, the band spent a large part of the year on the road.

Roy Milton—rhythm and blues, had many big hits. Caughey Roberts, my teacher, had played with Roy Milton, and they had come to a parting of the ways. And he had had another alto player, Cliff Noel. I think I, in a sense, replaced Cliff Noel. I played alto only with Roy Milton. Between the time my teacher left and I joined Roy Milton, Roy Milton had gotten even bigger and bigger and had better automobiles to travel in. And shortly after I joined him, he bought his first full-sized Flexible, a brand-new bus. Roy Milton was a fine job, marvelous job, great job.

I think I played my first job with Roy Milton at the Club Alabam. All the time I was with him, he was one of the neatest, best-dressed people, and his band was just immaculately dressed. I remember the first sets of uniforms. That's plural—sets of uniforms. The shoes impressed me more than anything else, because they were brown-and-white wing tips. That meant when you walked on stage, you will have had your shoes either shined and prepared properly, or you've done it yourself, which means you've got to have white polish. I've got a bunch of pictures, and I can't believe how good that band looked. They were wearing those brown-and-white wing-tipped shoes, gray pants, maroon jacket, and we had three or four changes of uniform. He had that when I joined the band, and he continued to keep the band extremely well uniformed, because he was a national name at that time. So I just moved right into something that was extremely popular.

Roy Milton was doing it first with just two horns. Hosea Sapp, trumpet player, and Buddy Floyd played tenor saxophone, Texas tenor saxophone player. Buddy Floyd had a unique Texas style. Not the Texas style that we associate with Arnett Cobb or Herschel Evans or any of those other people, but a more earthy type. When I say earthy, no attempt at hard technical swinging. Just sheer emotion. In fact, almost like—we were talking about this earlier—Kid Ory taking one or two notes and getting a whole lot of mileage out of one or two notes. Well, that's what Buddy Floyd would do with these tenor saxophone solos. Mainly, these were the solos that he had played on Roy Milton records that had been big hits. So Roy, being smart, and Buddy, being smart, both of them built their style around their hit records.

I stayed there eight, nine years, because I became quite valuable to Roy. When I joined, he had maybe a dozen real big national hits, recorded on Specialty Records. And Roy Milton's library was in everybody's head. The band performed from memory. None of it was written down. Now, get this. If Roy fired somebody or somebody quit or got sick, the tour had to end. Everything was canceled. The whole band would have to come back to Los Angeles, and they would rehearse for a month or so until the replacement—I'm talking about a horn player now—was able to sit there and find his notes. I said, "Roy, listen. I don't like to have to waste my time this way, and you shouldn't have to do this, either. Why don't you let me write down the charts, write down the arrangements? I'll even write out the solos." He was so thrilled and relieved and delighted. That's one of the reasons I became so valuable to him, because I had written the whole book.

During Jack's years with Roy Milton, the amalgamation movement within the musicians union was under way. Jack supported the movement, but his touring schedule prevented him from being active.

I missed being intimately involved with the demise of Central Avenue in the physical sense, because right after the war, as a result of trying to maintain steady employment, I had to join bands that went on the road. That was during the time of the amalgamation of the two unions and all. I missed all of that, except I happened to be in town during one of the meetings. I was in touch with what was going on at that time. The musicians union on Central Avenue was one of the main focal points of my life. Whenever I was in town, naturally, I was in and out of the union almost on a daily or weekly basis.

I remember speaking to Leo Davis about the amalgamation. Leo Davis was the president at that time. I said, "Leo, how can we not do this? You know, it's going to just increase everybody's work opportunities. We'll be rubbing elbows with everybody over there. We might not jump into the big money right away, but just being in the proximity of where the action is, some of us are bound to profit from it." I remember Leo's words precisely: "You go to that big organization, and you'll get lost." In other words, there's so many of them and so few of us, you'll just be swallowed up. And his word was "lost."

But my feeling was—and many people felt like—it's the principle of the thing, the concept of everybody being in the same organization. Separatism is not good. It limits everybody. It deprives everybody, males and females. And even now, yes, I would certainly be on the side for amalgamation. I have some very, very dear friends whom I respect very highly who still feel that we didn't get enough for our money when we went over there.

Decline of Central

World War II is the big dividing line, I guess, because things happened during those periods. The migration of various types of elements of the population. People were traveling all over the country. So that was one of the biggest things that influenced Central Avenue—in fact—the whole Eastside—along with the Supreme Court decision about restrictive covenants. That just allowed everything to just flow in all directions. But it's quite true that before World War II, that was Central Avenue at its most glamorous.

When we came back from the service after the war, there were still traces of the old— I shouldn't say traces. When you were on Central Avenue, you felt the same things again. But you could see that there were subtle changes. And I guess it was the Supreme Court decision that took place a couple of years after the war. That's what maybe really pulled the plug. And the fact that the plug had been pulled really wasn't evident for a few years, because just the physicality, the physical aspect of the property along Central Avenue, maintained its integrity for quite a while. But after a time, it just went down. Upwardly mobile human beings moved out of the area to better things. Then things began to deteriorate in a fashion.

But, in any event, as soon as the restrictive covenant thing went into being, Negroes began to move out of the area. I don't know, a year or two, three years after that court decision was handed down, my parents moved out. They moved quite far west. They moved to Fourth Avenue just off of Adams Boulevard. So it was a straight shot west.

Very gradually, I imagine, many elements in the population in the Central Avenue area began to expand into areas that had not been available before. And the fact that there had been such an influx of people from all over the country during the war to Los Angeles to take advantage of the job opportunities in the defense industries, that created a type of housing pressure that somehow couldn't be relieved until the restrictive covenant thing made it possible. In the thirties, the population of blacks in Los Angeles was less than forty thousand. And when I came back after the war, I sensed that there was something very different about that part of town. The pressure was there, because people hadn't been free to move out. There was a type of density there which intensified the uniqueness of the area.

After the war, it was almost as if there's this exhilaration of "We've got more money than we know what to do with, and we can't buy houses in any other area." And then, three or four years later [snaps fingers] "Yes, we can. Let me at it."

When I see what it looks like now, it's almost as if everybody just wanted to leave that area. It's almost as if "Free at last. Thank God Almighty, free at last. I don't know where I'm going, but I know I don't want to stay here." Because Central Avenue now is just unbelievable. The property values and the glamour and everything that was there—suddenly it's like a war zone. You know, vacant lots. How can this happen?

There was some talk about "Well, Western Avenue is the new Central Avenue." No way. Because before World War II, boy, that Central Avenue was like a jewel. And you didn't know it. There was no way to appreciate it and know what it was until after it had disappeared, and to see that it didn't reproduce itself anywhere else. Graffiti? No. Spic and span. And we just took that for granted. High quality, a good, beautiful, beautiful boulevard, beautiful street.

To me, Central Avenue was the heart and the focal point of existence. That was the street. And it drew everybody there, not because that was where all of the naughty things happened. No, everything that happened that was important happened on that street. Almost anybody of importance would have been on Central Avenue if they were in town. It was certainly the main street in my life. Everything worthwhile happened on Central or close to Central. Central Avenue had any and everything you might want. It was a complete street with the extra veneer of that mysterious glamour that you didn't find anywhere else.

11

William Douglass

Drummer *Bill Douglass was a lifelong Los Angeles resident. During his career he performed with Benny Carter, June Christy, Benny Goodman, Earl Hines, Lena Horne, Red Norvo, Kay Starr, Art Tatum, Cal Tjader, T-Bone Walker, Ben Webster, and Gerald Wiggins, among others. He also recorded with Red Callender, Hines, Norvo, Tatum, Tjader, and Wiggins.*

An early opponent of segregation in the musicians union, Bill was a leader in the fight to amalgamate the black and white Los Angeles locals of the American Federation of Musicians. He served as vice-president of the black local until the amalgamation with Local 47 in 1953. In 1985 he was elected Treasurer of Local 47, a position he held until 1991. Throughout the years Bill also taught drums.

Bill Douglass died on December 19, 1994.

Bill was born in Sherman, Texas, in 1923. His family moved to Los Angeles six months later.

They brought me out here for a fresh setting, away from the Jim Crow. Not that none of it existed here, but basically, by law, it was not supposed to exist. We have a very large family, and it seems that most of them migrated out here around about that time. We lived on Compton Boulevard and then a little later on just a few blocks from there, East Thirty-ninth Street, 1500 block. It's Forty-first Place right now. My grandmother and grandfather had a lot there with two houses on it, and we were living in the rear house. Then we moved out on East Fifty-sixth Street, where I did the majority of my growing up.

Early on I had a guitar and a ukulele, because I had an uncle, Peter Douglass, who was a guitar player with one of the real popular bands around town, the Les Hite Orchestra. People like Marshal Royal, Floyd Turnham, and a number of others, were in that same orchestra. But I always had an interest in music. My dad, James Douglass, was with a vocal group, a quartet called the Bilbrew Quartet. I guess that was basically a sideline, because he was a custodian in the school system, same as my uncle and grandfather. But I actually saw him on stage many times. And my dad's father, Calvin Douglass, was a violinist. He and Marshal Royal's dad played together in the same orchestra. The music was always around.

My grandmother used to have the windup Victrola, and they'd put these records on. I'd hear a little bit of Louis Armstrong, and then, once in a while, a little Lionel Hampton. You used to be able to turn on your radio and catch live broadcasts. And then Benny Goodman came along. I never heard a clarinet like that! I was very much wrapped up in that until I heard Gene Krupa get loose and they left him out there playing all by himself. That was "Sing, Sing, Sing." The first time I heard that, it was on the radio, and something just happened to me then. *Camel Caravan* was the name of that program. I never missed it; I never missed a broadcast. The whole thing was thrilling. That's what I had to do. That's all there was to it.

Early Days

The schools we attended were quite integrated. They were, I guess, predominantly black, but we had Caucasian, Japanese, Chinese, Hispanic. I mean, they all attended the same schools. My first school was the Ascot Avenue Elementary School, then Hooper Avenue, when we moved to Fifty-sixth Street. From there, I went to McKinley Junior High School, and that's where I first ran into Dexter Gordon. I mean, we looked at one another. We're both the same height, and this and that. People have said that we looked an awful lot like brothers. We just looked at each other kind of funny, and just kind of grinned and laughed. We just became very good friends, very close friends.

I had a cousin by marriage, Alvy Kidd, who was quite a little bit of a showboat type of guy. He played the washtub and had tin pans and things all set up like a drum set. I think that was when Dexter first got hold of a clarinet. I used to listen to the two of them together, playing with little groups and trying to jam. Naturally, I got attracted to that and wanted to get into it. So I kind of hung out with him and was fooling with the drums a little bit.

From there, we went to Jefferson High School, where we finally began to get our formal training. That was the first time I actually got a chance to get into a real instrument class. At Jeff we were under Sam Browne, our first music teacher. He was our band director and music teacher. You know, from this day, I still respect him. I thought he was just absolutely the greatest. He's the one who taught all of us how to play and what to do. That was the thing that made school so interesting. He not only conducted the regular high school orchestra and the marching band, but he organized the little swing bands and taught us how to jam together. We used to have little jam sessions at school. Of course, we were listening to the big orchestras. Like our idols were the Count Basies, Jimmie Luncefords, Duke Ellingtons, and he sort of helped us as we were all trying to emulate these people.

The first thing Sam Browne did in the instrument class was put a book in front of me with notes in it. I said, "Gee, I didn't know drummers were supposed to read notes." I've been a note fanatic ever since then. He was the one who encouraged me in the study of rudiments. And then he always encouraged everybody to get with a very good private teacher and really get into studying the instrument. We were always encouraged to study. And there were times when we got people like Lionel Hampton and the Nat King Cole Trio to come over to our school and perform. I got to know some of those guys real well.

I ran around with Dexter and Lamar Wright. Ernie Royal went to school with us there—he was a little older than we were—and I knew he was a great trumpet player then. Our guys, even before they got out of high school, they could play. We all held down jobs at night while we were trying to go to school. I mean, nightclubs, you know. We just didn't sleep. We used to try to sleep in class, and then we used to catch hell from the teachers. They knew what we were doing, and we had to get our studies together or else. Our teachers were always threatening to expose us and get us pulled off the jobs, but they sort of left us alone if we got through school and got our studies.

Perhaps the most influential private teacher in the Central Avenue area was Lloyd Reese, a talented reed and brass performer in Les Hite's orchestra.

Lloyd Reese was one of my private teachers. All of us studied with him. Buddy Collette, Dexter Gordon, Charles Mingus, myself, Hampton Hawes, Eric Dolphy. He taught everybody. I was a drummer, basically, but I was into studying music. So I studied keyboard with Reese. That happened with all these different guys that studied with Reese. Charlie Mingus. Now, Reese didn't play bass, but Charlie was into it, so Charlie studied keyboard. We studied what you call keyboard harmony, and he just kind of told me what to do on the drums. He told me who to watch, and this is right, and that's it. I never had a formal drum teacher. I had people that I got together with from time to time, and I just sought out the knowledge that I wanted and just worked at it.

To this day, I firmly believe that just playing drums means nothing unless it's related to the other instruments in the orchestra. I felt that by having some knowledge and some feeling as to what the other guys were doing, it made me more sensitive as a drummer. That's proved true throughout my career, because I've always managed to accompany all of the great pianists, such as Art Tatum, Erroll Garner, Gerald Wiggins, Earl Hines. They seemed to like me because I seemed to understand what they were doing.

Then Reese organized a band made up of all of his students, a big band. We used to go down to Local 767. We weren't members at that time, but they got it open on Sunday mornings for us. So we would go there and we would rehearse. We'd get stock arrangements. I think we all chipped in something like a quarter apiece per week, into the little treasury, so that we could buy music. Finally, we got Gerald Wilson, who was playing trumpet and writing with Jimmie Lunceford, to bring some of his arrangements for us to play.

So this band, we'd rehearse, rehearse, rehearse. Boy, if you could have seen us. I remember there was a fellow named Charles Martin, who was a pianist. He lived way out in the Watts area, and he would pick up Mingus. He drove a little Willys car, a very small car. Then he would swing by and pick me up. We had the bass, the drums, and I don't know how many musicians in that car, hanging in and outside of us, and then we'd make that trip all the way down Central Avenue until we got to Seventeenth Street, where the union was located. That was the ritual. We looked forward to that each and every week. We played and we played. Finally, we had a lot of real adult musicians who would come around and listen to us play.

I remember Reese mentioned to me what a great musician Cozy Cole was. I managed to meet Cozy after a while, and he was very influential. He was traveling with Cab Calloway's big band. They'd come into town. Fortunately, he would let me come by his house, usually after school. He's getting up around that time. He was one of those guys who practices very diligently at all times. I was able to just sit around there and watch what he did and all the things that he practiced. I never heard the rudiments move that fast. I was learning the rudiments, but the way he played them, they sounded so great and so musical. I sort of watched and saw it all go by, and I just maintained that in my head and decided that I was going to just keep after it until I had it the same way.

Cozy was a great influence. I mean he could read anything, he knew all the rudiments. I just couldn't imagine anybody knowing as much as he did. I know that Jo Jones and some of the other guys couldn't read like Cozy could. It wasn't really necessary. But Cozy was just thoroughly schooled. I just decided I wanted to be like that, also.

And then, when I went around other drummers— I mean I must have changed the way I held my sticks a dozen times. Every time I saw a new drummer, I'd try to hold my sticks the way he does. Or where he sets his snare drum or his cymbal. I just went through all kinds of things until I finally settled on something that seemed to work best for me. Then I admired guys like Sid Catlett. Sid was a big guy, but he had that finesse. There were so many good ones until you didn't know which way to go. [laughter] And I guess, in the long run, I finally wound up being myself. But during the years, it was always gratifying when somebody says, "Gee, you remind me of so and so." I've even had write-ups where somebody said that my brushwork was reminiscent of Jo Jones. To this day, that makes me feel great. It really does.

"That was a proud day, the day we all got our union cards in our pockets."

We were going around and soliciting jobs and playing the dances and things like that. I remember Dexter and I and probably Charles Martin had a job down on Main Street. These are just beer joints, beer and whiskey, little places where people just drank, you know. We'd play the music. With our little three pieces, we'd try to imitate the sounds that we heard in the big bands. I remember the salary was $1.50 a night. Of course, people always threw tips at you. You got well off the tips.

In fact, there was a point where we were giving a lot of the union musicians a pretty bad time for some of the jobs. [laughter] And the union had a business rep, Elmer Fain, who made us very aware of the union, because he was like a big policeman. We were always hiding from him, even though we didn't belong to the union. He just seemed to be so big, bad, and ugly. Musicians were always staying out of his way, because he was the type of guy who really went out and hunted you down. Unions had a lot of clout then. And he could pull you off the job. He would do it in a minute. He'd pull his mother off a job. But it was Lloyd Reese, who I think was vice-president of Local 767, and the union who came up with some sort of a deal where they got all of us to join by giving us a special joining fee. I think it was something like $25 apiece, instead of the usual $50, and we all joined at the same time. That was a proud day, the day we all got our union cards in our pockets. When you finally got your union card and you started playing with all the different guys, the union card meant that you were professional. You actually were a professional. We were really proud of it.

The local was at Seventeenth and Central. It was really just a large two-story frame house. I remember the Basie band rehearsing downstairs right beside our financial offices one day. And we had big bands rehearse upstairs. That's where our group, the Lloyd Reese band, would rehearse every Sunday. We had the offices on the first floor. I remember the financial office was run by a very popular fellow named Paul Howard, a famous saxophone player. His band was called the Quality Serenaders. We had a lady named Florence Cadrez, who was the recording secretary. Leo Davis was president then. We had a vice-president, boards of directors, and trustees. The highest policy-making body was the board of directors.

Yeah, I think it was an advantage for all of us. The fact that we were just there, we were on the spot and— I mean, next door to the local itself was Lester Young's family. They lived right next door to Local 767. It was just a great big two-story frame house. Lester was there whenever he was in town. His brother Lee was another one of the many drummers. If I wanted to learn something, I'd go watch—"Lee, how do you do that?" I

mean, when the Lee and Lester Young band was formed and was performing around here, I was just one of the young guys that Lee would
trust. He could get up from the drums and say, "Come on and play a few
tunes." Boy, that was just the thrill of a lifetime. I got a chance to play
with some awfully great people.

Central Avenue — "It was just home. It was just a way of life."

We didn't think of Central Avenue as being anything special. It was just
home. It was just a way of life. I had to go down Central to get wherever
I was going. We had all kinds of clubs all up and down the street, and
they stretched all the way out towards Watts way. There was the Dunbar
Hotel and the Club Alabam. That was a famous place. All of us as young
kids, when we got out of school and were on our way home, we would
walk right down Central Avenue just for a chance to pass by the Dunbar
Hotel, because that's where all the big bands stayed. We used to get the
word ahead of time that somebody's band was coming into town—it
might be Basie or whoever—but we'd stand there and wait on the bus.
We'd watch these guys climb off the bus and go upstairs to their hotel
rooms, and we just hung around. And then, if they opened in a theater,
no school for us! [laughter] We'd see that same movie. They always had
a movie and then the stage show, a movie and the stage show. We'd just
sit through that movie over and over again just to catch the next show.
And then, we'd run out in the alley and watch them come out of the
backstage entrance, in and out. That kept on until we got a chance to get
acquainted with the guys, and then they knew we were musicians. Once
in a while, I'd get a chance to carry Jo Jones's case or something like that,
and then you'd get in backstage. When I heard Jo, well, that turned me
around, all the way around. It was just a completely different thing, a
very loose, free style of playing.

The Club Alabam was where everybody went when they left their Hollywood jobs, Beverly Hills jobs, and whatnot. Around about 2 a.m., everybody came from all over everywhere, and they always gathered right
in the Club Alabam. The show would always run late, and then it just
seemed like they did that just because everybody was coming over there,
not only the musicians and whatnot, but the crowds. I guess I'd say that
the predominantly white crowds would just sort of follow the guys over,

and then, when that closed up, they would just migrate to the little after-hours joints.

The after-hours joints were all over the place. I remember the Ritz Club always used to have battles of the saxophones. We had a guy named Bumps Myers, a real hang-outer, a drinker. He was the other tenor saxophonist in the Lee and Lester Young orchestra. He worked with Benny Carter and just about everybody. Players were always nervous when Bumps was around. Yeah, we had all kinds of after-hours places. There was Lovejoy's, and there was Ivie Anderson's Chicken Shack, Jack's Basket Room.

The Elks Auditorium was where an awful lot of the action happened. The big bands came in and played the dances there. Basie, Lunceford, Earl Hines. It was a big auditorium with a balcony. And then above that, we had another little club room and facilities. And Saturday night, both ends of it were jumping. That's the place where everybody had their functions. Sometimes even school events like proms and things were held there. That's a very, very historical place. It's equally historical as the Club Alabam.

There was another big place on Central, out in Watts, run by Joe Morris, the Plantation Club. Buddy Collette, Charlie Mingus, Joe Lutcher, I, and a number of others used to work there in Snake White's band. Snake White was an arranger, trumpet player, good musician. The place was hilarious. People came out there to see who was going to fight who. One night Wynonie Harris, the great blues singer, kept cracking on Dorcester Irving, a real cockeyed bass player. Next thing Irving pulled the peg out of his bass and went after him. He had Wynonie begging for his life. It was really funny.

Black jazz artists also worked in other areas of Los Angeles. Billy Berg, who owned and operated several clubs during the 1940s, drew heavily on the musical talent of Central Avenue.

Heck, I worked all the Billy Berg spots and there were a lot of them, just before I went in the service. The first one was the Club Capri, and that's where Lee and Lester Young started their band. The Club Capri was located on Pico and La Cienega, right next door to a bank, on the corner. Most of the young kids came in there and bought nothing but Coca-Colas and jitterbugged. Boy, did they dance. I used to just go there and watch. And then, I got a chance to sit in with that band. You're talking about jam sessions. At two o'clock, things were just starting. The few people who were in the know got a chance to stay in the club, and then the bands like Duke Ellington or Basie, whoever was in town, they all came in there and then the jam session started. I remember seeing Jimmy Blanton from Duke's band and Ben Webster and people like that. I was just out there in the audience, and every so often they said, "Well, Bill, why don't you come up and play the next set?" That had to be a thrill. So I got a chance to play with all these guys.

Then Billy Berg bought another club called the Trouville. That was over on Beverly and Fairfax. The Trouville was a club that was kind of Beverly Hills–ish, kind of an exclusive-type nightclub. So when he opened the Trouville, he moved Lee and Lester over to it and then brought in Lorenzo Flennoy's group at the Capri. In that group, there was Flennoy on piano, Charlie Mingus on bass, Loyal Walker on trumpet, Buddy Collette on alto sax, and myself on drums. So we kept the Capri going. Over there at the Trouville, he's got the Lee and Lester Young group. He's got Leo Watson and the Spirits of Rhythm alternating. He also had Slim and Slam. That was Slam Stewart and Slim Gaillard. They were there at the same time. They had Joe Turner there singing the blues. They had Billie Holiday there at the same time. There's no let-up all night long. It was ridiculous. And then, while that's going on, he goes down Hollywood Boulevard and Las Palmas and opens up the Swing Club. He puts Benny Carter's big band in there. He's got three clubs going at the same time. He didn't even open Billy Berg's, which was down here on Vine Street, until all those other places had closed.

Even in suburban white enclaves such as Glendale, there were clubs interested in Central Avenue sounds.

There were always little places popping open here and there. I used to play over in Pasadena quite a bit. There was always a couple of clubs that were really happening over in Glendale. There was one place that jumped like mad, the Melody Club, run by a piano player, Poison Gardner. Bumps Myers and Brother Woodman would do these two-tenor type things. It just jumped like mad.

Glendale was the type of city where black guys didn't hang out on the streets, but in the clubs things were all right. But you wouldn't dare be caught walking around the streets there at night. As soon as your gig was over, you get into your little buggy and get back across town. We had a lot of places like that. We always referred to those areas as "Little Texas" or "Little Mississippi." Even a little place like South Gate, which is just south and east of here. I was always working over there, and I had my little problems, my little run-ins with various people, a lot of racial things. I know I had experiences where, when I laid a guy out cold, well, it seemed like, after that, we had peace and quiet.

When jazz pianist Art Tatum settled in Los Angeles after the war, Bill and bassist Red Callender joined him to form one of the most formidable trios in jazz.

I'll always remember Lovejoy's. It was an upstairs place. I was a very young guy in 1941 working on West Eighth Street at a place called the 331 Club with Dootsie Williams's Four Chocolates. That was when I really had gotten acquainted with Art Tatum, who was playing there, doing a single. I was just a little kid who was worshipping guys like Art. The guy who owned the club was named Herb Rose. So Art would tell me, "Tell Herb to give you a case of Pabst Blue Ribbon." Whenever I got that case, I'm supposed to take it over on Central Avenue to Lovejoy's and put it in the refrigerator. Art drank scotch, V.O., and then he chased it with the Pabst Blue Ribbon. When everybody saw me coming there with a case of beer, then the word went around town, "Art's coming in tonight." [laughter] You'd have all the piano players and everybody hanging around.

Art was just fabulous. I mean, I just couldn't think of anything to equal that. But I heard all the piano players. As great as Art was, I knew which ones he liked, also. Nat Cole was one of his favorites. He used to like Gerald Wiggins. I was working with Gerry for many years, and Art used to come into our club on Central Avenue. That was a little place called the Turban Room, which was inside the Dunbar Hotel. Just a little small lounge. But everybody hung out there. Ben Webster, Lloyd Reese. They all came to the Turban Room just to see what was going on. If you went all the way back, well, then, the big Club Alabam was in the back. It was Gerald Wiggins and myself—we worked as a duo—and then, later on, it was a trio with Red Callender on bass.

You never knew when Art was in town or not. He was in and out of town all the time, even though he had made this his home and had an apartment over on Adams Boulevard. I mean, you're up there jamming, you're playing, and then you look around: there's Art standing at the bar, just hanging over the bar with his scotch in one hand and Pabst Blue Ribbon in the other. Then Gerry would say, "Oh, my God, God's in the house." Then he'd decide that he wants to sit in and jam some. We had a little spinet piano with half the notes missing off of it. And they never tuned it. It was terrible. You've never heard anybody play like he could play when he gets on an old bad piano. He'd fool around, find out what's missing and what isn't, and then what he did to that piano was just something else altogether. It didn't stop him. He just knew what to do with it. Those are the things that are not on record—hearing him play a bad piano and what he could do with it.

Tatum eventually stole me and Red Callender away from Gerry Wiggins. We went into a place called the Royal Room, on Las Palmas and Hollywood Boulevard. Tatum would play just quiet, so that atmosphere was very, very quiet. It was so quiet you could hear a pin drop. Pretty soon the waitresses didn't move around and rattle their glasses. It was just like a concert. And we'd play as a trio. He was a drummer himself at one time. It was almost as if he was reading my mind because, while I'm playing my little patterns, he seemed to find little musical things to inject into what I was playing. He wasn't leading me, just complementing the little things that I did. I never could describe—I wish I could have recorded something like that.

Later we played Jazz City on Hollywood Boulevard at Western, and Zardi's at Hollywood and Vine. We attracted a terrific movie crowd and all kinds of celebrities, and, of course, musicians, just clamoring to get into the place. We had people like Leopold Stokowski. He would come in there and sit with his mouth, his chin hanging wide open.

Tatum could play anything. I've seen him do runs with these two fingers up here and then the other two fingers of the same hand playing something else down there. Two fingers on the black keys, and then the other two fingers would be playing something else on the white keys. He could do that in either hand; it didn't matter. Stretched tenths from here to here. He was just phenomenal.

I always felt good about the fact that he felt like nobody could play drums for him better than I could. I carry that with me everywhere. Yeah, nobody can say anything to me about how to play drums. If it was good enough for Art, it should be good enough for anybody. [laughter]

The other great jazz pianist in town was Nat King Cole.

You know, he was one of ours: 767, Los Angeles, Central Avenue. He was one of those on the scene. Among his peers, we looked upon Nat as just the greatest thing that ever happened around here. And the rest of his trio, his original trio, which is Oscar Moore, one of the world's greatest guitarists ever, and Wesley Prince from right out of here. When he succeeded at first, it was with his trio. It was the Nat King Cole Trio. Terrific musicians. The rest of us guys around here worshipped them. They were the greatest things that we knew and they were making it as a trio. They were equal, not a leader and two men.

And we were the people who used to go to the clubs where Nat played, and when he'd get two or three drinks, then we finally coaxed him into singing a couple choruses of the blues. He was actually sort of inhibited about singing, but after a couple of drinks you could get him to do it. I remember I was at Earl Carroll's Theatre Restaurant, and after we played a forty-five minute dance set, then this big show started. We were probably free for two hours or so. Nat was working right around the corner at the Radio Room on Vine Street. We'd just run in there and say, "Let's go down and have a couple of drinks and listen to Nat." We always listened to him because he played so fantastically. And then, if you hung around him long enough and drinks and this and that, then he'd loosen up, and then he'd sing the blues for us. We'd say, "Gee, that cat sure has got a good style." [laughter] Somebody else finally recognized the fact that he had a good style, and bam!, after that, you'd go in a store and say, "Well, just give me a pound of King Cole records." [laughter] You didn't care what they were.

That bass, guitar, and piano sound became the familiar thing in almost all the little trios around town and everywhere else. All patterned themselves after the King Cole Trio. Even the great Art Tatum, who was the greatest pianist who ever lived, probably will ever live, had the same thing. He added the bass and guitar. Everybody was on that kick. He was one of the world's greatest jazz pianists. Art and Nat set the pattern, and everybody else kind of went along that way.

War Years

I finished Jefferson High School in 1941. When the war broke out, I didn't have to go right away. I wasn't quite of age. But I did go one year later. We enlisted. Then, you enlisted for the sake of escaping the draft. Jackie Kelso, Buddy Collette, Charlie Mingus, myself, had this opportunity in San Francisco. They were recruiting guys, organizing a band at St. Mary's Pre-flight School near San Francisco. When you got in that band, you'd be a musician in the navy and probably exempt from any other duties, but it was a way to escape the draft.

All of us went up there together. Charlie Mingus didn't pass the physical, and I think by the time they told me to raise my hand to get sworn in, I got scared and chickened out. [laughter] I just didn't make it. We were supposed to go there and be stationed there for the duration. Then the guy said, "Well, there's nothing that says that you can't be shipped out." And I said, "Oh no, not get on the boat!" Mingus wasn't going, so we came back together. Buddy and those guys stayed there, and I don't think they've been on the water yet.

Just about a year later, another opportunity came up. There was a warrant officer and a lieutenant from the regular army who came down to our local. They were going to enlist the band for the Tenth Cavalry at Camp Lockett in Campo, California. So I said, "Well, we're going to be sitting right on the Mexican border for the duration." [laughter] So we jumped at that. Twenty-eight of us from Local 767 went into that band. My teacher, Lloyd Reese, went into that band. We had a fantastic band. We played all of the USO shows, came out here, did the Hollywood Canteen. We were always in San Diego, but any time we had any amount of time at all, well, then, bam, straight back to Los Angeles. We'd come in and hang out in the clubs and jam. The clubs were really swinging. And there were more clubs in the downtown Los Angeles area, up around First Street and San Pedro, places that were predominantly Japanese or used to be predominantly Japanese. That was when they put all of the Japanese and their families into the camps. The Avenue kind of moved and stretched on out that way. There were all kinds of clubs.

And then, after about fifteen months, we did go overseas. [laughter] Across five oceans. [laughter] I didn't want the navy because I didn't want that! And those guys at St. Mary's don't even know what water looks like! [laughter] But everybody was just trying to get out of it. People were doing whatever they could to beat the rap physically. I was just as bad as any of them. I started complaining about this and complaining about that, going on sick call. But there was just no way out, you had to accept it. It's a very uncertain thing when you get on that boat, go up that gangplank, and you look at that little bit of water, and you know that this is it. I saw a lot of guys—not in our band—jump overboard once they got on there. People panicked. And I'm talking about officers, the guys who ordered you around. They're the ones who just cracked completely when they got on board that ship.

The first place we went was North Africa. We landed in Casablanca, and from there we went to Oran, and later on moved to Algiers. We had some fun there. We played some good clubs. There was always a group of us, about five of us, who were the jamsters. Well, we'd get a regular gig in town. Get off in the evening and go on our regular little nightclub gig. Yeah, we had a ball.

When we left there, we had to cross the Mediterranean. We went to Italy, landed in Naples, and later on marched into Rome. At this point I was a sergeant and commanded the band. We were then, I think, the 118th Army Services Band and were attached to Allied Force Headquarters. Then they took another band and joined it together with us, another twenty-eight piece band. And because of my great height, they felt I would look good as a drum major. I took over the duties of actually leading the band. It was my job to lead the band in parade formations and things of that sort.

When we approached Rome, the Nazi army was pretty much on the run, and we were making this gigantic push up north from Naples. When we got outside the gates of Rome, a truce was called. The truce was for the sake of saving the city of Rome itself. It was called to give the enemy a chance to move farther north and clear out of the city, because the Allied Forces usually destroyed everything in their wake. Consequently, we stayed there at the gates overnight, and then we had to get up and prepare for a parade. The next day came the march into the streets of Rome. We were blowing our music, and the tanks and things lined up behind us, and the troops. It was quite a thing, just going down the streets of Rome with the people pouring champagne from the rooftops. And I was leading. I was the first man down the street. And over half the band were guys from Local 767 on Central Avenue.

The rest of the time, we split the band up into small combos and played the clubs, USO, Red Cross functions, and things like that. Eventually, we got our own hotel, room service, sheets, and even a banquet hall with Italian chefs who could take K and C rations and really just do it up grand style. We had a lot more going for us than a lot of the other troops. And we did not lose a man the whole time. All of us returned here.

Postwar Central

After being discharged, Bill took a job in San Francisco that lasted for the better part of a year. There, he met his first wife, Dorothy Burney. In 1947 he moved back to Los Angeles.

I should have stayed in San Francisco, but because I'd been away so long, I wanted to get back here. Then when I came back, well, the bottom dropped out of everything. Nothing was happening around here. One minute you're busy working, and the next minute there are no jobs.

During the war, more women musicians began appearing on the Avenue, some of whom maintained successful careers after the men returned.

Clora Bryant was around there at that time. She was kind of a young thing. She was playing in the Alabam. There was a violinist named Ginger Smock. She played jazz violin, played a little bit of everything. And I knew of Vi Redd, an alto saxophonist. She had a brother, who was a drummer, and I knew her dad, Alton Redd, also a drummer. Alton Redd was one of the guys that my uncle used to play with. And we had many people who were pianists. Nellie Lutcher was around and Betty Hall Jones.

Along with Buddy Collette and Marl Young, Bill was one of the key figures in the fight to eliminate segregated locals in the American Federation of Musicians.

Of course, all the white guys belonged to one local, Local 47, and all the black guys belonged to another. We didn't get really conscious of it until later years. I was playing with Benny Goodman at that time. I was the only black guy in his band, and I was doing a lot of recording and touring with him. I guess one of the things that impressed me about Benny was not only the Gene Krupa thing, but, I mean, when Lionel Hampton and Teddy Wilson played with him. Benny Goodman was just the ultimate, as far as I was concerned. All of a sudden, here the bands are all mixed up. I drummed along with all those Benny Goodman records and along with those radio programs. "Gee, maybe there's a chance for me, even a guy like me, to get into a band like Benny's." It was one of my ambitions as a kid. He started something. Many years later, when I least thought about it, I finally received a phone call. About 1949 I did my first date with him. That was a relationship that I was very proud of.

All of a sudden things began to hit all of us a little bit. There was always black and white. The white union did this, and the black union does this. When I was doing things with Benny Goodman in '49, '50, '51, I was the only black in the band, and there were a lot of times when he had to take care of business such as contracts. Well, he was always bitching about the fact that he'd have to come way across town to take care of business for me. Or he'd have to send my checks here when he sent everybody else's checks uptown there. So he would talk about that, and so, naturally, these things were ringing little bells in your head, like, "Yeah, what is it all about?"

There were a number of us like Buddy Collette, Charlie Mingus, Chico Hamilton, myself, who are moving around and working with some of the white guys from Local 47. Musicians, when they start digging one another and working together, well, then it happened. We met in Hollywood clubs, but you know, Central Avenue was the place. Everybody came to Central Avenue. "That's where the black and the white folks meet." They talk about Basin Street. Well, hell, you've got Central Avenue again. The people, when they'd leave those clubs, they'd come down here, and all the after-hours activity was all up and down the streets of Central. And, of course, musicians are going to get to know one another.

And then, we were talking with Lloyd Reese about it, who looked at the thing the same way. What we needed to do was progress. "Yeah, what you guys ought to do, you should buck against this thing. I mean, why should we have two unions here? It's discrimination."

All of a sudden we were becoming very, very conscious of the racial thing throughout the world, I guess, for that matter—what's happening with people here and what's happening with people there. And here in Los Angeles, we don't have those kinds of laws. We didn't have to go to the back of the bus and so on, yet you still knew the areas where you weren't treated quite like other people were. So there were a lot of things you resented. There were housing covenants, "No, you can't sell to so-and-so." Even where I live right now, we can pull out our deed to the house. The wording is right in the deed that they weren't supposed to sell this property to anybody other than the Caucasian race.

Okay, so now we began to get together in the union—Buddy Collette, Charlie Mingus, me. Marl Young would join us soon. Benny Carter supported us. It seemed like he was so great and so far above all these things. However, he felt the same way we did, and he could not stand to see this thing like it was. Basically, all of the younger guys, all of the progressive-style musicians. We finally decided to go to a union meeting, and we're going to bring this up on the floor. I was the individual who was going to stand up on the floor and ask to be recognized and then bring on this question of black and white unions. We tried to bring up the subject on the floor, and we were gaveled down. We were "out of order." They didn't want to hear it. We began to realize, "Well, you're not even going to get a voice in here. These old fogies, they're not going to let you say anything."

We had people who were deathly against it. Some of them were our best-loved people. Like our president at that time, Leo Davis—he was our opponent. Florence Cadrez, the recording secretary—she was against it. Paul Howard, our treasurer, was one of the most popular, most well-loved people in the world. I love him like a father today, but he was against it. We never could unseat those three people, no matter what.

Fortunately, they had elections every year. Nobody had ever opposed anybody down there, so we said, "Well, let's run for office. And if we get into office, then when we have a union meeting, then we'll get a chance to say what we want and let people say what they want." So that's the way it happened. I think we kind of caught those guys by surprise.

During this time Marl Young joined us. He was very knowledgeable in the ways of law. When they tried to find legalities and technicalities as the reason why we couldn't join the two unions, well then with Marl we got our books out and we'd study up on the bylaws, how to go about this. So then we knew what we were up to and what we were up against.

Then we had an organization and we started giving fund-raising parties at a place over on St. Andrews Place. Buddy Collette, John Ewing, and Jimmy Cheatham's place. We had little sessions and we'd sell booze, tickets, raised funds, to get a little money so that we could print pamphlets for the union election. Buddy was at the head of the ticket. I was running for vice-president, and we had several others. Well, the elections went down. I won the vice-presidency. But Buddy lost to Leo Davis, and whoever we ran against Florence Cadrez and Paul Howard, they lost. We did gain a majority on the board of directors. Benny Carter was on the board, and so was Marl Young, John Anderson, and I forget who else. We started to take control of those meetings, and we got ourselves heard. We finally had a real good turnout for a membership meeting. I was the one elected to get up and make the antidiscrimination speech. So we got them all riled up, and they went after it.

Naturally, with all of us working around with different musicians, there was also another faction of musicians working hard at Local 47 at the same time. Well, all those guys, you know, we all worked together, we mingled together, we had meetings together. Yeah, it was a combined effort of the black and the white musicians. So they're working on the membership over there. We've got to bring it to a vote in each local. And if the majority vote happens in each of the locals, well, then it has to happen.

Another election came around a year later. Trying to get the presidency, we ran Benny Carter. You know, like, how can Benny miss? [laughter] Buddy ran for the board and I ran for vice-president again. Buddy won, and I won, but Benny lost. [laughter] You couldn't move these guys! Everybody wants an amalgamation, but they all love these old leaders. Benny Carter got really riled up, pissed him off real bad. "Dumb so-and-sos, how can they vote against me?" So the next time we gave an event, a great big to-do at the Club Alabam, as the vote on amalgamation was coming up in both locals, Benny just called everybody he knew. He had every great singer, everybody of any renown. We had all of Jerry Fielding's entire orchestra. I don't know how many big bands, name artists. Nat King Cole appeared. All the big artists came down to appear on this one show, and they just packed this place. All of it to raise money for the amalgamation committee. So we made money and put out more pamphlets, bills, and whatnot.

Then people started playing dirty politics. They started to name many

of us as being "influenced," "communist-inspired." That was popular at
that time, to blacklist people. That was during the McCarthy days. So all
of a sudden we're getting this bad publicity. I'm a communist or Buddy's
a communist. Or "they're being led, they're communist-inspired, those
who want that." Even the people who are higher up in our local, they're
preaching this type of thing. And then, the people in Local 47, "Yeah,
that's what's wrong. That's what's stirring these poor young guys up." We
went out and got as much support as we could from everybody else. We
went to all of the black stars, entertainers, the baseball players, football
players. Then, we went to the NAACP, and they were scared to touch us.
To this day, I am not a member of the NAACP. I resigned my membership. I said, "Well, this is what we're supposed to be all about." But they
listened to all of the crap and got just a little bit nervous and a little bit
scared.

Finally, we won a majority vote in both locals for the amalgamation.
But now we faced the national union trying to block our way. In the
national bylaws there was a law that in places where there were two locals,
a black local and a white local, the white local would not be allowed to
take in a black musician, and vice versa. They were trying to use this
bylaw to block us. We decided that if they didn't go through with the
amalgamation, we were going to become more competitive against Local 47. We were going to start accepting white musicians into Local 767.
Marl Young and I called James C. Petrillo, president of the federation,
and told him. All the younger members coming in, we were going to
accept them. I think our initiation fee was $50 at that time, and 47's was
$100. So we said, "All the real good young musicians, white musicians
who are coming up, they want to get into the union, well, this is the place
to be. We'll take you." And they didn't mind because, hell, we had all the
damn stars belonging to our union. There were an awful lot of guys, the
jazz kids, white or Latino or whatever they happened to be, they were all
very anxious to join our local. And we made it clear to the federation.
There's no way in the world 47 didn't know it. And there was a faction in
47 that wanted the amalgamation. To this day, I almost wish that we had
gone the other way. [laughter] I think the whole scene would be interesting, to this day.

They finally decided they were going to go along with it. It was beginning to be a real unpopular thing. Petrillo said he was going to send

Herman Kenin, his right-hand man, out here to oversee our meeting. He sent us a telegram to that effect. We called Petrillo and told him, "Well, if he's coming out here, we'll let him attend the meeting, but we want him to keep his goddamn mouth shut." [laughter] "This is our fucking union, and we're going to do this thing." He said, "Well, this thing is a little bit too hot to handle right now." So he left us alone, and we brought the whole thing about.

We still had to draw up terms. We had to dispose of our property, and all of it goes into the 47 treasury, all of our assets. And then their death benefit was a little higher than ours. I think that it's always been $1,000, and I think ours was something like $600. So we agreed that, regardless of that, the members of 767 would maintain full death benefits. Also, that the years of seniority in 767 would be fully counted in Local 47. They wanted to designate certain offices in Local 47 for us. In other words, "Okay, you're over here, but now you'll be in control of the black population." But we wanted none of that. We said, "We depend upon you and your officers to represent us the way that we feel we will be represented, and if any of us ever aspires to become an officer in this new organization, we will run in the election like anybody else." We did not want to be singled out. We wanted to all be the same, no means of identification or anything else like that. We put all this down in our agreement. So we came over to Local 47 in 1953.

The pattern established in Los Angeles was followed by locals in other cities.

A lot of places all over the country, like Chicago and San Francisco, had two locals. So we were the beginning of a movement that was going to take place throughout the country. Our amalgamation was the first, and it's responsible for the fact that there is no more, or supposedly no more, discrimination of that sort within the American Federation of Musicians. We finally broke up that thing about separate locals for black and white throughout the federation. Other locals followed. They had to. We made it law.

But it wasn't the most popular thing in all of them, at least from my understanding. There are some locals, like in San Francisco, I think, that it's Local 10 plus something else, 300 and so-and-so, which means that there were two locals, and they're still identified by the fact that the two of them were put together. I also found out many years later that they allowed some locals a black delegate in the case of those who did not integrate voluntarily. In other words, all of the so-called amalgamations didn't happen exactly the same as ours did. But the main thing is we did get that wiped off of the national bylaws. We did away with that, and that was appropriate.

Of course, we still had to deal with problems after the amalgamation. We discovered, some time after the amalgamation, some things on the new file cards. You pull out Marl Young's card: Marl Young, such and such address, piano, and they would maybe underline *piano*. Then you might find Buddy Collette's card: underlined phone number. We noticed that if you found anything underlined, that means that was a black musician. We filed charges against the treasurer, who was in charge of membership and brought him up before the board. His whole thing was, "Well, I'm only trying to protect them." I got up and said, "Let me tell you one thing. I have been black all my life. I think I know more about how to protect me than you do."

And then I gave him an example. I once got a job in Oxnard with a trio. We've got Ronnie Ball—a white piano player, Ben Tucker on bass—he's black, and me on drums. We drove all the way out there, and we were walking in the club, bringing our stuff in, and the boss, a real screamer, sees us, "Oh, no! Oh, no! This can't happen. It's not me. I mean, it's the people I have coming in here, the customers. They cannot see this." I said, "Yes, sir, I understand perfectly. We can work it out like this, and we'll never go in the place. You know, I have a contract here. It says we're going to be here for two weeks. All you've got to do is just pay this thing off and we'll get the hell out of here." [laughter] Oh, man. You know, I'm just being very cooperative. "Well, I don't know. We'll just go on and give it a try, anyway." After that, we went in there, no problems. Next thing you know, we're sitting at tables drinking with the customers, and we had a complete ball for that thing. If it had been that treasurer's way, we would never have gotten a chance to go out there in the first place because he was going to protect us and see that we were never sent on jobs like that.

Thinking back on the amalgamation:

When we were fighting for the amalgamation, we got to a place where we could go in and do anything we wanted to. I wish we could have kept some of that. We could be out here fighting our own battles. Now, we got over here and we integrated. And what is integration? I don't know. It's like you take a bottle of chocolate milk and you mix it in with enough white milk, after a while, integration is an act of disappearing. [laughter] All of a sudden, "Oh, gee, we didn't know anybody over here was having any problems. We thought everything was okay." A lot of us were working with the white bands. But everybody wasn't. A few guys did get a show here and there, and they're not concerned about the guy who's not doing anything. In the union we're not really representing the people or getting a chance to represent them like we want to. There's a lot of activity going on, but there's still an awful lot of unrest. Things are not being done to sort of help the guys along.

Everybody's just making it the best way they can. And we do need to get a little bit of organization. Not a black movement or white movement, but just players in general to get together and then start to iron out the problems. We all need to sit down and talk about it. Maybe we'll get some ideas. Maybe somebody will come up with a direction that we should go.

12

Melba Liston

A *premier jazz trombonist and arranger, Melba Liston has performed with Quincy Jones, Dizzy Gillespie, and Gerald Wilson, and arranged for Count Basie, Duke Ellington, Johnny Griffin, Milt Jackson, and Abbey Lincoln, among others. Her long-standing collaboration with Randy Weston has produced six albums:* Blues to Africa, High Life, Little Niles, Spirits of Our Ancestors, Tanjah, *and* Volcano Blues.

Her credits include Mingus's Town Hall concert in 1962. During the 1950s, Melba relocated to New York and was continuously in the recording studios. She returned to Los Angeles in the 1960s and devoted most of her time to composing and arranging. In the late 1960s she began teaching and working with youth orchestras. She lived in Jamaica from 1973 to 1979, where she taught at the University of the West Indies and was the director of popular music studies at the Jamaica Institute of Music in Kingston.

A stroke forced her to give up playing, but she continues to compose and arrange, and is a frequent visitor to various venues around Los Angeles.

Born in 1926, Melba started playing piano as a youngster.

I was born in Kansas City, Missouri, but I was raised between Kansas City, Missouri, and Kansas City, Kansas. My grandparents were in Kansas, and my mother [Lucile Liston] was in Missouri. I got my trombone when I was seven years old. I was tall then, but I didn't reach to sixth and seventh position. I used to have to turn my head sideways. My mother wasn't around too much, because I was living mostly in Kansas. But my grandpa [John Prentiss Clark] used to take me out on the back porch and let me play for him. They admired music and listened to it all the time.

I was playing on the radio when I was eight years old. They heard me or something and said, "Come on," and I said, "Okay." It was piano and trombone or something like that, little solos.

I had a teacher, but he wasn't right. He was an old soul brother, and I realized that he was no good. I guess my mama found him somewhere. And he wasn't right. I don't know how I knew, but I knew. So I said no, canceled, and I just went on my own. I mean, I was always good in my ears, so I could play by ear. I didn't think of anything else.

Then I came out here in 1937. I was ten. My grandma and two daughters came out way before we did and set up housekeeping, and then we came out later. There was nothing in Kansas City for us, you know. Environment, work habits, everything. It was better here than in Kansas in those times.

I passed for the ninth grade, but they wouldn't put me in there because I was too young. But I was already past the sixth grade in Kansas. I was a good student. They finally put me in the eighth grade at McKinley Junior High School. My music teacher at McKinley was really nice. He rode home with me and asked my mother could he adopt me or something. I said, "No." I wanted to stay with my mom. He said he wanted to further my music. And he wanted to send me off to some teachers. He knew some people that would be better for me. But I didn't go. I just wanted to stay home with my mom.

We went to church all the time. Oh dear. I did like going. But I didn't like my horn at church.

Then Melba met Alma Hightower, a music teacher who was working with neighborhood kids in a local park near Jefferson High School on Forty-first Street. Alma Hightower was also the aunt of drummer Alton Redd.

She was an orchestra teacher, leading an orchestra. Fourteen or fifteen pieces. She played drums and piano. She would be in the playground from two o'clock to something or other, and then she would carry on with us when that was over. I started with her in, let's see, 1938 or something. Some of my friends, who were going to school with me, said "Come and meet Miss Hightower," and that was it. She was okay as a music teacher and I loved her. I would stay with her from time to time. She was all right.

It was boys and girls in the band. Predominantly boys. But also Alice Young, Minnie Moore, who was her daughter, Vi Redd, and me. And later more girls started joining, but I wasn't there. I know Lester Young's younger sister [Irma] joined the band when I wasn't there.

Our band went to Sacramento and played the fair there. And we worked all kinds of churches and everything.

Then I started at Jefferson High School, but I didn't remain there, because Miss Hightower, my teacher, sent me to Poly [Los Angeles Polytechnic High School]. She was down with the school, Poly, so I didn't question her. She was always Poly. And I liked my teachers there. My band and orchestra, harmony and those kinds of teachers were nice. It was just marvelous.

When I was sixteen, I joined the musicians union and I went and told her. She was adamant. She wasn't ready for me to join the union because the band hadn't joined the union at this time. Oh, she let me know. Anyway, I went on and did it. I had planned that all the time. I mean, you've got to work. You've got to join the union. That's that. So I filled out my application. I had my mother's signature. I had to get that. And that was it. And then I joined the band at the Lincoln Theatre, when I was seventeen. I was with her four years, five years, something like that.

I joined Bardu Ali's band at the Lincoln Theatre. There was one other girl in that band at the Lincoln. The piano player, Alice Young, that was with Miss Hightower, she came with the band for a while. But that was it. They would have a movie, and then the show would take over. It was a lot of girls, a lot of acts, Herb Jeffries and all of those people. Valaida Snow. She was an artist, a singer, and a trumpet player. I think it was one show a night on the weeknights and two shows on Saturday and three on Sunday. And the music changed once a week. Dusty Fletcher and Pigmeat Markham were there all the time. They had me up doing some stuff, too, now and then. Putting on the girls' costumes and singing on the stage.

We had the Sweethearts of Rhythm band at the Lincoln, all-girl band. They wanted to take me with them. I hid. [laughter] Oh, the other thing—oh, lordy. [laughter] Shit. When I heard that, boy, I had to run off and hide. Shit. I was riding with two of them and they got to carrying on—I mean, not carrying on with each other. And I said, "I'll be back," and I went and hid. Then I went and told my mother. [Bardu's] band had already let me go because I was going with the girls. But they didn't hire anybody, because they knew I was coming back. [laughter] So I went on back with the band. I didn't know anything about freaks or anything. Oh, dear. But there were some good girls in there, so that's all right. They couldn't solo and stuff as well as the boys, but they were good.

I was writing music by this time for different acts who would come in and didn't have their music. I mean, I didn't write for the band per se. I just wrote for the acts that came in. I didn't know whether it was exciting or not, because I had to do what I had to do, and I just went on and did it. You have to write, so you write. That's it.

At this time I wasn't attuned to all the things on Central Avenue. If the band was going to do something, well, I would do whatever they were doing. But other than that, I was just a homebody. When I joined Gerald [Wilson], then I got wind of Central and all of those things.

I was at the Lincoln about one year, I guess. And it was all right. I don't know what it was paying, a hundred and something a week. It was nice. Yeah.

On the Road

By 1944 trumpeter Gerald Wilson had left Jimmie Lunceford's band, settled in Los Angeles, and was organizing his first big band.

I moved right on to Gerald's band. I think he must have known something, because it was just a matter of "Be there at such and such a time." A few people from the band at the Lincoln went with his band, so it wasn't just me. The band was breaking up, because they didn't have any more shows in there.

Much of the music was Gerald's, and we rehearsed and rehearsed. And we traveled. We had hard times out there on the road. Once in a while we'd get stranded. But it was groovy then. We went to New York and played right behind Duke Ellington at the Apollo Theatre. We played the following week after he played. We did really good. Yeah. And all the time I didn't think about being the only female.

We also used to go to jam sessions on Central. It was nice. I mean, it was not profound or disheartening or anything. It was just nice. And it was a chance to see the other people whom you didn't see in your rounds. I didn't pick up on anything moral or amoral or something like that. No, it was nice to say hello to the people and all of those things. You don't get much musically from the jam sessions. I don't, anyway. You just happened to say hello and everything, that's all.

I was with Gerald about five years or so. Then Gerald and I went with Dizzy's band in '50 or so, and then we went to Lady Day [Billie Holiday]'s band. He put a band together for her. We went down South with her. That was something. But we got stranded down in South Carolina somewhere. I guess Lady didn't have any more gigs or something. And we were on the bus day and night. We finally made it to Kansas City and then sent for money from Los Angeles. It was two days getting to us. So we had a lot of oatmeal.

Then I quit the band and went to work for the Board of Education. I worked there for three years or so. I was just too disgusted, so for about two years I didn't do anything, and then I started getting back into it. I had little jobs in between I guess the third year or so, when I started leaving the Board of Ed.

And then Dizzy came out here, and I wrote a couple of charts for him, and he told me to get ready, because he was going to send for me when he got the new band. So I did.

I also worked a couple of movies for MGM. I played on the *Ten Commandments*. And that one with Lana Turner, *The Prodigal*, where I had a long thing with her. I followed her around and played the musical harp.

During her years on the road with the big bands, Melba was severely abused by several fellow musicians.

Rapes and everything. I've been going through that stuff for all my life. I'd just go to the doctor and tell him, and that was that. Anyway, that's not— I don't even want to hear about— I mean, I don't want to talk about that.

It was all right. When I started going with Gerald I was okay, because I had support. Then it was better because I had his support. So I didn't have to worry. But then I left in '55, and I went back to Dizzy's band, it was the same thing all over again. Yeah, well, you know, it's a broad, and she's by herself. That's that. But the older I got, the less it happened. [laughter] I don't know how old I was, but it stopped altogether.

Back Home

[The amalgamation] was going on, so I had to go along with it. It was good for getting us out of the place over there on Central Avenue. But it was bad for a lot of reasons, too. It was good and bad. The thing is, you've got no place in this white world. So that's the other side of it, you know.

[Central Avenue] got to be strange I guess around '49 or '50. I mean it just changed. You know. Whitey decided it was going to change, so it changed. Businesses failed and all of that. They moved west. Western Avenue did it for a while. It was trying. But it wasn't like Central.

I got a lot out of it. I can't remember all the things that I used to remember, but I was pretty thrilled about Central at the time. It was exhilarating or something. And it was a peak above. It was not ordinary. I'm sorry I don't remember, but it was all right. I don't expect anything to stay the same all over the world, but Central Avenue was great and that's that.

Marshal Royal, standing right, leads the band at the
U.S. Navy Pre-flight School at St. Mary's College,
Moraga, California, 1942. Other Central Avenue
musicians included: Andy Anderson, tenor sax
(front row, left); Jack Kelson, alto sax (front row,
third from left); Ralph Bledsoe, trombone (second
row, middle); Ernie Royal, trumpet (back row, left).
Among the other musicians was Jerome Richardson,
alto sax (front row, fourth from left). (Courtesy of
Jack Kelson)

William Green, Buddy Collette, Jack Kelson,
Al Aarons, Marshal Royal. Los Angeles, 1994.
(Photo by Ray Avery)

Drummer Lee Young in the
studio with trumpeter Gerald
Wilson, guitarist Irving Ashby,
bassist Red Callender, pianist
Phil Moore, circa 1944/45.
(Courtesy of Shades of L.A.,
Los Angeles Public Library)

Pianist Fletcher Smith with
drummer Henry Tucker Green
and bassist Chuck Hamilton,
circa 1960. (Courtesy of Lynn
and Gerry Wiggins)

William "Brother" Woodman, Jr.
(Courtesy of William Woodman, Jr.)

William "Brother" Woodman, Jr.
(Courtesy of William Woodman, Jr.)

Buddy Collette at the Jungle Room on
Central Avenue, 1947. (Courtesy of
Buddy Collette)

Britt Woodman at radio station
KLON's "Central Avenue Revisited"
concert, John Anson Ford Theater,
Hollywood, May 28, 1989. (Photo
by Steven Isoardi)

Josephine Baker addresses the audience and
musicians of the interracial orchestra in support
of the amalgamation of Local 767 and Local 47 of
the American Federation of Musicians. Humanist
Hall, circa 1950. On stage, left to right: Cliff
Holland, Buddy Collette, Eddie Beal, Vernon
Smith, Josephine Baker, George Kast. Leaning on
the stage, to the right: Seymour Sheklow, Jack
Trainor. (Courtesy of Buddy Collette)

Buddy Collette.
(Courtesy of Buddy Collette)

David Bryant, January 1995.
(Courtesy of David Bryant)

Big Jay McNeely at the Olympic Auditorium,
Los Angeles, October 6, 1951. (Courtesy of Big Jay
McNeely and Jim Dawson)

Big Jay and Bobby McNeely, somewhere in the Midwest, circa 1952. (Courtesy of Big Jay McNeely and Jim Dawson)

Big Jay McNeely at radio station KLON's "Central Avenue Revisited" concert, John Anson Ford Theater, Hollywood, May 28, 1989. (Photo by Steven Isoardi)

Lionel Hampton, standing left, and Joe Adams, standing right, parading past the Club Alabam on Central Avenue, circa 1940s. (Courtesy of Shades of L.A., Los Angeles Public Library)

MUSICIANS IN CONCERT JEFFERSON HIGH

The Second Annual concert, featuring the A Capella choir, the orchestra and band of the Jefferson High School, will be presented this coming Sunday at four o'clock at the Independent Church.

Warm reception last season resulted in the transformation of the event as annual, stated Band Director Samuel Brown, teacher at the Jefferson school.

X. L. Washington and Marie Salo are the students who will conduct the orchestra and band, respectively, it was announced. Edward White will be featured violinits and Miss Robert V. Edwards well known musician, will preside as guest organist.

A varied program will be presented. Special number will be Summertime from George Gershwin's Porgy and Bess, to be sung by the A Capella choir. Incidentally the entire opera, "Porgy and Bess" will be presented locally next month by the New York cast.

An address by Cyrus Keller, youngñ post graduate student at the Jefferson school, will be one of the highlights of the afternoon. Young Keller will speak on "Human Values in Music Education".

The program will commence promptly at 4 p. m., it was announced and admission is free.

TODAY'S GOOD DEED

Pretty Dolores Casey, who lost a Paramount contract when stricken with tuberculosis two years ago, found a part waiting for her in Major-Paramount's "Doctor Rhythm" when she was released from the hospital as cured. Bing Crosby, with whom she had worked in "Mississippi", had arranged it for her. And the part landed her another term contract with Paramount!

WRESTLER IN CHARACTER
Hans Steinke whom Cecil B. D-

WIELDS BATON

SAMUEL BROWN, young music professor, whose Jefferson High School music aggregation will be presented in concert Sunday.

Samuel Browne, Jefferson High School's innovative and inspirational music teacher, from the *California Eagle* newspaper, January 13, 1938.

The Al Adams Band with Jack Kelson and Buddy Collette on alto saxes, Elks Hall on Central Avenue, circa 1939. Left to right: Lady Will Carr, piano; vocalist (unknown); Al Adams, with baton; Clarence Pointdexter, guitar; Forest "Chico" Hamilton, drums; James Nelson, tenor sax; Crosby Lewis, trumpet; Jack Kelson, alto sax; Jack Trainor, trumpet; Buddy Collette, alto sax; Jake Porter, cornet; James Robinson, trombone; James Henry, trombone; Eddie Taylor, tenor sax. (Courtesy of Buddy Collette and Jack Kelson)

Jack Kelson with Harold Nicholas and Freda Payne
in *Sophisticated Ladies,* Long Beach, California, early
1990s. (Courtesy of Jack Kelson)

ll Douglass, 1941.
Courtesy of Deloris Douglass)

Bill Douglass.
(Courtesy of Deloris Douglass)

Melba Liston at the Salute to Dizzy Gillespie
concert in Los Angeles, June 12, 1996. (Photo
by Paula Ross)

Trombonist/arranger Melba Liston in Gerald
Wilson's first big band, debuting at Shepp's
Playhouse, Los Angeles, November 1944. Front
(standing): Gerald Wilson. First row, left to right:
Vernon Slater, Leo Trammell, Floyd Turnham,
Eddie Davis, Maurice Simon. Second row: Jimmy
Bunn (piano), Zeke Livingston, Melba Liston,
Robert Huerta. Third row: Henry Green (drums),
Robert Rudd (bass), Hobart Dotson, unknown,
James Anderson. (Courtesy of Gerald Wilson)

Art Farmer and Frank Morgan at radio station
KLON's "Central Avenue Revisited" concert, John
Anson Ford Theater, Hollywood, May 28, 1989.
(Photo by Steven Isoardi)

Jefferson High School Swing Band, summer 1950.
Samuel Browne (front row left); Frank Morgan, alto
sax (front row, fourth from left); Horace Tapscott,
trombone (middle row, second from left).

Horace Tapscott. (Courtesy of Horace Tapscott)

Gerald Wiggins with bassist Adolphus Allsbrook, possibly at the Cosmo Club, 1950s. (Photo by Howard Morehead)

Gerald Wilson leading his big band at the Elks Hall on Central Avenue, 1945. (Courtesy of Gerald Wilson)

Gerald Wilson on trumpet, with Buddy Collette,
Red Callender on bass, at the Pour House, La Jolla,
California, circa 1958. Seated in front is Archie
Moore, light heavyweight boxing champion.
(Courtesy of Buddy Collette)

Clora Bryant on stage at The Lighthouse, Hermosa Beach, California, 1950. Left to right: Sonny Criss, Art Pepper, Keith Williams, Clora Bryant, Howard Rumsey. The band also featured Hampton Hawes on piano and Shelly Manne on drums. (Courtesy of Clora Bryant)

Clora Bryant, 1959. (Courtesy of Clora Bryant)

Trumpeters Clora Bryant and Andy Blakeney
playing "When the Saints Go Marching In" at the
funeral of New Orleans pianist Alton Purnell.
Los Angeles, 1987. (Photo by Claire Rydell)

The Progressive Musicians Organization, which
ran jam sessions at the Crystal Tea Room near
Central Avenue, at the Crystal Tea Room, 1949.
Left to right: Bill Green, David Bryant, Jewell
Grant, Buddy Collette, Bobby McNeely, Clarence
"Tex" Thomas. (Courtesy of Buddy Collette)

Left to right: Bill Green, Jack Kelson, Lanny Hartley, Buddy Collette, 1992. (Photo by Guy Crowder)

Marl Young signing the document merging Local 767 and Local 47 of the American Federation of Musicians, March 1953. Seated, left to right: Maury Paul, secretary of Local 47; Marl Young, chairman of Local 767 Board of Trustees; Estelle Edson, secretary of Local 767. Standing: Leslie Bailey, executive director of the Los Angeles NAACP. (Courtesy of Marl Young)

Marl Young.
(Courtesy of Marl Young)

13

Art Farmer

rriving in Los Angeles in 1945 at the age of sixteen, trumpeter Art Farmer started playing professionally while attending Jefferson High School. He left Los Angeles in 1952 to join Lionel Hampton's band for a year of touring. In fall 1953 he settled in New York, forming a group with Gigi Gryce. He also played with Horace Silver, Gerry Mulligan, and Lester Young, among others. In 1959 he and Benny Golson formed the Jazztet, one of the definitive hard bop groups. A few years later Art teamed with guitarist Jim Hall to lead a memorable combo.

In the mid-1960s Art gradually abandoned the trumpet to play flugelhorn. In 1968 he moved to Vienna, married an Austrian, and they had two children. Art has toured the world and returns regularly to perform in the United States. He has appeared on dozens of albums, as sideman, bandleader, and co-leader.

Art and his twin brother, Addison, were born in Council Bluffs, Iowa, in August 1928. When they were four the family moved to Phoenix, Arizona. Art was attracted to music at an early age, and was studying piano by the time he was in elementary school. He studied and played violin and bass tuba before picking up the cornet at thirteen to play in the school band. Soon he was playing trumpet in a local band and met one of his idols, Roy Eldridge.

Artie Shaw's band came through on a one-nighter, and Roy Eldridge was working with him. I was playing in a little club, and he came by there, and he sat in on the drums first. Then he went to his room and got his horn and brought his horn back and played. Roy was a great person. The next night, at the dance hall, the Artie Shaw band played the first dance

261

from nine to one, and then our band played from like two to five, because there was a thing then called the swing shift, where there would be a dance held for the people who were working on what is called the swing shift at night—they would get off at midnight. So the guys from Artie Shaw's band, they stood around and listened to us.

When the bands came through, we would go to where they were staying and introduce ourselves and ask them if they would like to come by our house for a jam session. Some of them would, and they were very kind and gentle and helpful. There was never any kind of stuff about "Oh, we're tired and too busy" or something. They would come by.

There's a certain kind of community inside the jazz neighborhood, that's international. And there's a lot of mutual help going on. There always has been. This is what's kept the music alive until now, because it's been handed down from one person to the next. And as long as a young person would show that they were sincerely interested, nobody would say, "Hey, go to hell," you know, "I'm busy!" I never had that kind of experience with anyone. So these guys would come by the house and they would give us whatever help. If you knew what questions to ask, you would get the answers. A lot of time you didn't know the questions. But whatever you'd ask, they would help you.

When Art and his brother arrived in Los Angeles during the summer of 1945, Central Avenue was still booming with wartime prosperity.

Then when we were around the age of sixteen, we came to Los Angeles on a summer vacation, and there was so much musical activity here that we just decided to stay. We had one more year to go in high school, which was fortunate. And we just didn't want to go back to Phoenix, because we knew that we wanted to be professional musicians, and this was where it was happening. And the center of it was Central Avenue.

I can remember pretty well the first evening I went to Central Avenue. That block where the Downbeat and the Last Word and the Dunbar— all those places—are, that was the block. And it was crowded. A lot of people on the street. Almost like a promenade. [laughter] I saw all these people. I remember seeing Howard McGhee; he was standing there talking to some people. I saw Jimmy Rushing, because the Basie band was in town. And I said, "Wow!" I didn't really go into the Alabam, but I passed by there. I heard the big band sound coming out.

The other clubs were not large. They might hold maybe a hundred people at the most. And the stage might hold six, seven at the most. And they had a bar. There was no dancing in these little places. Just tables. Most clubs were like that. I think the first place I went into was the Downbeat. Howard McGhee was there with Teddy Edwards and another tenor player by the name of J. D. King. And Roy Porter was playing drums, and the bass player was named Bob Dingbod. It was crowded, so we just sort of walked in and stood around and stood up next to the wall.

As far as I know, that was the first organized band out here that was really playing bebop. Dizzy and Bird hadn't come out here at that time. I think Dizzy had been out here with other bands, but he and Bird hadn't come out with the quintet yet. Certainly people were playing bebop. We were playing it; we were trying to play it before Dizzy and Bird got here. It just sounded good to me. I didn't have to ask myself, "Gee, what is this? Do I like it or don't I like it?" because my mind was completely open at that time.

This time was the beginning of the bebop era, but it was also the beginning of the rock era in a certain sense, rock-pop, instrumentally. Across the street from the Downbeat was a place called the Last Word. I went in and listened to Jack McVea, who had more of a sort of a jump band entertainment type of thing, which wasn't as interesting to me as what was happening with Howard's group. There was a guy in Los Angeles by the name of Joe Liggins. He had a group called Joe Liggins and the Honeydrippers. I guess you might call this like a jump band. Well, they had this very popular record called "The Honeydripper," and it was very, very simple music. It didn't have any of the harmonic complexity that bebop had to it, but it was very popular. So while the bebop thing was going in one direction, which was musically complex and had some quality to it, I would say this other thing was going in a completely different direction. Very simple. The average person could get something out of it without any effort. So that's where things started going in a different direction.

Well, that kind of music didn't have any interest to me. Not at all. My attraction to music basically was the swing era with the big bands—Jimmie Lunceford and Count Basie and Duke Ellington—and that was a high level of music to me. It had a lot of things going on. And things like "The Honeydripper" was just completely watered down. It's like TV; it's watered down to the lowest common denominator, something that's made for idiots, you know, for morons. That's what the whole pop music has become.

But the music I liked was more complex. The big band music had a lot of depth and profundity to it to me. So it was a natural movement from big band to bebop as far as I was concerned. It really pleased me. Plus the fact that at the end of the war, big bands started fading away. And one of the reasons was the music became too complex for the audience, for one thing. The economic situation was against it—the cost of moving a band around the country. Plus the fact that the record companies and the promoters thought that they could make as much money with five pieces as they could make with sixteen or seventeen. So the big bands faded away. And in order to stay in music, you have to be able to work in the small group. To work in a small group, you had to be able to play a decent solo. My first ambition was just to be a member of that sound in a big band. I would have been very happy just to be a second or third or fourth or first trumpet player, whatever. At that particular time, I would say it was beyond my dreams that I would ever become a soloist.

And there were a lot of people our age hanging around. One thing led to another; we would meet guys. But that was the heart of it right there.

Jefferson High—"A whole new world."

When school opened, we went over to Jefferson High School and enrolled. Jeff to us was a great school, because we had gone to the schools in Arizona, which were totally segregated then and very limited, which I never will be able to overcome. Because I wanted to study music. There was nobody there that could teach me. I never had a trumpet lesson. I developed bad habits. And when you develop bad habits at an early age, and playing the trumpet is a physical thing, it's hard to overcome that. Like pushing the horn into my mouth, you know, pressure and all, when your teeth get loose and you get holes and sores on your lips. Well, I had to pay for that later on.

So we came over here and it was a whole new world, this big school with all kinds of white people, black people, Chinese, Mexican. Everybody was in this school. They had classes where you could study harmony. They had this big band. You could sign up for the big band and go in there and learn how to play with other people. It was just completely different for us. And you'd meet people your age who were trying to do the same thing, and we would exchange ideas, of course. So it was great.

And Samuel Browne was a nice guy. He was really ahead of his time in training kids to be musicians. To my knowledge, this was the only school in the country that had a high school swing band, and that was part of the curriculum. Well, see, this kind of music wasn't regarded as serious music in the education system. But at Jeff maybe a couple of hours a day were spent on music at school. I remember big band and harmony—I would say harmony and theory. But other guys were studying arranging, also. Some of the students were making arrangements for the big band. You know, guys who had been there for a year or so in front of us—they were at the level then that they could write arrangements for the big band. And they could hear their stuff played then. We also not only learned to play in that type of a setting, but we would have exposure to audiences also, because we would go around to other schools in this area and play concerts. So they were really at least thirty years ahead of the rest of the United States.

Sam Browne was a very quiet person. He kept order by his personality. He never had to shout at anyone. He never had to say, "Do this or do that" and you didn't do this and you didn't do that. Somehow you just felt that you should do it. Otherwise you just felt that you were in the wrong place. This was a serious thing. And everyone who was there really wanted to work. They wanted to play music, otherwise they wouldn't be there. You know, he loved music, and he wanted to help kids.

And he would bring other people. If somebody came into the town that he knew, he would go around and tell them to come around and talk to the kids. He would get the people to come around and play what we'd call an assembly for the whole student body and then talk to the band. Leave themselves open. You could ask them any questions that would come to your mind.

Art was also surrounded by many students just as interested in music as he was, and in some cases just as talented.

Sonny Criss was there. Ernie Andrews, the singer, was there. There was a drummer by the name of Ed Thigpen, who was the year under us.

There was a tenor player named Hadley Caliman, who is now a teacher at a conservatory up in Seattle, Washington. Another tenor player by the name of Joe Howard. I don't know what happened—I think he's dead now—but he was writing very nice arrangements by then. Alto saxophone player named James Robinson. We called him "Sweet Pea." He was a very good player. He's not alive any more, either.

You know, meeting these guys and exchanging ideas was just a great thing. Big Jay McNeely was there. I think he was in the class in front of us. But I was in the harmony class with him. And my memory is not so clear, but somehow the story is there that he asked the teacher, "Well, how much money do you make?" And the teacher told him. And he said, "Well, I already make more money than you. How do you think you can teach me anything?" But he had his little group, and he was working around town. The scale was sixty dollars a week, you know, for a sideman. Sixty dollars. And that was big money. So he was getting that much, because the union was strong then.

When we first got here we took what jobs we could get. I remember having a job in a cold storage plant. [laughter] Stacking crates of fruit and vegetables. We were kids, you know; we didn't take anything seriously. A lot of the time we didn't have any money, and we got thrown out of rooms and things. We got fired from that job because we started throwing these potatoes at each other. [laughter]

Art was soon playing in regular bands at night, while attending Jefferson during the day. Word quickly got around about the young trumpeter.

The worst thing I remember was hanging out all night. Of course, the clubs would close around one or two o'clock, and then the first class in the morning was physical ed. And I remember the lowest thing to me was trying to climb a rope.

A lot of good players were still in the army, and there were still some big bands around getting some shows. I think the first job that I got in Los Angeles was with Horace Henderson, Fletcher's brother. I don't remember how I met him. I think that he came by Jeff one day, and I was out on the playground.

He said, "Come over here."

I walked over there, and he said, "You're Arthur Farmer?"

"Yeah."

"Well, I got a band. I need a trumpet player." I don't know how that happened. I got some work with him. And one thing leads to another, and I would work with Floyd Ray.

It wasn't that easy, because sometimes we would work and wouldn't get paid, you know. Things started getting weird. I remember I went down to San Diego with Horace Henderson and didn't get paid. And I remember working somewhere around here with Floyd Ray and didn't get paid. That would happen sometimes. Club owners skipped out, or the people who would put on the dance, they skipped out. That was part of the business, and it still is. But it didn't take much to stay alive. Rent was very cheap, you know, and food was cheap. If you could get a gig every now and then, you could make it—if you didn't have any habits. We were too young to have any bad habits. [laughter]

Sometimes I had to go out of town for a week or two. Well, my brother and I, we were living by ourselves. So when we couldn't go to school, we would just write our own excuses. I'd say, "Please excuse my boy today because he has to do such-and-such a thing." And sign it "Mrs. Hazel Farmer," you know. Because the school didn't know we were living by ourselves.

When I got an offer to go on the road with the Johnny Otis band, the school year wasn't out yet. And my mother had told me I've got to get that diploma. So I went to the principal and I told him. I said, "Look, I have this chance to go on the road with this band. This is the beginning of my career, and I really don't want to lose it. I really need this. If my work has been okay, I would like to be able to get my diploma. I would like you to please consider this and write a letter to my mother to that effect." And the guy was nice enough to do it. And I said, "Would you put that diploma in the safe just in case you're no longer here?" I came out here with Gerry Mulligan's group around '58. This was in '46 when I left. I came back in '58, and that diploma was in the safe, and I went over there and got it.

Johnny Otis had a big band that was sort of styled after the Count Basie band. They had been working at the Club Alabam for some time. But when they got ready to go on the road, some of the guys didn't want to leave, so that left an opening in the trumpet section. He sounded me and asked me did I want to go, and I said certainly. So that was my first chance to go back east.

Charlie Parker—
"He was out here just like everybody else."

I met Charlie Parker and Miles Davis when they first came out here. I actually met Miles at the union, 767. And he said, "Yeah, I came out here with Benny Carter's band because I knew Charlie Parker came out here, and I'd go any place where Charlie Parker was, because you can learn so much. I would go to Africa." Well, our image of Africa at that time was people with bones in their nose, you know. Nobody would have thought about going to Africa. He said, "I would go to Africa if Charlie Parker was there because you could learn so much."

I met Charlie Parker at Gene Montgomery's house. He was a tenor player and was a close friend of Teddy Edwards. He used to run the Sunday afternoon matinee jam sessions at the Downbeat on Central Avenue, and he was what we would call the session master. The club would hire one man to coordinate the session, to see that there weren't too many guys on the stand at one time, and keep things moving along.

On the way home from school, well, we just got in the habit of stopping by his house. And I met Charlie Parker over there. He was a very nice, approachable person. To me he was not really a monster at all; he was just a nice guy. Well, my brother and I, we had a sort of a large room on Fifty-fifth and Avalon, and eventually Charlie Parker was over there staying with us sometimes. We had two twin beds and a couch, so he was sleeping on the couch.

We would walk the streets on Central Avenue. One night we went up to Lovejoy's. He always had his horn with him. There was one guy playing the piano, playing music that would fit the silent movies—stride music, or stride piano and stuff. And he just took out his horn and started playing. After that, we were walking back to the house, and I told him, "Hey, you really surprised me playing with somebody like that," because Charlie Parker was regarded as the god of the future. And he's playing with this guy, who's just an amateur. He said, "Well, if you're trying to do something, you take advantage of any occasion. Go ahead, ignore that other stuff. That doesn't mean anything. You have to concentrate on what you're trying to put together yourself." So I always kept that in my mind.

And none of us had any money. My brother was working sometimes because the bass players would get more work than trumpet players, you know, because many little places would have a trio. Sometimes Charlie Parker would say, "Loan me five dollars" or "Loan me ten dollars. I'll pay you back tomorrow." He always paid him back. Always. He developed a reputation of being a sort of a swindler, borrowing money and never paying people and all sorts of negative things like that. But that never happened.

And I remember one night we were walking on Central Avenue to go to one of those movie theaters. Well, you wait until the last feature had already started and then go to the doorman and say, "Hey, man, we don't have any money. Why don't you let us in to see the end of the movie?" [laughter] It worked sometimes. [laughter] So there was the great Charlie Parker, who didn't have enough money to buy a ticket to go in a movie. But he was a human being, you know. He was out here just like everybody else.

Charlie Parker was supposed to be a drug addict. Well, at that time he didn't have any drugs, and he was in pretty bad shape. I remember one night there was an incident, and he was about to have a nervous breakdown. We were on the second floor. There was a French window from the ceiling to the floor, and he opened it up, and he was standing there like he was going to jump out. And before that he'd been taking off, putting on his clothes, and taking them off and putting them on, taking them off. He was just going off. So I took him out of the window and I said, "Let's go for a walk." So he put on his clothes and we went right across the street. It was Avalon Park. We went and walked in the park. And he had a bad cold, like his lungs were falling apart. I said, "You ought to do something about this." He said, "Not a goddamn thing!" I mean, he was really down. We took him back to the room, and he finally went to bed. But he was having a hard time. He was starting to come apart, because he had nervous tics. His nerves were really shot. I guess it was just stress from the withdrawal, because he didn't have any drugs at that time. And he wasn't working. No money. At that time, in the forties, he was the first guy that I heard of that had a narcotics habit. Of all the younger guys I knew, nobody was into hard drugs.

In late 1945 Bird and Dizzy Gillespie arrived in town for a long engagement at Billy Berg's club in Hollywood. It was their first foray to the West Coast and opening night attracted a large crowd; but when the turnout fell, Berg canceled the rest of the gig.

Yeah, I was there the first night. It was crowded at the opening, but then it kind of fell off, because the music was too far advanced for the general audience. And Billy Berg's had two other acts there also—Slim Gaillard and a guy named Harry "The Hipster" Gibson. And they were very, very entertaining. Billy Berg decided to give this new thing a chance, but when he saw the audience reaction, well, I think that he actually cut the engagement short a couple of weeks. So Dizzy went back east and Charlie Parker stayed out here.

I remember one time, Howard McGhee was part owner of a place called the Finale Club in the Little Tokyo area. Howard McGhee worked there with his band, and Charlie Parker worked there one time with his own group, which Miles was in. Miles was working with Benny Carter and Charlie Parker. Benny Carter had a job at some dance hall or something. So there was a lady working for a weekly black newspaper called the *Los Angeles Sentinel,* I think. And she came and checked out the group and wrote a review in the paper, and was very negative. She said, "This group has this saxophone player who carries himself with the air of a prophet, but really not that much is happening. And he's got a little wispy black boy playing the trumpet who doesn't quite make it," you know. [laughter] "It has a moon-faced bass player with an indefatigable arm," speaking about my brother. She didn't have anything good to say about anybody.

Well, I saw that paper, and I went over to where Bird was staying at Gene's house and said, "Hey man, wake up!" [laughter] I said, "Wake up, man! You have to read what this bitch is saying about you, man!" He's still laying in bed. [laughter] Well, we couldn't get him to move unless you gave him a joint. You'd have to baby him. Anyway, he read this and said, "Well, she's probably all right. Just the wrong people got to her first." And then he got kind of in a self-pitying mood and he said, "Well, Dizzy left me out here, and I'm catching it." You know, "Dizzy got away, but he left me out here, and I'm catching this from everybody." That really brought him down, because he didn't see nothing strange about his music. His music was very melodic. And for somebody to say something like that— You know, he was proud to get good reviews. He liked that and would send the reviews to his mother.

Almost 99 percent of the younger guys really loved this new music. The disagreement came with the older guys, some of the older guys, who were more firmly entrenched in the swing era, and they just couldn't see anything else happening. But bebop was an outgrowth of big band, because all those guys had worked with big bands and they went into bebop because they were able to play more. It presented more of a challenge to them. If you played in a big band, you didn't get that much chance to really play. You jumped up every now and then and played a short solo. But if you were working with a small group, well, you had much more time to play, and you could play different kinds of tunes that were more challenging. There was more flexibility than in a big band.

So let's see. That was my introduction to bebop. So when I got this offer to go back east with Johnny Otis, I think Bird was already in the institution [Camarillo State Hospital], or else he went in shortly after that. And the next time I saw him was when he first came back to New York City. Someone had fixed a job for him, a one-nighter up at a place called Small's Paradise in Harlem. So I went by to see him. He said, "Hey, Arthur Farmer, we're in New York, man. You can get anything you want in New York!" [laughter] He was so happy to be out of California. [laughter]

Jam Sessions and Gigs on Central

After a few months on the road with Johnny Otis, Art returned to Los Angeles.

But there were sessions, jam sessions, on Central Avenue. The Downbeat and Last Word. Monday night was the off night, so there was always a session on Monday night in these clubs. Then the after-hours clubs— Lovejoy's was an after-hours club. And then there was a place called Jack's Basket Room, which was farther north. That was a big session place. And farther north from that, there was a little place called the Gaiety. That became the Jungle Room. We'd go from club to club.

These jam sessions were a great part of life, because that's the way you learn. They were well attended and the music was still a part of the ordinary people's community. People would come into the jam session. They liked music. You'd go into the restaurant and you'd have a jukebox there. There would be bebop tunes and tunes by swing bands and things. So we still hadn't reached that gap where the general audience sort of lost interest. So it was a different thing, because now the average person doesn't know anything about jazz at all, or they know very little. They go to a place like the Playboy Jazz Festival at the Hollywood Bowl for the spectacle. I played one in New York at a place called Randall's Island years ago. Every attraction was given a bulletin about what to do and what not to do. It said, "No ballads." [laughter]

In the late 1940s, the Los Angeles police increased their presence on Central.

The police started really becoming a problem. I remember, you would walk down the street, and every time they'd see you, they would stop you and search you. I remember one night me and someone else were walking from the Downbeat area up north to Jack's Basket Room or the Gaiety or some other place like that, and we got stopped two times. And the third time some cops on foot stopped us, and I said, "Hey, look, you guys are going the same way. Do you mind if we walk with you?" [laughter] We'd been stopped so many times we were getting later and later. So they said, "Okay." But we didn't have anything. It would be insane to be carrying some stuff on you on Central Avenue, because you'd get in trouble. You could get put in jail. You didn't have any money for a lawyer. If you had one marijuana cigarette, you could get ninety days. And if you had one mark on your arm, you'd be called a vagrant addict. Ninety days. The police were very obnoxious around there.

I remember working at a place, somewhere in the Fifties on Main or Broadway, some years later, in the late 1940s or early 1950s. It was a nice club, what we would call black and tan, because black people and white people went there too. I was working with a band that was led by Teddy Edwards. People went in there, and we could have stayed there a long time, but then the manager said we had to go, because the police said that they didn't want this racial mixing there, and if the club didn't change its policy there was going to be trouble.

This mixing thing, this thing about white women and black men, was really a hard issue. When the war came, all the people from the South came in, and they brought their racial prejudices with them. And that's why we've had the problems here.

And then there was a lot of prostitution going on. There were some cases where black men were pimps, and the white women were prostitutes. And the police, they would rather kill somebody than see that happen. And every time they saw an interracial couple, that's what they thought was going on, which was not the case. As far as they were concerned, the only thing they saw anytime they saw any interracial thing going on was crime. This was a crime. If it wasn't a crime on the books, it was still a crime as far as they were concerned. So their main worry was this interracial mixing, because it was a crime leading to prostitution and narcotics.

They weren't worried that much about robbery, because that wasn't the problem then, because people were working. The economic picture was better then than it is now. The people had a chance to get a job. And more people had what we call the work ethic. People would rather get a job that they were overqualified for than not to work at all. The members of the black community then felt more that it was a disgrace not to have a job.

Then everybody had a job, everybody was working, and if they were working they figured that they should be able to enjoy the fruits of their labor, and that would include entertainment. There were no TVs. The clubs were thriving. Johnny Otis's band would go into the Alabam and stay there for months. [laughter] At Joe Morris's Plantation Club in Watts, well, Count Basie would come out, and Billy Eckstine would come out. And they were supported by the community. Some white people would come in, but the white people were not enough to keep this going. They were really the fringe. It was the black audiences that supported these places.

Another important influence on Art was Roy Porter's big band. Porter also appeared on Charlie Parker's sessions for Dial Records in Los Angeles.

The Roy Porter band was important to us, to the younger guys. Roy Porter was the drummer who had played with Howard McGhee when I first heard Howard McGhee on Central Avenue at the Downbeat. Then later on Howard McGhee went back east again, and Roy Porter organized a big band. The members were younger guys like myself, mostly. A lot of us had gone to Jeff. Eric Dolphy was in the band. There were other good players. So that was like a training ground. The charts were patterned after Dizzy Gillespie's big band. By then Dizzy had come out to California with his big band, and that was the next earthquake. [laughter] Well, some of the kids that had gone to Jeff, who learned how to write arrangements at Jeff, were writing arrangements for this big band. We made some recordings for a company called Savoy Records. They're out now in an album called something like "Black Jazz in California."

Eric Dolphy was a prince. You know, he was an angel. He really lived for music. He lived for music, and he loved music. Twenty-four hours wasn't long enough for him. Eric was always a very enthusiastic guy, but he was 100 percent about music. He was a nice, nice, friendly, warm person, but he just loved to play. During that time I didn't feel it was necessary to spend all that time playing. I figured it would just come naturally. [laughter] I figured if I spent a couple of hours on it, why, heck, that's great. Somebody like Eric would practice all day long. All day.

At that time he was very much under the influence of Charlie Parker, as all the young guys were. Then later on, when he went back east, I think he got involved with Charles Mingus, and I think Mingus broadened his boundaries. It wasn't that he stopped loving Charlie Parker, but he started being interested in more of a less-structured type of music thing. He used to imitate the sounds of birds and things on his horn, on his flute. He'd listen to bird calls and play them, do things like that. Then he got hooked up with John Coltrane, and John Coltrane was the same way. It was like his wife said: he was 95 percent saxophone. They were really kindred spirits.

Charles Mingus, a graduate of Jordan High School in Watts, had been a mainstay on the Avenue until he left for New York in the late 1940s.

I never played with him in California, but I knew him. That was the first bass player that I heard of when I got here. They said, "Yeah, there's a guy here named Charlie Mingus. He's got a bad temper, too." [laughter] "Last week he took his bass stand and chased the vocalist off the stage with it." That was the first I heard of him. He didn't like the way she was singing. [laughter] He was a bad boy. [laughter] So nobody messed with Charles Mingus. Everybody was afraid of Mingus.

When I got to New York, I started playing with Mingus. I developed a reputation of being able to play anything that anybody put in front of me. So there was a certain group of guys back there who were getting into very difficult music. They were stretching out, venturing into areas where it wasn't just ordinary jazz. That's how I happened to have hooked up with Mingus out there, because that's the way his music was. You just couldn't play it the way you played everything else. You really had to work with it. You had to have the time to give it.

I remember one night he came into a place where I was playing. He had this fearsome reputation. And he was sitting in this club, and he hollered up to the stage, "Hey, Art Farmer, play a C scale!" And I'd say, "Oh, man." I didn't want to get any stuff. And I hollered back down, "I really don't know how you want it played." I got out of it some way. And then I found out later that he had told some people there with him, he said, "This guy here, he can play a C scale and make it into music."

Nights on the Avenue — "It was like the Wild West."

When rhythm and blues began to attract a large appreciative audience, some jazz players, including Big Jay McNeely, made the transition from bop to r&b.

I remember one night I was in the Downbeat, and Big Jay McNeely was working across the street at the Last Word. He came out in the street with his horn and came all the way across Central Avenue and walked into the Downbeat with his horn, playing it, honking, whooping and hollering. [laughter] And the owner, a little bald-headed guy, he must have been about seventy years old. I think he was an immigrant, European Jewish guy, with a heavy accent. He said, "Get the horn! Get the horn! Someone get the horn!" [laughter] It was like the Wild West. [laughter] That was the funniest thing. [laughter] Because the Downbeat was the bebop club that night, and this guy—he was like the enemy!

Well, Jay, part of his act was complete, total abandon. It was like somebody who had become completely possessed by the music. He throws off his coat and throws that down, then he jumps on his back, and he's playing the horn, he puts his legs up in the air, and he's playing all the time. So there was a place called the Olympia Theatre where he would play on Saturday night, a midnight show. I'm working with Dexter Gordon and Wardell Gray. They had a band—and these are highly respected jazz stars, and I was working with that band. We got a job there one Saturday night, and we figured, "Well, gee, this is a step up." [laughter] Dexter decides that he's going to pull a Big Jay. So he's up there, and he's playing his thing, and all of a sudden he starts to come out of his coat, and Wardell had to help him out with the coat. Wardell takes the coat and very civilly takes it and folds it and puts it on his arm. There's Dexter, and he's honking à la Big Jay, and he finally gets down on his knees à la Big Jay. And then the people in the audience, these kids, these teenagers, are looking up there like, "Gee, when is he going to do something?" He stayed down there so long like that. He stayed down there on his knees like he's praying, like he didn't know what to do then. So he finally got up off his knees, and the show went on. But that Big Jay, he was something else.

Earlier, Big Jay and Sonny Criss, the alto player, had a bebop quintet together. And he was getting gigs. But then his brother came back from the army and told him that he was going in the wrong direction. He said he wouldn't be able to make a quarter playing that. With Big Jay it was either one thing completely. Because when he was playing bebop, it was extreme. It was either everything had to be the hippest or the most corny with him. We called him "bebop" because everything he played sounded like bebop, like he didn't give a damn about any other aspect of music than that. So he changed. He made a radical change.

But Sonny was strictly a jazz player. The trouble with Sonny is that he never really studied. He took some lessons from Buddy Collette, but he never really learned how to read that well. He never learned how to read good enough to play with the big bands and things like that. He said, "I shouldn't have to do that. I'm a jazz player." So that just closed down a lot of possibilities, because if you play jazz, well, a lot of your income is going to be from making records. And you go into a studio, you have to be able to play whatever is thrown in front of you. If they call you one time and if you hold up the thing, they're not going to call you anymore regardless of how great a solo you play. And then most saxophone players double. They play flute or clarinet or something. He said, "Well, I'm an alto saxophone player." So he didn't get as far as he should have.

As a teenager, Frank Morgan was an extremely promising saxophonist. Unfortunately, his drug addiction led to his first prison term in the mid-1950s. Not until the 1980s was he able to realize his full potential.

I first met Frank Morgan in the late forties, and I guess Central Avenue was on its way down, but there were still some things happening then. Frank was about sixteen years old. Frank went to Jeff also. We were quite close. But then, when I left here in '52 with Lionel Hampton, after then, well, he started getting involved with narcotics and really got too deep into it, and spent a lot of time in prison.

But the tragedy is that a lot of guys didn't survive this narcotics thing. Too many. Between narcotics and the prejudice thing and I don't know what— The prejudice thing might have led to the narcotics in some cases, just feeling like the avenues are blocked anyway, so we might as well get high. Guys spent years and years in prison, and then they're just out of the music thing completely. Or else they take an overdose and they're dead. So a lot of guys didn't survive. Of the students who went to Jeff in Samuel Browne's band, when they left there a lot of them got hooked on narcotics, and they just fell by the wayside. Talented people.

But the narcotics killed white people, too, some talented white people. For instance, there was a saxophone player named Art Pepper. I used to make gigs with Art sometimes. We'd work in Latin bands around Los Angeles sometimes, playing montunos and things. Well, he got hung up in narcotics. It was sad because he said, "I'm a junkie, and I'll be a junkie till I die." You know, that's it. That's the reality. And Chet Baker is another one, too. I met Chet and guys like that coming into this part of town to participate in jam sessions.

It was a scourge. They'd get hooked, and they'd get arrested by the police. You go to jail, you come out, you have a record, and if the police want a promotion, then they arrest other people. They know who to come to. Like if they want to put another star behind their name, they look down the list and say, "Oh, here's so-and-so. He's been arrested before. Well, we'll go see what he's doing." Sometimes they might even manufacture some evidence, because you already have the record. If you go before the judge and you've already been arrested for narcotics and the police say, "Well, we found such and such a thing in his pocket," the judge is going to believe the police before he believes the criminal who has this record of being a narcotics offender. So guys started going in and out of jails. And the next thing they know, it's all over, because the music is highly competitive, and you have to be able to do what you're supposed to do. It's hard enough then, you know. But if you lose a year here and a year there, it's just impossible.

So Frank—I give him credit for at least being able to survive somehow, because he was a rare one from California. He's not without scars from all the stuff he's been through. It's changed him. He's not the sixteen-year-old kid that I used to know. After you spend some years in San Quentin, you develop something else. He's hardened. He has hardened a lot, which I guess you'd have to do in order to survive. But he still plays very well.

Union Musician—
"We figured that's part of being a professional musician."

I joined the union in Phoenix first, and I even had a problem getting in there because of race. When me and my brother and other guys had this little band and we were getting jobs, well, we decided we wanted to be in the union. We figured that's part of being a professional musician. So we went there and told them we wanted to be in the union, and they said no. There were no blacks in the union. So we wrote to the headquarters in Chicago. That's where Caesar Petrillo's office was. They said they have to let us join the union. So we joined the union in Phoenix, because the federation told the local that they had to let us in if we were qualified. So we got in.

When we came over here, we transferred to Local 767. The first time I heard Gerald Wilson was at the union. They had this house and the rooms on the second floor were used for rehearsal rooms.

By the late 1940s the amalgamation movement had begun.

Certainly I was supporting it. Everybody from a certain age group was, certainly. They didn't see any reason not to support it. Because it was a matter of territory, also. You see, Local 47 had the larger part of Los Angeles. There were certain territories that were allotted to each local. And we figured if we were all in the same local, then we would be able to play anyplace in town. And this whole studio thing, like the movie studios—that was Local 47 territory. In order to work in the studio, you were supposed to be a member of Local 47. But if you were black, then you had to be in Local 767. The white people could come and work on Central Avenue, but the blacks had trouble coming to work in Hollywood. They could work in some places, but there would have to be some kind of special dispensation to work like at Billy Berg's or a place like the Swing Club.

The Legacy of Central

I stayed in Los Angeles until '52, when I left with Lionel Hampton. So during that time, that's when Central went into history. I remember the Alabam was still going, and I heard Josephine Baker there one time. Sweets Edison was the musical director of her show. That was probably one of the last big events at the Club Alabam—that I was aware of, anyway. And things were just thinning out generally. I was working with Gerald Wilson or Benny Carter or whoever had a job. Dexter Gordon or Wardell Gray or Sonny Criss, Frank Morgan—people like that. You see, the downfall of Central Avenue was more than anything else economics. When the war ended, people didn't have money to be going out into clubs. Then television came into being and they would go home and watch TV. The attendance at these clubs became sparse and they eventually had to close.

Also there was a migration from the Eastside to the Westside. We would call Central Avenue the Eastside. The people who had work and had some kind of equity and property in that part of Los Angeles, they made a step up the ladder and moved to the west of Los Angeles, say, around Western Avenue or Normandie, places in that part of town. And what was left on the Eastside were people who didn't have the money to move. People were able to buy houses in what had until then been exclusively white neighborhoods. There were a few key cases that opened the thing up. There was something out here called restrictive covenants that were eventually beaten. So people were able to buy in other neighborhoods. And they got out of that neighborhood.

Then there were some clubs opening up over there on the Westside, like there was a place called the Oasis on Western Avenue and some other smaller clubs. It was nothing like Central Avenue, because Central Avenue was more compact. That's where everything was going on. The real center was located around where the Alabam and the Dunbar Hotel and the Downbeat were. Yeah, that was the real center. But then after that, as Los Angeles is, you have one place here and another place thirty miles over there, so there's nothing like Central Avenue.

Central Avenue was the neighborhood where I could go and hear people play and meet people. On Central Avenue, Count Basie and Duke Ellington were more accessible. They were part of the neighborhood. I got to meet people and got to hear them play, and I could go there any night, stand around and listen, and see what was going on. It was a matter of getting experience. And you could get that on Central Avenue more than you could get it anyplace else. Central Avenue was the main thing for Los Angeles. After you left Los Angeles, you had a long way to go to Chicago or New York City. By the time you got there, you were really supposed to be ready. But here you could start off.

I think Central Avenue was important also to groups that were really not regarded as jazz groups—like Roy Milton, blues groups, things like that—because they had a lot of work. I wouldn't want to give the impression that Central Avenue was just a jazz place, because it really wasn't. You had Roy Milton and Pee Wee Crayton and T-Bone Walker and Ivory Joe Hunter, Big Joe Turner. And they were much more successful than the jazz was, without a doubt. [laughter] This was their happy hunting ground. [laughter] But you see, groups like that had jazz players playing with them. That was certainly a big part of the street.

My final thoughts are kind of sad, because when you go there now, I feel like I'm stepping into a graveyard. It's very emotional to see something that played such a large part in your life, and now there's nothing left there. Nothing would give you the impression that this place had ever been anything other than what it is right now. And you have to stop and ask yourself, Well, is it all an illusion? Is it all an illusion? And that's the big question. You know, I'm sixty-three years old, and when I first went there I was, say, sixteen or something like that, and what happened then at that age has influenced me until now. But if I look at that street now, what could have influenced me? What was there? There's nothing there that would influence anybody now. Nothing at all. Not one brick. I mean, there's no sign of anything ever happening of any value or importance to anyone in the world.

It's a loss, because the kids come up and they don't have any idea. All they know is crack and shoot somebody, that kind of stuff. Basketball. Basketball is okay, but there's more to life than basketball. You know, everybody can't be six, seven feet tall and make a million dollars playing basketball.

So the kids come up, and their role models are so limited that they don't see any alternative to what's before them. And what's before them is almost totally negative, almost totally negative, in the black community. That's the pity. That's really the pity. And not enough is done to make the people aware of what could be, of what was and what could be.

One day things that happened here will be looked on with more interest than there is now. But the people who did it will be long gone. Some people made a great contribution, like Sam Browne. He is a good example for others to live by, to try to do something to pass on some knowledge to people who didn't come in contact with it. And that's about the best thing that we can do.

Horace Tapscott

Pianist, composer, arranger, and Arkestra leader Horace Tapscott left *Central Avenue in 1953 to join the Air Force, where he served in the band until 1957. For the next three years he played trombone in Lionel Hampton's orches-tra. By 1961 he had quit Hamp's band and committed himself to remaining in his Los Angeles community and working on social and cultural issues. In 1961 he formed the nucleus of the Pan-Afrikan Peoples Arkestra, which he continues to lead. For many years Horace was also a key member of a larger organization that encompassed the Ark—UGMAA, the Union of God's Musicians and Art-ists Ascension, which worked on a variety of community projects.*

Horace has recorded eight albums of solo piano music, as well as others in trio, quartet, quintet, sextet, octet, and large orchestra ensembles. Many of the pieces are his own compositions, and most are on small, independent labels, such as Nimbus and Interplay.

From leading a marching band in the annual Kwanzaa parade and teach-ing kids in the neighborhood, to late night jams in Leimert Park and standing on his front lawn near Crenshaw High School chatting with his neighbors, Horace remains an influential presence in his community.

Horace was born in Houston, Texas, in 1934. His family moved to Los Angeles when he was nine years old.

In the beginning, what I remember is darkness. And then, boop! It was from Robert Tapscott out of Mary Lou Tapscott on April 6, 1934, at a hospital in Houston in segregated Texas called Jefferson Davis. I was raised in Houston, where everyone was one family. The next-door neighbors were like my family when I left the house. It was the kind of neighborhood where everybody knew each other. I was coming up in this kind of environment.

In those days people were all in the streets. There wasn't any crime to speak of. The worst crime that would happen that I remember was the black male getting away from the white policeman, you dig, getting away from a lynch mob. And that's all I remember. I don't remember anything like purse snatching or fights down the street.

There was a guy who was a pastor in the church named Alexander Pleasants. He would walk through the community, from his home to the church house. He had a big ten-gallon hat, and he had one of those coats that used to swing, penguin kind of tuxedo with the tails back there. And everybody would stop what they were doing and say good morning to the reverend. The so-called prostitutes would come out of the beer joints, because he'd walk in there on his way to church. These things stayed in my head. On his way to the church to preach the gospel, he'd step into the dens of iniquity, so to speak, and talk to everybody, make them feel good. All the kids would be on the porch, "Hi, Reverend Pleasants." And he'd be tipping his hat everywhere, all the way to church. So immediately after he gets to the church, everybody goes back in and gets dressed, and [whooshing noise] right to the church. The only people that weren't at church were the so-called sinners, and they'd feel so bad they'd stay off the street, because there wasn't anybody on the streets, you dig? Everybody knew who everybody was at the church. Everything was hooked up with the community in the church.

That's the way I see churches today, and that's why I'm not at this moment a part of any particular church, because I remember growing up in a church where it took care of the community. No one starved. No one had any problems, because everybody was there at church. If you needed somebody to help you fix your outhouse, then there's a guy there that can do it. That's the kind of attitude that was rolling through the community. And everything was provided for the youths in the community. They had a playground for us. They had areas for us to go in and run and play while other things were happening. And the emphasis was on study at all times. They made people study hard all the time.

Everything was pushed toward brotherly love, to taking care of each other. And it was really dangerous for us during those days to be alone on the highway, because you might get pulled over, killed, or something like that. So naturally, it was like that, because there was no other way to be. And I enjoyed those days, those early days in Houston, Texas. They more or less shaped me for what was to come. I just enjoyed everything that was happening. It looked like everything was cool to me. And then, once again, that pain of segregation, that pain of prejudice.

In those days of segregation, there was a lot of activity going on at the time all around the world. But I was only surrounded by this block that I lived in. It was like sitting on your front porch watching the whole world pass you by, all in one color. But all these people that passed here made some kind of significant contribution toward the settling of this country. Have you ever heard of this black sailor, Dorie Miller? He was a black sailor in World War II, a cook in the navy. Blacks weren't allowed on top. So some kind of attack came from the Japanese, and Dorie Miller ran to his position as a gunner, and he wiped out several of the enemy aircraft. And that was hushed up for many years. He's just been written up, naturally, in the last twenty-five years, into the history. But the black community in Houston knew about it.

This person, Dorie Miller, came right into my pathway, right in front of me as a kid with his white uniform on. I'll always remember that. Everyone was sitting on the porch just talking and looking. He passed by, and he was waving at the folks. I ran and caught him and pulled him by his coattail and asked him, "Are you Dorie Miller?" He said, "Yes, I'm Dorie Miller." I spurted out something and ran back to my house.

With segregation in the South, for those heroes of those days, the only place they're coming is just that one place, this particular village. In that case, that particular village was the Third Ward in Houston. And I had a family there. I came out of the family of the Malones and the Tapscotts.

My stepfather, his name was Leon Jackson, was a real dynamite kind of a person. I guess he was half Native American and African American. He had a great look, and he could run fast. And I loved to run. [laughter] That was one of my biggest things. When I used to have a problem, I'd just take off running, because I felt like I was the wind. And this guy could run fast, because I remember him running from the police shooting at him. He had this gambling house on the railroad track, and every now and then the police would break up these gambling houses. I'd see these guys busting out, running all different ways, and my stepfather was whipping. I used to love to see him. They'd be shooting at him. Yeah, he'd be doing it, man. I liked him. We used to run a lot.

But I was raised in a house full of women, from my grandmother to my two great-aunts, my mother, and a rooming lady, a woman that she rented a room to up front. As usual, the men were dead, you dig? They made babies like the black widow, I guess, because they weren't going to last. Black men were scheduled to live up to thirty or something like that. If they made forty, they were lucky. So it was mostly the women. It has a lot to do with what I think about women now. I have a lot of respect for women because of the things they went through for us. My mother lived to be about ninety-two. You know how men are about their moms. They're the queen. There's nothing like them. And that's true, especially when you think of what they had to go through.

Men at that time had different families in the same block, two or three houses from each other. Everybody knew it, and this cat stayed in none of the places, but he could go in to eat. It was accepted in church that these are his children, and their brothers down the street. It wasn't like the women would get that friction, because they had to sit together and be together for the sake of the children, for the sake of keeping everything tolerable. I could go to some cat's house, see his daddy, and go three or four houses down and he'd be down there. It wasn't anything that was hidden.

Like my father, he had two or three ladies in church. They all went to the same church, and they all had his babies. I met him once. I was on the street one day in Houston. I was about six. I was standing on this corner, and this real tall guy reached down to pat me. "Hello, son," and he gave me twenty cents. That's all I can remember about him. I remember him being in the area, but I only had communications with him that one time. The next time I saw him was a picture of him in a casket. I was told that the guy died jumping off of a truck, helping his seventh wife move. He was in his sixties at the time, and I guess he was still pumping them. [laughter]

But everybody would be supportive of the family. That's the way it was. Everything that I remember had to deal with family. And everybody had that. Family values were actually valuable things that people passed on from one to another, from one family to another, and from one person within that family to another. Like at school functions, it was always a family thing. You get off from your job early so you can go and make your son's or your daughter's little recital at school. And everybody was there. You could walk down the street the next day, and the ice man might pull his truck over and say, "That was a good recital you had, son," that kind of thing.

I remember there were bad times as far as the economy and having food was concerned. I remember we used to get food from a barbecue place. My stepgrandfather would pay a nickel for a bag of garbage food they were throwing out, and then we'd eat that. But I don't remember ever starving. You can always go out in your yard, too, and get some food. People always made things for you. Grandparents would be sewing the sole on your shoes so you could go to church.

First Experiences with Racism

I had a real thing about racism as a little child. I have a vision that stays in my head. Even today I might have a dream and all of a sudden it's back to that day, that evening in Houston, Texas, when I was in bed. I was about five, six years old. I was laying in bed with my mother. It was late at night and it was dark. And I remember this white guy with a coat and hat on breaking my window, just coming through the window with his fist. He pushed through. He had this gun in his hand. My mother was laying in bed, and he put it to her head. He said, "Where's your brother? I'm going to kill that nigger tonight." This is the police. That's all I remember. I was crying, I guess. Years later I found out that they were looking for my uncle. But that vision stayed with me a long time. It stayed with me for so long that everybody I saw that was white I was afraid of and I didn't like, because of what they did to my mother, you dig? And that went on through the years. That was my first experience with racism. And I had never seen a white person in my life. That was the first time.

Every now and then you had to go downtown in Houston. That meant you had to ride in the back of the bus. The only time I saw white people is when I went to town. I remember this incident, me and my mother getting on this bus, and I sat down in the middle of the bus, because there wasn't anybody on the bus. I'm a kid, you know, I don't know I'm supposed to sit in the back. I was sitting in front of the colored sign. I remember the bus driver looking in the mirror. And I remember my mother saying, "Come back here. Come on." I said, "Why?" And she wouldn't tell me I wasn't good enough to sit up there. I'll never forget that. She never said I wasn't good enough. She said, "Well, I want you to sit back here," because of this, because of that, but never because I was black. I put her through a whole lot of things, because I can remember the pain in her eyes to have to tell me this, to come back with her.

"From day one it was music."

It started at home with my mother. She had her own group in the early part of the century playing jazz. Yeah, a woman jazz lady, Mary Lou Malone. We had this home on Dowling Street, and this house was a shotgun type of a house. You come through the front, and you see the back. She had a big old stand-up piano in those days. It was very large and it hung right near the doorway. It took up part of the doorway. So when you came in my house, you had to play the piano to get to the couch over there. [laughter]

From day one it was music. All I remember is when I came to being, all I saw and heard around me was music. All these blues cats would be coming by my house, Floyd Dixon and Amos Milburn. And they lived in the neighborhood. My sister [Robbie Tapscott Byrd] and Floyd Dixon were boyfriend and girlfriend. In those days, because of segregation, whoever you were, whatever class you were in, you still had to live in this area.

In those days blues singing was everywhere. You've got to have the music all the time. It was part of the fabric. And on Sunday that same blues became the spiritual. All of it to me was blues, because I could hear the blues running through every phase of all the music that came out of the community. It was all based on that "hmmm." Out of that came the spiritual and the blues and rock and roll, rhythm and blues, all of that. They were all trained the same way. Every woman singing the blues came out of the church choir. It all begins in church. The church was our thing, man. Everything happened at church. Anything that was organized was a church activity. The church was open every day until seven or eight at night. And children were learning different kinds of things, always being taught about African American history. That was part of it. That's how we learned about black people. It wasn't written in the regular public school books.

I remember listening to Marian Anderson. She had that look, that classy look of my grandmother and my aunt. Those high cheekbones, that stare, that open stare that's like an open forest, an evergreen. We would all sit in our homes and listen to her sing on the radio. Once she came through the community and sang at church. We got to see and hear all those people up close. The Hall Johnson Choir. Some of the early musicians that have made such a contribution even to European classical music, like Roland Hayes. We used to listen to him.

My mother saved her money from the jobs they had in those days and bought me my first instrument, a trombone. We already had the piano in the house, but I wanted a horn. Growing up in those days, if you'd play the piano and the violin, you'd go outside and the cats would want to beat up on you. That was just for girls, playing the piano. If you're going to play an instrument, you're going to play a horn or something. She gave me that trombone. And I remember the first time I blew on it, my neighbor said, "Oh, my God, the boy got a horn!" And every day they'd hear me. I was about eight or nine. But I had been playing piano since I was six. It got to the point where I'd spend four hours a day, two of those hours on one instrument, two hours on the other. I got to the point on trombone where instead of just practicing scales and stuff, I started taking one position to see how many notes were in there, and I started to try and hum while I was playing, all crazy kinds of things at the time.

Soon I had my first band. I would play the drums. I had the cats up front playing whatever instrument they had. It seemed like everybody had instruments or wanted to. And you'd always have an audience, because the whole family would sit down and listen to you sometime during the day.

And on Sundays, most parents might take their youngsters to some kind of sports activity. In my case, the activity was a musical activity, some kind of concert somewhere in the community at some church, anywhere, that featured orchestras. I had to go. My mother loved it, and she'd always take me and my sister to these concerts. My mom played in two bands at the church itself, two full orchestras, twenty and thirty people. And I was about to get in the band, but we cut out and came to California. But I had spent a lot of time with music.

"All these white cats, man. Where am I?"

The reason we got out here in 1943 was my stepfather came to work in the shipyards in San Pedro. During the war the jobs were opening up. The best job that black men had in those days was being a chauffeur or working on a train as a porter. Those were the two highest-paying outside the preachers in the community. When the wartime boom happened, that's why most of the people left Texas and Louisiana.

So I was on the train heading toward Los Angeles, California. It was segregated all the way. But nobody even thought about it. It was cool. I saw my first sexual act on the train. Some soldier got on and met this woman. I guess by the time they got to Arizona they were humping. I was sitting right behind them, and I was supposed to be asleep, you dig? I was a little old kid about nine, ten years old. And then I remember them getting off at Union Station in Los Angeles, saying good-bye to each other. [laughter] That was out.

Union Station was beautiful. It was busy and you'd see the movie stars coming through. I was really taken: "All these white cats, man. Where am I?" My first scene getting off at the Union Station was that city hall building. At the time it was the tallest building in the city. And, man, it was another kind of city. Then all of a sudden you'd start seeing palm trees. And all these fruit trees, right on the street. And it was cool for you to pick them as you're walking along the street. They didn't belong to anybody. All that was colorful. We got into this car, started driving down Central Avenue.

I got down on Central Avenue, and I started seeing things unfold in front of me. The first place we went, before I got to my house, my mother told the driver to stop the car. Our suitcase was still in the trunk. And I said, "This is where we live?" She said, "No, this is not where we live. I want to introduce you to your first music teacher." She's already picked him out. We hadn't gotten to the house yet. I don't know where I live. It's the first time I'd ever been in California in my life, and we're driving from Union Station to where I'm going to live. Before we got there, I was introduced to my first music teacher. That's the first person I met in Los Angeles, Harry Southard. He was a barber on Fifty-second and Central. I got out and met this guy. He said, "I'll be seeing you, son." The next day I was at music lessons.

We went to the 1900 block of Naomi Avenue. That's a street about a block east of Central Avenue between Washington Boulevard and Twentieth Street. That's the first place we lived. My neighbor was Etta James. She used to sing at the St. Paul Baptist Church every Sunday. She started breaking people up when she was about twelve years old.

But I only stayed there a few months, because it got really crowded, which meant I had to go somewhere else to live. And I went to Fresno, California, and stayed with my great-uncle and great-aunt about two years. I had to wait until the family got their money together to get a pad so that me and my sister could have different rooms. So I left and she stayed here.

I went to school in Fresno, my first mixed school, the first time I'd ever gone to school with anybody white, anybody. I walked to school with these other black cats that lived on the street. The first thing, I got on the school grounds, there were two white guys fighting. I ran over and pushed them aside and I looked at the big one: "Try that on me, man."

And this cat said, "What?"

"Do it, do it. Hit me." And I don't know this guy.

And he said, "Aw, go away."

I'm really mean, now. I'm in a mean stage. Prejudiced. Whew. I wanted to fight him. He didn't hit me, so I hit him. I hadn't even registered in school yet. First day of school.

So I'm going to class, and I looked over across the room, and there was this beautiful blond girl, blue eyes. I started looking at her, and she looked at me. That turned me around. And she became my girlfriend. Her name was Barbra. And we'd talk about race. She was trying to cool me down, because I was fighting white cats all day every day.

It was a colorful school. It was beautiful. They had this Indian girl there named Carmen. I'll never forget her. She had long black hair. And some of the things she made me do, I don't even want to mention. [laughter] My first Mexican friend was a cat I had a fight with. We fought all day. He wasn't giving up; he was macho. And I wasn't giving up. Me and this cat became great friends after that. And I started trying to get along with the rest of the people.

But I never could get along with the guys. If the guys saw me coming, they would move to the side, because I had gotten that rep by then, "It's that crazy kid from the South." And they had passed the word on to stay out of my way until I started getting used to the fact that there were other people in the world.

I do remember demanding how come the history course wasn't talking about black people. I wanted to know how come the history I was reading didn't have me in it, only as a slave. And I had some teachers, some white teachers, that I'll never forget that sat down and explained to me why. Told me the truth, why things were like they were. Then I began to understand more. I still had that prejudice, but I wasn't as crazy as I was at first. By now I'd made a friend, a white guy. I was learning very slowly, because all I saw was a guy with the gun at my mama's head each time. And I didn't get past that almost until I got into the service. And when I got into the service, there was a whole new set of rules. There was a whole new racial thing there, right after Truman had integrated the service. And it was hard for both sides to get used to each other.

But before that, during the time in Fresno, that's where I got to realize I should take it easy and smell the flowers, and listen and look and watch the ants, and check out different things. Open up your ears to what is and what isn't, and how you should guide yourself and your seed. And I enjoyed those years in Fresno. And I was practicing all the time in the backyard by myself.

SWU: Sidewalk University

Then I came back to L.A. The money got a little better, and my family moved across Central onto Twenty-first Street to a bigger house. I was different when I came back. I was really different. I started thinking about compositions. I started to think about dancing. I started thinking about plays I wanted to write. I started writing a play in high school. I wrote a tune, the first song I ever wrote, called "Bongo Bill." I remember doing it with Samuel Browne listening to it and critiquing it. Mr. Browne used to come over from Jefferson High School. My thought pattern started stretching out. I wanted to play different music. I remember the *Peer Gynt* suite that I used to play a lot, those kinds of things that had to do with composers. I started listening to other composers, cats that were looked upon as the revolutionaries or the outcast cats. And all their music was great, even the Beethoven and Haydn cats. I started listening to the other side of the coin.

I started going to Lafayette Junior High, just off Central and Fourteenth Street. Me and my wife, Cecilia, met during those days. We were fourteen years old. I became the student body president and she became the vice-president of the junior high. We were running things. We had concerts there. It was a lot of fun. I had all the ladies running after me. That was nice. Lafayette Junior High School was the second time being with such colorful groups, ethnic groups. Very mixed. I got a chance to hear a lot of different kinds of music and started to play a lot of different kinds of music, you dig, being at Lafayette. We had a band there. The bandmaster was Percy McDavid, who taught Illinois Jacquet and all the cats in Houston, Texas. And he had a band that played in different parks around the city every Sunday. He had Charlie Mingus, Britt Woodman. All the cats were in it. And I played with this band from junior high school until we all grew up. I just grew up with the band. On a certain night every week there was a rehearsal at the junior high school.

Cecilia and I used to walk the streets together and got to see all these people. We used to listen to Art Tatum, Red Callender, and Bill Douglass near the Clark Hotel, at the Clark Annex. Being so young, we weren't able to go into the club part, but we stood at the window. And then you'd go across the street and Billie Holiday is there. Down the street, a big band: Lunceford, Henderson, all of them playing all the way up Central. And that's what we used to walk through.

It's heartbreaking now. I hate to go down there, because when I came here it was just live. It was live. The main difference compared to Houston was that there were so many musicians at one time, playing all the time. And listening, getting a chance to listen to each other doing a job. During intermissions they'd come across the street or go next door to hear the other cats, and those in turn do the same thing, all night long.

My teacher, Mr. Southard, once took me down to the black musicians union. He said, "You'll be here a lot." I spent my time there sitting on the stoop. I couldn't join yet. I'm just twelve years old. [laughter] I wasn't even a teenager. Every cat in the world, every black musician in the world touched me on my head and my shoulder and my back and told me something. I was sitting there, just sitting there all those years. And me and Eric Dolphy and Don Cherry and the young guys at the time were sitting there all the time, man. That's where I met Larance Marable, the drummer. And it was just rich, very rich.

Naturally, I didn't realize it until afterwards, but I was taking advantage of it, because you didn't have any choice but to take advantage of it. Because one teacher knew the other teacher. "I teach you something, and then what I taught you you're teaching this other person, and it's coming back around to me with another flavor to it." In other words, they were putting things to you, and pulling it out of you. How many mentors you'd have in a day was impossible to count.

I learned how to write from those cats: Melba Liston, Gerald Wilson. Gerald Wilson was the first guy that got me into writing. I mean to arrange and compose for a big orchestra. I used to hang with him. Gil Fuller, I used to hang with him, one of the writers for Dizzy Gillespie. John Anderson, one of the great writers around here. So many cats were writing, and they'd always turn you on. You had to learn how. I didn't go to a class to learn to write. I went to the action to learn to write, looking and listening and asking questions, and hearing it right away, so you could know where you were from that point. And that way of passing on teaching was very good for me, because I could handle that—all different kinds of people telling you different things about the same thing and their approaches to it and how many ways it can be done. So I refused to go to the Juilliard School because of that. My mother had saved up some money. My sister had given away the money that was saved for her college so I could go to Juilliard. I said, "No thank you. I appreciate it. I love you. But I have the best right here. You already put me in the best atmosphere. And I can't leave." It was SWU—sidewalk university—because these cats would be on your case, all the time.

I've been looking at Duke Ellington's writing since I was thirteen. I could go into the union and walk right through the sections and look at the music while they were rehearsing. It was cool. Like the Fletcher and Horace Henderson band. I could walk through there and look and ask a question if I wanted. You were expected to be there. You were expected to ask questions. They know who you are. They've seen you. And you're welcome. All the cats were welcome.

It's like Duke said, the best part of having a band is that you can write anything you want and immediately you can hear it right away to see if it's cool. And that's why I always had the Ark [Pan-Afrikan Peoples Arkestra]. I would write something, and I could hear it right the next day, you dig? And I tried to make my relationship with other musicians on that kind of level. They are artists themselves, and I had them in mind when I was writing this, because you want to get all you can out of the person's creativity to put into this music.

Gerald Wilson used to come to my house and pick me up for rehearsal. My mother saw to that. Red Kelly, a trumpet player, used to come to my house to pick me up. All the musicians would come pick you up, the young cats, and take you to rehearsal and bring you back home. Yeah, it was something, wasn't it, man? You'd come out of the house, here's a well-known, world-renowned trumpet player waiting to pick you up to take you to a rehearsal. And they were serious, man. They wanted you to learn. All the time you were riding with them they're talking and they're jamming you.

That was most of my tutoring and all the mentors that I had. There was a main one all the time that you would report to, like Samuel Browne or Lloyd Reese. But then during the same period you're with Gerald Wilson, you're with Buddy Collette, you're with "Streamline" Ewing, you're with Red Callender, you're with Wardell Gray, you're with so-and-so. You've got somebody you want to ask questions, "How far could I write this for a trombone?" So Britt Woodman might be interested in that kind of thing. And that's how I learned most of it. I had so many mentors, up and down the Avenue at the black musicians union 767, you couldn't go wrong if you tried to. They were telling you about everything: the music and the dope that's coming in and what to do and what not to mess with. And Gerald Wilson later paid twenty-five dollars for me to join the union.

Jefferson High School

When Horace enrolled at Jeff in 1949, Samuel Browne was waiting.

I enjoyed going to the school because I was already scheduled to be in the band with Mr. Browne. When I was in junior high school, Mr. Browne would come over and recruit for his band at Jefferson: "So you're going to play in my orchestra. You're playing second horn." He'd be getting you ready for high school, get you in and get you started even before you graduate from Lafayette. The same way they do in sports, they did with music. And the cats, naturally, they'd be practicing, because they wanted to do it.

But coming to Jeff, it was something. There was a lot of activity. Anything you wanted to get into was available to you on the campus. Everybody stayed on campus. There were no gates, no fences, no locks, no graffiti. The only thing you went off school ground for was to get some hamburgers. During that time, Jesse Belvin was going there, Ernie Andrews, O. C. Smith. There were a lot of opera singers that went over to Europe to work that were under Samuel Browne. We had a choir under a guy named Mr. Moon, the school marching band under a guy named Stewart Aspen, and then you had the swing band, Mr. Browne's function. There were two harmony classes, there was a counterpoint class, there was a music reading class, there was a solfeggio class. Jefferson was a proud school, a very proud school. Everybody wanted to do their best for it.

Sixth period every day, about two o'clock in the afternoon, was the big band for an hour. Every day. Five days a week. And sometimes we'd have concerts at Fairfax High or out in the [San Fernando] Valley at Taft High. Or we'd go to one of Stan Kenton's early rehearsals in Hollywood. He'd introduce us to the legends. That's how I first met Shelly Manne, when Shelly Manne was in his band. He took us to the Hendersons' band, all these cats. And the cats would be coming over to the school to talk to you. Lionel Hampton always came over. He brought his big band. And I told Lionel, "Man, I'm going to get in your band one day." He said, "Okay." [laughter] That's in 1950 or something like that, you dig? They'd come over and play, and the whole school would be screaming and hollering and dancing up and down the aisles.

Some of the cats used to come back to Jeff. Like Sonny Criss might come back and be just playing upstairs. All the players around the city would come back. The band rehearses at the end of the day, and they might have some arrangements they want to play, because they were in the band when they were at school. Now they're on the Avenue or up and down the West Coast. But when they were at home, they'd come back to the school and sit in, and might say something to the cats and tell them where they're playing and all that. It was always some kind of hookup.

And Dr. Browne would come to certain musicians' houses to see that they're taking care of business. He'd be at my house all the time. Or at Frank Morgan's house. He knew your family, you understand? They knew him. He was making sure he was setting up the foundation correctly from the family on up. He was able to come in and to teach or to inspire, just come and talk with you. He made sure he kept an eye on you. He really dug you. He'd say, "I dig you, man." That's what he'd tell you. "You don't understand that yet. But I dig you."

He was also telling us how to survive. "You have to be much better than the guys that go to Hollywood High." That's what Dr. Sam Browne always said. "I don't care how good you are, because of the racist society you live in, you're going to have to be much better than the student over at Hollywood High School. You can fool around if you like, but those guys out at Palisades and Hollywood High, they're going to be the ones that took care of business. And you're going to be hip." [laughter] "All you're going to be is a hipster. That's all you want to be, is that it? Okay, you're going the right direction if that's all you want. But if you want more, you'll try to do more. You'll try to study and learn more." That was the thought of the day all the time: try to do better.

But at the same time, Horace saw heroin making its way into his community.

I'd say about 1951 the hard drugs were coming into Central Avenue. It was about over then, anyway. And it was a big deal. I mean, it was like being in a clique. If you didn't shoot smack— I don't care how good you play, but if I shot smack, then I wouldn't feel comfortable playing with you because you don't shoot up like I do. So a lot of that happened. I saw a lot of cats die early from not being able to handle the narcotics in the area. And the narcotics, when they came in, it was really a monster, because you'd start seeing cats changing personalities. Then all of a sudden you don't want them to come to your house anymore. They'd become like zombies and nothing else matters. That's when it really hit bottom. All you wanted to do was just get high and nod. And you've got too much talent for that and that's whipping you.

I've seen a lot of cats come out of it, on their own, "cold turkey." They just stopped, because what was around them was so well put together that they felt out of place themselves. Once they realized that they mean something, how important they are to the whole scheme, then they understand that they have a part. They don't have to try to kill themselves for no reason at all.

It didn't have to do with just narcotics. It had to do with more than narcotics. It had to do with everyday living in the kind of society at that time in the early fifties for black people, and the black male in particular. Maybe he had a family. Maybe he couldn't work the way he wanted to. Maybe he was worried about getting drafted and going to the front line, where they were putting all the black soldiers at the time, and dying. They had a lot of things on their minds. They knew it wasn't right. And then they got the attitude and got the jacket on them about not being black men, "weren't good fathers." That whole kind of downtrodden man started after the Korean War.

A Taste of College

Horace graduated from Jeff in the summer of 1952 and enrolled at Los Angeles City College.

When I graduated I didn't have any real plans. All you knew was that you were trying to stay out of the service. And then I went to City College. I was in the college band. That was the band that Stan Kenton and Woody Herman would hire their people out of. That was that kind of band. They put me out of it, though. There were still these problems, these culture problems going on, you dig? And me, I'm a young, cocky black musician, and I've got an older white instructor, Mr. Donaldson. We were playing a tune called "My Silent Love." I was playing the trombone with him. And there was kind of a solo; it was written. The cat who usually played it, the Tijuana Brass cat—I can't think of his name—he would play it just like that and a great sound. I played it one time and I played it all funny styles and shit. [laughter]

Donaldson said, "Wait a minute. Wait a minute."

I said, "What?"

He said, "Why don't you play it like it's written."

"Well, I don't hear it like that."

"All you guys from Jefferson, you're not God's gift to music."

I laughed with all the rest of the white cats in there. "Well, maybe I'm not *the* God's gift, but I'm one of them." [laughter]

"Get out." He put me out of the band. I was the only black cat in there, and they put me out.

Then I was in a class where one of these harmony teachers had the gall to stand up in front of the class and say, "Duke Ellington's music was wrong, was written wrong." He said that in harmony you're not supposed to double thirds and have parallel fifths going. "Well, why not?" is what I wanted to know. And he couldn't explain. "Because it's incorrect. You're playing the wrong notes." Then I said, "Okay." Then we finally got to that day. He played a little bit, just a tiny bit, of "Black, Brown and Beige" and said it was written wrong. I left. That did it for me, man. I said, "That's it." That was a waste of my time. I mean, it was a personal insult, as well as a standard. I just got up and left. I left City College before I got into trouble, because I wanted to hit him. He had pissed me off actually to that point where I wanted to just jump on this cat. The best thing for me to do was to leave. I left the whole school and went back to the U of S—university of the streets.

I only went there because these same cats from the university of the streets, my mentors, told me to go there, because that's what they're going to ask for when you go in the service. Did you have college music? So I went to college.

But there was one instructor there, Dominic DiSarro, that I had an open line to. He was the conductor of the symphony orchestra of the college, and he was really into it heavy. But he gave me time. He listened to my things. He asked what I was doing. We got a thing going. And he let me conduct the orchestra. He dug me. He stayed on my case. That's the reason I stayed as many months as I did was because of Dominic DiSarro. Even though he was a European master, and he knew all of it, he allowed. He said, "But there are no boundaries." When he said things like that, I said, "This is the cat to be with."

The Decline of Central

By that time, about '51, '52, Central Avenue was closing down. It was on its way. As a matter of fact, it didn't have but a few more feet to go before it was over. With the union amalgamation we were looking forward to making a little bit more money, having more gigs. It was supposed to get us better pay. It was supposed to get us jobs in the studios. That's what it was about. When they said, "Well, we're going to have better jobs, Tapscott. You'll be doing movie studios. And when television gets straight, we'll be doing that." I said, "Oh." Let's do it. So I didn't have too much to think about it until after the fact.

So what was the problem? The problem was that when they did have the amalgamation, some of the white musicians got called for jobs—and they were used to being called—then some of the black musicians came, and then the cliques started forming all of a sudden. Some of the white cats who were working would hire different black cats, and then they'd have their little old clique. And that particular black group of guys would work all the time because of being in that particular clique with these particular guys that run the studios. It wasn't a racial thing. It was really a clique.

But it all added to the music. It was always nice after a gig. Everybody was glad to be with each other, because they came to a center. We were all in the center now, and we had to play the music. That was the most important thing. If I'm playing with some cats now that live out in the [San Fernando] Valley, we've never seen each other before, we come right in. So it was easy for cats to get along, white or black, because the cats that were into the music had another thinking pattern going. And that's how I started working with some of the white cats. They'd call me, cats like Jack Millman, all the out cats, the so-called out white boys that were into the music. You would be together all the time because you had a hookup.

So the work was getting better, seemed to have gotten better for certain people, after the old Local 767 closed up. But a lot of the older players I didn't see anymore. They used to be around all the time on Central at one gig or another. All of them used to hang around the union. They'd just be there. When that closed down, they didn't have anyplace to go.

Just as the union was integrating, the Los Angeles police started paying more attention to Central.

It was a city hall crackdown. And that was because of the racial harmony that was happening. Well, mostly it was white celebrities that would come through there and bring attention to the place. Why couldn't they go somewhere else in Hollywood? But they'd come down here. Especially the blonds like Lana Turner and Ava Gardner. There's an old magazine, *Ebony* or *Sepia,* that Ava Gardner is in. It's in a black magazine by [John H.] Johnson, I'm sure. Ava Gardner is in there with Dizzy Gillespie, and the item says, "Diz and Bird show Ava Gardner how to eat a banana." I'll never forget that. I can't recall what date or edition that was, but it was in there. And all the cats at the union made a big joke out of it.

Even the bands that played in Hollywood, the white bands, after hours they'd come on Central so they could play in all-night sessions. And that wasn't too sweet. Yeah, it was integrated and the white ladies were coming down.

And to top it off that's when Local 767 was dissolved.

As the Central Avenue scene was winding down, Horace received his draft notice.

I got my greetings a few months after I graduated, very few months. I graduated in June, and I had my greetings I'm sure by October. They'd already told me that I'm on it. "You will be called." That's when we started talking with the cats, and they told us about the band, the navy band. Dr. Browne, Buddy Collette, Red Callender, "Streamline" Ewing, a cat named Red Kelly, and Gerald Wilson—all these guys had been in the bands. And they were saying that they had gotten us ready to go in these bands, because we could read anything now.

So my first thing was to join the navy. At the time, I couldn't swim, but I felt I could rectify that. But they told me, "Hey, man, the first thing you've got to do is jump off a twenty-foot tower into the water." [laughter] I backed out, walked around the corner to the air force. That's how I joined the air force.

The Pan-Afrikan Peoples Arkestra

After his discharge from the air force in 1957, Horace made good on his adolescent boast: he joined Lionel Hampton's band. Three years later, he set himself a much more powerful goal.

I was on the road with Lionel Hampton, when I said, "What is the point of all this? Why did I get into music in the first place?" And I questioned myself. Then the band was here on a gig, out on Sunset Boulevard, I'll never forget. We were going back to New York again. This was about 1959, '60. I got off the bus at four o'clock that morning and Oliver Jackson, the drummer, said, "Where you going, Horace?" I said, "This is it, brother." Four o'clock that morning, I said, "I've had it." I wanted to do something else. I wanted my own thing, and I wanted to write about it, and I wanted to help preserve the music. The music was just going off, and nobody knows who wrote the music or cares. With Hamp we played mostly in the South and New York. Those were two racist places and still are. I said, "Well, there's no point. What's the point of playing this music here? These people who come in don't pay any attention to it and don't have any idea what they're playing. Now, if it was a European orchestra, they'd be sitting there listening and trying to hear. So what is this? And how come so-and-so isn't getting the money that he's supposed to be getting?" And that's why my feelings got to the point where these people, these men and women who really were in the music, like Melba Liston and all those folks, they should be recognized, and their contribution to this whole scheme of things should be recognized.

That's why I got off the road to start my orchestra, to preserve black music. I wanted to preserve and teach and show and perform the music of black Americans and Pan-African music. To preserve it by playing it and writing it and taking it to the community. And that to me was what it was about, being part of the community.

And I didn't want to be away from home. My wife and I had a son. That's when I decided that what my family has gone through for me to get into the music is for this particular reason. And that reason is to make a point, to say something with it, for it to be accepted as good music and to be accepted as part of the fabric of the whole society that we all dream of having. Then I got off the bus, and that was the end of it, man. And I've been in it since then, up till now, until the dirt is thrown in my face.

Passing the Magic On

Me and Don Cherry were just saying last night that was a good time. We came up in a good time, real good times. There ain't nothing to do now but give it back in some kind of way. I can think of all the cats that passed on things to me, and I'll never forget these people. Sometimes the names might leave, but their faces I remember. Like Roy Porter, who is still around here. He was around here with his band playing. I mean we were just surrounded by music, just surrounded by it. It was more or less like musicians raised me. It was a good time to grow up in, when I came here.

I got the last good four or five years of it. Central Avenue. I saw it, I was in the middle of it, and I saw the end of it.

Central Avenue brought a lot of people together musically, artistically. I think Central Avenue is just as legendary a place as the Great White Way that they speak about. It had all of the musicians, the artists, that helped make the music of this country what it is today. That's what Central Avenue gave to this community, all these people, and they'd be right there on Central Avenue gathering together. It was like a bonanza. There was gold coming out of Central Avenue.

I can say I have been consistent in one way of thinking, and that is to demand respect, to demand recognition, and to demand that the children, and your children, benefit from all the things that we've contributed. That's why I came out of the womb—I found out before I go to the tomb—that they had to have that respect and understanding for a race of people and their contribution to this country. America might not be known as America for everybody while you and I are still here, but the contribution that's being made is constantly working that way, which means that it wasn't all in vain, even though things are still happening. But to get to the core, my idea is to be a part of that whole scheme.

"So what are you after? What are you trying to prove in this society?" I just want some respect. I want real respect, because I give real respect. That's all I'm looking for in this world, from man to man and woman to woman, man or woman, respect. That's all it comes down to. I'd like to be able, before they throw the dirt on me, to again walk through a neighborhood and everybody's speaking. Bars and windows are off the doors. I mean, that's really dreaming, but I'd love to see that one more time, to live in that kind of community. I grew up in that kind of setting, which made me like I am today, always ready to accept a person for who they are, and they accept me for who I am. Respect for one another.

You can't get that without giving it. So my way of giving it and getting it is in the little functions I'm into every day, and have to be done every day. Contact, information, actions, and passing it on. Like Mr. Browne told me, if I promised that I'd pass it on, he'd give me the magic. That's what I want to do, and I've been doing that.

I want to be able to say, to show, that I lived in the community and I appreciated it and I wanted to keep it up and I wanted to be a part of it, because I love people. And I wanted to be a part of it because I learned to love life. I know how I feel about things. I'm not bitter anymore. I worked my way out of that, because I knew I had to work my way out of that if I was going to try to do anything else.

Nothing feels better to me than being able to walk through the village and see functions happening. I like that. And I like to be a part of that. If I can do anything about helping that maintain itself, that's what I'll do.

Drawn by Central's Magic
—New Faces

The lure of southern California drew black musicians from all across the country to Central Avenue. Gerald Wiggins, Gerald Wilson, Clora Bryant, Bill Green, and Marl Young all moved to Los Angeles as adults eager to put their mark on the Central music scene. By about 1945 the era of big bands and swing was ebbing—bebop, rhythm and blues, and other sounds were on the way in.

On the lookout for great talent, Billy Berg hired Dizzy Gillespie and his New York–based bebop band to play his club in Hollywood. When Dizzy opened in December 1945, Charlie Parker was with him, offering West Coast musicians their first opportunity to hear two of the new music's originators in live performance. Bebop, however, was already familiar to many of the young musicians from Central who packed the club opening night. Some had heard the early Savoy recordings. Others had been listening to bop nightly on Central Avenue at the Downbeat, which featured the Howard McGhee–Teddy Edwards Quintet. Week after week during 1945 audiences had filled the club to hear the new sounds. Trumpeter Howard McGhee had come from the East Coast earlier that year as an apostle of bop, and the fire quickly spread. Young musicians on the Avenue and at the local high schools, in various bands and clubs, threw themselves into the new sounds. One of the best of these high school bands featured tenor saxophonist Cecil (not yet "Big Jay") McNeely, alto saxophonist Sonny Criss, and pianist Hampton Hawes. But although bebop was thriving on Central Avenue when Diz and Bird arrived, the rest of southern California was not impressed. Within a few weeks Billy Berg canceled the remainder of their appearances.

If it took bop a while to plant roots outside the circle of musicians and aficionados, success came quickly to what came to be called rhythm and blues. Originally a catchall term the record industry created to replace the "race records" tag, rhythm and blues emerged as an identifiable style in the postwar period. Drawing on a tradition of small jump and blues bands, confronting an economic climate inhospitable to orchestras, and reacting to the over-arranged excesses of the swing era, r&b offered a scaled-down big-band lineup playing music that represented a return to its roots—boogies and blues. Whereas bebop took jazz to new levels of harmonic sophistication and rhythmic complexity, r&b provided a return to a more basic, emotional, blues-drenched sound. On Central Avenue, and then nationwide, Joe Liggins, Roy Milton, and Big Jay McNeely enjoyed immediate and fairly long-lived success. Johnny Otis disbanded his nationally known orchestra and opened the Barrelhouse in Watts, a club that for several years served as an incubator for r&b talent. The sound had a new name and perhaps some different stylings, but to Johnny r&b was a return to his early days in the thirties as the drummer in Count Otis Matthews's West Oakland House Rockers.[1]

Despite the declining fortunes of big bands by the end of World War II, a few organizations managed to survive in Los Angeles through a combination of adroit leadership, original music, and great talent. Trumpeter Gerald Wilson, still in his mid-twenties when he formed his band in October 1944, had already made a name for himself as a composer and arranger with the Jimmie Lunceford Orchestra, and Wilson's band boasted such local talent as teenage trombonist and arranger Melba Liston. Drummer Roy Porter formed his band in 1948 and also tapped the local talent pool, including Eric Dolphy and Art Farmer, to play bebop charts.

Beyond Central Avenue, predominantly white audiences in Los Angeles enjoyed a New Orleans jazz revival. A New Orleans–style band put together for the Standard Oil Broadcasts of 1944–45 included Papa Mutt Carey, Zutty Singleton, Jimmie Noone, and Kid Ory, and was emceed by Orson Welles.[2] Ory then reorganized his band and spent the next twenty years playing and recording New Orleans jazz. Although the revival provided work and valuable training for many black jazz musicians, old and young, the Central Avenue clubs were too hip to book these bands. On Central, the sound had to be contemporary, and at the end of World War II that meant bebop and rhythm and blues.

Central's musicians and fans were, however, drawn to Norman Granz's Jazz at the Philharmonic concerts—the first sustained presentations of jam sessions in concert settings. Staged at Los Angeles's Philharmonic Auditorium, these concerts brought together some of the finest players in the country with some of the best local talent. By April 1946, however, the Philharmonic management complained that the concerts attracted "too many negroes," and Granz found a new home at the Embassy Auditorium.[3]

Despite the musical activity, Central Avenue's best days had passed. With World War II over, there were massive layoffs in the defense industry, and thousands of women and minorities lost their good-paying jobs. Disposable income fell, and patronage of the clubs declined.

But it was not only a foundering economy that forced clubs and entertainment establishments to close. In the late 1940s the Los Angeles Police Department, under police chief William H. Parker, took an increasingly belligerent stance toward the clubs. "Under previous police chiefs . . . Central Avenue's boisterous, interracial night scene had simply been shaken down for tribute; under Parker—a puritanical crusader against 'race mixing'—nightclubs and juke joints were raided and shuttered."[4] On orders from headquarters, the police routinely harassed, and at times arrested, interracial couples and white women attending the clubs on Central Avenue. The police also intimidated black businesses on the Avenue, including the popular Dolphin's of Hollywood record store at the corner of Vernon and Central: "According to Dolphin, Newton Division police had gone so far as to blockade his store, turning away all white customers and warning them that 'it was too dangerous to hang around Black neighborhoods.'"[5]

Despite the harassment and the restrictive housing covenants, the city's black population continued to increase; by 1950 blacks constituted almost 9 percent of the population of L.A.[6] But this ever-growing population remained confined to the same neighborhoods as before the war. The lawsuits challenging the restrictive covenants then took a paradoxical turn. David Williams, a veteran of these struggles who was appointed to the federal bench in 1989, recalled that initially, the United States Supreme Court "ruled that for government to enforce such covenants constituted unlawful action. The high court did not, however, rule the covenants to be illegal."[7] At the same time, a new series of cases, known as the Sugar Hill cases, were making their way through the California courts. In the late 1940s many whites left Sugar Hill on the Westside and sold to virtually anyone. Judge Williams continued: "All of a sudden an avalanche of lawsuits came upon them from the Whites that remained. They were trying to enforce those restrictive covenants. . . . and fortunately, those cases went before Superior Court Judge Thurman Clarke, who had a very liberal attitude. He declared those restrictive covenants unconstitutional."[8] On appeal the Supreme Court upheld Judge Clarke's decision.

The declining economy of Central Avenue and the opportunity to buy homes outside the traditional black areas led people away from the Avenue, primarily westward. The center of the black community shifted to Western Avenue, continuing on to Crenshaw Boulevard, about seven miles west of Central. Over the summer of 1950 the management of the Elks Hall spent $30,000 refurbishing the facility and announced an upcoming schedule of performers that included Amos Milburn, Count Basie, Big Jay McNeely, Jimmy Witherspoon, and Joe Liggins.[9] But a few months after the refurbished Elks Hall reopened, Dizzy Gillespie and his sextet bypassed Central to play at the Club Oasis on Western Avenue.[10]

By the mid-1950s Central Avenue was just another street.

15

Gerald Wiggins

An extremely versatile and exceptionally busy pianist, Gerald Wiggins has lived in Los Angeles since the 1940s. Members of his long-standing trio have included bassists Joe Comfort, Red Callender, Charles Drayton, and Andy Simpkins, and drummers Bill Douglass, Lee Young, and Paul Humphrey.

During his long career Wig has performed with, among others, Louis Armstrong, Louie Bellson, Cab Calloway, Benny Carter, Buddy Collette, Eddie "Lockjaw" Davis, Harry "Sweets" Edison, Teddy Edwards, Roy Eldridge, Duke Ellington, Dizzy Gillespie, Milt Jackson, Harry James, Jo Jones, Joe Pass, Art Pepper, Zoot Sims, Clark Terry, Joe Turner, Joe Williams, Gerald Wilson, and Jimmy Witherspoon. He has also been a much-in-demand accompanist for female singers, including Linda Hopkins, Lena Horne, Helen Humes, Eartha Kitt, Annie Ross, Kay Starr, the Supremes, and Dinah Washington.

Wig has recorded frequently as a sideman, leader, and, recently, as a soloist on the Concord label's Live at Maybeck Recital Hall series. He has also performed in studios, particularly for MGM, and on many film scores, including Don't Look Back, Harlem Nights, King Creole, Send Me No Flowers, and White Men Can't Jump.

I was born in New York City on May 12, 1922. I went to all the schools, P.S. 68, P.S. 24, Frederick Douglass Junior High School, which is P.S. 139, and the High School of Music and Arts, which La Guardia started. My mother [Eleanor Foster Wiggins] had me taking piano lessons when I was four years old, which was ridiculous. But that's what she wanted. It was all classical music. And this went on it seemed like for years until I found out I couldn't make a living in New York playing classical music.

There just was no place for us at that time. And I guess I just didn't want it bad enough. For one thing, in classical music, everybody plays the same notes. There's no variation, and so you have to get by on touch and interpretation and shading and all that. You know, everybody's got the same thing going on. There's no room for improvisation. You play what's written, and it gets pretty boring. So, when I found out the girls would crowd around you at the parties, I started getting into playing jazz.

While I was at Music and Arts, Benny Goodman used to come up with Teddy Wilson and Gene Krupa, and they'd play little concerts for us. The gymnasium was packed whenever they came, you know. You almost had to know somebody to get in.

At that time, Teddy Wilson was my favorite piano player. I said he was the greatest thing that ever happened, until I heard Art Tatum. [laughter] That changed everything. A cousin of mine bought me a couple of records. He bought me "Elegy" and "Humoresque" and a couple other 78s. I thought it was two guys playing the piano. I couldn't believe one man could do this. You know, it was just impossible.

Finally, I got in with the crowd that used to go to Ruben's. Ruben's was like a speakeasy, an after-hours place, one floor down on 132nd, 133rd Street. You'd get there, and all the piano players in town would be there. It was just one room with an upright piano in it. You'd open the door and hit the piano. And all the guys, the piano players, would sit down there and play until Tatum walked in. When he walked in, they scattered. [laughter] Yeah, and they left the piano there for him.

He would open a bottle of Pabst Blue Ribbon beer and put it up on top of the piano. He'd reach up there and get it, take a swig, and all hell would break loose when he started playing. The guys would just sit there with envy, you know. "How did he do it?" He was fabulous. He was unbelievable. I didn't give up on Teddy Wilson, but I knew Teddy would never be the piano player that Tatum was, or nobody else, as far as I could see. I just sat there. And the way he did it—effortlessly, you know. No mistakes, clean runs, speed to throw away. He could play as fast as I could pat my foot. It was amazing. And the time was right there. I don't care where he went, he'd go out of the tune, but he always was within the framework of the tune. And if you sang the melody, he was right there all the way. He was an amazing man. [Artur] Rubinstein, if he was within five hundred miles, he'd fly there to go hear Tatum. Oh, he loved him. And I got to meet Art, and Art got me my first job. He got me a job with Stepin Fetchit, of all people. I went on the road with Stepin Fetchit one summer. I was about seventeen years old. I thought I was hot stuff, but I really didn't know anything. [laughter]

By the time he went on the road with Stepin Fetchit, Wig had been playing various gigs in Harlem and in Greenwich Village. He had joined the house band at Clark Monroe's Uptown House, soon to be an important incubator of bebop, and hung out with Dizzy Gillespie and Bud Powell.

After I got out of high school in 1940, we were working at the Brooklyn Strand. The house band was Les Hite's band from Los Angeles. The army took his piano player, and the police took Stepin Fetchit off the stage for some charge. So Les said to me, "Well, you don't have a boss, and I don't have a piano player. How would you like to go to California?" I jumped at the chance.

I got out here Christmas Day, and it was a hundred degrees, and I loved it. [laughter] I said, "This can't be happening," because I knew what was going on in New York. I called my mother. "I have found God's country. This weather is not to be believed. I don't think I'm ever coming back to New York." I did go back, but California was it for me. That sunshine really sold me. And I've never regretted it. I remember Jo Jones used to say, "Wig, come on back to New York. I can make you rich." Until the day he died, he told me I should never have left New York. I told him it was too cold. [laughter]

I stayed at the Dunbar Hotel. And the first thing I did was wake up the next morning, jaywalked, and got a ticket! [laughter] I couldn't believe it. [laughter] I got even, though. Those courtesy tickets, cards that they carry, I must have had fifty of them, including Mayor Bradley's. He was a lieutenant at the time, I think. I had his card, too. I had all the cops' cards. As fast as they could catch me for something else, they'd take the cards away, and I'd get another batch of cards. I had one particular old cop, Todd Roark. He used to keep me and Sabu, the Elephant Boy— We were two wild youngsters in L.A. He'd keep us out of trouble. He'd kind of watch over us. .

Stints with Louis Armstrong's and Benny Carter's bands took Wig through much of the country. He remained with Benny Carter until 1944, when the army caught up with him in Los Angeles.

I stayed with Benny until I went in the army in '44. And that was the low point of my life. We were getting ready to go on the road with the Nat King Cole Trio, Savannah Churchill—who sang with the band—Timmie Rogers, who was a comedian, and the Benny Carter Band. We were going to tour all over. This was 1944. And I'm set for this. I hadn't been ducking the army, but all the time we were traveling, my papers would get there right after we left. This time, we got to Los Angeles, we played the Orpheum Theatre, but we didn't leave town. We went to Billy Berg's Swing Club. When I got to work that night, there were my greetings. So J. J. Johnson and Max Roach said, "Well, Wig, what are we going to do? How can we get you out of this?" Well, we tried everything, get a cold or—you know. Nothing. I was healthy as a pig. [laughter] I couldn't catch a cold, couldn't do anything. So I went in the army. I spent all my army time in Fort Lewis, Washington.

Postwar Central

After being discharged from the service, Wig spent time in Seattle and San Francisco before returning to Los Angeles.

When I got here, there didn't seem to be too many piano players, so I was working all the time. I didn't really have a chance to go anywhere. I was always in a club. On Central Avenue, there was the Dunbar Hotel, naturally. I worked at a place called the Turban Room. And there was Jack's Basket and a whole bunch of little after-hours places all up and down the street. Unfortunately, in those days I was drinking quite a bit. But I've stopped since. I was really into it, you know. I wouldn't say I was a drunk, because I was. I could always get to work and play, but I was living high then. Honestly, my first wife used to wonder how I got to work. She said, "Well, if you get him to the piano, you don't have to worry about him. Just get him to the piano." [laughter] At that time I was hanging out with Irving Ashby and—who else?—Joe Comfort, Bill Douglass, Ernie Freeman, and all the local guys. We were the wrongdoers, you know. [laughter] Yeah.

After-hours, yeah. There was Ivie's Chicken Shack. There was Love-joy's. Shirley's Ritz Club. I worked there. Central Avenue was it. It was a little Fifty-second Street. It really was a ball. This town was alive and really jumping. And crime was a word. It wasn't happening that way, you know. You could walk anywhere and nobody would bother you. It was just beautiful. Central Avenue could be as safe as it is in your own home. Now I don't go near. You know, it's like Harlem is. Bombed out, it seems. But we had a lot of fun there. Everybody had fun. It was really some good times. Everybody made money, and everybody had a job. Guys didn't worry about working, because you'd leave one job and go right to the next. As they say, it was happening.

T-Bone Walker was around. Wynonie Harris. Bad news. [laughter] Whew! Yeah, Wynonie. Now, that was a character, if you wanted a char-acter. He got into fights everywhere he went. And Witherspoon was around then, too, Jimmy Witherspoon. And, naturally, Ernie Andrews. Art Pepper was here. It was no segregated-type thing. Everybody was welcome. If you could play, you were even more welcome. In fact, a couple of good songwriters, Mike Stoller and Jerry Leiber, they used to hang out down there, and they must have been fifteen or sixteen or sev-enteen years old.

And there were a lot of good musicians in L.A. Some of them you never got to hear about, but they were here. I didn't know Lloyd Reese when he was playing. I met him after his playing days were over. I under-stand he was a great trumpet player. But he was like the patriarch. He was counseling all us youngsters. He was telling us what to do and what not to do. He used to hold court at his house, where he had about six pianos in different rooms. All the piano players used to hang out at his house. You'd find Hampton Hawes there or Lorenzo Flennoy. That was the place to go, if we weren't over at Lovejoy's, which was an after-hours joint.

Dexter Gordon, Wardell Gray. Boy, they used to wear me out. We'd go to a jam session and—Mingus and I used to walk out on them, be-cause they'd get up there, each one of them would play twenty or thirty choruses, and we're back there sweating, you know. And they never thought about giving us a solo. If they give a piano player a solo, maybe one chorus, and they were back in on him again. [laughter] One night, Mingus said, "Wig, come on. Let's get out of here." And he picked up his bass, I left the piano, we left, and they didn't stop. They went right on with the drummer. [laughter] Didn't miss us at all. Oh, they'd work you to death. Yeah, that's why I don't go to jam sessions anymore. [laughter]

The horn players seem to think that you're there for the express purpose of accompanying them. They don't care if you get a chorus or if you're heard. They don't mind you making the intros, and, after that, forget the piano player. They've got it. And they'd line up. There would be six or seven horn players. [laughter] And the rhythm section would go crazy. And they always wanted [claps hands extremely rapidly] tempos. "Let's do one up, man." "We just did one up!" "Well, let's do another one up." Oh boy. Yeah, those were some good days. I had a lot of fun.

Charlie Mingus was my man. Charlie and I got along. You know, we were two nuts together, crazy, and really didn't care. I think Joe Comfort made Charlie a good bass player, because four or five of us had this gig. They wanted a bass player, and they were auditioning Charlie and Joe Comfort. Well, Joe was up on his instrument; he read and could play. And Charlie couldn't read or do anything. You know, he just wanted to play. So they took Joe Comfort. And Charlie said, "I'm going to make you sorry you ever picked up a bass." [laughter] "I'll make all of you sorry."

We were all in our teens then, I guess. That's when I'd first gotten out here, I think. And Charlie did it. He got on that bass. He was doing things that nobody believed was possible. Yeah. And he made them sorry. Of all the bass players out here—Joe Comfort, Addison Farmer, Leroy Vinnegar—you never heard about them like you heard about Charlie Mingus.

But he was still a nut. [laughter] He was short-tempered. At the drop of a hat he was ready to fight. They tell me the story that he was on the big red car [public transit], and some sailor made one of those off remarks, and he cleaned out a whole train full of sailors by himself. He was very race conscious, and they said the wrong word. He went off on them. He would fight at the drop of a hat, and mostly all the time he won. He was a heavyweight. But that was my rhythm section. Boy, if there was a session, we'd be there. Whatever came up.

I met Chico Hamilton, and I met Buddy Collette, and I met all the local guys. Jackie Kelso. He was a wonderful saxophone player. Coming from New York, most of the guys here were strange. You know, they didn't dig New Yorkers at all. They said we had an attitude, and I guess we did. Well at that time I was under that false impression that these guys didn't know anything out here, you know, this West Coast jazz. Everything here was so laid back. In New York, when you opened your eyes in the morning, it was business. It was a hustle. I mean, in New York you can't lay around and wait for a job. You've got to go out and find a job. Here, guys didn't seem to worry about whether they played or not. You know, a job would show up for them.

In New York, every day was a scuffling day, and you had to be out there. When I got out here, guys didn't even want to rehearse. In New York, I'd rehearse with three or four groups with no job in sight, but just to play. Out here, you ask a guy to rehearse, he wants to know where the job is, when is the job, and how much does it pay. So I was an outcast. But then I finally made a lot of friends here, and that's where I stayed. I grew to love L.A.

Buddy and Chico and Jackie and Mingus, these guys, they wanted to play. And they were for real about playing. They didn't want to just sit on the job because it was a job. They wanted to try new things, write things and all that. At that time, nobody was very good at it, but they were all trying. I wanted to sit there and play and have fun and go out and hang out all morning, get home at daylight or whenever I got there. You know, that's when I would meet the guys. We were players.

"We had a whole bunch of good piano players out here."

When Wig arrived in California, Central Avenue's presiding piano genius was Nat King Cole. The two became good friends.

Yeah, well, Nat was something else, now. Oh, man, he was a whiz. He used to come down to Memory Lane all the time right after closing time. Larry Hearn would shut up the joint, and it would just be a few of the regulars and my trio. Nat would sit there and play till daylight, and you ain't never heard such piano. Oh, man. He was a good player. I was sorry he started singing. It made him a million dollars, of course, but anytime he was in town, he'd get by Memory Lane. Just to play piano. Oh, it was good for him. You know, even when he was very sick, he came by. Yeah.

He'd sit up there with us, and he couldn't do wrong. He was a marvelous piano player. Oh, man. He had all the little tricks and everything and a beautiful touch. A very distinctive style. Yeah. And Nat was a good friend, too. Yeah.

New arrival Carl Perkins quickly made a name for himself.

Carl was the piano player who played with his elbow. You should have heard him. Carl Perkins sat at the piano with his whole body angled to the right, playing bass notes with his left elbow. He'd run up and down with his right hand and hit bass notes with his elbow. Unbelievable. And never miss. I thought he had a finger in that elbow. [laughter] He was unbelievable.

Carl just could swing. He came to town and upset everybody. They'd say, "You've got to see this cat play piano. He must be deformed or some-thing, because he sits sideways, and he's doing something with his elbow." They didn't realize he was hitting bass notes. He made it sound so good. [sings, mimicking Perkins's piano style] When I saw that, I said, "Did I see you break out with something?" He said, "No, it's just that I couldn't reach tenths as a kid, so I did this." Which made sense. He couldn't reach it. It was a beautiful style.

By that time, we had a whole bunch of good piano players out here. Arnold Ross was fantastic. There's a whole lot. I can't even name them. There's Jimmy Bunn. He's still around. He's a good piano player. Hamp-ton Hawes, yeah. Let's see. Nellie Lutcher, and those guys like Lorenzo Flennoy. He *was* Central Avenue.

When Art Tatum got out here, he had like a little troupe that followed him around. There was Willie Hawkins, who was a guy that you probably never heard of and probably never will. He played everything in F-sharp, but he had all of Tatum's stuff. This just used to knock Tatum out. He'd try to play Tatum.

But, boy, I don't know anybody who could keep up with Tatum. Ta-tum wasn't really a good guy to jam with, because he was all over the piano all the time. It must have been his ego, although he wasn't an ego-tistical man. The way he played was all-out all the time. You know, you'd be trying to solo, and he's running all over the piano. So he wasn't too much of a guy to have in a jam session. He was the whole show. I don't care what you played, you couldn't match what he was doing, anyhow,

you know? I've got lots of albums with him that he made with Benny
Carter, Roy Eldridge. And it's the same thing. It's all Tatum.

Yeah, he was a solo pianist, see. That was his strength right there. And
his trio, it was— Well, there wasn't too much competition in the trio.
The guys kept time for him. But I always like him best by himself, because there was nothing to inhibit him or stop him from going wherever. With a bass player, you don't want to go too far and lose him, so
you can't stretch out that much. Although, I don't think he really cared.
He was going where he was going anyhow. And his sense of time would
drive a drummer crazy, because he knew where it was all the time. And if
you would pat your foot and hum the tune, the melody, he was right
there. But he'd go on some excursions sometimes where you'd wonder,
"Where's he going? Is he still in the same tune?" It would be the same
tune, but unless you had the melody in your mind and were singing it
along, you wouldn't believe it. Because he could get farther out than the
guys are today. But he'd always find his way back.

Oh, Lovejoy's was great. It was upstairs, and they had this big raggedy
piano, and that's where we'd all go because Tatum always used to come
in and play like he did in New York. He used to go to a place called
Ruben's and play after-hours. Out here it was Lovejoy's. And he'd make
that piano sound like a Steinway. Nobody else could do anything with it
but him. I don't know how he accomplished that. It's like the piano said,
"I'll sound good for him," and every note he played was a gem. Before he
sat down, he'd run his hands the length of the piano, and any clams, he
would never touch them while he was playing. I don't know how he did
that, but he did.

He used to play on Eighth Street. At one time, we were all working
Eighth Street: Nat Cole, Art Tatum, myself, all the different clubs. The
331 Club, and I think the Tiffany was down there. But that's when L.A.
was jumping, boy. This was a good town then. A lot of good musicians,
a lot of good clubs, and everybody was making a pretty fair buck for those
times.

All he wanted to talk about was baseball. He'd tell you what Ty Cobb
hit in 1903. Anything he wanted to do, he could have done. He had a
brilliant mind. But he was a guy you had to really know, because he was
a bunch of laughs. You know, he was good-humored and just a sweetheart. And the greatest thing of all, if I was playing somewhere, he'd come
to hear me play. And that really was a good feeling.

The biggest thing he ever did for himself was buy a brand new Steinway, and I think he died a few months later. They should have given him one, but he bought this new Steinway B. The morning he died, all the piano players in town were at his house. Carl Perkins, Eddie Beal, just everybody who was in town. We all played for him. He sat on the side of the bed while we played. The next morning, he was gone. That kind of left a void, because I'd known him quite a few years. It was 1938 when I met him. He was so helpful to the guys. You could ask him anything, and he'd show it to you, and you didn't have a chance of doing it. [laughter] He was just unbelievable.

By the late 1940s Los Angeles was a major center of r&b, and many jazz musicians moved into that sound—but not Gerald Wiggins.

I remember that I wouldn't play it, so they starved me to death. I said, "I'm not going to play that junk." I went into a session and the guy told me, "Wig, I want you to play a bad chord." And I'm trying to think of what can I lay on him and everything. And I'm stretching out. He says, "No. Play like you've got gloves on, like you don't know anything about the piano." That's the day I gave up that rock and roll and blues stuff. "Hey, forget it," and they didn't hire me anymore.

They were recording this stuff, you can't believe how much. It was so bad as far as I was concerned. It was mostly blues all the time. Any way you could think of it, it was blues, with the guitars wanging away, and the tenor honking, and the drums had a heavy backbeat. You know, it wasn't music at all. But it took the public's fancy, and they ate it up. In fact, guys like myself were saying, "Well, this won't last." It got bigger and bigger and bigger and bigger. All we could do was sit there and look at it and listen to it. But it was horrible. It really was.

Union Musician

I think everything on Central was more or less union. I know I usually filed the contracts on all the jobs I did. And they had one union guy, Fain, Elmer Fain. Talking about a policeman. He'd come by the job and look, and if he saw somebody on the stand he didn't know, he'd ask for their card, and if they didn't have a card or weren't in the union, off the stand you went. The guys hated—well, not hated him, but they sure hated to see him coming. [laughter] He was a big, burly son-of-a-gun, and he was all business. He had a smile that would freeze ice. [laughter] But he turned out to be a pretty good guy, though, really. But he was a businessman. Maybe a little bit too much. He was the unforgiving type, you know. Anything he caught you wrong at, that was it. There was no, "Well, don't do it again." That was it. You went before the board right away.

Needless to say, I stayed at the board. [laughter] But they liked me at the board, so I always got off. [laughter] For some reason, they never would do anything to me. I was jamming when I shouldn't have been, sitting in on somebody else's job when I wasn't supposed to be. A lot of little technical— Late with payment of the dues or whatever. Nothing earthshaking, but he was that much of a stickler for it. Yeah, he was a pretty tough customer. But I got to know him, and he wasn't that bad. At that time I was young and full of that ginger, and I didn't want anybody to interfere with my fun, whatever it was. [laughter] But Fain and I became pretty good friends.

Wig supported the movement for the amalgamation of Locals 767 and 47.

Oh, I voted for it. I thought it was a good thing, yeah. I think some of the guys felt at the time that, if it was amalgamation, they would lose the jobs that they had, but it didn't turn out that way. In fact, it opened up more opportunities for them. They weren't restricted to Central Avenue and things like that. Before, they never tried to go anywhere else. Now they had the whole territory open to them. It was open all the time, but there was that feeling, "Well, no, that belongs to 47, so we won't mess with it." There was no law that said you couldn't work the territory. But it was best that they all got together.

Wig spent much of his career in and out of town, accompanying Lena Horne, Kay Starr, Dinah Washington, and Helen Humes. He also worked on all of Marilyn Monroe's musicals in Hollywood.

My studio work came through Jackie Mills, who used to be a drummer with Tommy Dorsey. He got into the motion picture business, and choreographer Jack Cole was crazy about him. Every time they made a musical, they would hire Jackie Mills. Jackie swung me in on the deal. Jack wanted a piano player that was more or less jazz oriented. Jackie and I had gone to school together. He told Jack Cole about me, and Jack hired me. That's how I got to do so much work with Marilyn Monroe. We did the rehearsals and all that. I did the piano sketches for whoever was going to do the arranging.

In fact, I've got a couple of tunes in the picture *Let's Make Love.* They were original because we just made it up on the set. Another one was *Strip City.* They wanted something for, like, strippers, and I just made this thing up, no music or nothing, just played it. I still get checks from it. [laughter]

And Marilyn was a champ. I loved working with her, because she'd call us: "Gerry, I can't make it today. I'm sick." And I may not see her for two months, but I'm still on salary. Finally, she'd show up. Whatever she had to do, we'd get it done in a hurry. She was a hard worker and took care of business. But that was a great life. The pay was good, the work wasn't hard, and then I was left to my own devices most of the time. I did just about every musical that she did. I'd coach her for singing the tunes. She didn't have that much of a voice, but she made it work. So those were some of the good times.

The Decline of Central

Everything went west. All the guys started working on the Westside, and possibly the amalgamation had something to do with it. I don't know. The territory opened up. When I first came out here, I don't think Negroes could go past Central Avenue. I never got off of Central Avenue that I can remember. I was always there. But I think that it— Well, Central Avenue just went down.

Now Central Avenue is a wasteland. I used to go down to visit an old friend of mine, Luke Jones, who was a barber and also a saxophone player, and I think it got too rough for him down there. He just closed up his shop. It's pretty grim.

But it will build up again. It will do just like they do in Harlem. You know, Harlem was pretty bad. Now people are saying, "The heck with this good property up there. We're going to go back and build it up again." And that's what they're doing. So it will be a resurgence, I'm sure. I probably won't see it, and I really don't care. Everything goes in cycles.

I would say Central Avenue was very important for the fact that not only the musicians but all the movie people came down there all the time. All the stars would go to Central Avenue. That was their hangout, you know. You could see the biggest stars come down there. Someplace to go, I guess. It was pretty wide open, and you could hear good music. And they had to come down there, because we couldn't go over there! [laughter] And that's where all the famous musicians at that time would gravitate. When a guy came in town, he went to Central Avenue, because that's where the action was.

A lot of good musicians came off of Central Avenue. I mean very good guys. It should have a place in history, like Bourbon Street and Beale Street and Fifty-second Street. Central Avenue's right up there with them as far as being important, I think. Central Avenue was probably the closest thing to Fifty-second Street than anywhere else that I know of. Maybe New Orleans, but that was strictly Dixieland-type stuff. But I think for jazz you'd have to rate Central Avenue right along with Fifty-second Street.

Central Avenue was great, especially for me. I enjoyed every moment of it, even in my befuddled condition. [laughter] You know, guys from out of town would come in, and we'd listen to them and they'd listen to us. It's funny, I'm talking like I'm a Los Angeles person. Although I'm from New York, I've been here so long, I feel like I am part of it. Some wonderful things happened down there.

I'm glad I was part of it. It's a very important part of my life. Not only me, a lot of other guys, too. It was educational in quite a few ways, in fact, better than Fifty-second Street, I think, because you got a chance to participate mostly in Central Avenue, whereas Fifty-second Street, it was always the name groups. If Art Tatum was playing at the Three Deuces or somewhere in Chicago, or wherever in New York, you couldn't go up there and sit in with him. But on Central Avenue, if he was playing, you could jump on in there and nobody would say anything. Oh, yeah. They had a chance to play and learn. Yeah.

There were a lot of good musicians in this town who never got anywhere, but they were still good musicians. They went into some other things. A couple of guys I know went into electronics. Everybody has their own calling, I guess. Myself, this is all I ever wanted to do. As the song says, "As the curtain falls, just think, 'I get paid for this.'" You know? [laughter] That pretty much sums it up for me.

16

Gerald Wilson

Trumpeter, composer, arranger, and educator, Gerald Wilson has been at the top of his profession since joining the Jimmie Lunceford band in 1939 at the age of twenty. He has performed with and written for most of the top bands, including Count Basie and Duke Ellington, as well as Cab Calloway, Ray Charles, Ella Fitzgerald, Benny Goodman, Lionel Hampton, Woody Herman, and Billie Holiday. The Gerald Wilson Orchestra has been a mainstay for decades and is still performing and recording.

Gerald's talent for composing and arranging has taken him beyond the jazz field. He has written and scored for films and TV shows. His compositions have also been performed by the Los Angeles, Israel, and New York Philharmonics.

A long-time educator, Gerald has been a faculty member at several southern California universities. He is currently on the faculty at UCLA, where he teaches a course on the history of jazz. He has also been a musician in residence at colleges and universities throughout the country. Of the many awards that have come his way, one of the more recent is a National Endowment for the Arts American Jazz Masters Fellowship.

Gerald was born in Shelby, Mississippi, on September 4, 1918. His mother, Lillian Wilson, was a schoolteacher at the Shelby Grammar School, a position she held for some forty years.

My mother was educated and she graduated from Jackson College, which is now Jackson State University. She was also a musician. She played piano. She taught some of the early classes in music in Shelby. And then she also played in the church. So I got my beginning in music with my mother, who started all of us. The Wilson kids, my brother [Shelby James Wilson] and sister [Mildred Wilson]—we all got a start in music very young. So being around music all my life, it was easy for me to pick up on it and begin to like it.

My sister was a fine classical pianist. I had already heard her play compositions by Mendelssohn, Paderewski, Rachmaninoff, Mozart, Beethoven. In my early days I knew of these composers, besides being interested in the music of the day, which was jazz coming out of New Orleans. When I was a child around five or six, I was already hearing Jelly Roll Morton and King Oliver and Papa Celestin. Before I left Shelby I already knew of Louis Armstrong and Earl Hines and Duke Ellington and Jimmie Lunceford. I was already listening to jazz before I left Mississippi.

I left Mississippi at the end of the eighth grade because there was no other place to go there. So I went to Memphis. I attended Manassas High School, where Jimmie Lunceford had once been a teacher. I started trumpet lessons there with Mr. Love, who was one of the pioneer music teachers of Memphis. But I had started playing trumpet before I left Shelby, only because it was a shiny instrument, I guess. I really should have stayed on the piano. It is the master instrument to my mind, because it has everything there.

Then my mother arranged for me to study in Detroit—had friends there from Shelby. When I started attending school in Detroit in 1934, mostly all of the schools were integrated. And besides, they had such a great music department where I attended, Cass Technical High School, which is one of the greatest music schools in the world even to this day. So I enrolled there, and I stayed in Detroit for five years, where I studied.

I played in the area with different orchestras and different musicians. I learned so much playing with members of McKinney's Cotton Pickers, members of bands that had been led by Don Redman and Benny Carter. And many of the fine bands they had in Detroit: Stutz Sanderson's band, Gloster Current, Harold Green, Bob Perkins—these were all bands that were very musical. It was a place to really learn about music.

Gerald remained in Detroit for five years, until 1939, when a wire arrived from Jimmie Lunceford, the leader of perhaps the most popular black band in the country. Sy Oliver—Lunceford's long-time arranger, composer, and trumpeter—had left to join Tommy Dorsey, and Gerald was asked to take his place.

Jimmie Lunceford had been to our school, Cass Tech, to hear our jazz band, and he had met me there. However, I had people in the band that knew me because I used to hang around the band every time they would come to Detroit, which would be two or three times a year. Sy would sit me up on the bandstand beside him at the Graystone, just let me sit there. I knew Eddie Tomkins and Paul Webster and Willie Smith and Joe Thomas, Earl Carruthers, Dan Grissom.

I received a wire asking me if I would like to join the Jimmie Lunceford band. I said yes. I just went down the next morning, picked up my ticket, some money, on the train, and I went to New York. Then, from that time on, I was on top because they were on top. They were not a struggling band. They were on the very top. June of 1939. They were at the height of their fame. But the Lunceford band went higher after Snooky Young and I joined the band. He came six months after I did. We stayed there almost three years.

We made the film *Blues in the Night* here in Los Angeles for Warner Brothers in 1941. We played the Casa Mañana in 1940, the Paramount downtown, the Shrine Auditorium, where they had so many people they had to stop the dance. We were the biggest draw in the United States at that time, the Jimmie Lunceford band.

I was twenty-one years old. But you must remember, we were coming up at a different time. I was coming up out of Cass Tech. I could already read music, I could already write music. I was already into the modern things going around at that time in jazz because I was an aficionado besides. I had already met Dizzy Gillespie in 1938. I already knew Lester Young and Count Basie. So this gives you an idea of what we had to draw on as young musicians. You're right there with people that are doing it, and they're doing the very best.

The Jimmie Lunceford band, besides being an outstanding musical organization, had everything else. They had made it to the top. They knew what the top was supposed to be. Our costumes would take half of this room we're sitting in here to hold them. If we did seven shows, we changed seven times, from top to bottom. So you can see what kind of an organization the Jimmie Lunceford band was. But they were strictly on their music. They were a tough band to reckon with. You had to be really tough to get past us. [laughter] Yes. We would really tell you the real deal. You can go and listen to our records now. That proves it. Go and listen to their records today, and you will see how far ahead they were at any time during that period. The first number that they recorded of mine, "Yard Dog Mazurka," is just as vibrant today as it was then, and just as modern. You can see how far ahead I was.

My harmonic techniques at that time were very far ahead. When I left Detroit from Cass Tech, they were barely into four-part harmony. I'm still the only person that's very deep into eight-part harmony. I'm an orchestrator and an arranger and composer. That's my business. Of course, I'm one of the innovators of that. Much of my stuff you have to use if you're in modern music. If you're in orchestral music, you must use some of my inventions. Colleges don't even know what we're talking about here. They have an idea of what we're talking about, but they don't really know. I know all of the people that teach at colleges. We know what they do. They're not out here, they're not competing in the world. We know how much they know.

My band today is far ahead. I don't have just a band. I have an orchestra, really. A band is a commercial business. I'm not in it for the commercial business. I'm a musician. The music is what is important to me. That is my central drive. That is really what it's all about with me. I know that I have one of the greatest bands in the world. I don't know anybody in jazz today that would want to come up against me in writing. If he does, he's a strong man, and he's got a tough row to hoe. [laughter] And I don't know any you can find out there who will tell you that he wants to go up against me. And if you do, tell him to come on. [laughter] But that's not for an egotistical purpose. That is what I have done. I have studied all my life. I'm still studying.

Seduced by Sunshine

In February of 1940 I came to Los Angeles with the Jimmie Lunceford band. We had just finished playing a week at the Regal in Chicago, and we boarded the train there. By the way, it was like eighteen degrees above when we left. We had a Pullman and everything. Big-time band. I'll never forget that day in February. As I looked out the window of my bunk in the sleeper, I see this beautiful sunshine. We were somewhere like San Bernardino. And I said, "Well, this is going to be the place for me." [laughter] And when I got to Los Angeles and I saw how pretty it was, I said, "This will be my home." I was very impressed with Los Angeles. I made up my mind that day that I was going to live in Los Angeles.

I got off the train there at Union Station. They had a parade for us. This is how big we were. They had a parade from the station to the Dunbar Hotel, where we were going to stay. Snooky Young and I, we didn't follow along with the parade. We were just milling around at the station and looking around. The parade was moving on, and there was this white guy who came up to us and said, "Are you guys with the Jimmie Lunceford band?" We said, "Yeah. We play with the Lunceford band." He introduced himself. "My name is Carlos Gastel." He managed Stan Kenton, he managed Benny Carter, he managed Nat King Cole. Later. Right then, he was just booking some little dances, so he had been the booker for us at a dance at the Glendale Civic Auditorium. So he was just looking for some guys in the Lunceford band to talk to. He had missed Jimmie, but he offered to drive us to the hotel, which he did. He drove us up Central Avenue to the Dunbar Hotel, where we registered. That was my first day in Los Angeles.

Central Avenue. I didn't think about it as anything so special other than the fact that it's where I can stay. It's the only place I can sleep. [laughter] Having been everywhere in the United States, I had seen all the black streets. Central Avenue is like Saint Antoine in Detroit or like South Park in Chicago or like 125th Street in New York or like Central in Cleveland. So at that time I didn't realize what it would mean to me later. Los Angeles would become my home, and Central Avenue would become an integral part of me.

The Dunbar was a very fine hotel, coffee shop, bar, dining room. The rooms were impeccable. The Nelsons, who owned it and ran it, saw to it that you had to be right on top of everything. You couldn't come in there with a lot of loud behavior. So it was a place of class. I enjoyed staying there. And it was near everything. It was right in the center. A couple of doors down was the Alabam; a couple of doors from that was the Downbeat; across the street was the Last Word; over here on the other side was the Memo; the Five and Ten was there; down a few blocks, Dynamite Jackson's; the Lincoln Theatre was up a few blocks. All of these places— the Elks. This is all Central Avenue. This was our place to go.

The first job we played was the Civic Auditorium in Glendale. Our next date was at the Shrine Auditorium down on Jefferson. Packed and jammed. Couldn't get in, there were so many people. And then we played a return engagement there before we left. But then we played the Paramount Theatre downtown for a week. We even went to the Casa Mañana out in Culver City, where we played for six weeks. That was located on Washington Boulevard right out near the Helms Bakery. It was the old Sebastian's Cotton Club and was a big place. It would hold about, oh, I'd say fifteen hundred or two thousand. Then we'd stay here while we'd play San Diego. And we may go to Bakersfield, Fresno—because we'd play everywhere.

During this first trip, I went into the Alabam. It was a beat-up club. I said, "Why would anybody want to come in here, anyway?" [laughter] And I went in. But I heard some fine musicians that night. I went in and I heard Marshal Royal, his brother Ernie Royal, Lloyd Reese. Reese was playing trumpet and alto sax. [laughter] He was playing both of them and was recognized as being one of the finest musicians around the country. They were all playing with Cee Pee Johnson's band.

They had little groups playing at different clubs. Lorenzo Flennoy and his trio. A lot of trios around. Lee Young, Lester's brother. They had their group. They were working with Billie Holiday at the Trouville, which was in Hollywood. The Memo Club—they'd have some kind of maybe a piano player, a trio, a duo, or something like that. That was across the street from the Dunbar, like catty-corner. Lovejoy had a place where they used to have jam sessions. Upstairs place on Vernon Avenue and Central. All the guys would go there to jam—Art Tatum, the heavies. Duke's band came in town while we were here one time. I saw Jimmy Blanton, and he was up there jamming.

There were bands around Los Angeles. There was George Brown's band, Phil Carreon, and other groups that were playing at different clubs around. Of course, Red Callender—he was very popular at that time. He was a fine bass player. He was playing with Lee Young's group, Lester Young had joined them, and they were playing with Billie Holiday out at the Trouville.

So it was a lot of musical things going on during that period. Benny Carter was in town with a band. Les Hite had a band. Lionel Hampton formed his band in '40. I think it was '40. We were all talking down in front of the Dunbar there with Dexter Gordon, Illinois Jacquet, Ray

330 Drawn by Central's Magic

Perry—this kid with Chick Carter's band. Dexter was very young. He was just joining Lionel's band.

We played our first engagement here in 1940. We came back again during the early part of 1941. And this time, I believe we played the Orpheum Theatre. We made a movie for Warner Brothers, *Blues in the Night.* We were in that movie with Lloyd Nolan, Richard Whorf, Rosemary Lane, and Elia Kazan. We played the Casa Mañana, because that's where Ray Heindorf, who was one of the music directors at Warner Brothers, used to come to see us every night.

Wartime

I left the Lunceford band in April 1942. It was the time of World War II. I was 1-A, and I knew I was going to be called soon. I wanted to spend a little time kind of relaxed. I'd been with him a long time and needed a little time to kind of get ready for the service. And that's what I did. I came here.

But I didn't go for a while, so I went with Les Hite. I stayed with him for about six months. We played a long engagement at the Wilshire Bowl, which had become the Louisiana Club. The Wilshire Bowl was a fine nightclub that changed its name in the early forties to the Louisiana Club. It was on Wilshire near the Miracle Mile. But the Miracle Mile was nothing but open space in there. We played there for like two or three months. Every night. Big show. Big, big, big chorus line, big acts, big-time acts. All white acts, like the Rio Brothers and different kinds of singers. They had a black band, though; we were the black band. Mingus played with us there. And then Snooky was in the band. He joined Les Hite, too. He moved out to the coast, and he moved in.

Les Hite was always recognized as having a good band. He had good music. I did a lot of writing for him while I was in his band, and Gil Fuller did a lot of arrangements for him. He had been successful, and he knew how to front a band. And he was very popular. We toured, we played all up the coast here. Finally, he just gave it up. After all those years, he probably just really got tired of it.

And then we went with Benny Carter. Our whole trumpet section from that band, we just went into Benny's band one night. We were tough. In fact, those four trumpets—we also went out and played the music for the special dance that the black dancers did in *This Is the Army* with this huge orchestra, Warner Brothers orchestra. And the four trumpet players were black: it was Snooky Young, myself, a fellow named Jack Trainor, and another kid named Walter Williams. We were the only trumpets in the band. But we guaranteed that we could play anything. [laughter] We could play anything you had between the four of us. We handled it all. So we went into Benny's band one night. And from that night on, his band was lifted from here to here. Do you understand what I'm saying? From here to here. [laughter]

J. J. Johnson was in the band. They had Teddy Brannon and Bumps Myers. Oh, he had some good guys. He had Shorty Horton, J. J., "Big" Matthews, trombone. These were guys right out of New York. That was the trombone section. And he had Kurk Bradford. We had taken him from Les Hite's band.

We went on back up the coast with Benny. Then we were playing at Hermosa Beach, a place called Zucca's Terrace. It was right in front of the Lighthouse. Upstairs. Benny played out there a couple of weeks, I think. I was drafted, inducted, while I was there. I was inducted into the navy. It would have been probably June of 1943. June, maybe July. In fact, some of the guys in the band took me to the induction center down on Main Street. I thought I was going to be rejected, but they took me. [laughter]

Anyway, I was off to the navy, which was a fine experience, by the way. I was lucky. I got in the ship's company band at Great Lakes. It's just about, I'd say, thirty-five or forty miles from Chicago. We were very privileged people. We lived in Chicago. Come at eight in the morning and leave at four in the evening unless you were performing that night. And then whenever you finished, you could go. In fact, I never slept another night on the base after I got out of boot camp.

My friend Willie Smith from the Lunceford band was there. Clark Terry was there. It was a band of fine musicians, so it was a great experience. It was good for me because it was another chance to just study and do music, because we did music all day. That was it. We played for things: graduation, we played for happy hours, we played for colors. Then we had our jazz band. And we broadcast every week, every Saturday night, over CBS, so it kept us busy. A lot of writing. We had some fine writers there: Dudley Brooks, who was from Los Angeles, a great writer. He worked out at MGM, many of the studios. He was a fine pianist. He also did a lot of work with Elvis Presley.

So it really was a fine time at Great Lakes, because all I had to do was write and play. It gave me a great chance to study, experiment all of the experiments you wanted because we had like five trumpets in the band, five trombones, French horn, six reeds. That's the jazz band I'm talking about. Of course, our marching band was very large, and we did everything. They had handpicked all of the musicians.

But anyway, I only spent a year in the navy. I had a very bad sinus infection, so I had a medical discharge.

Then I came back to L.A. Oh, that was about July or August of 1944. When I got back, Central was getting into full swing. The Lincoln Theatre—they were starting to have stage shows every week. Before it was mostly movies. They had a pit band, they had acts, chorus girls, and they would change the shows every week. They had some great performers there like Pigmeat Markham, Bardu Ali. Bardu was the leader of the band, too. By the way, let me tell you some people that were playing in that band. Charles Brown, the great blues singer. He played piano. Yeah, he's a fine piano player. And Melba Liston was playing trombone in the band. She was very young. About sixteen or seventeen. Floyd Turnham, fine alto player that had been with Les Hite.

Bardu, he was a performer. He was like a straight man, and he would direct the band. He had been in New York, and he did the same thing in New York. He had a brother, also, who was in show business. He was a dancer. They used to call him the Beachcomber. And that was his deal. He was a showman.

The Alabam was now really looking good, had been remodeled. Curtis Mosby had it. Curtis was a nice man. He had been in the business. You know, he was a musician and had a band. And he had fixed the club up real nice. They were having regular shows in there. The Downbeat was coming on the scene. Across the street, the Last Word was happening then. In all, there were a lot of things going on now on Central Avenue and things were looking good. They were really looking good. You could tell that things were in good shape, because you could tell by how the clubs looked—real nice clubs, nice acts playing in the club, nice groups.

I played in the Downbeat with Lee Young during that period, Lee Young and one of the Woodman brothers. We called him Brother Woodman. He's the one that plays sax and the trumpet. And Joe Liggins was the piano player, and I was the trumpet player. In fact, we were the first people to do "The Honeydripper." Joe Liggins wanted us to do his number, "The Honeydripper," which later became a nationwide hit.

So Central was looking real good. The Dunbar was still nice. All the bands still came there. Duke and Count, Jimmie Lunceford. Joe Morris owned the Plantation. Oh, a beautiful club. Large place. They'd have shows, acts. I finished out an engagement with Billie Holiday with my band, which was a little later on. It was in '45. And Shepp's Playhouse was not on Central, but it was on First and Los Angeles, where the New Otani Hotel is. I played more than one engagement there.

From the Plantation to the Apollo

I organized my band in October of 1944. I was not really ready yet to form my band, but the opportunity came. Actually, I was going to join a band. I did a lot of work during that period with Phil Moore as trumpet player. I made many recordings with Phil on his own records. And he was also Lena Horne's musical accompanist and director, and I did all of her dates with Phil. He worked at MGM all the time. He did work for Nathaniel Schildkret. It's like ghostwriting. I've never seen his name on the screen. They did him really a bad deal. I kicked because they didn't put my name in *Where the Boys Are* and the other movies that I scored for. I kicked. That was even in the late fifties. But this guy was already writing music for MGM and other studios, too. Not only him—Calvin Jackson wrote many scores at MGM, many. I'm not speaking like one or two or three. I'm talking like ten or fifteen. Heavy, heavy scores, you know.

So I was very busy when I first got back from the navy. But, as I said, the opportunity came for me to get my band. From the time that I was ten years old, I knew that I was going to be a bandleader. I knew that. And I knew that I was going to be a bandleader that wrote music for my band to play, because I was already a great admirer of Duke Ellington. And listening to their records and listening to them on the radio, I knew that I was going to be a bandleader and I was going to be an orchestrator, an arranger, composer.

So my opportunity came, and I didn't let it pass. Herb Jeffries wanted to have a band, so he asked me to form his band. And I did. And things were going so good for Herb, I guess, that at that time he really didn't have time to be fronting a band. So there I was with the band. So Leonard Reed, who was the producer at Shepp's Playhouse, booked us in there. So that's how I got started with the band.

It was very good, because we broadcast two or three times a week over the radio. Had a fine show there. They had chorus girls and acts. And they had a lounge there, too, which was downstairs. It was like a bar. And Eddie Heywood's band was there while we were there, the band that had such great success with "Begin the Beguine," which was a big hit record for him and his band. That was in 1945. And we also played the Orpheum Theatre that year together, Eddie Heywood and I. We played a lot of things, a lot of dances and club dates over at the Elks Auditorium, which is on Central Avenue.

Now, my band, we were all from California. We had some fine players. We had Melba Liston; Jimmy Bunn was on piano, a fine young artist; Henry Green, who later became the mainstay drummer with the Treniers. We had some fine trumpeters: Snooky Young came with my band; we had Jack Trainor, who had been with Hite's band and Benny Carter's band. So we really had a fine band.

Melba was a fine trombone player. She was such a good trombone player, she could play it all. She could play lead, she could play solos, too—usually play it better than the guys. She joined my band in 1944, so she was maybe about seventeen. She was with my band when it disbanded, and she was with all of my other bands at that time. Really a fine musician. Still a fine musician. She's one of the finest writers that I've ever heard. In fact, I recorded a couple of her arrangements in 1945. I had another girl in my band too. Her name was Vivian Fears. She was a fine pianist. I had picked her up in Chicago. She had been playing with Fletcher Henderson's band. She was from Saint Louis. Another fine pianist, played real great jazz.

I played at the Plantation, which was on Central but way out in Watts. It was a large place with a lot of tables and chairs and a dance floor. It attracted big crowds, all different kinds of people, but you must remember that the bulk of the people that came there were black. And all the big bands played there: Count Basie, Jimmie Lunceford, Erskine Hawkins, Earl Hines, Billy Eckstine. Billie Holiday sang there—I played there with Billie Holiday. I finished out the engagement she had there when Billy Eckstine left. As I say, it was a very, very nice place, a very nice place. Joe Morris owned it.

And also I played with my big band at the Downbeat club. I was the first big band to ever play in the Downbeat. I think it was owned by Hal Stanley, whom I knew very well, and Elihu McGhee. Now, Hal Stanley was also at one time managing Kay Starr. Hal was managing Kay when I worked at the Casbah Supper Club as a trumpet player with Benny Carter.

The Downbeat was a small club. I'd say it would maybe seat 125 people. As you walk in, to your left there's this fine bar. You'd walk around, and you could stand at the end. Because I remember when I played there, Art Tatum used to come in every night and stand right over there to hear my band. He loved my band. He would come in every night. He wanted me to play some of my numbers that at that time were considered to be far ahead, because I was already using harmonies that no other bands were actually utilizing. I was deep into six at that time. Yeah, deep into six-part harmonies. Anyway—we're getting technical here now—but yeah, you'd see that bar and then the tables and chairs. And the bandstand was in the center of the building over on the right side, and there were tables all out from there.

We played all kinds of things and throughout the West over the next couple of years. We went to New York in 1946. We played the Apollo Theatre, and we were sensational there. I followed Duke Ellington at the Apollo, and Jimmie Lunceford followed me. So we were in top company. But we were very good. At that time we had recordings. I had about, oh, I'd say twenty or twenty-five sides by that time. I recorded my first recording date in 1945 on the Excelsior label. That's Otis René's label, the same label that Nat King Cole was on at the time. So my records were going very good. I had a couple of mild hits.

We left the Apollo, went to Pittsburgh, and then we went on into Chicago and we played there at the El Grotto for ten weeks. They built the whole show around my band. Marl Young, who's now on the board at the union [Local 47], he came in and subbed in my band for a few nights while we were in Chicago. This is before he came to L.A. I did six weeks at the Riviera in Saint Louis with Ella Fitzgerald. Joe Williams was my singer. And we packed this club—it would hold about twelve hundred people—every night for six weeks. And to really top it off, they had a special night there, I remember, where Ella Fitzgerald and Louis Armstrong battled my band. [laughter] And people were lined up around the corner.

Walking Away from It

While I was in Saint Louis, I realized that I had already hit the top. I was already on top now. It was getting to be that way. My time was getting so that I would hardly have any time. The band was very popular. I had these weeks already signed with Louis Jordan, and then Eddie "Rochester" Anderson wanted me to tour with him. So everything was happening. I realized that I had hit the top too soon. I was not even near where I wanted to be as a musician, and I knew this. And, of course, when I said this to people, they said, "Well, what's wrong with the guy?" They just don't understand what you're trying to say.

Anyway, I made up my mind during the engagement in Saint Louis. I realized that this was not it. This was not it. And, of course, many people thought I was making a very big mistake, especially my booking office. I made up my mind that I was going to disband and return to Los Angeles, and I did just that. I paid off my men, and we came back to L.A., and I disbanded.

And then I started working with Phil Moore again, other people around town. I still had a lot of work to do musically. I started writing for a lot of people and studying, just studying and writing and playing— just doing all kinds of stuff, and studying, as I said, studying very hard. I studied the classics, Stravinsky, Shostakovich, Prokofiev, Khachaturian, d'Indy, Bartok, Manuel de Falla, Villa-Lobos. I'm looking for everything. I'm looking for music to broaden my knowledge of music. I wasn't studying them to be classical. I was studying them to broaden my knowledge so that I could broaden my jazz. But as far as jazz writers, who was I going to study with? I was just about one of the best then and I knew it. Of course you're going to say, okay, there's a guy bragging. But I was doing it.

So I'm studying. I played with Benny Carter, with his small group. We played eight weeks out on Figueroa near Manchester at the Casbah with Kay Starr. Then we went into the Million Dollar [Theatre] with Nat King Cole. I played the Avedon Ballroom with Nat King Cole. That was downtown on Spring Street, right in back of the Orpheum Theatre. Fine ballroom. All the bands played there. And after that, I joined Count Basie in 1948, at the end of 1948. But in between this time, I'm making recordings and playing all kinds of record dates, blues dates with people, artists, writing arrangements for different people, rhythm and blues, too. I was doing it all. So in 1948, about near the end of the year, Snooky Young had to leave to go back east, so I joined Count Basie.

Well, here was another opportunity. Here's Count Basie's band, and I was already writing. In fact, I made my first arrangement for Duke Ellington in 1947 that they recorded here on Columbia Records. So my first orchestrations for Duke Ellington ["You've Got to Crawl Before You Walk" and "You're Just an Old Antidisestablishmentarianismist"] were in 1947, which came off very well.. Billy Strayhorn and I were great friends. He's one of my—I would say, a mentor, because he is one of the few people that actually helped me. That was way back in the early forties. You know, showing me things, how to do some things. Anyway, that started an association with Duke for me. He actually wanted me to join his band. Duke asked me to join his band the minute I got back from disbanding my band, at the Dunbar Hotel. [laughter]

Anyway, Count Basie needed someone to fill in for Snooky until Snooky would come back. He was supposed to come back right away. But I ended up leaving town with the band. They were at the Lincoln at the time. I played the Lincoln Theatre with him, and I left with him. I stayed with Count until way up into—that was '48, '49. I returned to Los Angeles in '49. So I did a lot of writing for Count during that period. I wrote a whole show, a theater review, for him. I did some other stuff for him that we played on dances. And when we went to New York, we did some recordings for Victor. I did most of the writing for all of the dates.

The Amalgamation

So when I got back in '49, Central Avenue was still hopping. And the union, of course, that's when they were getting into the amalgamation. So Buddy Collette and Red Callender—you know, they were my friends, my dear friends. And I remember they asked me to go with them and get in on the amalgamation thing. I joined their group. And I remember we went out to Los Angeles City College that first night that I went with them. We went out getting white musicians to sign the petition.

Hey, you know, I was from Detroit. There's no segregated unions in

Detroit. And besides, what we were going for, I'm really for. So there was no problem there. So I joined their group and then I left, went back with Basie and finished out the year, '49, with Basie. In fact, I was with Basie when he disbanded. Nineteen fifty. So I stayed in New York, and I worked with Illinois Jacquet, and then I joined Dizzy Gillespie's band. I was with Dizzy when he broke up to get his small group. So big bands were folding. I went out on a tour with Billie Holiday. And then, after that, I came back to Los Angeles—that was '50—and did some things around town here, played, and then I decided to do a show. I wrote a show called the "California Frolics Revue." We presented it at the Riverside Rancho. We were rehearsing at the union, over at 767.

Anyway, while I was doing this rehearsing, I said to Buddy, "How are things going with the union?" He said, "Well, we're not doing too much right now." So I took it upon myself— I had a friend of mine, I ran into him, he was a lawyer. His name is Calvin Porter, still in business here. He was a friend of mine from Detroit when I was going to school. So I ran into him one night, we were just talking. And I said, "You know what? Calvin, I'm with a group of people. We're trying to get these unions amalgamated. We've been getting petitions signed and trying to get it going."

So he said, "Well, it sounds to me like there's something you're not doing. Obviously, the people who are in power at the union are running the union just as they want to, because there's nobody to stop them. First you've got to go in there and get this thing on the floor at the union. You slip in there on a day, on a general meeting, but you don't let them know you're coming. You go in. You will say, 'I move to make a motion that there will be a special meeting called for the specific purpose of discussing the amalgamation of Local 767 to Local 47.'"

I immediately told Buddy what we had to do. We immediately got in touch with everybody that was concerned with the movement and people that we knew would be for the movement. But we didn't have too much to worry about, because my band was already big enough to outvote them—the band that we were rehearsing upstairs. So we went about it exactly like that. The next general meeting, they didn't know what was happening. All of a sudden, all of these people come walking in. We picked up people in automobiles.

As the meeting got started and things were moving, I held up my hand to make a motion. I stood up and made it to the president—Leo McCoy Davis was his name—and I made that motion. "I would like to make a motion that a special meeting will be called for the specific purpose of discussing the amalgamation of Local 767 to Local 47." I was talking with Bill Douglass recently, who recently was the treasurer here [at Local 47]. He says he seconded it, but I don't remember. I thought it was Percy McDavid. It could have been Bill.

Now, what did this do? This enabled the amalgamation people to be able to go in and then vote their people into the Local 767 leadership, where Bill Douglass, I believe, became the vice president. Now, the reason I'm getting into this is because this has all been forgotten. I don't remember seeing Marl there that day, and I don't remember seeing Benny Carter there that day. I didn't remember Benny into it at any time until later, because we all wanted Benny to be with us. We wanted Marl because of his ability and his legal background at the time. But that was the day that happened.

I fought for the amalgamation. When I sit here [at Local 47] tonight, I know that I am the one that made the motion for the first special meeting called for the amalgamation of Local 767 and Local 47. I know that I said those words because I found out what to do to give us another spur in that movement, although you never heard of it. That was an important battle in the battle.

And then, later, after that show that I did, I got a job with the *Joe Adams Show* on KTTV, and my band was working that. Buddy was in it, and Red Callender was my assistant on it. I was the music director for the show. We were on TV every week with the *Joe Adams Show*. And I played a benefit to raise money to support the amalgamation movement at the Humanist Hall on Union Avenue. And you couldn't get in the place that day.

Then I left. I went to San Francisco, so I don't remember how they went on from there. I went to San Francisco, where I stayed for a couple of years. I had a band up there before I came back in 1954.

Those were the years that the Avenue really declined. By the time I got back in 1954, things had moved. The Oasis was the big thing. It was on Western Avenue. When I got back the blacks had gotten over to Western Avenue and over in there, Exposition and Figueroa. And Central Avenue, I guess, just kept declining. The theaters were gone, the Lincoln and all of that stuff was kind of just going down, and it was not happening anymore. Everything had moved west.

"There's no place like Central Avenue."

Central Avenue was a place where my people lived. So the point is that Central Avenue was just like 125th Street in New York, that's where all the black people were. They couldn't go any other place. Where were they going to go? They could work at a couple of places out here, but they couldn't go in the front door. So they were all there together, just like that. They had to stay here, they had to live here. Duke Ellington: you'd catch him right there at the Dunbar. Count Basie, right there. [laughter] We all had the same thing in New York. No different in New York.

Central has a lot to do with me. You must remember that I organized my first band here. It was here that I had a chance to determine which way I wanted to go, and I had inspiration here. As I say, Phil Moore was one of my biggest inspirations as a writer. And Calvin Jackson, who later moved here. I didn't mention it, but Calvin Jackson also wrote arrangements for Jimmie Lunceford when I was with Jimmie Lunceford's band. That's when he was just a freelance piano player and writer around New York. He later joined Harry James. Wrote a lot of stuff for Harry James. Then he went to MGM and did so much work over there for them. But all these people were here. And the other people were coming in and out all the time. Count's band was coming in and out. In fact, I rehearsed my first number with Count Basie here at the Aragon Ballroom when they were playing out there on the beach—Venice somewhere—another ballroom that blacks couldn't even go into.

Central is just as important as 125th Street in New York City, or South Park in Chicago, Cedar Street, I think, in Pittsburgh. They all have it. All of the cities have a street. It's the street where the black people live. And I think it's important to Los Angeles, no matter what color you are. And it was very important to the music, jazz, because it was a place where it lived. And everyone came there, all of the biggest. You don't come any bigger than Duke Ellington. You don't come any bigger than Jelly Roll Morton. He died here. He's right out there in the Calvary Cemetery on the Eastside here.

So jazz is very important in Los Angeles, and Central Avenue— There's no place like Central Avenue. Because I'd rather come here. When I got here that beautiful day, and there was this beautiful street with a beautiful hotel to stay in, the Dunbar, which I didn't have in New York City— They didn't have a decent hotel for you to stay in there. But Los Angeles had the Dunbar Hotel and had that nice street, beautiful street. That's all I can say about it.

I would like to see a lot of my people into this [music] today. I'm not seeing that. In fact, I'm seeing less and less as I go about the United States lecturing on orchestration and composing and arranging. And I look up in a class of a hundred, and I only see one black, or I see no blacks. Two weeks ago, at the Grove School of Music, I lectured to the arranging class, and there was not one black there. That disturbs me. Where are we going to be, then? What are we going to do? Will there be one day that there will be no more?

But I'm talking about these things because I'm trying to explain to you what music, jazz, means to me and my people. Where are my people now? I'm a member of the board of governors of NARAS [National Academy of Recording Arts and Sciences], the Grammy people, for the second time. I had two nominations. I have two first-place *Down Beat* [magazine] awards. I have many awards. But where are my young people that are coming up to carry on the thing for these people? We are a people here. As much as we can be swallowed up, we are still a people. Where are we going? What are we doing? These are the things I'm thinking about now.

17

Clora Bryant

After honing her craft as a professional on Central Avenue, Clora moved to New York in 1954. She traveled and performed regularly on the East Coast and in Canada for a few years. After spending a year in Chicago, she returned to Los Angeles in the late 1950s, where she freelanced, led her own groups, and continued to travel. During the 1960s she toured with Billy Williams.

Clora has played with many musicians and organizations, including Louis Armstrong, Count Basie, Jeannie and Jimmy Cheatham, Duke Ellington, Dizzy Gillespie, Stan Kenton, Johnny Otis, and Charlie Parker. She has recorded frequently as a sideman and as a leader, cutting the album . . . Gal with a Horn. During the 1980s she toured the Soviet Union at Mikhail Gorbachev's invitation.

Clora continues to perform, compose, arrange, teach, and write about jazz. She has written a five-part suite for her mentor, Dizzy Gillespie, and has received three grants from the National Endowment for the Arts for composition and performance.

Clora was born in 1927 in Denison, a small Texas town near the Oklahoma border. Her mother, Eulela Lewis Bryant, died when she was three, and Clora and her two older brothers, Mel and Fred, were raised by their father, Charles Celeste Bryant, a laborer earning about seven dollars a week in a hardware store during the Depression.

I loved music. Everybody in my hometown had a piano, an upright piano. I always had a good ear. I could always go to the piano and pick out anything I wanted to play. I started on piano, when I must have been about five or six. I wanted to play so badly. It was just in me. You know, the music was in me. My dad didn't have money to give me lessons. But there was a white lady that came from Sherman over to Denison to teach the black kids. And she would teach me and my brother, Mel, for free. Miss Lindsay was her name. I can still see her soft, caring face.

That's how I got into it. Plus, I was singing with the children's choir in church. We were Baptists, and every time the doors opened we were in church. So I sang in the choir. We'd always have a preacher who sang and could holler and scream and preach. And we always had a good adult choir. We'd bring in people like the Blind Boys, musical groups to come in and do concerts. And we'd have fish fries. I'm telling you, you've never tasted fish until you've had it fried in these big black pots, deep pots.

We had one of those "His Master's Voice," the RCA Victor, the one you wind up. I'd sit there in front of that thing and listen to Louis Armstrong, Fats Waller, Andy Kirk and his Clouds of Joy, and, of course, Duke and Basie and those people. In the early evening, on the radio shows, you'd have Glenn Miller, Tommy Dorsey, Charlie Spivak. It was all-white shows in the early evening. The radio was very good for your imagination, because you could make it whatever you wanted it to be. And I had a vivid, live imagination.

Then, when we'd go to bed, I'd sneak into my brother's room, and we had the crystal set radios. My brother would put on one earphone and I'd put on the other, and we'd dig around in that little piece of crystal and find stations. I'd hear Earl Hines, Cab Calloway, and all those bands. I can't describe it, but it has stayed with me until it's just like it's in the pores of my skin. That's how deep music is. That's why I can sit here from day to day and just be absorbed into putting down what I feel about the music and what I feel about my life, my beginnings, and what I've gone through, because the music outweighs the bad part of me not having things. I never had a bicycle when I was a little girl. I never had roller skates. There are so many things I never had, you know, but I didn't really miss them, because once I found out about music, that became my friend, my companion.

My father would take us to see and hear bands like Count Basie, Duke Ellington, Lionel Hampton, T-Bone Walker, Jay McShann, Jimmie Lunceford. All the bands came through there. And you know what fascinated me the most? I'll never forget. It was the trumpet section with the hats. That's what drew me. I never knew at the time that I would be playing the trumpet, but that's what struck me. It was seeing those horns. They had a choreography, so to speak, with the hats.

We were coming into the war years when I realized I wanted to play the trumpet. My brother Fred went to the service in 1941—he was drafted—and left his horn, and that was when our principal brought in the marching band. Naturally, I wanted to be a part of that. So my dad said, "Well, the only thing here is the trumpet." So I took the trumpet to my uncle, Henry Young. Buddy Tate and my uncle played in one of those southwest bands. He took and placed my fingers on the right valves, and he taught me the scales. The first time I did it, the sound came out, and my uncle was amazed. [laughter] So right away, he wrote the fingering down for me.

So I had something to stay at home for. I'd work on the trumpet. And I wanted to play the high notes. I'd heard Harry James and seen him in the movies playing all that stuff. And then, when I heard Cat Anderson with Duke Ellington, I wet my pants. [laughter] But it was a challenge. In the school band there were girls, Elizabeth Thomas and myself, in the trumpet section and two guys. And I was playing just as good as the guy who was playing first. Just that quick. It was just like my life had been waiting for me to find out about the trumpet, and, when I did, that was it. And it has been tunnel vision ever since. That's all I wanted to do.

By the next year, my senior year, most of the guys were going off to the service. They were glad to have females who could play. I came along at the right time. And the parents were all behind the kids who played. And they finally had car washes and things and bought us uniforms.

By the time I graduated, I had scholarships to Oberlin Conservatory and to Bennett College. But my professor got a letter from Prairie View Agricultural and Mechanical University, which is down near Houston. The band director there, Will Henry Bennett, knew our band teacher, Conrad Johnson, and he'd heard about me. They wanted me to come to Prairie View, although they didn't offer a scholarship. But when I found out they had an all-girl band there, the Prairie View Coeds, that's where I was going. The scholarships be damned! And the way I got through school was, my brothers, Fred and Mel, were in the service, and they made out their allotment checks to me to pay my tuition. That's the way

I got through college in those two years down in Prairie View, through my brothers.

When I got to Prairie View, I played some first trumpet and the solos. They had never heard a female playing the trumpet like I was playing. The Sweethearts of Rhythm had been out, but most of them were playing solos that the guys wrote note for note, except girls like Vi Burnside or Jean Starr and Tiny Davis. I was creating my own solos when I got to Prairie View, except on some songs they expected to hear the same solo that was on the record, the solo on Erskine Hawkins's "Tuxedo Junction." I was so happy I was there, and I was playing what I wanted to play. I wasn't cocky about what I was doing, but I was confident in what I could do.

During the school year, on weekends, we'd play Houston, Dallas, Fort Worth, San Antonio, Austin, Waco, Port Arthur, Corpus Christi. We'd play all the large cities in Texas. We did one-nighters up and down the coast, the eastern coast, from Florida up to New York. We ended up playing the Apollo Theatre! We played the Howard Theatre in Washington, D.C., the Royal Theatre in Baltimore, the Stanley Theater in Pittsburgh. We played all the big theaters.

We played all the military bases. And they didn't love it any more than all of us girls loved all those good-looking guys in those uniforms at that time! Whoa! [laughter] We got to Tuskegee and saw these black guys in these airmen uniforms, flyers! Holy shit! I was overwhelmed. [laughter] I'm telling you. But we had a chaperone. She must have weighed about three hundred pounds. [laughter] When she was in bed, it looked like there was a mountain in the bed. [laughter] But she was a nice lady, classy lady. But I was the youngest one there. The other girls knew how to sneak out. Heck, I was scared. I had been raised by my father and had been sheltered. I didn't know too much about street life. I mean, I was very naive. I was still naive when I got out here. I still had a lot of my naivete almost until I was fifty years old. But I said, "I had to come to California to learn how to be a Texas bitch!" [laughter]

We played this camp in Alabama, and there was this good-looking guy in the audience. [laughter] He kept coming up to the bandstand and told everybody he was a musician, he played drums. And this girl, his girlfriend, was getting jealous. It seemed like he had three or four girls in this town, because he was so handsome. You know who it was? Chico.

Chico Hamilton. And one of the girls got mad and threw a Coke bottle up at the bandstand. There was a jukebox on the side, and it hit the jukebox. Boy, we hit the floor. Everybody hit the floor. Wow, did that break up the dance! [laughter] People scattered. It sounded like a gunshot. In those days, Coke bottles were Coke bottles. But Chico and I laugh about that now.

At that time, they had so many all-girl groups. They had the Prairie View Coeds, the Sweethearts of Rhythm, the Darlings of Rhythm, the Texas Playgirls, Jean Parks and her All-Girl Band, and then they had a man, a trombone player from Houston, who had an all-girl band. There were all kinds of girls bands. The men were scarce. There were still bands, but they weren't the same.

I stayed there until January 1945. I came home for my semester break and Dad said, "We're going to California." And that's what we did.

Los Angeles

After Dad found out that we liked music and we were musically talented, he kept telling us he was going to bring us to California. Because when he was in the navy, he spent some time in California. He was stationed down in Long Beach. Later, when we were small, he would tell us about the palm trees and the oranges growing in the yards and how the weather was warm all the time. No way in the world you could make us believe that. But he always told us he was going to bring us to California so that we could be discovered. He really did encourage us. And that's what I've always cherished in my heart and admired about my father. He encouraged me doing what a lot of parents wouldn't have done.

Clora transferred to UCLA in 1945, and her father had lined up work in the shipyards in Long Beach. In the dead of a Texas winter they boarded a train for Los Angeles.

On the train, there was a lot of military, guys who were coming out here to be shipped out to the Far East. Even though my dad and I were on the trip for a good, happy reason, you would still talk to some of those guys, and they would be talking about who they were leaving. You didn't know if they were going to live or die or come back hurt or whatever. So you had kind of mixed emotions. But in the front of my mind, I always kept the fact up there that I was going where I was going, and why I was going was for a good reason. My dad wanted me to better myself. There were trains everywhere, and convoys of guys in these trucks up and down the highways. We'd ride alongside a highway, and we'd see them moving tanks and those long guns, anti-aircraft guns and stuff. So it was a learning process, and it was an emotional thing for you to deal with. You'd see families transferring along with their military husbands from camp to camp.

We didn't have the money to go in the dining room every day. We had some sacks of fried chicken. In those days, when you traveled on the train or the bus, you always fried up a bunch of chicken and cake and stuff and some kind of rolls or something and had these greasy bags. [laughter]

When we got off the train in Los Angeles, it was in January 1945, and the sun was shining bright. I had just left all the snow, and we'd come through ice and sleet and snow and rain. Oh, I said, "Now I know what Daddy's talking about." So we stopped at Pasadena and then the train started coming into the Union depot in downtown Los Angeles, and all of these tracks and all of these trains— I'd never seen anything like that. My eyes popped. I looked at all the trains coming and going and backing up and pulling out. It was a point in my life that I will cherish. All of those early years of my life I'll cherish, because there was something exciting happening just about every day.

When we walked down into the station, you'd look and you'd see people waving, and they'd see somebody whom they knew was coming in. I looked and saw my brother, Mel. I hadn't seen him in a year, because he had mustered out of the Marine Corps and came to California and didn't come home. I saw my brother and I started crying. My daddy was right behind me. We jumped into each other's arms. He swung me around, and we had our Bryant meeting there.

Then we went on into the station, and there was this big huge room. They had these big overstuffed chairs where you sat, and the loudspeaker was calling the trains. Everything was magnificent. You'd go into the dining room and there was china and crystal and silverware, not the plastic nothing and no paper this and that. And the linen napkins folded neatly and the starched tablecloths, and the waiters had on their starched jackets with the gold buttons. It was just thrilling.

We get off the train and the sun is shining bright. It was in the afternoon, and there was a light breeze. I started shedding clothes. We got into the cab and started riding down the street. Soon I was living in a beautiful mansion. St. John's Hospital is there now. It's St. Andrews Place and Adams Boulevard, right on the corner.

Clora's brother Mel was employed as the first black usher at the Wiltern Theatre and a bit actor. That first night, he took them to dinner at actor Ben Carter's home. Dinner conversation included instruction in racism, southern California style.

They were trying to tell Dad what to expect on his job. They were telling him that there would be prejudices here in California, but they weren't blatant like they are down South. You know, you could walk into it. Nobody would tell you you can't do this and can't do that, but you could walk into it and be hit in the face with "You can't go here or you can't do that" or somebody might call you a nigger. They were telling us not to be so relaxed and think that everything is just what we see on the surface. There were things to ponder. They told me how UCLA could be, which it was. Because I had applied to USC, too, and then, at home, I heard that they were very prejudiced. But when I got out to UCLA, I found out that they were just as prejudiced. [laughter] It was the same thing, but it was subtle.

When I got here and went out to UCLA, the classes I needed were filled or weren't being offered. So I tabled my entrance and said I'd go the next semester, which I did. But it gave me a chance to discover Central Avenue. [laughter]

Registering to Wolf Whistles at Local 767

I had my brother take me over on Central Avenue so I could deposit my union card, because I had joined the Dallas local. The Prairie View Coeds had to join that local before we went to New York. I had called Florence Cadrez, who was the union secretary, and told her that I wanted to put in my transfer. I'd had the man from the union in Dallas and my teacher from Prairie View send letters of recommendation, which they did. We caught the U car downtown and took it down Central. We got off at Eighteenth.

The black union, Local 767, was at 1710 South Central, on what would be the west side of the street. It was a frame building. We got off the streetcar, and I see these guys are sitting there. It was just a big house, a two-story house. We walked up, and the guys were sitting on the banisters and standing out on the street and sitting in their cars. I was pulling back. My brother said, "Come on." And the guys are looking. I really got nervous. [laughter] I said, "Oh, my God." Mel said, "You'd better come on. Some of these guys who are looking at you, you're going to have to depend on them to get you work." So we're walking up the steps and then I hear this [wolf whistles]. My brother said, "They're complimenting you." I said, "Really?" [laughter] "That's a compliment?" Boy, dumb! I mean, I was dumb that way. Streetwise, I was very dumb.

I walked into the union and I was met by this man, Baron Moorehead. He was a little short man. His head was bald in front, and bowlegged, very bowed legs. But he was one of the first black pilots out here in California. He was a business agent at the union. He had the first office. When you walked in the door, his office was to your right. It had been a living room, and there were couches around the room. I told him what I had come for and he took me into the next room, which had been the dining room, I think, because Florence's desk kind of sat in the middle of the floor. She was a nice-looking lady, a pleasant smile, red hair, and freckles.

She said, "You come highly recommended."

"Oh, thank you, ma'am." [laughter] I'm still ma'aming everything.

She said, "Oh, I like the way you talk." [laughter] Why not, huh? You always respected your elders. I'd been taught that. So she gave me an application to fill out. She said, "Well, you know, you can't work a steady job until you've worked off your transfer, and that takes about six weeks."

And then she took me around and introduced me to the president. His name was Edward Bailey. And then she introduced me to Elmer Fain. He was a business agent. Paul Howard was the treasurer. And I met him. Then she took me to the kitchen where they had their fish fries and showed me the backyard where they had the homemade barbecue pits, like they're doing now. They're made out of those oil cans. They cut them in half. And then she took me upstairs to the rehearsal rooms. There was a big room, and then there were smaller rooms. And I'll never forget, there was one room that had these pictures on the wall of these bulldogs dressed like men. They had on these derby hats and these big fat cigars and these loud suits. I mean, I'll never forget it. They're sitting there playing cards and shooting pool. You know, different pictures.

Then my brother and I came outside, and just as we walked out the door Ginger Smock, a great violinist, jazz and concertwise, was coming in the door. My brother knew her, and he introduced me to her. I met a lot of other guys. When I came out, there was Gene Montgomery and Cake Witchard, Clarence Jones—a bass player—and I met about four trumpet players.

We left there, caught the U car, and went on down Central. As we rode along, my brother pointed out the places where they had music, like the Jungle Room. That's where Ernie Andrews's future wife, Dolores Andrews, at that time was the hat-check person. And there was the Elks Hall. Mel told me that's where they had dances and jam sessions on Sundays. The Lincoln Theatre. Bardu Ali had his band in there. Melba Liston was working in the band at that time. There were all kinds of theaters, the Bill Robinson Theatre. What's that black woman's name who was a singer in the twenties and thirties? Florence Mills. And they had about four theaters. Mel showed me Brother's after-hours place. Then we got to the Downbeat, the Last Word, the Alabam, the Turban Room. And on the corner was Cafe Intime. Upstairs was Dynamite Jackson's.

But it was around four o'clock and I told my brother I was hungry. So we went to this place called the Nickel Spot. It was a cafe where you could have a meal ticket. It was a weekly thing. So we ate there. He introduced me to the waitresses. We hung around there until almost early evening. The guys were out on the street, all of the night people: the pimps and the hustlers and the ladies of the evening. There were a lot of musicians. My brother introduced me to some of the guys he thought I should meet. We stood around while Mel talked with them, the guys hanging on the corner, the young guys listening to all this bullshit the guys are talking. A lot of young kids just hanging there just to be on the scene and to learn. See, in those days, there was a lot of camaraderie. That's why I became a part of it. Because there was a caring and a sense of hooking up, or what we call networking now. That was our area. Central Avenue was our area.

And finally, when the Downbeat opened up, we stood outside and listened to that great bebop band. Teddy Edwards and J. D. King were the tenor men. Howard McGhee, Roy Porter the drummer, Bob Dingbod was the bass player, and Vernon Biddle was the piano player. I couldn't go in. I was under the age. That was the first time I'd heard bebop live in L.A. I couldn't figure out what they were doing. Howard was a very good trumpet player. He was wailing his ass off. I said, "My God, what is this?"

I liked anything that's different. It's like the kids nowadays. They like anything that's different. I'd been inundated with swing, and I was ready for the next step, just like the kids are now. So after I heard that, I listened to the broadcasts from Billy Berg's club. I listened to Joe Adams in the daytime on the radio. I listened to Hunter Hancock. I listened to Gene Norman's jazz show. And then after-hours the broadcast from the Bird in the Basket, where they had live jam sessions. Wardell Gray and Dexter Gordon would lock horns there. Bill Sampson would broadcast live from there. And then, at Dolphin's of Hollywood, they had live broadcasts from their window with Charles Trammell. He sat in the window at this record shop—Dolphin's of Hollywood on Vernon Avenue off of Central.

There was Cafe Society, and downtown was Shepp's Playhouse at First and San Pedro. Gerald Wilson's band played down on First and San Pedro. Howard McGhee and his wife later had a place, Club Finale, down there too. And later, after Billy Berg closed his place out there on Sunset and Vine, he had the Waldorf Cellar downtown, down on Main Street. I played down there, too. It was downstairs. He'd have shows, and he'd have jazz groups in there. There was a lot of activity down there. It was kind of Japanese town down in that area. The Japanese people had been relocated.

There was so much activity on Central Avenue when I got there. It was like a beehive. It was people going in and out of everywhere, out of the clubs, out of the restaurants, the stores. There were all kinds of stores up and down the street, like furniture stores, five-and-ten-cent stores, doctors' offices, dentists' offices, restaurants, barbecue joints. There was so much activity. And there was just as much going on on the street as there was in the clubs, as far as standing out there talking to people and listening and learning. The camaraderie of the guys just hanging together and going around the corner, smoking their pot, or doing whatever else they were doing. There were some stories that I've got to remember. Because that's the way I learned how to deal with the male part of— When I got tired of playing with girl groups, that's the way I learned how to deal and cope with things.

The people were into each other, interrelating. And it was all black, except at night. At night, that's when the movie stars would come over. I saw Rita Hayworth, Cesar Romero. Alan Ladd was there quite often. Sonny Tufts. Later on, Ava Gardner. But there were lots who I don't even remember the names of. There were always some fine cars lined up outside the clubs on Central Avenue from the movie stars or people just from Beverly Hills.

You could get anything. Drugs, women, whatever. Night or day. There was a place called Brother's, an after-hours place, where you'd go and sit around on the floor on the pillows, and the incense and the music and the soft lights, and that was it. People would go off into other rooms. I don't know what they were doing, but they must have been getting loaded or something. It was called Brother's. He was a guy who wore all these long robes. There was a mystique there, you know. It was a hangout for guys to go for guys and whatever. You could get whatever. But he was a nice man, a nice man. And he stayed open a long time after Central Avenue started to break down. He was on Central Avenue kind of off the alley. I remember you had to go down a walkway to the back. You had to know somebody who knew somebody to take you there. That's the way it was. There were movie stars. And the entertainers. I only went there a couple of times, because that wasn't my shtick at all. There was no live music! They had soft records.

The Jungle Room was kind of jungly, you know, dark and mysterious. It was run by a lady named Fat Ann. I never learned her full name. Everyone called her Fat Ann. She was married to a white guy, so I don't know really who owned it. She was the boss. She was the one who paid and everything. They called her Fat Ann because she was a big fat black chick. It wasn't a jam place. They'd have a show, not like you'd see at the Club Alabam or at the Lincoln Theatre or downtown. It would be local talent, good talent. That's where Al "Cake" Witchard played, and— What was that trumpet player's name? Sammy Yates. A guy by the name of Jack La Rue, piano player. He was a little, thin guy. Clarence Jones, bass player, very good bass player. He died with a needle in his arm. They just got off into that dope.

I saw a lot of my friends, guys whom I'd met and hung out with, dying. Heroin. Marijuana was the main, main thing. And if you just wanted to be completely wild, then you went into heroin. If you wanted to be like Charlie Parker— Like Frank Morgan says. He figured that's why he played like he did, but it wasn't. All these guys I knew started out with marijuana and then went to the needle. I've seen them run off the bandstand so they could go throw up. Yeah.

"I didn't want them to feel like I was a namby-pamby little tippy-toe female."

The Downbeat was run by a man we all called Pops. He was a little short Jewish guy. I didn't have that many dealings with him. But he knew who I was, and I'd come in there. Half the time I wouldn't have any money. The waitresses would let me sit there with one Coke or else they'd buy me a drink. I made a point to learn the waitresses. And if I didn't have the money, either somebody who I knew who was up there playing would buy me a Coke or else the waitresses would just bring me one.

It was a small place. You'd come in the door and the bandstand was kind of up against the wall. I remember the tables and the chairs in the front. Between the door and the bandstand, there was a row of tables, small tables. The bar was along the wall. It stayed packed all the time. And they had jam sessions on Sunday afternoon. That was a biggy. That was one of the biggies on Central Avenue.

The people were so creative all the time; it would have to be an ass kicker, so to speak, for me to really remember something spectacular. Every time somebody played, it was sensational, because everybody was playing, everybody was motivated, and everybody was dedicated. Everybody was just tunnel vision playing their music. And it came out that way. It was challenging to get up there. There were some who couldn't play who would get up there, and then they'd start calling tunes at ninety miles an hour. They'd call "Cherokee." [laughter] That was their pet tune to get guys off the bandstand. Race-neck speed. [sings fragment of melody to "Cherokee"] You'd see the guys drifting off the stage and sitting down.

But they never did that with me. I knew how to play it. I'd sit there, and when they started playing something that I thought I wanted to play, then I'd walk up there. I'd take my horn up and walk on up there. A lot of times you'd have to sign your name and they'd call you down. Well, I wouldn't do that. If they played, they'd just let me do it. They let me do whatever I wanted to do, because I told them I wanted to learn. I was there to learn, and the only way you're going to learn is to be a part of it. That's what you have to do. You have to go out there and be a part of that.

And I'll do it now. Sometimes when Dizzy's playing and I hear something he's doing that I know, I won't get out my horn. [laughter] I'll go up and take his horn! Because we play the same size bore, the same mouthpiece. Same rim. The mouthpiece I have he gave to me in the sixties. So I take it on. They were interviewing him, and he was saying, "Yeah, she had the nerve to come up and take my horn and try to play the rim off of it!" That Dizzy, he will pump you up. Thankfully. [laughter] You can just feel when people are being for real. Especially musicians and especially a trumpet player. You can feel if they are genuinely secure with knowing that you do play the same instrument they do and knowing that it's a difficult instrument too. Dizzy has no insecurities. He's not intimidated by anybody or any sex or anything. No matter if you're female, male, or whatever, he'll give you a chance to come up there and play. I loved him for that, because I could feel that he had no inhibitions. He knew who he was, but he never shoved it down your throat like a lot of people I know do. And that's why I admired him, because he was just Dizzy.

I've heard J. D. King at the Downbeat—you don't hear anything about him—he was a very good tenor player. And Teddy Edwards. Teddy Edwards was something. Teddy Edwards and Howard McGhee together were ass kickers. They were playing. That's why Teddy gets kind of depressed and disgusted, because he knows what he has done. He knows who he is and where he should be and that he isn't. He was a tall, good-looking guy, too. He had the chicks falling all over him. Oh boy, oh boy, oh boy.

You know it's sad. People in Europe know who I am. And right here in L.A., for forty-some years, people don't know who I am. Sonny Criss was the same way. He was very depressed when he had to go to Europe, and they recognized him over there like that. Over here he couldn't get a job. If he did, they were paying him twenty and thirty dollars. That does something to your ego and to your manhood or to your feeling of self-worth. You lose your self-esteem, you lose your motivation. You just lose it, because people don't give you credit for being who you are, what you are, and what you can do.

The major place for jamming was the Bird in the Basket. It was a restaurant. There were tables with the checkered cloths. It wasn't too big of a bandstand, but the atmosphere was tremendous. It was conducive to jam sessions because everybody came there and they were listeners. They had done their research. They had their records. There was a tall guy who came in selling records. He had a bebop nickname. He used to come around with a stack of records and sell them—strictly a bop person. But the people would have the records, so they knew what was going on. They knew when you were playing whatever, and they knew everybody's solo. The laypeople knew the solos.

The Bird in the Basket had a clientele of people who were there every night. Like I said, the pimps who were hanging on the street. My brother explained to me the first night we were there that the number-one lady of the night would be the one who had made the most money on that day. That's who he would go out and spend the money on in the clubs. You could depend on the pimps to come in the clubs and spend money. They had to show off how much money the ladies had made that day. They hadn't made a penny, but they'd come in there spending the women's money. And they'd get sharp. The women would go home and get sharp, and the number-one lady was the one who they'd bring out. There was a lot of that. You got good tips.

And the feel, it was infectious, you know. I think I saw a fight maybe one or two times the whole time. The war was over, but the guys were still gone. There were still a lot of sailors and soldiers. But in the jazz places, I never saw anybody fight. Where it wasn't just jazz oriented, you might run into people who would have too much to drink and they'd start a fight or something.

The Bird in the Basket had a lot of famous jams between Wardell Gray and Dexter Gordon and Teddy Edwards. Hampton Hawes. And my ex-husband, Joe Stone, played bass there a lot. That's where I had the challenge with the trumpet player with Duke Ellington, Al Killian. He got into an argument with a guy in his hotel room down on Fifth Street, and the guy killed him. He was a high-note man with Duke before Cat Anderson. I was not cocky, but I accepted a challenge for what it was. Because I didn't want them to feel like I was a namby-pamby little tippy-toe female just because I played the trumpet. I didn't want men to think of me like that. I wanted to be on their same level, as far as the profession was concerned.

But I never let them forget that I was a female, because I always dressed as a female. Not sexy like Marilyn Monroe or anything, but I was a female-looking woman, you know. [laughter] And I had big legs, and at that time they had the mesh stockings with the seam up the back. I'd get a whistle every time. [laughter] I knew what to do! [laughter] I was naive towards certain things, but not when it came to that, because I'd learned that in college, how to dress so that I wouldn't have that stigma on me that I was a— When you play the trumpet, you had to be a man. That was my main purpose for doing that. Because when I was in college, we played some of these places. They'd say, "Aw, that ain't nothing but a bunch of lezzies in that—" I didn't want to hear that. I didn't want to become one of those kind of people where people thought you were playing the trumpet because you had masculine tendencies, which I didn't have. So that's why I dressed to impress. A female.

I even played a place that used to be up on Vermont. It was a place called Ebb's, and it was a lesbian place. I was playing with a half-girl group and a half-boy group. I remember that the girls would go into the bathroom— I never went to the restroom the whole time I was working. I'd see the women in the booths kissing on each other.

Club Alabam, the Last Word, and Billie Holiday

The Alabam was run by Curtis Mosby. He was a little crooked. He owed a lot of people money. They'd pay you under the table. Finally, the union got after him, so you'd have to go to the union to collect your money. He'd pay you the right money on the union check. But then you'd have to come back down there and kickback some money. They finally caught him and put him in jail for taxes, I think it was. He still owed me.

Once we were playing behind Al Hibbler, the blind singer, at the Alabam, and pay night came. Mosby was farting around and wasn't showing up or was behind the bar fiddling around again. And Al Hibbler said, "You dirty MF. You'd better give me my money or I'll shoot you." [laughter] He says, "Say something so I'll know where you are." [laughter] I mean, Al Hibbler was serious. He couldn't see, but he didn't take no shit. I mean, we got our money that week. That was really funny.

But he had made the money. The place was doing good business. And then we played there with Billie Holiday. When I played there at rehearsals, she'd babysit my daughter [April Stone] while we rehearsed. My daughter must have been about three months old. I'd go and sit and talk to her in the dressing room. She always wanted children. She loved children. She never talked about men. She wanted to hear about women who had a home life, a married life. Mine wasn't shit, really, because after my husband got off into the dope, after my daughter was born, it was down the tubes. But she wanted to hear about women who were living what she called a normal life with a husband and kids. The image that you got from that movie [*Lady Sings the Blues*] was not the impression that I got the week that I worked with her.

It was like most of the people who I know that get off into drugs. Like the Frank Morgans and the Charlie Parkers. It was like they were looking for love, and it seemed that they thought they had found it in the needle, because they couldn't get a human being to really give it to them. You'd come in the dressing room, and sometimes she'd just be sitting there looking around at nothing in particular, because there wasn't nothing in there to look at. I knew she was doing that because she either wore those long gloves or she'd always hold her arm up.

In that band we had Wardell Gray on tenor, Frank Morgan on alto. Another tenor player by the name of Donald Wilkerson. He died a couple of years ago. He was with Ray Charles for a long time. Damn good tenor player, but he got on the needle. Harper Cosby on the bass, Oscar Bradley on the drums. The leader of the band was Lorenzo Flennoy. And Lester Robertson on trombone. We were the house band. We also played behind Josephine Baker. Redd Foxx and Slappy White came in. There was a chorus line. Norma Jean Miller was the choreographer. And then we had this lady—Marie Bryant—and they all thought we were related, but we weren't. Later on, she did a lot of choreography for people like Betty Grable and Marilyn Monroe in the movies. She was a very good dancer. Johnny Otis had a big band in there. Gerald Wilson had his big band in there. Marl Young had a group in there.

It didn't have a huge dance floor, but it was big enough. You'd come in the room, and the stage was in front of you, and our dressing room was on the left side of the stage as you face it. And the bar was back on the left corner. Then I think there was a balcony up there. It was a nice room.

And next to the Alabam there was a little bar, in the Dunbar Hotel—the Turban Room. People like Gerald Wiggins played there, and Art Tatum played there. It was jumping in the day and night. Yeah.

Across the street from the Alabam and the Downbeat was the Last Word. Now, that was owned by Esvan Mosby, who was Curtis Mosby's younger brother. And at that time they had a mayor of Central Avenue. Well, Curtis was the first mayor. It was an honorary position. It gave him a feeling that we had control of our Eastside. We called it the Eastside. We didn't call it South Central L.A. It was the Eastside. There were only two mayors. Curtis was the first one, and then Esvan was the second and last one. I think they picked themselves! [laughter] They had a parade and the whole thing, you know, and they rode in the open touring cars with their family, and the school bands. It was great. Once a year.

They were slick. I worked at the Last Word with a girl group. We had to go to the union and get our money too, and bring it back and kick back. You were only making a few dollars, but at that time a dollar was a dollar. But you had to kick back five or six dollars apiece. Esvan was a nice man, but they were businessmen. And Esvan's first wife had a place called the Crystal Tea Room, over there on Avalon. She had music in there every night. But the jam sessions were on Sunday.

Well, you found the whole scope, the whole gamut of what I call the tree of jazz. The only thing that I didn't really encounter on Central Avenue was New Orleans jazz. I don't remember anyplace that had that on Central Avenue. You heard rhythm and blues. The blues, swing, bebop, and just, well, always in between bebop and swing was jazz. You'd hear blues singers like Charles Brown, T-Bone Walker, and Witherspoon. My first husband [Joseph Stone] played with T-Bone, Pee Wee Crayton, Jimmy Witherspoon. That's where Charles Brown and Johnny Moore and the Three Blazers played, Central Avenue.

Of course, Johnny Otis had his big band at the Alabam when I got there. And then, later on, Gerald Wilson had his band there. Bardu Ali had a band at the Lincoln and, of course, Melba Liston was in that band. And Gerald Wilson got Melba and some of the other guys that had taken lessons from Miss Alma Hightower, like Lester Robertson and Anthony Ortega, an alto player. He did real good with Lionel Hampton's big band.

Miss Hightower got started in the thirties with the Roosevelt thing, the WPA [Works Progress Administration]. She was employed at South Park on Avalon and Fifty- or Forty-something. There was a piano there and she would make the kids come in and play music. She started having bands, and then she started teaching. She got a studio in the back of her house where she taught kids. I took lessons from her then, and her school was in the back of her home.

And Lloyd Reese, of course. When I first came out here, I wanted to take some lessons. I only took about four lessons, because I couldn't afford it. But he showed me how to breathe from the diaphragm, and he was teaching me, like, you put the trumpet on a string, you know— [laughter] That embouchure, little trumpet thing. You'd hit high notes, hit altissimo C, with a trumpet hanging up there. That's the kind of embouchure he had.

All-Girl Groups

When I came out here, my first job was with a man, a piano player, who called me up right after I got my transfer, got my real union card. We played at a place called the Cup and Saucer out in Norwalk. It was just three of us—drums, piano, and myself, which was a different thing for me. And this place, it was prejudiced. We had to sit in this back room where they kept the liquor, the storage room, and there was no going out. No talking to the customers. But that was the first gig that I had, and the only one I had for a long time after that, because I started working with girl groups.

I started getting calls, because this man, the piano player, hung out at the union. He went back and told them that I could play. There was another guy named Clint. I can't think of Clint's last name. He got an all-girl group together. And then Floyd Ray organized an all-girl group. And, oh, there's another guy who was a trombone player. He had a group, the Darlings of Rhythm. I joined them and we played the Plantation Club out there in Watts on 108th and Central.

The first summer I came out here, I worked with the Sweethearts of Rhythm at the Million Dollar Theatre. I worked one week with them down there. They had a chaperone, Miss Rae Lee Jones, and she wanted me to travel with them. My dad and I were still living out here on Adams and St. Andrews Place, and I went home the first day and told my dad about how these girls were feeling on each other's boobs and patting each other on the butt and kissing. Daddy said, "You come home." I had to come home at every intermission. From downtown on Second and Broadway, I had to come all the way out here on Adams and St. Andrews Place. My dad said, "Ain't no way you're going on the road with them." I didn't know. I didn't know what a lesbian was at that time. [laughter] I wouldn't have bleated it out to my father! [laughter] Then his eyes got big, "What?" I'm telling you, I was so naive it's not even funny. I didn't know my ass from a hole in the ground at that time. But that was the beginning of my bebop Central Avenue days.

The girl groups were plentiful at that time because of the military. The guys were still gone, most of them, and we were a novelty. I worked with just about all of the groups around town. I was with the Queens of Swing for about three or four years. I played trumpet and drums. Doris Meilleur, Minnie Hightower—Moore is her married name. That's Miss Alma Hightower's daughter. Elyse Blye. Do you know what? I just saw where [San Francisco longshoremen leader] Harry Bridges died the other day. She used to go with Harry. We were working in Frisco, and he used to come down to the club every night. Perry Lee was the piano player. Frances Gray was the leader. She also sewed and made all these homemade costumes for us. [laughter] There was always somebody pregnant in the group, so every time she turned around, she was having to make these loose things. But then she'd make them sexy. We wore the midriff things and the strapless and the—you know. She made them sexy because she was an ex-dancer. She decided she wanted to play the drums and sing. Then she got into an argument with the piano player, and that's when she left. That's when we had to have a drummer.

We played nothing but standards, and we played blues. We didn't have any originals. But we played some bop things. Everybody improvised. I even took a solo on the drums. [laughter] Yeah, I loved to play "Caravan." I'd be playing drums, and I had that mallet going around there. Yeah, I could do it. I'd worked it out.

We played and traveled quite a bit, places like Caldwell, Idaho, and Eureka, California. We played Boise, Idaho, Tucson, and Las Vegas. And I got married in '49. After I had my son [Charles Stone], I'd take him on the road with me. I'd come off the stage and nurse him backstage. That's another thing that women have to deal with, you know, having children and going right back to work. I did that with both my young kids.

Women on the bandstand were sometimes resented by women in the audience and by the musicians' wives.

I was working over in Pasadena at a club, the Onyx Club, on Fair Oaks. Charles Norris was on guitar and Elyse was on piano and George Morrow was the bass player, the one who played with Clifford Brown and Max Roach. The women would just sit there. I played with my eyes closed. I never saw what was going on. And they would sit there and just get very upset. This woman was pulling her knife out of her purse, too, and I had my eyes closed, and Elyse said, "Look out, Clora!" [laughter] I said, "Oh, my God." I'm telling you, it's no fooling. I wasn't the only one. I mean, any girl musician you know can tell you stories like that.

You'd call the fellows up about rehearsal or something and they'd say, "Well, who's that bitch?" You know, "Is that your bitch?" I heard one woman asking her husband that one day. I said, "Tell that bitch I ain't no bitch." [laughter] I'd get a lot of flak calling guys for rehearsals. But I hurry up and let them know who I am and why I'm calling. I found that out. "Look, tell them that Clora Bryant the trumpet player says so-and-so," and they kind of cool it out. But I've been through some stuff with women, really.

In 1951 Clora was a member of the first women's jazz group to appear on television.

I worked with a group that went on TV. Actually we were the Queens of Swing. When we did the TV show, they changed our name to the Hollywood Sepia Tones. The girl who played guitar was Willie Lee Terrell. Anne Glascoe was the bass player. Her uncle was Gene Ramey, the bass player with Basie, a well-known bass player from Texas. The drummer was Mattie Watson. Anyway, we had a good group. We had been working at the Last Word and quite a few places. At the time when Benny Carter and Phil Moore were getting this TV show together, we were working down on Fifth Street at a club. I think it was the Waldorf Cellar, that was owned by Billy Berg. It was downstairs.

We were on TV for six weeks. It was called *The Hollywood Sepia Tones* and it was our own television show. Half-hour show. It was channel five. All the jazz things came on five, eleven, or thirteen. We were the first jazz female group on television. I was pregnant with my daughter. She was born in October of '51. I was about seven months pregnant with her. But we couldn't get a sponsor. That was at the same time that Nat Cole was on and couldn't get a sponsor.

And also at that time, after my daughter was born, I got a call from the union to do Ada Leonard's all-girl orchestra show on TV. She had an all-girl band. So did Ina Ray Hutton. I was on there a week, and they got letters, "Get that nigger off there." And Xavier Cugat's wife had an all-girl show, an all-girl band on TV at that time. What was her name? Lorraine Cugat. There were three white all-girl orchestras on there. I think that's where Benny Carter and Phil Moore got the idea to bring our group on, because at that time we had a pretty tight little group. But we were more jazz, and with a smaller group. We had guitar, sax, trumpet, bass, drums, piano, and two singers—Vivian Dandridge, who was Dorothy's sister, and Evelyn Royal, who was Marshal Royal's wife. We didn't have sections, but we had a tight little group. The TV show was on kinescope, so I've never been able to get any copies of it. There was another show that had some women. Oh, it was that country and western guy, Spade Cooley. He had a lot of women violin players. Ginger Smock played on it.

After that I got so fed up with girl groups because there was so much confusion and so much bullshit going on with them. There was always one, "You said this," and the other one's saying, "You said that," and just petty stuff. I didn't have time for it, like I don't have time for it now. Because I get into my music. But there was always one who would keep some shit going.

And I found out it wasn't just the women's groups; it was with men too. As soon as I started working with men, I found they're the same way. There's always somebody going to keep some stuff going. But I found that I had outgrown— You know, there was no challenge. You get so far, and nobody's challenging you. You find yourself playing the same thing. There was no inspiration there. So I just stopped working with girl groups. It was in 1952 or '53.

My first job doing a single was then at the Oasis Club. Eric Dolphy had the band there. He'd come to my house and we'd listen to records. Just before he went to New York, he came by to tell me he thought he was going to go to New York. He was going to make the move. He said Gerald Wilson had told him he should do it, and he wanted to know what I thought about it. That's the kind of friends we were. He was a couple of years younger than I was, so it was like I was his big sister or whatever. He was very shy, and he wasn't that talkative. But when he did talk, he had something to say.

In the early fifties, I played jam sessions over in Glendale at a place that was called something Perry's Melody Room. At that time, you know, blacks weren't really welcome in Glendale. [laughter] The club owners usually had to put your name down with the police department so that if they stopped you they knew that you had a reason for being there. [laughter] Yeah. And I was working with Bumps Myers. The man who had the session, Poison Gardner, he was the piano player for Al Capone in Chicago. And a very good pianist. A little short guy.

And those sessions were famous too. Everybody went over there. Conrad Gozza lived in Glendale, so he used to come in all the time—the trumpet player who was the first trumpet on the *Dinah Shore Chevy Show* and all those big TV shows. He wouldn't rehearse. He'd just walk in and cut the show down. Just give him his cues. He was that kind of trumpet player. And Manny Klein, trumpet. Who's the guy who would play the accordion who was on the Spade Cooley show, but he liked jazz too? Tommy Gumina.

The Union Amalgamation

I wasn't a part of it. They weren't looking for any females to be a part of that. It was a male thing. They didn't have women's lib. It was the ones who had the desire to be a part of the studio scene—like Buddy Collette and Marl Young and Benny Carter. And nobody was knocking the door down to record women. Melba Liston had gotten in on a date with Dexter Gordon simply because he made her. He almost had to pick her up and take her to do it. But at that time they weren't knocking the door down to record women. There was no push for us to do it. And the men were trying to get themselves in, so they definitely did not want that kind of competition.

There were about fifteen women that I know of in Local 767. Let's see. There was Ginger Smock, Vi Redd, Minnie Hightower, Elyse Blye, Ann Brown, Nellie Lutcher, Betty Hall Jones, Hadda Brooks, Marie Coker, Martha Davis. I'm not sure of the number.

The older guys—like Vi Redd's father [Alton Redd] and the president of the local [Leo Davis] and the treasurer [Paul Howard]—spoke about the minuses of amalgamating the union. We lost money. There was a little prestige there that you could never capture over at the white local. And it's become even less than when we first went there. Now there's no— Oh, they treat you like a piece of dirt over there now. There's no pride. You had a pride. You had somewhere to go and see your peers who were on the same level with you and could talk about the same things you talked about. So I wasn't really for the amalgamation at first because we did lose. It's the same as integrating the schools. You lose some of your roots; you lose some of your togetherness.

There was a need for blacks to be in the studios, but there should have been another way to do it, because we lost something that we'll never get back, and that was a togetherness. Central Avenue was a togetherness. We'll never have that again. Like every culture should have their own space—not being segregated—but just have a space where you feel free to do whatever you want to do. It doesn't mean that you don't want nobody else in there, but just have a space where you can— Like you have your own home.

It's the same way with that local over there. You'd walk in there, and there would be Basie's band upstairs rehearsing or Duke Ellington's band or Benny Carter or Nat King Cole, you know, or Lloyd Reese would be rehearsing those kids on Sunday, upstairs. There was a thing. But we go out here [to Local 47], and the minute you walk in, you feel a coldness, because there are so many people there who don't want you there in the first place. Even now that it's been integrated for thirty-some years, it's getting a coldness there again.

What they did, it made history, and it was good for some people. But you can name them on two hands, the people who really benefited from that, as far as the studio work is concerned. And that is what it was all about. The studio work. So, to me, I don't know if it really served a good purpose. I really don't.

The union, to me, was a meeting place. Not for meetings per se, but it was a congregating place, where you go and socialize or get a job. There was a clique there. There were certain people who they always called for certain gigs or background studio work, extras and stuff like that. But there was a camaraderie that you can't replace. There was a camaraderie that musicians had then that they'll never have again, because now we're pitted against each other. Like, Quincy [Jones] never comes over on this part of town. Benny Carter never comes. They all hung out in Hollywood that way. That's where they made their money. It was good for some, but for the majority it hasn't been that good.

"Central Avenue closed up when they found out how much money was being dropped over there."

I was talking to a guy on the radio in Denver, who had gone to UCLA. He was teaching a music class at the University of Denver, and he interviewed me when I was up there at the Fairmont Hotel. He said he had heard that what caused Central Avenue to go down was when they took the buses and the streetcars up.

I said, "What are you talking about? That had nothing to do with the activity on Central Avenue."

He said, "Well, the people stopped coming when they stopped those services."

I said, "The people weren't coming on public transportation. When they came over there, they came over to show their fine cars, their clothes, and their furs. They weren't about to take public transportation to come over there to show their diamonds off. Think about it for a minute." I said, "Central Avenue closed up when they found out how much money was being dropped over there and City Hall started sending the cops out there to heckle the white people." All the movie stars were coming over and dropping a lot of money. All the white playgirls were coming over and dropping a lot of money with the black guys. They would stop the women and pat them down and call them nigger lovers and that kind of stuff. And the men, they would do them just as bad. You'd be up against the wall spread-eagled, and they'd be taking your pictures and all that kind of stuff. And they'd catch you over there, and you'd better not have a ticket out or something. The least little thing and you were going down.

That's what stopped Central Avenue. It was the insults, the heckles, raiding the after-hours places. That's what stopped it. The money wasn't flowing. That was the whole point, to close them down. They started closing up one by one. Well, time was passing. I guess it was time to move on. But that helped to close it up.

See, the businesses began to hurt out west, northwest. Places like the Mocambo, Ciro's, and all those places, they were losing a lot of business with the people coming down in there, coming south to see the shows over there. That hurt. The businesses were hurting up in Hollywood, so it got to City Hall.

And then it started moving west. When we left Central Avenue, we went straight to Western Avenue. That became the hub. And up to Washington Boulevard. There were some clubs up there. The late forties and the early fifties. Then it moved to Crenshaw.

Musically, Central Avenue contributed music, musicians, clubs, theaters, and hotel show rooms that were just as important as contributors or contributions to the history of jazz as New York City's 125th and 52nd Streets, Chicago's 63rd and Cottage Grove, Kansas City's 18th and Vine, Memphis's Beale Street, New Orleans's Bourbon Street, or any other city that has been duly documented as a contributor to the history of jazz.

It gave me the motivation, the inspiration, enthusiasm, the desire, joy, you name it. Central Avenue was it for me. It started in Texas, but that was my fulfillment. When I got to Central Avenue, it was like I was where I was supposed to be. At that point in time, I was where I was supposed to be. And at that point in time, that was the place to be.

Hey, Central gave me the stamina. It gave me the wherewithal that I needed to take that step. That's where I really took the giant step to get into my music, because when I wasn't on the Avenue, I was at home doing what I had heard on the Avenue. I just breathed it in like osmosis. Central Avenue was my thing. It really was my thing.

And when Central Avenue shut down, I still carried Central Avenue to Western Avenue, to Glen's, and to the Oasis Club, over there on King Boulevard to the California Club, where Max Roach and Clifford Brown started. Central Avenue was the name. The street was over there, but it was all over L.A. Central Avenue was all over L.A. Wherever we congregated, that was our Central Avenue.

It became more than a street. It was a spirit. It was your goal. It was my life, really. It really was. That's where I found out who Clora was and what Clora wanted to be. It's something I can't really tell. It was everything. It started everything. It's like that song, "The Start of Something Big." Central Avenue was. I knew it the minute that I walked onto the Avenue, the minute I rode there and my brother was showing me all these places that day from the streetcar, the U car. I knew. When I walked up to that union, I knew. There was an aura. There was a feeling. No matter whether it's music or if you're a clerk or a steel-mill worker. If you're really into that and you feel it, you know that this is where you're supposed to be. You know, it's just a feeling. It really is.

And now I can get my Central Avenue in a lot of different places. Like when I'm around Count Basie's band and they're swinging their butts off, that's Central Avenue. It's held over into my genes now, my whole being. That Central Avenue is there. That's how deep Central Avenue is to me. I was in Russia and I heard some music. That was Central Avenue. I take it with me. Central Avenue is a part of me. It's in Clora Bryant. It's in a lot of people and they probably don't even know it. They've shut it off. But I never closed it off. I carried it with me. I've had it in New York, sitting there listening. And Birdland? Hey, they thought that was New York, but that was Central Avenue. There's a Central Avenue in every large city or any city that had a black congregation where they started their music. Kansas City has a Central Avenue. It might be called Main Street or whatever. And 125th was a Central Avenue. By any other name, it's Central Avenue to me.

And that's how deep it is with me. It's me. Central Avenue is me. That's how much a part of me it is. It was a continuation of the things that I felt when I would hear music in my hometown. And I knew I was reaching for something. I knew there was something there. It's just like being pregnant. You know you've got a baby, but you don't know what it is till it comes out. [laughter] That's what my hometown was. I knew I was going for something. It was in me. But when I got to L.A. and to Central Avenue, I knew that baby was it. It was Central Avenue. It's me. It's just that deep.

I don't know if I'm really putting into words exactly what I feel about it or what it has meant to me, but it's still there. Central Avenue closed down, but I didn't feel any distress or any sadness because, by the time it stopped going, we'd moved on over here, and Western Avenue became Central Avenue. Then Crenshaw became Central Avenue. Vine Street was Central Avenue. Central Avenue—it's history.

Central Avenue could be my heaven on earth. Really. I was in heaven when I was standing outside of that Downbeat club. I've heard a lot of guys say that's strange to hear a female say that, because they think they're the only ones that are able to experience those kinds of things. But I did, because that's how deep the music had gotten into me.

Can you imagine that feeling every night? From club to club? Can you imagine that? It has to be felt and lived. You have to live it. And I'm so glad that I did. But I want to leave something where the kids can understand that that's the way it was.

1 8

William Green

Multi-instrumentalist Bill Green was one of Los Angeles's most sought-after freelance performers. A first-call studio musician, Bill played in various studios and on many TV shows. He performed on a number of occasions with the Los Angeles Philharmonic and played with a wide variety of musicians: Burt Bacharach, Louie Bellson, Tony Bennett, the Capp-Pierce Juggernaut, Benny Carter, the Clayton-Hamilton Jazz Orchestra, Natalie Cole, Nat King Cole, Sammy Davis, Jr., Ella Fitzgerald, Lionel Hampton, Gladys Knight, Peggy Lee, Frank Sinatra, Dionne Warwick, John Williams, and Nancy Wilson. He recorded as the leader of his own jazz group and frequently as a sideman.

Bill carried on the excellent teaching tradition of Central Avenue. From 1952 to 1962 he was an instructor at the Los Angeles Conservatory of Music and regularly offered jazz workshops and seminars at universities throughout the country. Beginning in the late 1940s he also taught privately, and his studio on La Brea Avenue in Los Angeles was a training ground and meeting place for several generations of musicians. Bill died on July 29, 1996.

Bill was born on February 28, 1925, in Kansas City, Kansas.

My mother [Sarah Grant Green] would take me to school right along with my sisters [Lillian and Doris Green] and brothers [Thomas and Herbert G. Green]. I'm from a large family. I'm in the middle of the family. But my father [Thomas Green] was kind of good at drinking. I can always remember that. He had a habit, but he made a living, a very basic living. He was kind of like a mechanic and just did little odds-and-

369

ends jobs, but he did have a steady job. At that time twenty dollars a week was quite a bit of money, seemingly. I didn't ever really get to know my father because he wasn't around.

My mother would sing in the choir at church every Sunday. She was pretty good. That was nice exposure. And my older sister [Lillian] was studying piano, so she learned to play well. Now she plays in church and she has quite a talent. If you start singing, she'll know how to back you up, no matter what key. So I was exposed to some music. My father was able to play the saxophone, alto saxophone. He played a few songs, and that inspired me. I liked the sound of it.

So, many years passed. I was ten years of age. I took a stab at taking the horn out of the house, because we were all offered an opportunity to study music at the Dunbar Elementary School in Kansas City. My lessons were quite strange. They were like ten cents an hour, and there were about sixty people who would stand in line for this one teacher to teach individually. He would only come once a week, and I'd take a lesson for ten cents and maybe get to see him twice. The time that I spent with him was a few seconds, because he was trying to get around to sixty people or more in the one hour with all of the instruments that everybody plays. So he knew quite a bit. He was good. His name was Carl Brown.

On the way home from school, about three in the afternoon, there was a WPA [Works Progress Administration] organization—band members, older guys, adults. It was more or less a work project they had in this little church house on I think it was Fifth Street, Fifth and Cleveland in Kansas City. This big band of people would be playing, and I couldn't stand it. I had to nose my way in. I opened the door to this church, stood in the back room. Nobody said anything to me. I had the horn in my hand, in the case, naturally. I'd stand there maybe an hour.

So one day, after about a week or so, the conductor called me up: "Go over there, take your horn out. Sit with that fat fellow over there." He was speaking of a fellow by the name of Virgil Hill. Virgil was good enough to make a living at it. He played in nightclubs, and he was in this band just doing a little reading. There were about forty members in this band. And he said, "Just look over my shoulder. Take your horn, and when you feel you know your way around, just start blowing." So I learned something there, just watching the notes. And I would take the music home.

Then about the age of twelve I ran into Louis Whitworth, who was in the band. He was playing first clarinet and had been studying with a symphony player in Kansas City, Missouri. He was quite good. So that whole band, knowing that I was interested in playing clarinet— I'd learned how to play the saxophone part in the band, and I didn't think it was challenging anymore, so I asked if I could have a clarinet. They all chipped in without any question and bought a clarinet for me.

So Louis Whitworth, who is now here—in fact, I played a job with him just yesterday. Such a nice guy. Beautiful. I thought of him as being my father. I idolized him and tried to pattern my life after him. So there came a point where I stopped trying to be like Louis Whitworth. Louis had begun to play with knives, and he would take two very sharp knives and throw them up and juggle and catch them by the point. He had gotten pretty good until he cut a couple of his fingers.

In the meantime, I'm studying clarinet with him and had gotten pretty good. And I've learned the part, the first clarinet part. This was when I was around thirteen, close to fourteen. He had cut his fingers and couldn't play. I had been sitting with him, and they gave me that chair while he was recovering from his knife wound. I started playing the cadenzas and all and doing a very fine job of it, I must say. I really enjoyed it. But, like I said, all the time I would be practicing the clarinet now. No saxophone. I put that aside. And they started to pay me a salary out of their pocket. I wasn't old enough to be affiliated with the WPA association, but they gave me a salary. They chipped in each month out of their pockets, and that really was complimentary. When Louis Whitworth came back, we both played together.

Well, when that ended I must have been about fifteen.

When I was fourteen some lady came up to me and asked me if I would teach her son. I said yes. I had learned my scales, I was playing very well and could play these overtures. So he was failing. He was getting like F's, you know, in the band, playing clarinet. His name was Harvey. So I would go over to his house once a week, and, in about a couple of months, he started getting better grades.

But that's the beginning of my teaching career, really. I took time with him. I really enjoyed it. So I've been teaching since I was fourteen. And one student brought another student.

Military Service

When I was eighteen, I graduated from Sumner Senior High School. I played in the high school band. Naturally, I played the lead clarinet, solo clarinet. But I was drafted after graduating from senior high school. The next week after getting out of school—let's see, 1942—I was in the navy, and, by being drafted, I had to take what was given; I had no choice. I was pretty good in mathematics, in fact, excellent. So they decided to send me to service school, but for machinist mate. I told them I was a musician and I wanted to be a musician. "We don't have any openings, so you'll have to take this."

I was sent to service school up in Great Lakes. I stayed there nine extra months, coming out as a third-class machinist mate. After that, I was shipped down to San Diego by train. I liked it out here. California. Warm. I'd been used to all of that cold weather. It was so cold in Chicago that you could be going down a street and decide you wanted to go to the right when you got to the top of the hill or at the corner, and when you got to that corner the wind would be blowing probably the opposite direction. You would go with the wind. [laughter] This is true. But I liked California. And on weekends I would try to come to L.A.

Also, I learned to play pool very well in Kansas City as a youngster. So that came in handy. Money was scarce; I needed money. I could go down to the pool hall as a sailor and win some money to spend before the checks came. But I got away from that and started taking my liberty time going down to the navy field, where every weekend they would have dances. The band at navy field would play.

At first I went down to just dance. Then I decided, "I'd like to play with these guys." So I walked up to the bandstand and talked with Floyd Acklee. He was the lead alto man. On one of the breaks, I asked him if he needed someone to just sit in once in a while on sax. Would you believe, he said, "Well, we'll try you out on baritone. Just come over to the barracks where we rehearse." I did. I went over there and I sat in the band, and they liked me very much. I could read the part and everything. So I started a new career, you might say. And that lasted for the duration of the war. I had a nice job and was developing friends and getting more popular all the time with my instrument.

In April of '46 I was released from the service. I went back to Kansas

City, my hometown, and stayed at home with my mom and had some more of that good cooking. [laughter] I even learned how to cook a little bit watching her. And I stayed six months. I got a job playing in a nightclub, Eighteenth and Vine, which is now still a popular spot. We were playing at Scott's with a four-piece group. I started learning how to play bebop at that time and being exposed to Willie Rice, who was a great trumpet player and also pianist. Oh, he really was responsible for my understanding. He had like an open house every day for all musicians who wanted to come. Excellent musician.

I really enjoyed that part of my life. For six months I'd go spend most of my days from, say, at least twelve noon. I'd take the bus over to Kansas City, Missouri, every day from twelve noon until six or seven that evening and have a job that night from nine until one in the morning. I was playing mainly alto sax at that time. On trumpet Nat Ratler, with Bobby Stafford on drums, and Willie Rice at the piano. I think once in a while we'd have a bass player, but mainly four pieces.

I did that through the summer, say from June through August. And at that point I decided to come out here to go to school. Now, Nat Ratler and John Smith had already left Kansas City a couple of weeks before. They called me and told me that they had found a place for me to stay. And it was around Forty-first Street on the Eastside.

L.A. on the G.I. Bill

So I moved in, came to town in I think it was the first part of September before school started. I liked it out here because of the climate. I had a choice to go to New York, anyplace I wanted to on the G.I. Bill to study. So we decided to come back out here and study because of the weather mainly. And things were happening here too.

When I arrived in town here, they met me at the airport, and I came back to my room, which was on Forty-first Street. I heard a saxophone in the background, in the backyard, being played. It was a guy living on the same property. He had a room, just one single room. I found out a couple of days later it was Sonny Criss. He lived in the back house, you might say, of this place that we were renting. It was kind of crowded, three of us sleeping in maybe a small area, a room. We had three beds, staying in the same room and going to the same shower and what have you, so we didn't stay there too long. I found a place, and John went one direction, and so did Nat, and we all separated. So I stayed there I would say about three months.

We got started in the L.A. Conservatory of Music. There were a few blacks at the conservatory. I would say out of the four or five hundred, there were no more than fifteen to twenty, at the most, black. Nat, I think, was the best musician of all at an early age. He was a trumpet player. I learned quite a bit from him. He was able to hear chord changes without the need of any instrument. He had nearly perfect pitch, and he wrote well. All of his compositions in the conservatory were really outstanding. He spent all day just writing. When we were told to bring in one or two compositions, say, maybe twenty-four bars each, he'd bring in at least a dozen.

I was playing at a nightclub on the beach in Long Beach from, say, nine-thirty to one every night making a salary such as seven dollars a night. Only four pieces. This is while going to school at the L.A. Conservatory in the daytime. In fact, Buddy Collette got the job for me; he recommended me to El Herbert, who had the group. El was a trumpet player who took after Louis Armstrong. He used all of his expressions, and it was beautiful. His playing was reasonable. He couldn't read a note, but his ear was pretty good. The place was called the House of Rhythm.

So I worked there really quite a while making money, enough to live on, because the G.I. Bill hadn't paid off. It took about six months after I'd arrived here and started in school. I had to make out however I could. I had two friends, but neither one was working. I was kind of supporting them until they got their check, the same as I, waiting for it. We drank milk and ate bread—made out however we could. We had a few friends around who would cook and invite us over, and that helped some. But I really know what a bean tastes like. [laughter] Slim pickings.

I stayed with the conservatory until I got a bachelor's degree, and then I went on to a master's degree, mainly on clarinet, spending most of my time on the clarinet. I got some very good jobs out of doing it. I studied with Mitchell Lurie, and he sent me on a couple of shows he was playing on when he couldn't get back on time from other events that he was involved with.

That was my saving grace. I had studied in the conservatory and that really saved me. I learned to play flute and the clarinet and how to read the classical music and play it as well as the jazz. So whenever they needed something in the studio that needed just a little touch of classical, the background, I was ready and prepared. Especially with Motown. All of the stars that had something, they needed a little flute that had a touch of classical in it.

I was at the conservatory until 1952 as a student. Then, after that, I stayed on for ten more years as an instructor or a teacher at the L.A. Conservatory.

In the meantime, naturally, Central Avenue was jumping. The very night that I came to Los Angeles, we all went up on Central Avenue, and, oh, it was jumping. The Last Word had someone playing there, Emma "Ginger" Smock, a lady violinist, played jazz. She was a good looker too. I ran into Benny Carter at the Club Alabam, maybe not that particular night but one of the nights in that period of time, when I first came here. The Downbeat was jumping. I had never heard so much music, and all in, say, one block between Forty-second and Forty-third on Central Avenue. There were about four clubs, maybe five.

Redd Foxx was around during that time, and he would practice on us. He'd tell jokes and see how they took with us before he would go up on stage. [laughter] That's the truth. But I can tell you Redd Foxx was quite a guy. He was always practicing. He kept a crowd around him. He'd come in the pool hall, and right away he was number one. They'd stop shooting pool just to have him talk. And he loved it. On his intermission from the Last Word or wherever he was performing, he would come down and practice a couple of lines, thoughts that had come to mind, and see how it would take. Just beautiful, really.

It seems like there was so much talent around during that period. Johnny Otis was on the scene then also. He knew how to get things going. He'd be playing probably at the Club Alabam, but he managed to get around to all the clubs, even the Downbeat, with some kind of a group. And Johnny Otis was a good talker. They loved him.

I hardly go over in that vicinity now that I've been living on the Westside. I guess once you get away from it, you don't go back. And there's nothing really over there happening. There's a good eating house still over there I visit once in a while. But Central Avenue is just like blah, nothing. One time there was—what was it called—the Bird in the Basket. We used to go down to that place. It was a little small club and always packed, and it had some great jazz players to participate.

I think every Monday night was jam session night at the Downbeat. I sat in quite often. There would be so many guys up on the stand, trumpet, any instrument you could name. And it wasn't a very large bandstand, either. But it seems like guys can make room when it comes to jamming, if they can get a part of it. [laughter] And especially if he hears a song he feels he knows. "I've got to get a little bit of that song," you know. He takes his horn out and runs up on the bandstand, "Let me have a chorus or two." It was fun. Really, it was unbelievable, those days.

I met Miles Davis during this period, too. He was over on San Pedro and Vernon. There was a club there. I don't remember the name of it, but Miles Davis and, I think, Dexter Gordon were playing with a rhythm section at this club. I walked up to Miles Davis and asked him, "Miles, how could you help me understand what to do with jazz? How would you describe it?" "Well, Bill, I take one note that I like, and I add another and another—" he started walking off. "And another and another—" Until he disappeared. [laughter] And that was it. And, truthfully, that is the answer. [laughter] That's what he said. Keep adding a note that you like.

The Downbeat would close maybe one-thirty or two o'clock. Most of the clubs did. There was a club called Lovejoy's—that's at Central and Vernon—that would go from twelve o'clock midnight until six, seven the next morning. That is where we also went to jam. And there was quite a bit to learn and was learned there. You'd walk up this hallway, up the stairway into the hallway, into this little room. Somebody's playing. And a drummer might come. People would look forward to going afterhours to Lovejoy's to just listen and sit around the bar. That was like a training ground that we don't have these days. You could go anytime and jam.

Wardell Gray was on the scene at the time, Dexter Gordon, Teddy Edwards, Lucky Thompson, who I thought was the greatest of all on tenor sax. He was smooth, fast, and a beautiful tone. Nothing ever went wrong with his playing. It was just unbelievable. He said he practiced every day, mainly scales, eight hours a day. And he did that many, many years. Excellent player. I'd never heard such smoothness. But he had an attitude. That's what killed him. He never got going because he couldn't get along with anybody. Yeah. Great player. I liked him better than Paul Gonsalves.

But back to Central Avenue. Every night I'd have to go up on the

Avenue. I moved around about two blocks from Central Avenue so I wouldn't have far to go, because I knew I had to be there. [laughter] That's what I was out here for, to learn how to play music, and that's where it was. I lived on Forty-first and Naomi. And I stayed there at least a year. This room that I had was like a front porch to someone's home. They leased it out to me for six dollars a week. I only had a room, and I had to go around the back to the restroom to take a shower. But I even taught in that little room. Just enough room for me, really. [laughter] And in the closet I had a hot plate. That was it. And a bed.

So I stayed there, and I even did some teaching. Guys who were going to the school, Jefferson High School, which was a block away from Naomi and Forty-first—it was on Forty-first and Hooper, only a block away—they'd stop by. I'd be practicing, and I picked up a few students right there. They'd stop in, wanted to study with me, and I started my clientele. [laughter]

Teaching, Learning, and Jamming

I went over to Lloyd Reese's studio one day. In fact, he called me over and asked me if I wanted to teach at his studio. He'd heard the good I'd been doing, and he wanted me to join with him. And when I found out what he wanted to pay me, I said, "No, I think I can do better on my own, and thanks a lot for the offer." He seemed to be a nice guy. He had an attitude of really making all of his students unusually good. I liked that spark, and I tried to use that theory in my teaching. If I teach, I want you to really know what you're doing and be as good as anyone possibly can be.

But, as you live and learn, you know that most of what you say must be worked at by the student. If it isn't, well, it won't flourish. It's like watering a plant. If you don't put water on it, it won't grow. You have to apply yourself as a student. No matter what you study, it's mainly left up to the student. We all know this. Talent, sure. That means how fast, how well do you catch on to whatever it is you're studying and how much interest you have in it to pursue and to continue learning.

But Lloyd Reese, he impressed me the most. I knew of Caughey Roberts, because I played in a band with him. I didn't know of him as a teacher, but I know that he did teach Jackie Kelso, and he did a wonderful job with him. [laughter] Caughey was the clarinetist with Millard Lacey, who was the conductor of a park concert band. We played the various parks in town here in Los Angeles. South Park. Also MacArthur Park when they built it. And others: Hollenbeck, which is over on the Eastside. We were just all around Central Avenue. Buddy Collette used to play in one of the bands.

Before Millard Lacey, we had Percy McDavid. He was a nice man. He had great influence on all of us. He emphasized finesse in music. He was really into reading and dynamics and little things, tuning. I still admire his playing. I didn't know anyone with the same touch that he had when he played. He had gone to school in France and so forth, but he was a bandleader out here.

During the late 1940s, Bill and Buddy Collette carried their teaching activities into a restaurant, the Crystal Tea Room, for Sunday afternoon jam sessions.

We had to have someplace, and this place was available to us. You have to have someplace to perform, whatever you do. But we didn't really have an organization. It was kind of like a group of guys who would meet there, a rhythm section, and the horns would come and bring their instruments. Nobody really appointed. But somehow it took place. It didn't last long. I don't know why, but possibly the rental of the building or whatever. It's usually finances that bring about an end or a beginning to anything. [laughter]

It was in the vicinity of South Park there around Fifty-eighth and San Pedro, in that neighborhood. Avalon, that was the street, yes, where it was located. On Sunday afternoons they'd have jam sessions. I'd say the session started at noon and last maybe until four. You'd walk in and the house would be jumping. People were just on top of each other. You could hardly walk. There were always drinks available, but mainly the musicians were there to play their horns. It seems that we don't have days like that anymore.

I had one student, Walter Benton, coming to these sessions. Walter Benton was one of the best saxophone players ever at that time. He played tenor sax, and he sounded quite a bit like Lucky Thompson. Pee Wee Johnson was very good, and Hadley Caliman, who's doing very well up in San Francisco now.

A very interesting point is how does one know what to practice to play at a jam session. Well, mainly, you have to know what tunes are popular at jam sessions, so you have to attend jam sessions to know that. You could even take a notebook with you—you should—and note the tunes that are being played. Make sure you learn all of those tunes, like "You Stepped Out of a Dream." When that became popular, everybody jumped on that and was playing it. [sings fragment of melody] "Whispering." Now, you remember when all of the fellows jumped on that. When I came here, a very popular tune was "How High the Moon." And it still is popular. Some things never change. That song has changes in it either you know or you don't. I think a musician starting out today should learn "How High the Moon" or he really hasn't gotten his feet wet, you might say, in jazz. The changes are very nice. You kind of learn to live inside of them.

Then I left the Central Avenue scene to go to Glendale to sit in with Bumps Myers. This was in the early fifties. A place called the Melody Club. Bumps Myers and William Woodman were the two tenor saxophone players that I joined after the Central Avenue thing kind of slowed down. I don't know how to describe what really happened. It just kind of slowed down a little bit, Central Avenue. I don't know what the reasons were.

But they'd bounce me around like a rubber ball. [laughter] They're such great players. [laughter] I loved it. I kept going downtown to buy a mouthpiece that would just come halfway up to their volume level. [laughter] And every night they would let me sit in. So, evidently, I must have gotten pretty good, because the manager hired me to be the third saxophone with them.

As I look back upon the Central Avenue days, I feel that I achieved quite a bit, mainly through exposure to the great musicians. And I was able to play with them, such as Dexter Gordon; and Wardell Gray, who's gone long ago; Big Jay McNeely was on the scene; Lucky Thompson; Sonny Criss was around at the time. And there were others such as Gene Montgomery, who also passed shortly after the Central Avenue days. He was a fast liver. He did many things wrong; he was drunk all the time, drinking and smoking, naturally, and doping it up. So he didn't last very long, but a great player. He sounded and sort of looked like Lester Young.

At the Downbeat I would take out my horn and sit in once in a while with the guys. Even Benny Carter would play there sometimes, and I'd sit in with him. I even have pictures when I was sitting in with Benny Carter and Wardell Gray on this bandstand at the Downbeat. Those were wonderful days.

So what I gained, mainly, as I said before, was the exposure to these great players and attitudes that were taken by them with their instruments, and the kind of music they played. The average musician could get up on the stand if he felt he was good enough to. There was a fellow by the name of Sweet Pea Robinson; he was reasonably good. He'd take his horn out and get up on the bandstand and play, and he sounded good. During that period, Eric Dolphy came along too. He'd take out his horn and wasn't so good at the time. And they would let him sit in. And then, shortly after that, Frank Morgan came on the scene. I remember seeing him in one of the clubs. It was the Club Alabam. That was my first time hearing him. He was an unusual talent. He learned fast at an early age of sixteen, seventeen. They let him in because he could play.

Those were rough days but good days, fun all the way. The music made it all like a dream. I wish I knew then what I know now about what it really takes to do all that you'd like to do, but I guess that's where time pays off. It takes time to learn all of those things. And you need someone who has the experience. It's good to be around experienced people who can help you out and make your life easy, because they've experienced what they know you need to know. It's like some of the things I'm teaching you. For the most part, I know that you need that to improve. That's what I'm trying to teach right now: what I know will make you improve. So that about closes it up for me with Central Avenue.

Marl Young

ince his arrival in 1947, pianist Marl Young has been a mainstay of the club scene in southern California. His versatile skills have also landed him numerous television gigs. By the late 1950s he was working at the Desilu Workshop Theater, and in the early 1960s for The Lucy Show. *His association with Lucille Ball continued into the early 1970s, when he was director-composer-conductor for* Here's Lucy *during the show's four-year run.*

Marl's leadership in the amalgamation of the musicians locals propelled him into union politics. He was the first black to win a seat on the board of directors of Local 47, in the 1956 elections, and he served several terms on the board over the years. In 1974 he was elected secretary of the local, the first black elected as a full-time executive officer, and served in that capacity for eight years. Marl also chaired and co-chaired Local 47's legislative committee. In all, he has served his union in some official capacity for about nineteen years.

Marl was born in Virginia on January 29, 1917. Seven years later, his family moved to Chicago. He was attracted to the piano at an early age and, through the influence of schoolteachers and the church, became immersed in the European classical tradition.

I started when I was about six. I just started playing on my own. My mother always had a piano in the house. She liked music and had played some. When they saw that I had some talent, I started studying, because I wanted to learn it right. I guess that's why I'm not a hell of a jazz player now—I very seldom practiced jazz at home. I practiced classical music at home always, and then I would go out at night and make a living playing jazz. But I enjoy all kinds of music.

The black churches were the only places where black people could really go and play classical music. There was no place for them. There was no outlet. And I would say most of the classical music that's dispensed by black vocalists and instrumentalists now is still in the black churches. And I enjoyed playing in church.

In high school Marl played regularly around Chicago in a variety of venues, from speakeasies to clubs.

By the later part of 1932, I was still in high school, but I was playing music. I was playing music at night. They had speakeasies and bawdy houses and all those places. You played where people wanted you to play.

In 1940 Marl married Stella Traylor. Having finished junior college, he was attending the John Marshall Law School, from which he graduated three years later, and was writing and arranging for many club shows around Chicago.

At one time I was writing the music for all of them, the Rhumboogie, the De Lisa, and a place called the El Grotto, which was later on called the Beige Room. I became expert at rehearsing, sketching, writing arrangements, and conducting nightclub floor shows. That was my specialty. When you play piano, arranging becomes almost natural, because you're playing all the parts on the piano. I taught myself to arrange, and then I just started writing. And sometimes, even if I wasn't working, I just made a living arranging.

I never did get away from music enough to really sit down and study properly for the bar exam. I'll always regret that. But, you know, I was working, making money. However, the knowledge has just been invaluable.

Los Angeles —
"My God, where has this been all my life?"

Not long after finishing law school, Marl was ready for a change from Chicago. His marriage had broken up, and the winters seemed far too long.

I was getting tired of the weather in Chicago, which is very easy to do. [laughter] I never will forget that winter in 1944. Snow fell on the ground in November, mid-November, and in March of 1945 that same layer was still there except that there were maybe eight or nine layers on top of it. I got pneumonia that winter. I said, "I'm going to leave this fellow. I've got to get out of here." Finally, I got a chance to go with Louis Jordan's band. And I left Chicago—I'll never forget—on November 17, 1947. I had a raggedy Pontiac and fifteen dollars in my pocket.

I remember going through Pomona [California], and I put my hand out the window, and I felt that warm air. "Jesus Christ, this is November!" And I remember the first Christmas that I spent here. I'm walking down the street, and I had to stop, because I was dressed like this. "My God. Here I am, this is Christmas day, and I'm walking down San Pedro Street in my shirtsleeves, my short, short sleeves." I said, "My God, where has this been all my life? I'll never leave this town." [laughter]

I thought I had forever to get here. I got here on November 24, and Louis said I should have been here three days before. [laughter] I went down to Decca Records—they were recording there—and he had hired a pianist by the name of Bill Doggett, who wrote a tune called "Honky Tonk," which made a whole lot of money. I hope he got some of it.

But I started working. I called Benny Carter. He was going to do some things for Freddie Slack. I had written for Benny before. He had come by the Rhumboogie in Chicago one night and saw me conducting the band. He said, "Well, I want you to do some things for me." So I did quite a few things for him, sent them wherever he was, all over the country. This is in 1944, '45, those two years. Then I did some arrangements for Martha Davis, and got some work through Jenny Le Gon and Marie Bryant. And it's all because I could accompany people. I could play the shows, things like that. And I knew how to rehearse people. So I started doing fine.

On the Avenue, however, business was slowing, ensembles were getting smaller, and musicians were looking further afield for work.

When you come into a new town, you can't play a regular engagement, because of union rules, for at least three months. But the night three months were up, I started working at the Last Word Cafe with Jimmy Witherspoon. I worked there a few weeks.

Then I met my second wife, Judy Carol, at Marie's house. In three days

I'd asked her to marry me. I wasn't divorced a year before I got married again. You get used to being married, man, which is maybe something you shouldn't get used to. [laughter] Same way with my first wife. I went to see her. The first time I walked out, I said, "I'm going to marry her." And I'd just met her that day. [laughter] Of course, the way it turned out, maybe I shouldn't have. [laughter]

Judy was a professional and had sung with Lucky Millinder. She appeared in *Jump for Joy* with Duke Ellington. We got a band together, and work opened at the Downbeat, across the street from the Last Word. This was 1948. But things were getting economically worse. We had to cut down to a trio, but we still worked all the time. We worked places in El Monte, Ontario, Pomona. Nice clubs. We never worked Central Avenue again. I think we did work one place that was called the Oasis, about four days filling in for somebody else. But that was the only black club we played.

I started going out to the outlying areas in '49. I didn't have any problems. But there again, there were just three of us. Also, I always made it my business, no matter where I worked, that nobody is ever going to have to tell me to dress properly, nobody is going to have to tell me to come there sober, nobody is going to ever have to tell me to get on the bandstand when my intermission is up, nobody is ever going to have to tell me to work. When we go there, we go there to work. No bullshit. We work. When our intermission is up, we don't say, "Let's get on the stand." When the intermission is up, we are on the stand, we're ready to play. So that's the way we handled our jobs. So we didn't have any problems.

I never had anybody that was associated with dope. That's where you get the problems. When you have somebody that has a dope record, then the cops follow you. And the dope scene seemed to be more prevalent out here than in Chicago. But, mind you, I emphasize the word "seems," because you just don't know. Most of what I ran into in Chicago was marijuana, even in the mid-forties, which I really think should be decriminalized. It makes no sense the way they're doing it now. Cigarettes kill almost half a million people a year, and marijuana never killed anybody. But that's another subject. [laughter] I've never touched marijuana, lit or unlit, so I'm completely neutral on the subject. But I think it's stupid to arrest somebody for smoking a joint. The joint might make you a little giddy, but that cigarette is going to kill you. It makes no sense.

Then my wife and I separated. We did all right as long as we were in bed, but after that we didn't agree on anything. [laughter] I was at UCLA working on a degree in music, and I met Estelle Edson, who was at UCLA. She had been a professional singer, too, so we started working together. And we worked all the time with a trio. So I came back from a twelve-piece band down to a six-piece band to a four-piece band to a trio. Then the last ten years, before I became secretary of the musicians union, I worked in nightclubs as a single. [laughter]

Estelle was also instrumental in involving Marl in the musicians union. Marl's legal training provided much-needed expertise to the pro-amalgamation forces of Local 767. Along with Buddy Collette and Bill Douglass, he quickly became one of the prime movers for a merger of the two locals.

Until thirty or forty years ago, all the unions in the big cities, with the exception of Detroit and New York, were segregated. There was a black union, there was a white union. The first musicians union that I joined in Chicago in 1933 was Local 208, and it was a black union. Local 10 was the white union, and [James C.] Petrillo was the president of that, before he became national president of the American Federation of Musicians.

Well, one thing about the Chicago local, it was well run, and they fought for you. I wasn't fond of Harry Gray, but he was a good president. He fought for you, and they enforced the rules. He and Petrillo were good friends, and I guess they accepted things as they were.

At that time I wasn't gung ho to get rid of the segregation. It was a way of life. I took some interest in union politics. But I was busy. I made most of my money on the South Side, anyway, unlike when I came to Los Angeles. I did very little in the black neighborhood in L.A. I did everything in outlying white sections. So it was a different type of city.

Local 767 functioned all right, except that they set their scales according to what the white union did, and they would call the white union for this and the white union for that, and I thought that just made no sense at all. If you're going to have an organization, run it. The people were all right, too. There was one business agent there, Elmer Fain, who did his job, and that's the main thing with a union, for the people who are representing the musicians to do their job. A lot of people thought he was a bully, and I guess in a sense he was, but he was just the business representative. He would go around to the nightclubs and see that the union rules were being kept, etc., etc.

So the union seemed to be running okay, but it was a poor union because it didn't have that many members. Local 47 had fifteen thousand; we had maybe seven hundred or eight hundred. How the hell are you going to do anything? They're out there where the jobs are; you're over here where nothing is. And besides, every time they wanted to do something, they would call the white union for advice. Well, hell, if I'm running a union, I don't want you calling anybody for advice. So that was one thing I didn't particularly like. Bagley, the vice-president at Local 47, also wrote the bylaws for Local 767. And, you know, that looks like the man is taking care of your business, don't worry about it. "Mr. Charlie will do it." That's bullshit.

The Amalgamation: Getting Involved

Out here, with the amalgamation thing coming, I wasn't particularly interested. When I arrived I just went in to the union and dropped my transfer. I very seldom went down there, because I was working, and I was in school. And my wife and I were feuding, I guess.

When I went to UCLA, I met Estelle Edson and she was writing a thesis, "The Black Man in Radio." Of course, there weren't any black musicians in radio. So then she said, "Well, does the fact that the unions are segregated have anything to do with it?" I said it certainly could, because if somebody's looking for somebody, they aren't going to come over here. They're going to go to Local 47. She said, "Well, do you think we could have some discussions about this at the union?" So I called the president and we had a meeting. There were a lot of prominent musicians attending: Buddy Collette, Bill Green, Billy Hadnott, Red Callender.

I think people like Percy McDavid, Russell McDavid, Ernie Freeman, Buddy Collette, John Anderson, others, were just beginning to talk about the fact that segregation was not right. The white musicians like George Kast, Gail Robinson, Seymour Sheklow, Henry Roth, Esther Roth, his wife, Joe Eger, and others, were beginning to talk about this. The whites and blacks were getting together. Jerry Fielding was very prominent. This was '49 or '50.

And we held the meeting. I made two or three speeches at the union.

Because of the way I spoke, they thought that maybe they might have an ally. But we were working.

Then when a fellow named John Anderson came by my house one morning and said they had been fired because of their amalgamation activity, I got mad. Because if they can do it to them, they can do it to you. They had a municipal band sponsored by the city and the union, by what we call the Music Performance Trust Fund. Because of their activity in favor of amalgamation, they were fired by the black union officers. It was Percy McDavid's band. Bill Douglass, who later became vice-president of the black union, was in it, John Anderson, others.

So then I got started. John said, "We want you to come to a meeting." They had heard me speak at the meeting that we had, and they felt that I was aggressive and also seemed to have a command of parliamentary procedure. So I went around. Buddy, John Ewing, and Jimmy Cheatham had a place at Fifteenth Street and St. Andrews Place, right around the corner. I went by, and they said, "We need somebody like you to join us." I said, "Okay, I'm in." Then we all got together, Benny Carter, Bill Douglass, John Anderson, Buddy, John Ewing, and Estelle, and then the white guys were George Kast, Gail Robinson, Henry Roth, Esther Roth, Joe Eger, Seymour Sheklow, and a lot of others, and we started meeting.

The leadership of Local 767 unanimously opposed ending the segregated locals. Marl understood their reasons.

Hey, you have to look at the economic issue. They had jobs. They were working. Their jobs were to run the union. They were being paid. They got full-time salaries. And I can understand that. When your economic existence is threatened, you fight, black or white. And it's happened all over the country with integration. So that's the human element there, and you have to understand that. At that time, I didn't give a damn about it. I said, "It's wrong. To hell with their jobs. We're going to get rid of it, anyway." But I can still understand the economic threat. When your economic existence is threatened, you'll do a lot of things.

Also, remember, we had to form our own unions because the white unions didn't want the black guys. So they said, "Okay, now we've got our union, now you want to get rid of it." Because I remember one meeting where one black guy said, "I don't want to have nothing to do with no white man." He had grown up in the South, where they were treated like dogs. I could understand his not wanting to have anything to do with white people.

But still, to have two unions is wrong. If you're going to get any opportunities, you've got to be where the work is. And also, it's just basically wrong.

So anyway, we started talking about getting rid of segregation. The only way you can get rid of the segregation is to get some power in the union. We said, "The only way that we're going to get rid of this is to become officers in the union and then demand or ask that we have negotiation proceedings with the white union." So we ran for office. Buddy ran for president, Bill Douglass ran for vice-president, Estelle ran for secretary. We didn't oppose the treasurer, Paul Howard; everybody liked him. I ran for trustee. Russell ran for director. The election was in November of 1951 to take office in 1952.

We campaigned strictly on the matter of amalgamation. We wanted to get rid of the two unions. We ran on that one issue. We talked to people, called people, put out literature, wrote letters, the same way you run any campaign. We had talks, meetings.

Leo Davis beat Buddy for president by a good margin. Bill Douglass, on our side, won for vice-president. Estelle lost. Their candidate, Florence Cadrez, who had been there for years, won for secretary. And we didn't oppose the treasurer. But then we got enough on the board that when the votes came down we could win on the issues. We had a majority. These four officers, plus three trustees and two directors, comprised the board of directors. I was a trustee. Russell McDavid, a director. Bill, vice-president. John Anderson, a director. Oh, and Benny Carter. He was a trustee. We had a five-four majority. They had Leo, Florence, Paul, and Harvey Brooks as trustee.

We then had a meeting of the board of trustees to choose a chairperson. Now, I could have had it easy, because Benny was in our faction. But Harvey said, "Well, I want it, you want it. Why don't we flip for it?" I said, "Okay." So we flipped, and I lost.

Negotiating and Campaigning

We immediately said that we wanted to start negotiations for the amalgamation. Our amalgamation committee consisted of Benny Carter as chairman. He wanted me to be chairman, but I thought that his name was more widely known, so he should be the chairman. It was Benny Carter, Estelle, Buddy, me, Leo Davis, Paul Howard, and Harvey Brooks.

We contacted the white union. They said that they would be glad to talk with us. We had a meeting. The election was in '51. We are now in '52.

The first hurdle was to formulate a method for integrating the union. Local 47's leadership proposed that Local 767 dissolve and its members then apply individually for membership in 47. Marl's solution was an amalgamation by merging the two locals.

The first thing they told us was, "Well, if you fellows dissolve your union, we'll be glad to take you in as members." Charles Bagley, Local 47 vice-president, said all you have to do is to get the written consent of your membership. But they knew we couldn't dissolve. Our bylaws required, in order for us to dissolve, that you have the written consent of nine-tenths or maybe four-fifths of the entire organization. That meant those that did not vote were the same as a no vote. You know you're never going to get that. And we knew that. That's why when I wrote the merger proposal I knew precisely what I was doing. I wasn't guessing at all.

When we started the amalgamation fight, I made it my business just to become completely conversant with the bylaws of Local 767 and Local 47 and of the federation. That's why I was able to write a merger proposal, and I knew the specific difference between an amalgamation that calls for a merger and an amalgamation that calls for consolidation. The two are different, the two are drastically different. In consolidation, each organization goes out of business and reorganizes as one organization. In merger, one organization is just absorbed by the other. That was the practical way for us to do it. That's why I wrote the amalgamation proposal as a merger proposal.

Another issue raised by Local 47 concerned the death benefit—the money allotted to cover a member's funeral expenses.

Then they said that the issue that was hanging us up, strangely enough, was the death benefit. At the time in Local 47, if you were forty or over when you joined, you could not be covered by their one-thousand-dollar benefit. It was the same way in Local 767, except the death benefit in 767 was only four hundred dollars. We didn't have as many members, you know. So that was the hang-up. They said, "A lot of your members are more than forty. And even though they're covered at Local 767, when they come over here we can't cover them, because they will be in violation of our bylaws."

So I volunteered to solve the problem. I had a lot of guts. [laughter] "I'll write a proposal to take care of it." I didn't know what the hell I was doing. [laughter] So what we did, Buddy and I and a lot of others, we went down to the black union, we got all the members, and we made a table as to the number that were over forty and those that were under forty. We found that a third of our membership was over forty, two-thirds was under forty.

In my proposal I wrote that for the first year, if there was a merger, all the members of what had been Local 767 would be covered by the four-hundred-dollar death benefit that was in vogue at Local 767 at the time we merged. And the money from our assets—we had twenty-five thousand dollars in our treasury assets—would be used to cover any deaths from this. Now, I said, "My God, if we have an earthquake or a catastrophe, we're in deep trouble." [laughter] You think of all these things. So then I said, after the first year, those who, in accordance with Local 47's bylaws, were under forty at the time of the amalgamation would then be covered by Local 47's one-thousand-dollar death benefit just like everybody else. Those who were over forty at the time would continue to be covered by the four-hundred-dollar death benefit. The beauty of that was two-thirds of us under forty would gain, and the other third wouldn't lose anything. So while they wouldn't be getting as much in a death benefit, they wouldn't get any less than they had been getting at Local 767.

The final point of contention was union seniority for Local 767 members. The number of years of union membership was used to determine eligibility for life membership: After thirty years of dues paying, members in good standing receive a life membership, which exempts them from any further dues.

And also part of the plan was that, as far as seniority and your eligibility for life membership is concerned, the date that we joined Local 767 would be listed as the date that we joined Local 47, so that when your life membership came around you wouldn't lose. So in other words, we had seniority. For instance, I joined Local 767 in 1948. In Local 47's record, I'm listed as having joined Local 47 in 1948, although I actually went over there in 1953.

When I wrote the proposal, we said that as a result of the merger the resulting organization—that's the way it's done in legal terms—the resulting organization will be Local 47, and Local 767 will be merged and absorbed into Local 47. And everyone who was eligible to become a member of Local 767 is now a member of Local 47. Then I put out the matter of the death benefit and how would it apply, and the life membership, how that would apply.

Local 47's leadership didn't think we would be able to work it out. They didn't want it. Some of them probably just didn't want any black people over there. So they said, "We cannot accept this."

Then we said, "We want you to present this to your membership and put it on your ballot at your December election." Well, we had people over there who were working for us, too. We had people like George Kast and Gail Robinson and others who were going to meetings and saying, "This is the right thing to do. Why, the democratic thing to do is to let the membership vote. If the membership turns it down, fine. But if the membership wants it, why not?" So they were in a position where they would have looked like real bigots if they said, "We aren't even going to present it to our membership." Finally, they said, "Okay, we'll put it on the ballot."

So I wrote an article that appeared in [the Local 47 publication] *Overture,* not under my name—I think it was under George Kast's name—urging people to consider it and vote yes on it.

Also we had a setback, because remember, our election was every year. Theirs was every two years. We had another election coming up in November of 1952. This time Benny Carter ran for president. We lost the majority on the board. Russell McDavid, a director, lost, and Benny lost for president. Leo Davis beat him by fifteen votes. We were devastated, boy, because, remember, the next month the amalgamation proposition is coming up on the ballot at Local 47, and the amalgamation forces have just been kicked downstairs by the Local 767 membership.

But then our membership dissolved the amalgamation committee and said, "From now on, just let the board of trustees handle the amalgamation." The election of '52 is over. Now the board of trustees is Harvey Brooks, Marl Young, and Buddy Collette. So on the trustees we did have a majority. We called a meeting of the trustees and said, "Well, what about a chairman?"

I said, "Well, I want it."

Harvey said, "I want it. Why don't we flip a coin?"

I said, "No way." [laughter] "The Dodgers lost the World Series. Stevenson lost the election to Eisenhower. There ain't no way we're going to flip a coin this time. I want it. You want it. It's up to Buddy."

I said, "Buddy, who do you want to be chairman of the board of trustees?"

He said, "I want Marl Young to be chairman."

I said, "The meeting will now come to order." [laughter]

Harvey Brooks got so mad. He stood up over me this close. A foot or two away. For fifteen minutes he cursed me. He called me every name, some names that I'd never heard of before, and I grew up in the streets of Chicago. He called me SOBs and MFs. He talked about my mother, my father, my sisters, my grandmothers, my grandfathers. And I just sat there.

I said, "Are you through?"

He said, "Yes."

I said, "The meeting is adjourned." I walked out. [laughter] Oh, he was mad. I've never been called so many names in all my life. I've never seen a man that mad in all my life. He was strongly opposed, and he was a very intelligent man, a very articulate man, a good man. But I just told him, "Harvey, there ain't no way I'm going to leave this up to chance."

Then Maury Paul, the secretary of and the power in Local 47, wrote an article in *Overture* about the amalgamation proposal, and he didn't come out against it. And I think we can thank George Kast for that. I think George, who was on our side, talked to him and got him to be neutral on it. Well, that helped a lot, because people liked Maury. He was a very smart man, and they respected him.

The media gave us no help at all, except one person. The night before the vote at Local 47, my girlfriend, Estelle Edson, and I got in my car. We went to every newspaper, every news association, Associated Press, United Press, International Press, *Los Angeles Times, Los Angeles Examiner, Los Angeles Mirror.* And we went to every radio station. We went to

ABC, and I went into Chet Huntley's office, and I told him about it. I said, "There's a vote tomorrow. It sure would help if you could say something about it." He was about to go on the air, and I stuffed it in his hands. We got in the car. Right at the end of his program, he said, "Incidentally, tomorrow the all-white Local 47 will vote as to whether to accept and merge with the all-black musicians Local 767." Boy, I'm telling you, that was a thrill. And we heard this on the radio. [laughter] The black newspapers helped us, but the white ones didn't do a damn thing. The only white press that helped us was the *People's World*.

Anyway, we won by 233 votes. There were about two thousand people voting in that election. Estelle and I were up all night, and George Kast called and said, "Marl, we won!"

Now the black local had to vote on it. And remember we don't have a majority on the board, but we said, "Well, now we'll put it up to the Local 767 membership and have a special election." And we had to win by two-thirds of those voting. But we won easily. The black press helped us, and we campaigned like hell. We went on the radio. And we won. It was in January of 1953.

Getting AFM Approval

The next day, we had a board meeting. The national office had heard about it, and they wanted us to come to New York before the international executive board of Petrillo to talk about what we're going to do now that both unions had voted in favor of the merger. We hadn't contacted them before. We did it purely on a local basis. Our president, Leo Davis, said, "I will not go to New York, because they know that I've been against this, and if I go there and make a statement it will seem as though I'm fighting something that the union has voted in. I just won't go." He was a good man, and he was a good president. He just happened to be president at the time that we wanted to get rid of the damn organization.

So we went to New York, John te Groen, president of Local 47, and me. We finally got in to see the international executive board. I was dressed in a pure black suit, black tie, white shirt, white handkerchief. You know, strictly conservative. I walked in.

Petrillo said, "You're a lawyer?"

I said, "No."

"I don't like lawyers."

"I don't blame you."

Everybody relaxed. So we get rid of the bullcorn; now they want to hear the proposal, because the members of the executive board were skeptical as to how we were going to work it out. Petrillo said, "Johnny, your union has voted for it, their union has voted for it. What are we going to do about it?" Bagley, who was vice-president of Local 47 and on the international executive board, said, "They have to dissolve their membership. They can't merge. The merger is not the proper way to do it." And I remember Rex Ricardi, Petrillo's assistant, stood up, pointed his finger at John te Groen and Bagley and said, "Now, we told you that this merger was legal. We don't want to hear any more about it!" That's when I found out that there had been correspondence between the white union and the black union and the national body, and they were all attacking the process that we were following. They—the local officers, not the national officers—said this was not a legal merger.

Well, when I wrote it, I mentioned the word merger about ten times, and I was very clear about the matter of amalgamation. It was not a consolidation; it was a merger. And that's what the argument was over at the international executive board, when Bagley said that it could not have been done that way, that we had to go out of business and then consolidate. Or else, if not consolidate, if we had gone out of business, they would have accepted us as members of Local 47. When I got through, their mouths were open. [laughter]

So when we get ready to leave, Petrillo said, "Well, what is your schedule here? How long can you stay?"

I said, "I can stay here forever. I'm on an expense account." [laughter] "Whatever it takes I can stay here."

So we went out. They said, "We'll let you know."

When we got outside the door, I said, "Johnny, it looks like your union and my union have been corresponding about this merger without telling me. And it's in my hands, because our union has put this in the hands of the board of trustees, and I'm the chairman of the board of trustees. I want every goddamn one of those letters right now or else when I get back to Los Angeles the [*Los Angeles*] *Times* is going to be selling for two dollars a throw!" [laughter]

He said, "Here."

With te Groen attacking the amalgamation at the board, I got on the phone. I called George Kast: "You guys go to the board meeting of Local 47 and tell them that te Groen is trying to fuck up the merger." You know, I heard that they stormed the board meeting here. [laughter]

And so now 47 is getting in touch with te Groen saying that the members there are protesting. So te Groen called me and said, "You've got to pull me out. The guys are there protesting, saying that I'm trying to kill the merger."

I said, "Okay, Johnny, I'll be right up." He was at the federation. So I got in a cab and went to New York Local 802 and went to lunch with the black member on the board, Tiny Walters. And he's sitting down there waiting for me to come and pull him out. So I went to lunch. Tiny took me for a tour of Local 802, and we sat down and talked. After about three or four hours, I went up to the federation. He is there waiting. [laughter] I said, "I'm sorry, Johnny, I just got tied up. I'll send a telegram to Local 47."

So to the lady, "Will you take this telegram? This is to attest that John te Groen has assured me that he is in favor of this merger." How can he deny that he's for the merger now? "John te Groen has assured me that he is in favor of the merger and he will do nothing to block the merger. I'm sure that the merger will now go through because everybody's for it." So that's the telegram that I sent. [laughter] He just stood there. What could he do?

So we went back to the board, and Petrillo said, "We're going to send out a committee to oversee the merger and the transition. Herman Kenin will be the chairperson of the committee." It was Herman Kenin, their secretary, their treasurer, and another board member. I think there were four of them. Herman Kenin in 1958 became president succeeding Petrillo. But anyway, he was the president of the Portland local. So they tentatively approved it.

Wrapping It Up

In the meantime we had to take care of some housekeeping here at Local 767, because our corporation owned the property, not the union. It was called the Rhythm Club. At Local 47, Local 47 doesn't own the real estate. The Musicians' Club of Los Angeles, a corporation, owns it. So it was the comparable corporation. Each corporation was linked to the union through the board of directors. The board of the club is the same as the board of the union. So the elections to union office are dual elections, really.

We had to have a meeting of the Rhythm Club to approve merging our assets with the Local 47 assets. We were in control of the meeting, so I was elected president of the corporation. Estelle was elected secretary. Florence Cadrez had resigned by this time. Estelle had become secretary of the black local. Bill Douglass, who was the vice-president of the union, became vice-president of the corporation. And we didn't oppose Paul Howard. We had the same treasurer.

Herman Kenin from the international was there. He spoke and made a prophetic statement. "This will probably be the first of many mergers in the AF of M as far as black and white locals are concerned." Yeah. We did it, and we did it without any help from the federation. We got the votes without any help from the government or anybody. We did it purely through negotiations between the unions. It took a long time, but it was a prophetic statement.

Then we started having meetings with the federation officers and with our people and the people at Local 47. There were a lot of people still at Local 767, the old heads, who still were saying, "Well, I'm not going to join Local 47." The attorney said that the people in the corporation still had to sign a release as far as the assets were concerned. A lot of guys said they were not going to sign. So I told te Groen, "Look, when the guys come over on April 1 to get their card, they either sign the waiver or else they don't get a card." The waiver stated that they will not protest the transfer of the property from one corporation to the other, that they accept the merger, and that they're going in as members of Local 47 without any chance of a lawsuit being filed, as far as the transfer of assets was concerned. And te Groen took the idea.

Sometime in March of 1953, Estelle and I went to Local 47, I as the president of the corporation, she as the secretary of the corporation, and we signed the papers and the deeds to transfer the property. Then on April 1 Local 47 started accepting members. After everything was done, the international board just passed a resolution approving the merger, and everything was fine.

But it was quite a fight. We had a lot of setbacks and then a lot of victories, and that's the way politics is. You win some, you lose some, but the big fights we won.

If we hadn't amalgamated, I had plans. I was going to take the federation to court, because they had a bylaw in there—it shows you that people don't read—I think it was article seven of the federation bylaws that said no two locals shall do business within the same county boundary lines. You just go all over the country where they had a black local and a white local— [laughter] So I just read that. I said, "Fine. I'll just keep this in my pocket. If they don't—"

Also, another tack I was going to take— Even then it was against the public policy of the state of California to discriminate. If we hadn't amalgamated, I was going to run for president of Local 767 and open up our membership to everybody, white, black, everybody. And if anyone complained, I'd say, "I am just complying with the public policy of the state of California." If they said anything, we'd be in a court, because segregation is against the public policy of the state of California.

We didn't have to go that route. But I was going to bring the membership fee down to twenty-five dollars and have a dispensation period of a ten-dollar joining fee for three months and invite white, black, and everybody in it. Come on in. A couple of us had planned it. This is what I intended to do. I told Buddy and two or three others. But beyond that, we didn't mention this. I don't think more than four people discussed it.

So there were ways to do it, but we did it the right way. We brought it to a head. We had a vote of the white local under their bylaws, and we had a vote of the black local under our bylaws. Theirs took a simple majority, ours took a two-thirds, but we won it all easily.

Aftermath

We had some problems in Local 47. They started flagging black members. When I got on the board in '57, we went down to look at the membership cards and membership files. Every black member had a flag on his card. So the board got rid of that.

And then Jimmy Clark, a black business agent who was hired immediately in 1957 when I went on the board, kept coming to me. "Marl, there's something wrong with the guys at the casual office." Members give their name and addresses and telephone number so that if there's a gig that they can field, the guys will call them. "Marl, there's a way that they're identifying the black guys. I don't know what it is."

So one night at a meeting, I talked to Elliot Daniel, the president, and I said, "Elliot, something is going on in that office that I don't think is right. I'd like for you to look at it." Earlier that day I had gone down, and I went through all the files, and I saw a circle on a card, a circle around the address. Then I saw another circle, but this circle was around the name. Next, the circle is around the instrument. Now the circle is around the telephone number. But it was always a circle. And I found that every card that had a circle on it was a black musician. So we called the casual guy in and got it straight.

I wanted to have the guy expelled. But Red Callender and the guys came down and said, "Marl, no, just make it straight." I said, "You guys are too soft. We ought to get this son of a bitch out of here." We made him straighten it out. We should have fired the son of a bitch. But the guys wouldn't push. Anyway, those two things were straightened out.

Herman Kenin's prediction proved correct: The Los Angeles amalgamation spurred a national movement to eliminate segregated locals in the American Federation of Musicians.

We found out that each local was a different proposition. For instance, the white musicians turned down amalgamation twice in San Francisco. And San Francisco is supposed to be such a liberal town. Chicago, some of the guys didn't want it because it was really a better-run union than the white one. They had a good treasurer and everything. But by this time, the federation was saying, "This stuff has just got to go. We can't have this."

In some instances it worked out well. In some instances I guess it didn't. Some of the black guys feel as though they're still isolated. And suddenly the number of black delegates to the convention dropped, because the black guys were absorbed into the white union. It has its good points and it has its bad points.

The only thing is, segregation is wrong, period, and you had to proceed from that. Could you imagine in 1991 still having a black musicians union and a white musicians union? It's crazy! But there again, I must admit, when I joined, I didn't think anything of it. It was a way of life, although

I'd never gone to a predominantly black school in my life, because we always moved and went to where the whites were in the majority. I learned early that when a school becomes predominantly minority, the establishment just doesn't give a damn about it anymore. So I made it my business to always go to a school where the establishment was in a majority. I said, "That way, if they educate them, they've got to educate me." [laughter] They can't escape it, you know. [laughter]

But, as I said, we did it. Remember, we started accepting all members in Local 47 a year before the Supreme Court decision of May 17, 1954, of *Brown v. the Board of Education*. And that decision started the modern civil rights movement. We did it well before that. So what we did, I think, was rather remarkable.

We did it on our own through cooperation between white and black musicians. And they were just as important to it as we were, because without the white musicians we couldn't have made it at all, man. So you can't look at a person and say, "He's white, he's against me." I said, "We are not interested in a person's politics. We're not interested in a person's religion. We're not interested in a person's anything. All we're interested in is, is that person in favor of amalgamation? And if he's in favor or she's in favor of amalgamation, we don't care how they think otherwise. That's the person we want to come and support us."

This struggle brought me out of my shell, I guess, because then I got on the board of directors of the NAACP, and I became a political power. When John Anderson first came by here and said they got fired because of their activity, I got mad. I guess I've been mad ever since. Because that was something that you can't tolerate. That started me fighting, and I've been fighting ever since. So I guess it did change me.

An unexpected consequence of the amalgamation was a request from Paul Robeson to meet Marl.

I had the honor of sitting in a room like this, just him and me, for two hours, and we just talked. Isn't that something? That is the highlight of my life.

Conclusion

In some ways Central Avenue through the early 1950s was a typical black urban neighborhood rooted in the cultural soil shared by black communities nationwide. Like most such communities, Central did not have a unique secular musical style until the emergence of rhythm and blues in the late 1940s. For the first half of the twentieth century it absorbed styles and influences. Into the conservative musical environment of turn-of-the-century Los Angeles came New Orleans jazz, and blues migrated from the southwest, especially Texas. Although many swing bands played in and around Los Angeles during the 1930s, there was no identifiable Central Avenue swing style. Bop, of course, came from the New York hothouse in the mid-1940s, stoked by musicians from almost every corner of the country. Buddy Collette was one of the few native sons to achieve an international reputation while remaining in his hometown.

It was not until shortly after the Avenue's decline that Los Angeles became tagged as the home of the West Coast Cool sound—a label in many ways misleading about the music of Los Angeles, especially black Los Angeles. Not only did Cool receive its first significant presentation in Miles Davis's East Coast *Birth of the Cool* recordings, but the emergence of Cool on the West Coast coincided with independent and very different "hot" goings-on in Los Angeles. Abandoning a sideman's role and becoming a leader for the first time in his career, Max Roach teamed with Clifford Brown and shaped their decidedly hot quintet nightly at the California Club on the Westside. Rhythm and blues was exploding, as numerous L.A.-based independent labels competed for the large local

401

talent pool. Ornette Coleman and friends were forging a freer approach that revolutionized jazz a few years later. And boppers followed the black population west from Central Avenue to light up clubs on Western Avenue and beyond. There were also many white and Latino musicians, such as Art Pepper, Anthony Ortega, Gil Bernal, and Barney Kessel, who musically came of age on Central Avenue. It's hard to think of Art Pepper, who spent his formative years hanging out on Central and playing in Benny Carter's and Lee Young's bands, as a West Coast Cool school improviser.

Although Central Avenue had no identifiable style or sound, Central was special in many ways. The sheer number and variety of artists it produced and nourished made it a unique source of black music. Central's constituent parts—the families, neighborhoods, schools, and performance venues—may not have been exceptional in themselves, but the whole provided an unusually fertile milieu for creative artists.

Music was a part of everyday life. There were instruments, as well as radios and records, in many homes, and families regularly patronized the various theaters, ballrooms, halls, and auditoriums to listen to, among others, Louis Armstrong, Duke Ellington, Count Basie, and Jimmie Lunceford. And after the Saturday evening concerts, there were Sunday morning services with more music. Many parents viewed music as a legitimate and desirable professional goal for their children, and many parents and other relatives supported and launched youngsters in their musical careers. Within the community, the sons and daughters of Central found teachers and role models who emphasized the value of serious music training. Of course, some denigrated blues and jazz and encouraged young musicians to study only classical European music. As more than one person has recalled, you were considered a bad boy or girl if you frequented the clubs on Central. But the power of the music could not be denied.

Rigorous musical education was also supported by the public school system. Jefferson High School, in the heart of the Central Avenue community, and Jordan High School in Watts offered extensive music programs, with classes in theory as well as performance. Samuel Browne's program at Jeff was especially noteworthy for giving students the opportunity not only to learn to play jazz but also to arrange and compose. Alongside the public school system, private teachers such as Lloyd Reese and Alma Hightower, and in the late 1940s Bill Green and Buddy Collette, provided superb musical training and offered wise counsel.

Central's young aspiring musicians also benefited from the instruction and friendship of visiting artists. Black visitors had no choice but to stay at the Dunbar, and all the leading black musicians played in the Central Avenue clubs. So a novice could easily meet and perhaps practice or even play with them. Many members of Ellington's, Basie's, and Lunceford's bands made time to talk and work with the kids who were hanging around stage entrances and the Dunbar Hotel waiting for their heroes. Friendships developed; knowledge was imparted; and the culture was passed along.

Finally, Central Avenue offered aspiring artists places to jam, to perform, and to grow, to craft their art before spirited and knowledgeable audiences. Many young musicians were working regularly in the clubs by their mid-teens, and the generally open, casual atmosphere in most venues encouraged younger players to express themselves and find their own voice. Because there was no one Central Avenue style, a variety of sounds emerged from this community, and passion, originality, and individuality were prized. The result was a profusion of talented artists representing many different approaches and innovations. In addition to the artists represented in this book, even a short list of Central alumni must include Hadda Brooks, Lawrence Brown, Red Callender, Don Cherry, Nat King Cole, Joe Comfort, Sonny Criss, Maxwell Davis, Eric Dolphy, Teddy Edwards, Dexter Gordon, Chico Hamilton, Lionel Hampton, Hampton Hawes, Billy Higgins, Roy Milton, Charles Mingus, Anthony Ortega, Johnny Otis, Roy Porter, Vi Redd, and Ernie Royal.

The story of Central Avenue also includes serious political struggles, one of which was fought by most of the musicians represented in this book. Their pathbreaking struggle from the late 1940s through the early 1950s to unite the two locals of a segregated musicians union in Los Angeles was one of the first civil rights victories of the post–World War II period. And their success sparked a nationwide movement that led to the elimination of segregated locals within the American Federation of Musicians. As related by the three principal movers within the black local— Buddy Collette, Bill Douglass, and Marl Young—the source of the growing political consciousness of this postwar generation of black artists lay in their early years. Young people coming of age on the Eastside or in

Watts in the 1930s and '40s invariably found themselves among people of all races and ethnicities. In their neighborhoods and in their schools, friendships crossed the line drawn by L.A.'s segregationist political and police leadership.

By the early 1950s, then, political victories for union amalgamation and against restrictive housing covenants—all antedating the landmark U.S. Supreme Court decision in *Brown v. Board of Education* in 1954—had seemingly prepared a brighter future for Los Angeles's black community. Thus, Central Avenue's history offers further evidence of the importance of the struggle for political equality in midcentury America. Its significance goes beyond that, however. For the history of these struggles, and the decades since, have at the same time revealed the limitations of strictly political victories won in the context of a socioeconomic system whose driving force and ethic is inequality and individual aggrandizement.

Despite these successes, an undercurrent of disillusionment, if not outright regret, runs through some of these accounts. In the struggle for equality, a vital communal bond was forfeited. The black musicians' Local 767 was a cultural and social center that fostered social interaction, acted as a clearinghouse for jobs, and provided practice and rehearsal space. The amalgamated Local 47 operated as a business, not as a social and cultural institution. Although it provided many benefits and furthered the careers of some black musicians, for others these advantages were not adequate compensation for the loss of 767. In striking down segregation, the merger destroyed a source of community and fellowship.

Nor were the amalgamation, the termination of the restrictive covenants, and legislation banning housing discrimination followed by a lessening of racial antagonism or an improvement in the economic situation in which most black working people found themselves. For professional and middle-class blacks, new jobs in the previously white areas north of Wilshire Boulevard opened irresistible opportunities. But their departure deprived the Central Avenue community of its leadership. Blacks who could not afford to move out found themselves surrounded by the walls of hate erected by a racist City Hall and a Los Angeles Police Department determined to prevent "race mixing." Thus, while part of the black population successfully fought for political equality and increasingly worked and lived away from the historic center of the community, pressure from City Hall, the LAPD, and racist gangs intensified against those remaining. The police started to systematically raid clubs and harass white patrons, particularly women, to break up the integrated atmosphere and the flourishing business of the clubs. In *City of Quartz,* Mike Davis suggests that even the rise of black gangs may be traced to the racial harassment and confrontations in the late 1940s.

> The earliest, repeated references to a "gang problem" in the Black community press, moreover, deal with gangs of *white* youth who terrorized Black residents along the frontiers of the southward-expanding Central Avenue ghetto. Indeed, from these newspaper accounts and the recollections of oldtimers, it seems probable that the first generation of Black street gangs emerged as a defensive response to white violence in the schools and streets during the late 1940s.[1]

Although Coney Woodman (see Chapter 4) recalls the presence of gangs in the 1930s and early 1940s, Davis's contention that black gang activity became more noticeable during the late 1940s, as hostility toward the black community around Central Avenue increased, seems plausible.

In this context, the civil rights successes—the musicians union amalgamation, the striking down of the restrictive covenants—improved the lot of some but worsened that of the rest, by depriving them, for example, of the sort of sanctuary that such organizations as Local 767 offered. A difficult lesson, then, from Central Avenue is that political integration *by itself* does not bring equality.

By the mid-1950s the Avenue was finished as an entertainment and music center. The Watts upheavals of 1965 destroyed much of what remained in South Central from those earlier days. The Dunbar Hotel structure survived and is now protected as a historical landmark, but there is little else to remind us of the days when one could *walk* from club to club, block to block, and enjoy great music. On Saturday night, April 6, 1996, a small blues club on Central Avenue, Babe's and Ricky's, held its farewell performance and then closed its doors. The passing of the last club on Central was noted by the *Los Angeles Times* in an editorial headlined "Make It a Dirge for Blues on Central."

> Play it sad and slow for Babe's and Ricky's Inn. The last blues club on Central Avenue—the historic heart of Los Angeles' black community—closed over the weekend, ending a rich era when Angelenos came from all over the city to its hotels, theaters, ballrooms and after-hours joints to hear

such greats as Count Basie, Duke Ellington, Billie Holiday and, always, the blues.[2]

Of course, black musical creativity and artistry continued to flourish in Los Angeles after Central Avenue faded. In the 1950s doo-wop groups lined up to record at Modern Records in Culver City; crowds turned out to hear rhythm and blues shake the 5-4 Ballroom at Fifty-fourth and Broadway; Max Roach and Clifford Brown arrived, put together a quintet, and rehearsed day and night until it was right; newcomers Ornette Coleman, Bobby Bradford, and Charlie Haden jammed with Jefferson High alumni Don Cherry and Billy Higgins during endless exploratory sessions in saxophonist George Newman's garage—truly a garage band with a difference; and dozens of boppers and hard boppers burned in clubs throughout L.A. In the 1960s, before as well as after the fires of 1965, 103rd Street in Watts was sprouting poets, the Watts Prophets, painters, writers, musicians—all to the pulse of Horace Tapscott's Pan-Afrikan Peoples Arkestra rehearsing at the Watts Happening Coffee House and filling the neighborhood with the sounds of "The Dark Tree," as people danced spontaneously in the street.

It continues now along Crenshaw Boulevard, in hip-hop venues, in the precious few junior high and high schools that have adequate music programs, in the Leimert Park area, and around L.A., where Central Avenue elders pass the magic to the next generation. For everyone, the history of Central Avenue should be a constant reminder of what can be accomplished in even the most adverse circumstances. May Central Avenue serve as an inspiration for future generations to continue learning, creating, and contributing to the culture.

Notes

Foreword

1. Ross Russell, *Bird Lives! The High Life and Hard Times of Charlie "Yardbird" Parker* (London: Quartet Books, 1976), p. 201.
2. Carolyn Kozo Cole and Kathy Kobayashi, *Shades of L.A.: Pictures from Ethnic Family Albums* (New York: New Press, 1996).
3. See the bibliography for a complete citation for each source.
4. Ronald Grele, *Envelopes of Sound: The Art of Oral History*, 2d ed. (Chicago: Precedent Publishing, 1991), p. 135. On the uses of oral history, see also Alan Lomax, *Mister Jelly Roll: The Fortunes of Jelly Roll Morton, New Orleans Creole and "Inventor of Jazz"* (New York: Duell, Sloan and Pearce, 1949; reprint ed., New York: Pantheon Books, 1993), pp. xv–xvi; Ron Welburn, "Toward Theory and Method with the Jazz Oral History Project," *Black Music Research Journal* (1986): 79–95; Burton W. Peretti, "Oral Histories of Jazz Musicians: The NEA Transcripts as Texts in Context," in *Jazz Among the Discourses*, ed. Kim Gabbard (Durham, N.C.: Duke University Press, 1995), pp. 117–33.
5. Marl Young, "The Amalgamation of Locals 47 and 767," *Overture* (December 1988): 8–9.

Introduction

1. Lawrence B. de Graaf, "The City of Black Angels: Emergence of the Los Angeles Ghetto, 1890–1930," *Pacific Historical Review* 39 (1970): 327. See also William M. Mason and James Anderson, "The Los Angeles Black Community, 1781–1940," Los Angeles County Museum of Natural History, History Division Bulletin no. 5: *America's Black Heritage*, 1969, p. 44, and Carey McWilliams, *Southern California: An Island on the Land* (Salt Lake City: Peregrine Smith, 1946, 1973), p. 125.

2. J. Max Bond, "The Negro in Los Angeles" (Ph.D. dissertation, University of Southern California, 1936), p. 22.

3. Photo in Mason and Anderson, "Los Angeles Black Community," p. 51.

4. Bond, "Negro in Los Angeles," pp. 288–89.

5. McWilliams, *Southern California*, p. 324.

6. De Graaf, "City of Black Angels," p. 329.

7. Arna Bontemps and Jack Conroy, *Anyplace But Here* (New York: Hill and Wang, 1966), p. 266.

8. Bond, "Negro in Los Angeles," pp. 25–26.

9. Mason and Anderson, "Los Angeles Black Community," p. 44.

10. Bond, "Negro in Los Angeles," p. 74. See also de Graaf, "City of Black Angels," p. 334.

11. Bond, "Negro in Los Angeles," pp. 46–54 passim.

12. Ibid., p. 54.

13. Ibid., p. 65.

14. Lonnie G. Bunch, "A Past Not Necessarily Prologue: The Afro-American in Los Angeles," in *Twentieth-Century Los Angeles: Power, Promotion, and Social Conflict*, ed. Norman M. Klein and Martin J. Schiesl (Claremont, Calif.: Regina Books, 1990), p. 103.

15. Mason and Anderson, "Los Angeles Black Community," p. 44.

16. *Vernon-Central Revisited: A Capsule History* (Washington, D.C.: A NeighborWorks Publication, 1989), p. 8.

17. De Graaf, "City of Black Angels," p. 335.

18. Bond, "Negro in Los Angeles," pp. 70–71.

19. Ibid., p. 70.

20. Mason and Anderson, "Los Angeles Black Community," p. 45.

21. Bond, "Negro in Los Angeles," p. 66.

22. De Graaf, "City of Black Angels," p. 338. See also Mike Davis, *City of Quartz: Excavating the Future in Los Angeles* (London: Verso, 1990), pp. 162–63.

23. Bond, "Negro in Los Angeles," p. 85.

24. De Graaf, "City of Black Angels," p. 335.

25. Michael B. Bakan, "Way out West on Central: Jazz in the African-American Community of Los Angeles before 1930," in *California Soul: Music of African Americans in the West*, ed. Jacqueline Cogdell DjeDje and Eddie S. Meadows (Berkeley: University of California Press, in press).

26. *California Eagle*, August 28, 1931, p. 10.

27. Lawrence Gushee, "How the Creole Band Came to Be," *Black Music Research Journal* 8:1 (1988): 91. Reb Spikes claims the band arrived in 1907; see Tom Stoddard, *Jazz on the Barbary Coast* (Chigwell, Essex, England: Storyville Publications and Co. Ltd., 1982), pp. 56–57.

28. Gushee, "How the Creole Band Came to Be," pp. 93–95. See also Frederic Ramsey, Jr., and Charles Edward Smith, eds., *Jazzmen* (New York: Harcourt Brace

Jovanovich, 1939; reprint ed., New York: Limelight Editions, 1985), pp. 20–22; Barry Kernfeld, ed., *The New Grove Dictionary of Jazz* (New York: St. Martin's Press, 1994), p. 942.

29. Bakan, "Way out West on Central."

30. See Lawrence Gushee, "A Preliminary Chronology of the Early Career of Ferd 'Jelly Roll' Morton," *American Music* 3:4 (Winter 1985): 389–412; Lomax, *Mister Jelly Roll*, p. 158.

31. Lomax, *Mister Jelly Roll*, p. 195.

32. Bricktop, with James Haskins, *Bricktop* (New York: Atheneum, 1983), p. 64.

33. Frank Driggs and Harris Lewine, *Black Beauty, White Heat: A Pictorial History of Classic Jazz, 1920–1950* (New York: William Morrow, 1982; reprint ed., New York: Da Capo Press, 1995), p. 182.

34. Lomax, *Mister Jelly Roll*, p. 197.

35. Bakan, "Way out West on Central." Advertisements for two separate New Year's Eve events, both featuring music by the Black and Tan Orchestra, ran consecutively in the December 11 and 18, 1915, issues of the *California Eagle*. The band's evolution into a jazz orchestra is evidenced by an *Eagle* advertisement on August 30, 1919, for the Dreamland Cafe, which promised "Music by the Black and Tan Jazz Orchestra." A few months later in an ad for the Black and Tan there is also mention of a Westside Jazz Band (*Eagle*, January 31, 1920, p. 3). No other information is available, and the group's personnel remains unknown.

36. Lawrence Gushee, "New Orleans–Area Musicians on the West Coast, 1908–1925," *Black Music Research Journal* 9:1 (Spring 1989): 1–18.

37. Lomax, *Mister Jelly Roll*, pp. 198–99; Bontemps and Conroy, *Anyplace But Here*, p. 251.

38. Floyd Levin, personal communication to the author, 1996.

39. Ibid. Levin further notes, "In an interview with Reb Spikes forty years ago, he told me: 'Mutt, who was actually the leader of the band, called the tunes and set the tempos. When we hired them to play at our Wayside Park Cafe at Leek's [*sic*] Lake in Watts, we billed the band as Ory's Creole Orchestra. The tune "Ory's Creole Trombone" was so popular that we used it as a drawing card—but Mutt led the band.' Wayside Park's advertisements always included the phrase 'Till Mut [*sic*] plays "Farewell".'" See also Driggs and Lewine, *Black Beauty, White Heat*, p. 183; Leonard Kunstadt, "Some Early West Coast Jazz History—The Black and Tan Orchestra & Kid Ory's Orch.," *Record Research* 61 (July 1964): 12.

The spelling of "Leek's Lake" by Levin, Lomax, and other scholars seems wrong. Advertisements in the *California Eagle* on June 24 and August 5, 1921, one of them a Spikes brothers ad, spells the location "Leak's Lake." Two years later an ad in the same paper refers to "Leakes Lake" (September 23, 1923).

40. Driggs and Lewine, *Black Beauty, White Heat*, p. 183.

41. Bond, "Negro in Los Angeles," pp. 76–77.

42. De Graaf, "City of Black Angels," p. 344.

43. *Vernon-Central Revisited*, p. 15.

44. McWilliams, *Southern California*, p. 135.

45. Bond, "Negro in Los Angeles," p. 78.

46. McWilliams, *Southern California*, p. 136.

47. Both quotations are from de Graaf, "City of Black Angels," p. 343.

48. Bond, "Negro in Los Angeles," p. 292. See also de Graaf, "City of Black Angels," p. 345; Mason and Anderson, "Los Angeles Black Community," p. 45.

49. Mike Davis, "Trojan Fortress," *LA Weekly*, December 1–7, 1995, p. 13. See also Davis, *City of Quartz*, p. 162; Mason and Anderson, "Los Angeles Black Community," p. 45.

50. De Graaf, "City of Black Angels," p. 346.

51. Ibid., p. 349.

52. Bunch, "A Past Not Necessarily Prologue," pp. 110–14.

53. "Ode to Central Avenue," *KCET Magazine*, October 1989, p. 15.

54. *Vernon-Central Revisited*, p. 8.

55. De Graaf, "City of Black Angels," p. 351; see also Bond, "Negro in Los Angeles," p. 108.

56. Quoted in Jeffrey Book, "Jamming on Jazz Street," *Angeles*, July 1991, p. 44.

57. Driggs and Lewine, *Black Beauty, White Heat*, p. 180.

58. Driggs and Lewine, *Black Beauty, White Heat*, p. 186. See also Bruce M. Tyler, *From Harlem to Hollywood: The Struggle for Racial and Cultural Democracy, 1920–1943* (New York: Garland, 1992), p. 95; Lionel Hampton with James Haskins, *Hamp* (New York: Warner Books, 1989), pp. 28–30. In his conversations with Alan Lomax, Jelly Roll Morton claimed that "Someday Sweetheart" was his idea: "I was in the music-publishing business with Reb and Johnny Spikes, whom I had met on the stage in the old days. Johnny played piano, and Reb, sax. They could read, but had no ideas. Occasionally I condescended to play with these cornfed musicians. Two of our early tunes became big hits and made the Spikes brothers famous. The first, 'Someday Sweetheart,' was my idea and the second, 'Wolverine Blues,' was my tune" (Lomax, *Mister Jelly Roll*, p. 212).

According to Reb Spikes, he was usually running nightclubs as well. In 1921 he opened the Dreamland Cafe at Fourth and Central, followed by the Watts Country Club, and later the Jockey Club, back in L.A. at Twenty-third and Central. He also remembers taking over the Club Alabam with Will Heflin in the 1930s, shortly after Curtis Mosby had to close it (Benjamin "Reb" Spikes oral history interview, Jazz Oral History Project of the National Endowment for the Arts, Institute of Jazz Studies, Rutgers University, May 1980, pp. 116–19). On Spikes's career see Floyd Levin, "The Spikes Brothers—A Los Angeles Saga,"

Jazz Journal 4:12 (December 1951): 12–14; Ray MacNic, "Reb Spikes—Music Maker," *Storyville* 21 (1969): 100–103; Stoddard, *Jazz on the Barbary Coast,* pp. 52–79; and Bakan, "Way out West on Central." On Lawrence, see Berta Wood, "Charlie Lawrence," *Jazz Journal* 9:10 (October 1956): 6–7, 12.

59. Joe Darensbourg, as told to Peter Vacher, *Jazz Odyssey: The Autobiography of Joe Darensbourg* (Baton Rouge: Louisiana State University Press, 1987), p. 56. See also the Spikes oral history interview, pp. 104–5.

60. Red Callender and Elaine Cohen, *Unfinished Dream: The Musical World of Red Callender* (London: Quartet Books, 1985), p. 27.

61. The date of this recording is often given incorrectly as 1922. See Floyd Levin, "Kid Ory's Legendary Nordskog/Sunshine Recordings," *Jazz Journal International* 46:7 (July 1993): 6–10; Bakan, "Way out West on Central."

62. Kernfeld, ed., *New Grove Dictionary of Jazz,* pp. 945 and 1152. After exhaustively researching these recordings, Levin was unable to determine the recording sequence of the six sides and has concluded that there is no way of knowing (personal communication with the author, 1996).

There have been references to earlier recordings, but none have surfaced to date. Pops Foster recalled the Black and Tans recording and Jelly Roll Morton claimed that he recorded for the Spikes brothers in 1918. Reb Spikes, however, denied that those recordings were ever made. See Pops Foster, as told to Tom Stoddard, *Pops Foster: The Autobiography of a New Orleans Jazzman* (Berkeley: University of California Press, 1973), p. 131; Ted Gioia, *West Coast Jazz: Modern Jazz in California, 1945–1960* (New York: Oxford University Press, 1992), p. 8; Lomax, *Mister Jelly Roll,* pp. 359–60; and MacNic, "Reb Spikes—Music Maker," p. 103.

63. On the various bands, see Albert McCarthy, *Big Band Jazz* (New York: G.P. Putnam's Sons, 1974), pp. 167–74; Bakan, "Way out West on Central."

64. Driggs and Lewine, *Black Beauty, White Heat,* p. 184. On Paul Howard and the Quality Serenaders, see Berta Wood's three articles: "George Orendorf—Quality Serenader," *Jazz Journal* 10:2 (February 1957): 4–6; "Paul Leroy Howard," *Jazz Journal* 10:11 (November 1957): 6–8; "Paul Leroy Howard, Part II," *Jazz Journal* 10:12 (December 1957): 13–14.

65. Driggs and Lewine, *Black Beauty, White Heat,* p. 184; Hampton, *Hamp,* pp. 30–33.

66. Driggs and Lewine, *Black Beauty, White Heat,* p. 186. On Clay's career see John Bentley's articles, based on a lengthy interview with Sonny Clay: "Sonny Clay: A Veritable Giant," *Jazz Report* 3 (November/December 1962): 7–8 and (January/February 1963): 13–14.

67. Brian Priestley, *Mingus: A Critical Biography* (New York: Da Capo Press, 1983), p. 6. He also played in Reb Spikes's Majors and Minors Orchestra; see MacNic, "Reb Spikes—Music Maker," p. 103.

68. *California Eagle,* August 19, 1937, p. 4B.

69. Tyler, *From Harlem to Hollywood,* p. 87.
70. Ibid., p. 90.
71. Driggs and Lewine, *Black Beauty, White Heat,* p. 248. For a brief profile of Wood Wilson, see the Spikes oral history interview, p. 17.
72. Ibid., 248–59 passim. See also Bentley, "Sonny Clay," part 1, p. 8.
73. Floyd Levin, personal communication with the author, 1996. See also the Spikes oral history interview, pp. 113–15.
74. Callender and Cohen, *Unfinished Dream,* p. 30. Unlike the musicians, some black actors were able to find regular employment, though their numbers were few: "Out of a total of 4,451 actors, only 128 were black. Three blacks were among the 1,106 'directors, managers, and officials, motion picture production' in the 1930 census. Of 2,909 actresses and showwomen, only 85 were black. The census did not even list a category for female directors, managers, officials, and motion picture production workers" (Tyler, *From Harlem to Hollywood,* p. 99). By the outbreak of World War II the percentages of blacks on these rosters had decreased.

Part One

1. Bond, "Negro in Los Angeles," p. 177.
2. Ibid., pp. 170, 273.
3. Chester Himes, *If He Hollers Let Him Go* (London: Falcon Press, 1947; reprint ed., New York: Thunder's Mouth Press, 1986), p. 3.
4. Bond, "Negro in Los Angeles," pp. 193–94.
5. Gilmore Millen, *Sweet Man* (New York: Viking Press, 1930), p. 262.
6. Darensbourg, *Jazz Odyssey,* pp. 68 and 103.
7. Wood, "Paul Leroy Howard," p. 8.
8. Driggs and Lewine, *Black Beauty, White Heat,* p. 189; Hampton, *Hamp,* pp. 34–39. On the Cotton Club, see Ralph Eastman, "'Pitchin' up a Boogie': African-American Musicians, Nightlife, and Music Venues in Los Angeles, 1930–1945," in *California Soul,* ed. DjeDje and Meadows. For an overview of Hite's career, see McCarthy, *Big Band Jazz,* pp. 176–79.
9. *California Eagle,* August 28, 1931, p. 10.
10. Ibid.
11. *California Eagle,* December 18, 1931, p. 10.
12. On Floyd Ray's career, see Frank Driggs, "Floyd Ray's Orchestra: The Story of the Harlem Dictators," *CODA* (July 1968): 2–7; McCarthy, *Big Band Jazz,* pp. 179–80; Driggs and Lewine, *Black Beauty, White Heat,* p. 191.
13. Quoted in Driggs and Lewine, *Black Beauty, White Heat,* p. 191.
14. Tyler, *From Harlem to Hollywood,* p. 55.
15. Callender and Cohen, *Unfinished Dream,* p. 29; Driggs and Lewine, *Black Beauty, White Heat,* p. 193.
16. *California Eagle,* March 11, 1932, p. 10.

Part Two

1. De Graaf, "City of Black Angels," p. 347.
2. Arna Bontemps, *God Sends Sunday* (New York: Harcourt Brace Jovanovich, 1931; reprint ed., New York: AMS Press, 1972), pp. 118–19.
3. Bond, "Negro in Los Angeles," pp. 87–88.
4. Bontemps, *God Sends Sunday,* p. 119.
5. De Graaf, "City of Black Angels," p. 347.
6. Bond, "Negro in Los Angeles," pp. 87–88; de Graaf, "City of Black Angels," p. 347; Bunch, "A Past Not Necessarily Prologue," p. 115.
7. De Graaf, "City of Black Angels," p. 347.
8. Stoddard, *Jazz on the Barbary Coast,* p. 74; and the Spikes oral history interview, pp. 20–21.
9. Bontemps, *God Sends Sunday,* pp. 160–61.
10. Bricktop, with Haskins, *Bricktop,* p. 62.
11. Leak's Lake, one of the largest and most popular venues in its time, provided a large space for dancing. The ubiquitous Reb Spikes took credit for its success: "I built up Leek's [*sic*] Lake out in Watts. Made a pile of money, too. They call it Wayside Park today, but it's still Leek's Lake to me" (Lomax, *Mister Jelly Roll,* p. 198 n).
12. Bontemps and Conroy, *Anyplace But Here,* p. 252.
13. Lomax, *Mister Jelly Roll,* pp. 198–99.
14. *California Eagle,* August 28, 1931, p. 10.

Part Three

1. *Los Angeles Times Sunday Magazine,* June 18, 1933, p. 10.
2. Bond, "Negro in Los Angeles," p. 280.
3. *Los Angeles Times Sunday Magazine,* June 18, 1933, p. 5; Bunch, "A Past Not Necessarily Prologue," pp. 115–16.
4. *Los Angeles Times,* November 20, 1991, p. B8.
5. Michael Ullman, *Jazz Lives: Portraits in Words and Pictures* (Washington, D.C.: New Republic Books, 1980), p. 93.
6. Mason and Anderson, "Los Angeles Black Community," p. 45.
7. *Vernon-Central Revisited,* p. 10.
8. *California Eagle,* May 16, 1940, p. 2B.
9. Eastman, "'Pitchin' up a Boogie.'"
10. *California Eagle,* June 26, 1941, p. 2B.
11. Eastman, "'Pitchin' up a Boogie.'"
12. Quoted in *Los Angeles Times,* June 11, 1989, calendar section, p. 52. Jack Kelson claims that Jacquet had switched to tenor earlier. Jack and Buddy Collette held the alto chairs in a local band, and for Illinois to get a gig with them he had to switch to tenor (personal communication with the author, 1995; see also Buddy Collette's discussion of the incident in chapter 7).

13. McWilliams, *Southern California,* p. 371.
14. Mason and Anderson, "Los Angeles Black Community," p. 45.
15. GP [Gary Phillips], "Boppin' on Central," *Heritage,* Winter 1994, p. 2.
16. Bunch, "A Past Not Necessarily Prologue," pp. 117–18.
17. Chester Himes, *Lonely Crusade* (New York: Knopf, 1947), p. 43.
18. Davis, *City of Quartz,* pp. 163 and 163–64.
19. Himes, *If He Hollers,* p. 4.
20. Bontemps and Conroy, *Anyplace But Here,* p. 4.
21. *California Eagle,* June 24, 1943, p. 2B.
22. *California Eagle,* May 7, 1942, p. 2B.
23. Linda Dahl, *Stormy Weather: The Music and Lives of a Century of Jazz-women* (New York: Pantheon Books, 1984; reprint ed., New York: Limelight Editions, 1989), pp. 45–58.
24. *California Eagle,* June 22, 1944, p. 12; see also *California Eagle,* June 1, 1944, p. 13.

Part Four

1. Johnny Otis, *Upside Your Head! Rhythm and Blues on Central Avenue* (Hanover, N.H.: Wesleyan University Press, 1993), pp. 53–55. For an overview of the early Los Angeles r&b scene, see Ralph Eastman, "Central Avenue Blues: The Making of Los Angeles Rhythm and Blues, 1942–1947," *Black Music Research Journal* 9:1 (Spring 1989): 19–33.
2. Driggs and Lewine, *Black Beauty, White Heat,* p. 196.
3. *California Eagle,* April 11, 1946, p. 14, and May 9, 1946, p. 14.
4. Davis, *City of Quartz,* p. 294.
5. Ibid.
6. Bunch, "A Past Not Necessarily Prologue," p. 119.
7. David Williams, quoted in *Los Angeles Sentinel,* February 15, 1990, p. 24. Senior Federal District Judge Williams was also a Jefferson High alumnus.
8. Ibid.
9. *California Eagle,* July 28, 1950, p. 15, and August 25, 1950, p. 15.
10. *California Eagle,* October 12, 1950, p. 16.

Conclusion

1. Davis, *City of Quartz,* p. 293 (italics in origiinal).
2. *Los Angeles Times,* April 8, 1996, p. B12.

Bibliography

UCLA Oral History Program Projects

Central Avenue Sounds project, interviews taped as of December 31, 1996:

Ernie Andrews	William Green	Marshal Royal
Joseph Bihari	Leroy Hurte	Fletcher Smith
René Bloch	Jackie Kelso	Horace Tapscott
Hadda Brooks	Melba Liston	Gerald Wiggins
Clora Bryant	Larance Marable	Gerald Wilson
David Bryant	Cecil McNeely	Britt Woodman
Buddy Collette	Frank Morgan	Coney Woodman
William Douglass	Anthony Ortega	William Woodman, Jr.
John Ewing	Johnny Otis	Lee Young
Art Farmer	Minor Robinson	Marl Young

Related projects: "Black Leadership in Los Angeles," "African American Artists of Los Angeles," and "African American Architects of Los Angeles"; consult the following catalogs for details:

Barnett, Teresa, comp. *The UCLA Oral History Program: Catalog of the Collection.* 2d ed., supplement. Los Angeles: Oral History Program, Department of Special Collections, University of California, Los Angeles, 1996.
Jayanti, Vimala, comp. *The UCLA Oral History Program: Catalog of the Collection.* 2d ed. Los Angeles: Oral History Program, Department of Special Collections, University of California, Los Angeles, 1992.

Memoirs

Bricktop, with James Haskins. *Bricktop.* New York: Atheneum, 1983.
Callender, Red, and Elaine Cohen. *Unfinished Dream: The Musical World of Red Callender.* London: Quartet Books, 1985.

415

Darensbourg, Joe, as told to Peter Vacher. *Jazz Odyssey: The Autobiography of Joe Darensbourg*. Baton Rouge: Louisiana State University Press, 1987.

Foster, Pops, as told to Tom Stoddard. *Pops Foster: The Autobiography of a New Orleans Jazzman*. Berkeley: University of California Press, 1973.

Hampton, Lionel, with James Haskins. *Hamp*. New York: Warner Books, 1989.

Hawes, Hampton, and Don Asher. *Raise Up Off Me: A Portrait of Hampton Hawes*. New York: Coward, McCann and Geoghegan, 1974; reprint ed., New York: Da Capo Press, 1979.

Lomax, Alan. *Mister Jelly Roll: The Fortunes of Jelly Roll Morton, New Orleans Creole and "Inventor of Jazz."* New York: Duell, Sloan and Pearce, 1949; reprint ed., New York: Pantheon Books, 1993.

Mingus, Charles. *Beneath the Underdog: His World as Composed by Mingus*. Edited by Nel King. New York: Knopf, 1971.

Otis, Johnny. *Colors and Chords: The Art of Johnny Otis*. San Francisco: Pomegranate Artbooks, 1995.

———. *Listen to the Lambs*. New York: Norton, 1968.

———. *Upside Your Head! Rhythm and Blues on Central Avenue*. Hanover, N.H.: Wesleyan University Press, 1993.

Pepper, Art, and Laurie Pepper. *Straight Life: The Story of Art Pepper*. New York: Schirmer Books, 1979.

Porter, Roy, with David Keller. *There and Back: The Roy Porter Story*. Baton Rouge: Louisiana State University Press, 1991.

Spikes, Benjamin "Reb," oral history interview. Jazz Oral History Project of the National Endowment for the Arts. Institute of Jazz Studies, Rutgers University, May 1980.

Young, Marl. "The Amalgamation of Locals 47 and 767." *Overture* (December 1988): 8–9.

Secondary Sources

Bakan, Michael. "Way out West on Central: Jazz in the African-American Community of Los Angeles before 1930." In *California Soul: Music of African Americans in the West*. Edited by Jacqueline Cogdell DjeDje and Eddie S. Meadows. Berkeley: University of California Press, in press.

Bentley, John. "Sonny Clay: A Veritable Giant." 2 parts. *Jazz Report* 3 (November/December, 1962): 7–8, and (January/February, 1963): 13–14.

Bond, J. Max. "The Negro in Los Angeles." Ph.D. dissertation, University of Southern California, 1936.

Bontemps, Arna, and Jack Conroy. *Anyplace But Here*. New York: Hill and Wang, 1966.

Book, Jeffrey. "Jamming on Jazz Street." *Angeles*, July 1991, pp. 44–50.

Britt, Stan. *Long Tall Dexter.* London: Quartet Books, 1989; reprint ed., *Dexter Gordon: A Musical Biography.* New York: Da Capo Press, 1989.

Buchmann-Moller, Frank. *You Just Fight for Your Life: The Story of Lester Young.* New York: Praeger, 1990.

Bunch, Lonnie G. "A Past Not Necessarily Prologue: The Afro-American in Los Angeles." In *Twentieth-Century Los Angeles: Power, Promotion, and Social Conflict,* pp. 100–130. Edited by Norman M. Klein and Martin J. Schiesl. Claremont, Calif.: Regina Books, 1990.

Cole, Carolyn Kozo, and Kathy Kobayashi. *Shades of L.A.: Pictures from Ethnic Family Albums.* New York: New Press, 1996.

Cox, Bette Yarbrough. *Central Avenue—Its Rise and Fall (1890–c.1955): Including the Musical Renaissance of Black Los Angeles.* Los Angeles: BEEM Publications, 1996.

Dahl, Linda. *Stormy Weather: The Music and Lives of a Century of Jazzwomen.* New York: Pantheon Books, 1984; reprint ed., New York: Limelight Editions, 1989.

Dance, Helen Oakley. *Stormy Monday: The T-Bone Walker Story.* Baton Rouge: Louisiana State University Press, 1987.

Davis, Mike. *City of Quartz: Excavating the Future in Los Angeles.* London: Verso, 1990.

———. "Trojan Fortress." *LA Weekly,* December 1–7, 1995, p. 13.

Dawson, Jim. *Nervous Man Nervous: Big Jay McNeely and the Rise of the Honking Tenor Sax.* Milford, N.H.: Big Nickel Publications, 1994.

de Graaf, Lawrence B. "The City of Black Angels: Emergence of the Los Angeles Ghetto, 1890–1930." *Pacific Historical Review* 39 (1970): 323–52.

Driggs, Frank. "Floyd Ray's Orchestra: The Story of the Harlem Dictators." *CODA* (July 1968): 2–7.

Driggs, Frank, and Harris Lewine. *Black Beauty, White Heat: A Pictorial History of Classic Jazz, 1920–1950.* New York: William Morrow, 1982; reprint ed., New York: Da Capo Press, 1995.

Eastman, Ralph. "Central Avenue Blues: The Making of Los Angeles Rhythm and Blues, 1942–1947." *Black Music Research Journal* 9:1 (Spring 1989): 19–33.

———. "'Pitchin' up a Boogie': African-American Musicians, Nightlife, and Music Venues in Los Angeles, 1930–1945." In *California Soul: Music of African Americans in the West.* Edited by Jacqueline Cogdell DjeDje and Eddie S. Meadows. Berkeley: University of California Press, in press.

Gioia, Ted. *West Coast Jazz: Modern Jazz in California, 1945–1960.* New York: Oxford University Press, 1992.

Gordon, Robert. *Jazz West Coast: The Los Angeles Jazz Scene of the 1950s.* London: Quartet Books, 1986.

Grele, Ronald. *Envelopes of Sound: The Art of Oral History.* 2d ed. Chicago: Precedent Publishing, 1991.

Gushee, Lawrence. "How the Creole Band Came to Be." *Black Music Research Journal* 8:1 (1988): 83–100.

———. "New Orleans–Area Musicians on the West Coast, 1908–1925." *Black Music Research Journal* 9:1 (Spring 1989): 1–18.

———. "A Preliminary Chronology of the Early Career of Ferd 'Jelly Roll' Morton." *American Music* 3:4 (Winter 1985): 389–412.

Horricks, Raymond. *The Importance of Being Eric Dolphy.* Tumbridge Wells, Great Britain: D J Costello Ltd., 1989.

Kernfeld, Barry, ed. *The New Grove Dictionary of Jazz.* New York: St. Martin's Press, 1994.

Kunstadt, Leonard. "Some Early West Coast Jazz History—The Black and Tan Orchestra & Kid Ory's Orch." *Record Research* 61 (July 1964): 12.

Levin, Floyd. "Kid Ory's Legendary Nordskog/Sunshine Recordings." *Jazz Journal International* 46:7 (July 1993): 6–10.

———. "The Spikes Brothers—A Los Angeles Saga." *Jazz Journal* 4:12 (December 1951): 12–14.

Lomax, Alan. *Mister Jelly Roll: The Fortunes of Jelly Roll Morton, New Orleans Creole and "Inventor of Jazz."* New York: Duell, Sloan and Pearce, 1949; reprint ed., New York: Pantheon, 1993.

MacNic, Ray. "Reb Spikes—Music Maker." *Storyville* 21 (1969): 100–103.

Mason, William M., and James Anderson. "The Los Angeles Black Community, 1781–1940." Los Angeles County Museum of Natural History, History Division Bulletin no. 5: *America's Black Heritage,* 1969, pp. 42–64.

McCarthy, Albert. *Big Band Jazz.* New York: G. P. Putnam's Sons, 1974.

McWilliams, Carey. *Southern California: An Island on the Land.* Salt Lake City: Peregrine Smith, 1946, 1973.

"Ode to Central Avenue." *KCET Magazine,* October 1989, pp. 14–15.

Peretti, Burton W. "Oral Histories of Jazz Musicians: The NEA Transcripts as Texts in Context." In *Jazz Among the Discourses,* pp. 117–33. Edited by Kim Gabbard. Durham, N.C.: Duke University Press, 1995.

[Phillips, Gary] GP. "Boppin' on Central." *Heritage,* Winter 1994, pp. 2–3.

Priestley, Brian. *Mingus: A Critical Biography.* New York: Da Capo Press, 1983.

Ramsey, Frederic Jr., and Charles Edward Smith, eds. *Jazzmen.* New York: Harcourt Brace Jovanovich, 1939; reprint ed., New York: Limelight Editions, 1985.

Reed, Tom. *The Black Music History of Los Angeles—Its Roots: A Classical Pictorial History of Black Music in Los Angeles from the 1920s–1970.* 2d ed. Los Angeles: Black Accent on L.A. Press, 1994.

Russell, Ross. *Bird Lives! The High Life and Hard Times of Charlie "Yardbird" Parker.* London: Quartet Books, 1976.

Simosko, Vladimir, and Barry Tepperman. *Eric Dolphy: A Musical Biography and Discography.* Washington, D.C.: Smithsonian Institution Press, 1974; reprint ed., New York: Da Capo Press, 1979.

Stoddard, Tom. *Jazz on the Barbary Coast.* Chigwell, Essex, England: Storyville Publications and Co. Ltd., 1982.

Tyler, Bruce M. *From Harlem to Hollywood: The Struggle for Racial and Cultural Democracy, 1920–1943.* New York: Garland, 1992.

Ullman, Michael. *Jazz Lives: Portraits in Words and Pictures.* Washington, D.C.: New Republic Books, 1980.

Vernon-Central Revisited: A Capsule History. Washington, D.C.: A Neighbor-Works Publication, 1989.

Welburn, Ron. "Toward Theory and Method with the Jazz Oral History Project." *Black Music Research Journal* (1986): 79–95.

Wood, Berta. "Charlie Lawrence." *Jazz Journal* 9:10 (October 1956): 6–7, 12.

———. "George Orendorf—Quality Serenader." *Jazz Journal* 10:2 (February 1957): 4–6.

———. "Paul Leroy Howard." *Jazz Journal* 10:11 (November 1957): 6–8.

———. "Paul Leroy Howard, Part II." *Jazz Journal* 10:12 (December 1957): 13–14.

Newspapers

California Eagle
Los Angeles Sentinel
Los Angeles Times

Fiction

Bontemps, Arna. *God Sends Sunday.* New York: Harcourt Brace Jovanovich, 1931; reprint ed., New York: AMS Press, 1972.

Himes, Chester. *If He Hollers Let Him Go.* London: Falcon Press, 1947; reprint ed., New York: Thunder's Mouth Press, 1986.

———. *Lonely Crusade.* New York: Knopf, 1947.

Millen, Gilmore. *Sweet Man.* New York: Viking Press, 1930.

Mosley, Walter. *Devil in a Blue Dress.* New York: Norton, 1990.

Index

ABC Radio, 127, 393
ABC Records, 51
Adams, Al, 141, 142, 171, 212, 213
Adams, Joe, 115, 168, 226, 351
Adams, Pepper, 139
Adler, Mrs., 29
After-hours clubs, 35, 48, 81, 84, 108, 171,
    183, 184, 189, 193, 199, 239–40, 271,
    300, 314–15, 317, 319, 325, 350, 351, 352, 366
Ain't Misbehavin', 114
"Alabam Mi-Tee Orchestra," 19
Albans, Ben, Jr., 93
Ali, Bardu, 85, 257, 332, 350, 358
Allen, Henry "Tin Can," 40
Allen, Steve, 164
All-women bands, 202, 344, 345, 346,
    358, 359–62
Amalgamation of musicians unions, 43,
    55–56, 71–72, 102, 112–13, 154–59,
    176–77, 191–92, 229–30, 247–54,
    260, 278–79, 321, 322, 337–39, 363–
    65, 381, 385–99, 403, 404, 405
American Federation of Musicians, 158,
    247, 251, 252, 337, 348, 385–96, 398,
    403; Chicago Local 69, 12, 252, 398;
    Local 10, 252, 385; Local 208, 385; Los
    Angeles Local 47, 43, 57, 71, 72, 79,
    131, 154, 158, 177, 191, 192, 233, 247,
    248, 250, 251, 252, 278, 279, 321, 335,
    338, 339, 364, 381, 385, 386, 389–99,
    404; Los Angeles Local 767, 42–43,
    44, 57, 71, 72, 79–80, 98, 106, 113, 125,

131–32, 145, 154, 157, 158, 176, 177, 181,
    191, 199, 201, 214–15, 220, 233, 236,
    238, 244, 245, 246, 251, 252, 257, 268,
    278, 279, 294, 299, 300, 320, 321, 338,
    339, 348, 349–50, 358, 359, 364, 385,
    386, 387, 389–97, 404; New York Lo-
    cal 802, 395; Portland Local, 395
American Indians, in Los Angeles, 2, 4
Ammons, Gene, 183
Amos 'n Andy, 35
Anderson, Andy, 145, 221
Anderson, Cat, 344, 355
Anderson, Eddie "Rochester," 54, 336
Anderson, Ivie, 37, 54
Anderson, John, 129, 132, 149, 157, 174,
    187, 250, 293, 386, 387, 399
Anderson, Marian, 288
Andrews, Dolores, 350
Andrews, Ernie, xvi, xix, 184, 265, 295,
    315, 350
Andy Kirk's Twelve Clouds of Joy, 202
Anthony, Ray, 22, 189
Apex Club (Los Angeles), 10, 18, 32–33,
    34, 36, 39, 54–55, 58, 205
Apollo Theatre, 258, 335, 345
Appomattox Country Club, 92
"April Skies," 154
Arbuckle, Fatty, 92
Armstrong, Louis, 18, 38, 40, 70, 136,
    166, 225, 226, 234, 311, 314, 325, 336,
    342, 343, 374, 402
Art Tatum's "Swingsters," 42

Ascot Avenue Elementary School, 234
Ashby, Irving, 314
"A Ship at Sea," 214
Aspen, Stewart, 295
Avalon Park, 269
Avedon Ballroom, 336–37

Babe's and Ricky's Inn, 405
"Baby, Take a Chance on Me," 154
Bach, J. S., 187, 209
Bacharach, Burt, 369
Bagley, Charles, 389, 394
Bailey, Edward, 43, 72, 349
Bailey, Joe, 40
Bakan, Michael, 5
Bakeman, Ralph, 181
Baker, Chet, 174, 277
Baker, Josephine, 156–57, 279, 357
Ball, Lucille, 381
Ball, Ronnie, 253
Bal Tabrin, 131, 143
Banks, Buddy, 85, 86
Baquet, George, 5
Baranko, Wilbur, 145
Barbary Coast (San Francisco), 6
Barefield, Eddie, 19, 126
Bargain with Bullets, 213
Baron Long's Tavern, 92, 201
Barrelhouse (club), 180, 308
Bartok, Bela, 336
Basie, Count, 20, 22, 36, 37, 43, 44, 47,
    48, 51, 57, 59, 61, 62, 84, 87, 109, 143,
    148, 183, 201, 202, 210, 235, 238, 239,
    240, 241, 255, 262, 263, 267, 273, 280,
    310, 324, 326, 333, 334, 337, 338, 340,
    342, 343, 361, 364, 367, 402, 403, 406
Bass, Ralph, 186
Bay Area (Calif.), 220, 221
Beachcomber, 332
Beacon Theatre, 182
Beal, Eddie, 20, 65, 320
Beale Street, 323, 366
Beatles, 218
Bebop, 146, 175, 179, 184, 221, 263, 271,
    272, 275, 276, 307–8, 351, 358, 360, 373,
    401, 402, 406
"Bedspread," 154

Beethoven, Ludwig von, 291, 325
"Begin the Beguine," 334
Beige Room, 382
Bellson, Louie, 311, 369
Belvin, Jesse, 188, 295
Beneath the Underdog, 137
Bennett, Tony, 369
Bennett, Will Henry, 344
Benton, Walter, 153, 181, 378
Berg, Billy, 62, 199, 201, 240, 241, 270,
    307, 314, 351, 361
Bernal, Gil, 181, 402
Berry, Bill, 203, 208
Berry, Chu, 103, 104, 110
Berry Brothers, 80
Bert, Eddie, 139
Bethune, Mary, 165
Beverly Hills, 26, 32
Beverly Hills Riding Club, 27
B-girls, 213
Biddle, Vernon, 351
Big Apple (club), 81
Bigard, Barney, 224, 225
Big bands, 36, 39, 41, 45, 61, 126–27, 131,
    207–8, 226–28, 235, 258–59, 262, 263,
    264, 271, 307, 308, 326–27, 401
Bilbrew Quartet, 234
Bill Berry's L.A. Big Band, 22, 114
Bill Robinson Theatre, 350
Billy Berg's club, xv, 47, 48, 62, 63, 84, 85,
    86, 101, 145–46, 149, 241, 270, 279, 351
Bilo and Ashes, 34
Bird in the Basket, 351, 355, 375
Birdland, 367
Bird Lives! xv
Birth of the Cool (recordings), 401
Bizet, Georges, 159
Black and Gold (club), 81
Black and Tan Jazz Orchestra, 6, 10, 11,
    13, 409 n35, 411 n62
"Black and White," 6
"Black, Brown and Beige," 298
"Black Coffee," 70
"Black Jazz in California" (album), 274
Blacklisting, 161–62, 251
"The Black Man in Radio" (thesis), 386
Blainwell's, 81, 82

Blanton, Jimmy, 59, 64, 67, 143, 171, 200, 241, 329

Bledsoe, Raleigh, 136

Bledsoe, Ralph, Jr., 136

Bledsoe, Ralph, Sr. (Dr.), 136, 144, 178

Block breakers, 49

Blues, 358, 360, 401, 402, 406; blues bands, 280, 308; blues singers, 166, 287, 358

Blues in the Night, 326, 330

Blues to Africa, 255

Blye, Elyse, 360, 361, 364

"Body and Soul," 42

Bogart, Humphrey, xvi, 182

"Bongo Bill," 291

Bontemps, Arna, 2, 91, 92

Boogie woogie, 308

Bootleg whiskey, 31, 83, 84

Bostic, Earl, 74

Boswell, Connee, 27

Boswell Sisters Trio, 27

Bourbon Street (New Orleans), 323, 366

Bowron, Fletcher, 199

Boxing, 99

Bradford, Bobby, 406

Bradford, Kurt, 80, 124, 331

Bradley, Oscar, 19, 80, 86, 129, 131, 132, 149, 357

Bradley, Tom, 56, 313

Brannon, Teddy, 331

Breakfast Club (Beverly Hills), 27

Breakfast Club (Central Avenue), 35, 60, 80

"Bricktop" (Ada Smith), 5, 92

Bridges, Harry, 360

Brooklyn Strand, 313

Brooks, Dudley, 80, 331–32

Brooks, Hadda, 364, 403

Brooks, Harvey, 35, 388, 389, 392

Brooks Bathhouse, 143

Brother's (club), 35, 81, 108, 171, 350, 352

Brown, Ann, 374

Brown, Carl, 370

Brown, Charles, 332, 358

Brown, Clifford, 361, 366, 401, 406

Brown, George, 119, 142, 171, 329

Brown, Joe E., 119

Brown, Lawrence, 11, 18, 20, 40, 140, 403

Brown, Les, 70

Brown, Ray, 146

Brown, Roy, 182

"Brown Broadway," 20, 199

Browne, Samuel, xx, 24, 25, 28, 141, 142, 146, 171, 182, 198, 209, 210, 235, 265, 281, 291, 294–96, 300, 402

Brown Sisters, 82, 106, 116

"Brown-Skinned Models," 78

Brown vs. Board of Education, 399, 404

Bryant, Charles Celeste, 342, 343, 346, 347, 348, 359–60

Bryant, Clora, iii, 164, 202, 247, 307, 342–68

Bryant, David, 96, 164–78

Bryant, Eulela Lewis, 342

Bryant, Fred, 342, 344

Bryant, Indiana Herrington, 164, 169, 174, 178

Bryant, Joseph, 164

Bryant, Marie, 357, 383

Bryant, Mel, 342, 343, 344, 347, 348, 349, 350

Bryant, Roscoe, 164, 167

Buckner, Teddy, 105, 110

Buddy Collette Day, 134

Bunn, Jimmy, 153, 318, 334

Burbank Burlesque Theatre, 208

Burdette, Fannie, 9

Burlesque shows, 111, 117, 183

Burney, Dorothy, 247

Burnside, Vi, 345

Butterbeans and Susie, 131

Byas, Don, 19, 59, 63, 104

Byrd, Robbie Tapscott, 287, 293

Cabin Inn, 81

Cadaly, Joseph, 185, 186

Cadillac Cafe, 5, 6

"Cadillac Rag," 6

Cadrez, Florence, 249, 250, 348, 349, 388, 396

Cafe Intime, 350

Cafe Society (L.A.), 81, 101, 351

Cafe Society (N.Y.), 64

California Club, 366, 401

California Eagle, xvii, xx, 5, 19, 20, 93, 199, 409 n35, 409 n39
"California Frolics Revue," 338
Caliman, Hadley, 266, 378
Callender, Red, xxvii, 11, 44, 62, 78, 86, 123, 134, 138, 155, 161, 170, 171, 222, 227, 233, 242, 243, 292, 294, 300, 311, 329, 337, 339, 386, 398, 403
Calloway, Cab, 19, 126, 237, 311, 324, 343
Camel Caravan (NBC program), 71, 234
Campbell, Paul, 62
Canard, Pete, 186
Capone, Al, 363
Capp-Pierce Juggernaut Band, 22, 114, 203, 369
Capri (club), 199, 240, 241
"Caravan," 360
Carey, Papa Mutt, 6, 11, 13, 18, 29, 56, 57, 225, 308, 409 n39
Carillo, Leo, 38
Carmen, 159
Carol, Judy, 383–84, 385, 386
The Carol Burnett Show, 158
Carreon, Phil, 329
Carruthers, Earl, 326
Carter, Benny, 51, 53, 74, 78, 114, 157, 164, 177, 203, 233, 240, 241, 249, 250, 268, 270, 279, 311, 314, 319, 325, 328, 329, 330–31, 334, 336, 339, 361, 362, 363, 364, 365, 369, 375, 380, 383, 387, 388–89, 391, 402
Carter, Chick, 330
Carter, John, 164
Casablanca (club), 153
Casa Mañana, 199, 326, 329, 330
Casbah Supper Club, 70, 335, 336
Cass Technical High School, 325, 326, 327
Catalina Island, 211
Catalina's Bar and Grill, 134
Catlett, Sid, 200, 237
Cavalcade of Jazz, 188–89
CBS, 62, 331
Cedar Street (Pittsburgh), 340
Celestin, Papa, 325
Central Avenue: black businesses on, 9–10, 19, 20, 143, 197, 309, 351; clubs on, 10, 18–19, 32, 46–47, 80–81, 108,

125–26, 148, 174, 182–83, 184, 199, 201, 215–16, 239–40, 262–63, 271, 273, 292, 314–15, 328, 332–33, 350–52, 358, 375–76; decline of, xv, xvi, 49, 72–73, 86–87, 113, 132–33, 177–78, 192–93, 230–32, 279–80, 298–300, 309–10, 322–23, 339–40, 356, 358, 365–66, 405–6; early jazz on, 10–11; emergence of, xv, 2–4; heyday of, xv, xvi, 46–47, 87, 108, 109, 113, 143–44, 148, 163, 182–83, 185, 198–200, 215–17; 232, 239–40, 262–63, 280, 292, 323, 328, 340–41, 351–52, 366–68, 375, 402, 403; post–World War II, 46–48, 109, 146–49, 185, 247, 309, 314; pre–World War II, 108, 143–45, 215, 231–32, 328–30; race mixing on, 148, 177, 272–73, 299, 309, 365, 404–5; visiting celebrities on, 143, 177, 182, 193, 217, 280, 299–300, 323, 352, 403; wartime years, 109, 145–46, 201–2, 262, 332–33
Central Avenue Jam Session, 134
Central Avenue Sounds committee, xxi, xxii
Central Avenue Sounds project, xviii, xx
Central Gardens area, 135, 181, 191
Central Street (Cleveland), 328
Chaplin, Charlie, 92
Charle Records, 191
Charles, Ray, 115, 169, 226, 324, 357
Chateau (club), 93
Cheatham, Jeannie, 342
Cheatham, Jimmy, 155, 250, 342, 386
Check and Double Check, 35–36
"Cherokee," 353
Cherry, Don, 152, 292, 301, 403, 406
Chestnut, Charles, 9
Chicago, 10, 278, 366, 384
Chico Hamilton Quintet, 134
Chinese, 2, 4, 115, 135, 180, 198, 234, 264
Chopin, Frederic, 187
Christian, Charlie, 59, 86, 200
Christy, June, 70, 233
Church, 95, 115, 256, 283, 381; music in, 287, 343
Churchill, Savannah, 314
Circle Bar, 84, 85

Ciro's, 366
City Hall, 35, 199, 365, 366, 404
City of Quartz, 405
Civil rights, 403, 405
Clark, Jimmy, 397
Clark, John Prentiss, 256
Clark Annex, 216, 292
Clarke, Thurman (judge), 310
Clark Hotel, 77, 125, 216, 292
Classic (club), 81
Classical music, 155–56, 162, 311, 336, 381, 382, 402
Clay, Sonny, 11–12, 13
Clayton, Buck, 20, 51, 57–58, 59, 204
Clayton-Hamilton Jazz Orchestra, 369
Cleghorn, Arthur, 156
Clouds of Joy, 343
Club Alabam, 18, 19, 33, 34, 35, 54, 61, 62, 80, 81, 85, 87, 108, 109, 113, 125, 143, 144, 148, 157, 182, 192, 199, 202, 215, 216, 228, 239, 240, 242, 247, 250, 262, 267, 273, 279, 280, 328, 329, 332, 350, 352, 356, 357–58, 375, 380, 410n58
Club Araby, 58
Club Finale, 270, 351
Cobb, Arnett, 229
Cobb, Ty, 319
Cocoanut Grove, 51, 65
Cohen, Mickey, 126
Cohen, Peter, 156
Coker, Marie, 364
Cole, Carolyn Kozo, xvii
Cole, Cozy, 237
Cole, Jack, 321–22
Cole, Natalie, 369
Cole, Nat King, xvi, 20, 44, 45, 51, 59, 60, 63, 70, 82, 86, 157, 164, 179, 184, 199, 235, 242, 244, 250, 317–18, 319, 328, 335, 336, 362, 364, 369, 403
Cole Dance Studio, 79
Coleman, Ornette, 151, 402, 406
"Collette," 153
Collette, Buddy, xx, xxii, 45, 46, 53, 83, 96, 104, 112, 121, 122, 129, 130, 132, 134–63, 164, 168, 169, 171, 175, 176, 180, 186, 192, 201, 203, 212, 213, 214, 215, 218, 219, 221, 236, 240, 241, 245,

247, 248, 249, 250, 253, 276, 294, 300, 311, 316, 317, 337, 338, 339, 363, 374, 378, 385, 392, 397, 401, 403, 413n12
Collette, Goldie, 134
Collette, Louise, 146
Collette, Willie, 134
Collette, Zan, 146
Coltrane, John, 114, 152–53, 274
Columbia Records, 337
Columbia Studios, 67, 68, 69, 70
Comfort, Frank, 97
Comfort, Joe, 82, 96, 97, 104, 105, 199, 140, 167, 171, 212, 222, 311, 314, 316, 403
Community Symphony Orchestra, 132, 133, 135–36, 159, 176
Concord Jazz records, 311
Coney Island Chili Parlor, 125
Conroy, Jack, 2
Cook, Sam, 203
Cooley, Spade, 362, 363
Cool jazz, 401, 402
Cooper, Bob, 142
Cooper, L. C., 225
Corcoran, Corky, 86
Cosby, Harper, 154, 357
Cotton Club (New York), 55, 182
Cotton Club (Sebastian's), 11, 18, 32, 36, 37, 38–39, 40, 41, 44, 58, 60–61, 78, 80, 126, 199, 329
Cotton Club Orchestra, 60
Covington, Floyd, 197
Cox, Bette, xvii
Coycault, Ernest, 5, 6
Craig, Mr. (junkman), 144
Crawford, Ernest, 153
Crayton, Pee Wee, 148, 280, 358
Crenshaw Boulevard, 310, 366, 367, 406
Crenshaw High School, 282
Criner, Lawrence, 213
Criss, Sonny, 134, 141, 148, 163, 164, 181, 182, 184–85, 185–86, 222, 265, 276, 279, 295, 307, 354, 373, 379, 403
Crofton, Vera, 127
Crothers, Scatman, 101, 116, 183
Cruise, Terry, 119
Crystal Tea Room, 153, 358, 378
Cugat, Lorraine, 362

Cugat, Xavier, 362
Culver City, Calif., 11, 38, 406
Cup and Saucer, 359
Curfew, 35, 46, 83, 199
Curson, Ted, 124
Curtis Mosby's Blue Blowers, 11, 40
Cutting contests, 47, 65, 85

"Daddy Dear," 6
Danceland, 30
Dance marathons, 55
Dandridge, Dorothy, 119, 214, 362
Dandridge, Vivian, 119, 214, 362
Daniel, Alfred, 115
Daniel, Elliot, 398
Daniels, Boogie, 181
Daniels, Leroy, 183
The Danny Kaye Show, 158
Darensbourg, Joe, 7, 11, 18
"The Dark Tree," 406
Darlings of Rhythm, 346, 359
Davidson, Leonard "Big Boy," 76
Davies, John, 29
Davis, Eddie, 82, 168, 169
Davis, Eddie "Lockjaw," 311
Davis, Leo, 19, 39, 43, 130, 157, 230, 238, 249, 250, 339, 364, 388, 391, 393
Davis, Martha, 364, 383
Davis, Maxwell, 61, 70, 71, 97, 103, 106, 109, 403
Davis, Mike, 405
Davis, Miles, 114, 184, 185, 268, 270, 376, 401
Davis, Sammy, Jr., 83, 109, 148, 369
Davis, Tiny, 345
"Deacon Rides Again," 191
"Deacon's Hop," 186–87
Decca Records, 42, 383
De Falla, Manuel, 336
De Franco, Buddy, 224
De Lisa (club), 382
Delta Rhythm Boys, 164
Depression, the, 17–19, 21, 26, 165, 170, 200, 204, 342
Desilu Workshop Theater, 381
Detroit, Mich., 325, 326, 327, 337–38
Devil in a Blue Dress, xvii

Dial Records, 273
Diamond, Carrie, 23
Dietz Music, 75
Dig Records, 203
Dinah Shore Chevy Show, 363
d'Indy, Vincent, 336
Dingbod, Bob, 263, 351
DiSarro, Dominic, 298
Disc jockeys, 189, 190, 351; first black in L.A., 169, 226
Disneyland, 105, 219, 226
Dixieland, 224–25, 323
Dixieland Blue Blowers, 11, 40
Dixon, Floyd, 287
DjeDje, Jacqueline Cogdell, xviii
Doggett, Bill, 383
Dolphin, John, 153, 309
Dolphin's of Hollywood: record label, 153; store, 153, 309, 351
Dolphy, Eric, 123, 134, 139, 142, 147, 150–53, 163, 171, 181, 236, 274, 292, 308, 362–63, 380, 403; family, 151
Domino, Fats, 182
Donaldson, Mr., 297
Don't Look Back, 311
Dootsie Williams's Four Chocolates, 242
Doo-wop groups, 406
Dorsey, Tommy, 97, 120, 174, 321, 326, 343
Double V (club), 79, 81
Douglas Club, 5
Douglass, Calvin, 234
Douglass, James, 234
Douglass, Peter, 234
Douglass, William, 112, 142, 145, 157, 172, 197, 201, 233–54, 292, 311, 314, 339, 385, 387, 388, 396, 403
Down Beat (magazine), 72, 341
Downbeat Room, 46, 67, 68, 81, 108, 129, 148, 149, 150, 174, 182, 183, 184, 185, 192, 201, 216, 227, 262, 263, 268, 271, 272, 273, 275, 280, 307, 328, 335, 350, 351, 353, 367, 375, 376, 379–80, 384
Drayton, Charles, 311
Dreamland Cafe, 409 n35, 410 n58
Driggs, Frank, xviii, 13
Du Bois, W. E. B., 9
Dudley, Roberta, 11

Dunbar Hotel, 9, 17, 18, 34, 47, 78, 87, 119, 125, 126, 197, 198, 215, 216, 239, 242, 262, 280, 313, 314, 328, 329, 333, 337, 340, 341, 358, 403, 405
Dunhill Records, 51
Dusen, Frank, 6, 93
Duvivier, George, 139
Dwan, Bob, 161
Dynamite Jackson's (club), 81, 328, 350

Earl Carroll's Theatre Restaurant, 244
Earls of '44, 182
"Earth Angel," 191
East Coast, 307, 342
East Coast Jazz, 307
Eastside, 195–202, 230, 279, 358, 378, 403
Ebb's, 356
Ebony, 188, 299
Eckstine, Billy, 71, 74, 86, 154, 183, 273, 334, 335
Edison, Harry "Sweets," 70, 156, 201, 311
Edson, Estelle, 385, 386, 387, 388, 389, 392, 393, 396
Edwards, Teddy, 47, 130, 147, 150, 163, 184, 185, 263, 268, 272, 307, 311, 351, 354, 355, 376, 403
Edythe Turnham and Her Dixie Aces, 19
Eger, Joe, 156, 386, 387
Eldridge, Roy, 104, 105, 110, 261, 311, 319
"Elegy," 312
El Grotto, 335, 382
Elks Hall, 81, 97, 106, 119, 125, 142, 182, 199, 205, 214, 224, 240, 310, 328, 334, 350
Ellington, Duke, 11, 12, 13, 20, 33, 35–37, 40, 51, 59, 64, 78, 94, 114, 120, 123, 126, 131, 132, 136, 140, 143, 167, 171, 174, 175, 182, 199, 207–8, 214, 223, 235, 241, 255, 263, 280, 293, 297–98, 311, 324, 325, 329, 333, 335, 336, 340, 342, 343, 344, 355, 364, 384, 402, 403, 406
Ellington, Mercer, 114
Embassy Auditorium, 309
EMI Records, 191
Ernie Andrews: Blues for Central Avenue, xvi
Europe, 175, 186, 191, 295, 354
Evans, Charlie, 80

Evans, Herschel, 58, 59, 84, 229
Evert, Nan, 159–60
Ewing, John "Streamline," 155, 250, 294, 300, 387
Excelsior Records, 335
Executive Order 8802, 200

Fain, Elmer, 56, 98, 106, 113, 171, 172, 214, 238, 320–21, 349, 385
Fairfax High School, 170, 295
Farlice, Bob, 142
Farlow, Tal, 160
Farmer, Addison, 261, 262, 268, 269, 315
Farmer, Art, 154, 182, 197, 261–81, 308
Farmer, Hazel, 276
Farmer brothers, 184
Fat Ann (club owner), 352
Fears, Vivian, 334
Feather, Leonard, 22
Feldman, Jerry, 161
Fielding, Jerry, 135, 159, 160, 161, 250, 386
Fields, Ernie, 185
Fifty-fourth Street Drugstore, 126, 143
Fifty-second Street (New York), xvi, 323, 366
Filipinos, 29, 30
Finale Club, 270, 351
Finley's restaurant, 125, 143
Finney (guitarist), 74
Fitzgerald, Ella, 324, 335–36, 369
Five and Ten, 328
5-4 Ballroom, 406
Five Hot Shots, 80
Five Spot, 124
Flame (club), 71
"Flamingo," 64
Flennoy, Lorenzo, 19, 80, 148, 241, 315, 318, 329, 357
Fletcher, Dusty, 257
The Flip Wilson Show, 158
Floyd, Buddy, 229
Floyd Hunt Quartet, 84
"Flying Home," 111, 189
Follies Burlesque Theatre, 94, 97, 98, 103, 117, 120, 122, 141
Foster, Pops, 7, 411n62
"Four Brothers," 70

Fourteen Gentlemen of Harlem, 58, 59
Fox Studios, 67
Foxx, Redd, 34, 357, 375
Freeman, Ernie, 314, 386
Frishberg, Dave, 22, 203
Frutkoff, Gary, xvii
Fuller, Gil, 293, 330
Fulson, Lowell, 142
Furlong Tract, 7, 17

Gaiety Theatre, 221–22, 271, 272
Gaillard, Slim, 85, 101, 241, 270
Galloway, Fletcher, 167
. . . *Gal with a Horn*, 342
Gambling, 31, 39, 284
Gangs, 95, 404, 405
Gangursky, Nat, 176
Gardner, Ava, xvi, 299–300, 352
Gardner, Poison, 110, 241, 363
Garland, Ed "Montudie," 7
Garland, Judy, 65
Garner, Erroll, 236
Garvey, Marcus, 98
Gastel, Carlos, 328
George, Shorty, 100
G.I. Bill, 131, 147, 373, 374
Gibson, Andy, 63
Gibson, Harry "The Hipster," 270
Gillespie, Dizzy, xv, 70, 114, 145, 146, 148,
   149, 184, 212, 221, 255, 259, 263, 270,
   274, 293, 299–300, 307, 310, 311, 313,
   326, 338, 342, 354
Gioia, Ted, xviii
Gipson, J. T., 202
Givens, Spaulding, 129, 149, 150
Glascoe, Anne, 361
Glendale, Calif., 101, 110–11, 241–42, 363
Glenn, Tyree, 59
Glen's, 366
God Sends Sunday, 91, 92
Golden Gate Quartet, 74
Golden West (club), 5
Golding Room, 119
Golson, Benny, 261
Gonsalves, Paul, 85, 376
Gonzalez, Louis, 62, 101
Goodman, Benny, 44, 51, 64, 104, 114,

127, 202, 203, 218, 227–28, 233, 234,
   247–48, 312
Gorbachev, Mikhail, 342
Gordon, Dexter, xvi, xx, 25, 119, 127, 141,
   142, 144, 147, 153, 163, 164, 171, 181, 198,
   210–11, 212, 234–35, 236, 237, 276,
   279, 315, 329–30, 351, 355, 363, 376,
   379, 403
Gordon, Robert, xviii
Gower, Fuzzy, 80
Gozza, Conrad, 363
Graas, John, 156
Grable, Betty, 357
Grand Hotel, 7
Grand Terrace, 60
Grandview Hotel, 33
Grant, Jewell, 97, 147
Granz, Norman, 63, 64, 86, 309
Grape Street Elementary School, 95, 96,
   103, 115
Graven, Sonny, 40
Gray, Frances, 360
Gray, Harry, 385
Gray, John A. "Professor," 96, 116, 209
Gray, Wardell, xvi, 85, 147, 153, 154, 163,
   164, 276, 279, 294, 315, 351, 355, 357,
   376, 379, 380
Gray Conservatory of Music, 209, 212
Great Lakes Naval Training Station (Ill.),
   45, 145, 331, 332, 372
Great White Way, 302
Green, Doris, 369
Green, Harold, 325
Green, Henry, 224, 334
Green, Herbert G., 369
Green, Lillian, 369, 370
Green, Mr. (teacher), 186
Green, Sarah Grant, 369, 370, 373
Green, Thomas, Jr., 369
Green, Thomas, Sr., 369–70
Green, Urbie, 139
Green, William, xviii, xx, xxii, 147, 153,
   155, 174, 307, 369–80, 386, 402
Green Mill Club, 18
Greer, Sonny, 64
Grele, Ronald, xix
Griffin, Johnny, 255

Grissom, Dan, 326
Gross, Mrs., 209
Groucho Marx show, 134, 161
Grove School of Music, 341
Gryce, Gigi, 261
Guedel, John, 161
Gumina, Tommy, 363

Haden, Charlie, 406
Hadnott, Bill, 172, 386
Hall, Jim, 261
Hall, Minor "Ram," 225
Hall Johnson Choir, 288
Hal Roach Studios, 67
Hamilton, Forest "Chico," 83, 114, 134,
    141, 142, 152, 164, 206, 207–8, 212, 214,
    218, 248, 316, 317, 345–46, 403
Hamilton, Jimmy, 114
Hamilton, Ralph, 110
Hampton, Gladys, 45, 188–89, 226
Hampton, Lionel, xvi, xvii, 11, 18, 20, 22,
    24, 40, 44, 45, 54, 58, 61, 74, 79–80,
    110, 120, 121, 130, 179, 181, 182, 187, 188,
    200, 203, 206, 218, 219, 221, 226–27,
    234, 248, 261, 277, 279, 282, 295, 300,
    301, 324, 329–30, 343, 358, 369, 403
Hancock, Hunter, 189, 190, 351
Hard bop, 261, 406
Hardiman, Leonard "Tight," 188
Hardin, Lil, 202
Harlem, 12, 133, 271, 313, 315, 322; Har-
    lem Renaissance, 12, 91
Harlem Dictators, 19
Harlem Dukes, 80
Harlem Nights, 311
Harper, Buddy, 78, 181
Harris, Wynonie, 218, 240, 315
Harvey, Bob, 110
Hawes, Hampton, xvi, xvii, 148, 182, 184,
    236, 307, 315, 318, 355, 403
Hawkins, Coleman, 85, 104, 147
Hawkins, Erskine, 334, 345
Hawkins, Willie, 318
Haydn, Josef, 291
Hayes, Roland, 288
Hayworth, Rita, 352
Hearn, Larry, 317

Heflin, Will, 410n58
Heifetz, Jascha, 36
Heindorf, Ray, 68, 70, 330
Hellman, Marco, 26, 27
Hellman National Bank, 26
Henderson, Fletcher, 103, 119, 136, 227,
    266, 292, 293, 295, 334
Henderson, George, 5, 92
Henderson, Horace, 119, 266–67, 293,
    295
Henderson, J. M., 11
Henry, Walter, 181
Hep Cats, 169
Herbert, El, 374
Here's Lucy, 381
Herman, Woody, 297, 324
Herriford, Leon, 6, 19, 40, 60
Herrington, Hixie, 164
Heywood, Eddie, 130, 334
Hibbler, Al, 70, 356–57
Hi-De-Ho (club), 81
Higgins, Billy, 403, 406
High Life, 255
High School of Music and Arts (N.Y.),
    311, 312
Hightower, Alma, 181, 256–57, 358–59,
    360, 403
Hi Hats, 124
Hill, Reverend, 5
Hill, Virgil, 370
Hilliard, Harriet, 65
Himes, Chester, 17, 200, 201
Hines, Earl, 60, 233, 236, 240, 325, 334,
    343
Hinton, Milt, 139
Hip-hop, 406
Hite, Les, 11, 13, 18, 36, 37, 39–40, 41,
    42, 44, 56, 58, 60, 61, 74, 78, 80, 84,
    99, 122, 126, 127, 129, 142, 234, 236,
    313, 329, 330, 331, 332, 334
Hoboing, 75–76
Hodges, Johnny, 36, 63, 114
Hole in the Wall, 184
Holiday, Billie, 51, 62, 70, 174, 241, 259,
    292, 324, 329, 333, 334, 335, 338, 357, 406
Holland, Milt, 155
Hollenbeck Park, 378

Hollywood, 12–13, 26, 32, 84–85, 224, 300, 365, 366
Hollywood Boulevard, 62, 225, 243
Hollywood Bowl, 272
Hollywood Canteen, 245
Hollywood High School, 296
Hollywood Sepia Tones, 361
Hollywood Sepia Tones TV show, 362
"The Honeydripper," 263
Honeydrippers, 110, 181, 263, 333
Honey Murphy's (club), 81, 108, 199
"Honky Tonk," 383
Hooper Avenue School, 234
Hopkins, Claude, 40
Hopkins, Linda, 311
Horne, Lena, 124, 233, 311, 321, 333
Horne, Marilyn, 156
Horton, Shorty, 331
Hot rod cars, 31
House of Rhythm, 374
House Un-American Activities Committee, 161
Housing covenants, discriminatory, 4, 7, 8, 26, 91, 200, 230, 249, 309, 310, 404, 405
Houston, Texas, 282–84, 286
Howard, James, 116
Howard, Joe, 266
Howard, Paul, 6, 11, 40, 57, 177, 226, 238, 249, 250, 349, 388, 389, 396
Howard Theatre, 345
"How High the Moon," 379
Hughes, Howard, xvi
Humanist Hall, 156, 339
Humanist Orchestra, 176
Humes, Helen, 311, 321
"Humoresque," 312
Humphrey, Paul, 311
Hunter, Ivory Joe, 280
Hunter, Lloyd, 84
Huntley, Chet, 393
Hurd, Martin, 119
Hutton, Betty, 161–62
Hutton, Ina Ray, 362

"I Am Woman," 203
If He Hollers Let Him Go, 17, 201

"I Got Rhythm," 30
"I'm Crying for You," 6
Improvisation, 223–24
"In a Mellow Tone," 140
"Indian Love Call," 120
Ink Spots, 74, 115, 153, 179
Integration, 1, 25, 49, 55, 104, 109, 113, 135, 177, 179, 199, 264, 272–73, 290, 291, 292, 299–300, 404
International Sweethearts of Rhythm, 202
Interplay Records, 282
The Invisible Man, 207
Irving, Dorcester, 240
Irving Brothers band, 105, 167
Israel Philharmonic, 324
Italians, in Los Angeles, 25, 29, 111
"It's April," 153, 154
"I've Got My Love to Keep Me Warm," 42
Ivie's Chicken Shack, 81, 240, 315

Jack's Basket Room, 46–47, 85, 86, 126, 148, 174, 183, 184, 185, 192, 240, 271, 272, 314
The Jack Smith Show, 154
Jackson, Calvin, 68, 333, 340
Jackson, Dynamite, 35
Jackson, Eugene, 214
Jackson, Freddy, 214
Jackson, James, 181
Jackson, Leon, 284, 285, 289
Jackson, Milt, 146, 255, 311
Jackson, Oliver, 300
Jackson Trio, 94
"Jack the Bear," 143
Jacquet, Illinois, 108, 119, 120, 127, 142, 199, 292, 329, 338, 413 n12
Jacquet, Russell, 48, 67
Jade Supper Club, 225
James, Etta, 290
James, Henry, 311, 340, 344
James, William, 222
Jam sessions, 46, 59, 63, 85, 86, 108, 110, 145, 153, 156, 172, 174, 183, 189, 235, 241, 243, 258–59, 262, 268, 271–72, 277, 309, 329, 350, 351, 353–54, 355, 358, 375–76, 378–79
Jan & Dean, 203

Japanese-Americans, 2, 3, 4, 8, 29, 49, 85, 91, 116, 135, 166, 180, 198, 201, 234, 245, 351
Jazz at the Philharmonic concerts, 63, 86, 309
Jazz City, 243
Jazzland, 81, 82, 92, 201
The Jazz Singer, 12
Jazztet, 261
Jean Parks and her All-Girl Band, 346
Jefferson High School, xx, 25, 28–29, 30, 35, 37, 40, 43, 78, 141, 142, 146, 169, 178, 182, 198, 209, 210, 212, 235, 245, 256, 257, 261, 264–65, 266, 274, 277, 291, 294–95, 297, 377, 402, 406, 414n7
Jeffries, Herb, 257, 333–34
Jelly's Last Jam, 114
Jews, 2, 3, 25, 29, 49, 96, 103, 110, 176, 275, 353
Jockey Club, 410n58
The Joe Adams Show, 339
Joe Liggins and the Honeydrippers, 110, 181, 263
Johnson (union president), 42–43
Johnson, Bill, 5
Johnson, Cee Pee, 44, 45, 107, 109, 144, 218, 219, 329
Johnson, Clarence, 203
Johnson, Conrad, 344
Johnson, Happy, 86, 108
Johnson, Jack, 143
Johnson, James Weldon, 9
Johnson, J. J., 314, 331
Johnson, John H., 299
Johnson, Marvin, 39, 41, 47
Johnson, Oliver "Dink," 5
Johnson, Pee Wee, 378
Johnson, Plas, 53
Johnson, Teaque, 115
Johnston, Merle, 147, 151
The Jolson Story, 51
Jones, Betty Hall, 247
Jones, Charley, 39, 41
Jones, Clarence, 350, 352
Jones, Duke, 94
Jones, Gus, 54
Jones, Henrietta, 107

Jones, Jo, 237, 239, 311, 313
Jones, Luke, 61, 83, 322
Jones, Parr, 70, 71
Jones, Quincy, 192, 255, 365
Jones, Rae Lee, 359
Jordan, Connie, 101
Jordan, Louis, 336
Jordanaires, 101
Jordan High School, 96, 104, 109, 121, 135, 165, 169, 178, 182, 274, 402
Jump for Joy, 384
Jungle Room, 148, 221, 271, 350, 352

Kansas City, Kans., 255, 256, 369, 370, 372
Kansas City, Mo., 202, 255, 256, 366, 373
Kast, George, 386, 387, 391, 392, 393, 395
Kazan, Elia, 330
Kelly, Red, 294, 300
Kelson, Jack (Jackie Kelso), 46, 141, 142, 148, 171, 197, 201, 203–32, 245, 315, 317, 377, 413n12
Kenin, Herman, 252, 395, 396, 398
Kennard, Peter, 167
Kenton, Stan, 68, 69, 86, 131, 295, 297, 328, 342
Keppard, Freddie, 5
Kessel, Barney, 85–86, 154, 402
Kestenbaum, Milt, 159, 160
KFVD radio, 189
KGFJ radio, 115
Khachaturian, Aram, 336
KHJ radio, 60, 199
Kidd, Alvy, 234–35
Kid Ory's Original Creole Jazz Band, 6
Killian, Al, 86, 385
King, Dr., 178
King, J. D., 263, 351, 354
King Creole, 311
King Kolax Orchestra, 20
King Oliver's Creole Jazz Band, 7, 202
King Records, 191
Kinsler, Julie, 155
Kirk, Andy, 202, 343
"Kiss of Death," 123
Kitt, Eartha, 311
Klein, Dave, 68–69
Klein, Manny, 61, 363

Knepper, Jimmy, 139, 140
Knight, Gladys, 369
Korean War, 297
"Krooked Blues," 11
Krupa, Gene, 234, 248, 312
KTTV television, 339
Ku Klux Klan, 8, 9, 92

Lacey, Millard, 377
Ladd, Alan, 352
La Doma Ballroom, 41
Lady Sings the Blues, 357
Lafayette Elementary School, 95
Lafayette Junior High School, 55, 208, 292, 294
La Guardia, Fiorello, 311
Lane, Rosemary, 330
Largo (Sunset Strip), 110
Largo Theatre, 116, 166, 180
La Rue, Jack, 352
Last Roundup, 81
Last Word Cafe, 33, 46, 81, 148, 150, 182, 183, 184, 192, 201, 216, 262, 263, 271, 275, 328, 332, 350, 356, 358, 361, 375, 383, 384
Las Vegas, 76–77
Latinos, xxi, 2, 29, 91, 198, 251; dances, 54, 119–20, 212; musicians, 277, 402
"Laura," 150
Lawrence, Charlie, 10
Leak's Lake, 92, 93, 409n39, 413n11
Leak's Lake Ballroom, 106
Lee, Billy, 65
Lee, Peggy, 369
Lee, Perry, 169, 360
Lee, Ruth, 11
Lee and Lester Young Band, 62, 239, 240, 241
Leer's Cafe, 81
Le Gon, Jenny, 383
Leiber, Jerry, 315
Leimert Park, 406
Leonard, Ada, 362
Lesbians, 257–58, 260, 356
Let's Make Love, 322
Levette, Harry, 19, 20, 199
Levey, Stan, 146
Lewis, Baby, 33, 58

Lewis, Crosby, 136, 141
Lewis, Ernie, 80
Lewis, Henry, 156
"Liebestraum," 65
Life magazine, 188
The Life of Riley, 159, 161
Liggins, Joe ("The Honeydripper"), 48, 103, 110, 181, 263, 308, 310, 333
Lighthouse, 94, 331
Lincoln, Abbey, 255
Lincoln Theatre, 33, 40, 56, 78, 81, 85, 106, 125, 126, 148, 183, 199, 218, 222, 227, 257, 258, 328, 332, 337, 339, 352, 358
Lindsay, Miss (teacher), 343
Lippi, Joseph Louis, 118, 121, 135, 168
Lipschultz, Schull, 171
Liston, Melba, 197, 202, 255–60, 293, 301, 308, 332, 334, 350, 358, 363; family, 255
"Little Bird," 35
Little Harlem, 81, 116, 167, 218
"Little Man, You've Had a Busy Day," 65
Little Niles, 255
Little Richard, 179
Little Tokyo, 201, 270
"Liza Jane," 6
Lloyd Hunter Serenaders, 74
Lomax, Teddy, 84
Lonely Crusade, 200
Long Beach, Calif., 32, 180
Los Angeles: arrival of jazz in, 4–6; black home ownership in, 4, 8, 10, 135, 310; black population in, 1, 2, 3, 7–8, 9, 198, 200–201, 231, 309; black working class in, 8, 17–18, 47, 144, 197–98, 200, 204, 205, 404; ethnic diversity of, 2, 25, 234, 264, 404; land boom of 1887–90, 1; oil boom, 7; pre–World War II, 215–18; post–World War II, 7, 101, 173–74, 221–22; racial boundaries of, 4, 7, 8, 17, 26, 48–49, 91, 115–16, 200–201, 230–31, 310, 403; schools in, 115–16, 135, 198, 234, 264–65, 348, 402; wartime, 84–85, 145–46, 200–201
Los Angeles City College, 218, 219, 297–98, 337
Los Angeles Conservatory of Music and Art, 147, 174, 369, 374, 375
Los Angeles Neophonic Orchestra, 134

Los Angeles Philharmonic, 324, 369
Los Angeles Public Library, xvii
Los Angeles Sentinel, xvii, 198, 205, 270
Los Angeles Times, xvi, xx, 10, 394, 405
Louis, Joe, 35, 98
Louisiana Club, 330
Love, Mr., 325
Lovejoy's, 81, 171, 199, 240, 242, 268, 271,
   315, 319, 329, 376
Lowe, Curtis, 221
Lubinsky, Herman, 187
The Lucy Show, 381
Luke, William, 115
Lunceford, Jimmie, 68, 109, 124, 126,
   182, 183, 199, 201, 202, 207, 214, 235,
   236, 240, 258, 263, 292, 308, 324, 325,
   326–27, 328, 330, 331, 333, 334, 335, 340,
   343, 402, 403
Lurie, Mitchell, 374
Lutcher, Joe, 240
Lutcher, Nellie, 164, 247, 318

Mabley, Moms, 34
Mack, Red, 86, 124, 224
MacMurray, Fred, 65
Madison, Paul, 181
Majors and Minors Orchestra, 10, 411n67
Mallory, Eddie, 59
Malone, Mary Lou, 287
Malone family, 284
Manassas High School (Memphis), 325
Manetta, Manuel, 6
Manne, Shelly, 295
"Maple Leaf Rag," 6
Marable, Larance, 175, 292
Marijuana, 32, 101–2, 270, 272, 351, 353,
   384
Markham, Pigmeat, 148, 183, 257, 332
Martin, Charles (Charlie), 136, 236, 237
Martin, Verne, 135, 168
Martyn, Quedellis, 145, 221
Marx, Groucho, 159, 161
Mason, Fred, 77, 78
Mason, George, 101
Masonic Temple, 97, 106, 124
Matthews, "Big," 331
Matthews, Count Otis, 308
"Maybe Some Day," 11

Mayer, Louis B., 36, 65, 66, 67
Mayfield, Percy, 74, 164
Mayor of Central Avenue, 43, 227, 358
McCarthy, Albert, xviii
McCarthy era, 251
McCullogh, James, 155
McDavid, Percy, 292, 339, 378, 386, 387
McDavid, Russell, 386, 388, 391
McGhee, Elihu "Black Dot," 81, 129,
   149, 335
McGhee, Howard, 184, 185, 262, 263,
   270, 273, 307, 351, 354
McKibbon, Al, 138
McKinley Junior High School, 29, 234, 256
McKinney, Nina Mae, 141, 213
McKinney's Cotton Pickers, 37, 325
McNeely, Cecil "Big Jay," 82, 96, 104,
   111, 134, 148, 163, 179–93, 266, 275–76,
   307, 308, 310, 379
McNeely, Dillard, Jr., 179, 188
McNeely, Dillard, Sr., 180
McNeely, Robert (Bobby), 179, 180, 181,
   188
McNeely brothers, 136, 141, 142
McShann, Jay, 343
McVan's (Buffalo, N.Y.), 84
McVea, Jack, 61, 86, 127, 183, 218, 263
Meadowbrook Ballroom, 60
Meadows, Eddie, xviii
The Mediterranean, 246
Meilleur, Doris, 360
"Melancholy Baby," 6
Melody Club (Glendale), 110–11, 241,
   363, 379
Melody Club (Los Angeles), 109
Memo (club), 34–35, 81, 108, 199, 328, 329
Memory Lane, 317
Memphis, Tenn., 325
Mendelssohn, Felix, 325
Mendez, Raphael, 61
Metlock, Kenneth, 153
Mexicans, 3, 4, 98, 103, 104, 109, 115, 119,
   135, 165, 179, 234, 264, 290
MGM Studios, 38, 61, 65–66, 67, 68, 71,
   259, 311, 332, 333, 340
Migration: to Los Angeles, 6, 7–8, 12,
   47, 109, 200, 231; to Westside, 279–
   80, 310, 366

434 *Index*

Milburn, Amos, 287, 310
Military service, 45–46, 99–100, 108,
    127–29, 172–73, 219–21, 245–47, 291,
    300, 314, 331–32, 346–47, 372
Millen, Gilmore, 18
Miller, Dorie, 284
Miller, F. E., 78
Miller, Glenn, 60, 186, 343
Miller, Johnny, 44, 63, 80
Miller, Norma Jean, 357
Millinder, Lucky, 384
Million Dollar Theatre, 141, 154, 155, 212,
    222, 336, 359
Millman, Jack, 299
Mills, Florence, 350
Mills, Jackie, 321–22
Milton, Roy, 184, 185, 203, 206, 228–29,
    280, 308, 403
Mingus, Charles, xvi, xvii, 45, 68, 70, 71,
    82, 83, 95, 96, 104–5, 114, 121–22, 123–
    24, 129, 130, 131, 136–40, 141, 142, 143,
    145, 149, 153, 154–55, 160, 168, 169, 170,
    171, 172, 175, 181, 184, 212, 213, 218, 221,
    222–23, 230, 240, 241, 245, 248, 249,
    274–75, 292, 315–16, 317, 330, 403
Mingus, Grace, 121
Mingus, Mrs., 122
Mingus, Vivian, 121
Mingus Town Hall Concert, 255
Minstrel shows, 205
Mrs. Dawson's (cabaret), 5
Mob, 84, 126
Mocambo (club), 366
Modern Jazz Quartet, 179
Modern Records, 406
Monroe, Clark, 313
Monroe, Marilyn, 321, 322, 356, 357
Montgomery, Gene, 147, 163, 268, 270,
    350, 379
Moon, Mr., 295
"Moonlight Waltz," 30
Moore, Johnny, 358
Moore, Leon, 148
Moore, Minnie Hightower, 257, 360, 364
Moore, Oscar, 60, 63, 132, 244
Moore, Phil, 124, 333, 336, 340, 361, 362
Moore, Wild Bill, 47

Moorehead, Baron, 125, 349
Moreland, Mantan, 213
Morgan, Al, 126
Morgan, Frank, 134, 147, 148, 151, 153, 163,
    175, 277, 278, 279, 295, 353, 357, 380
Morgan, Stanley, 153
Morris, Joe, 201, 240, 273, 333, 335
Morrow, George, 361
Morton, Jelly Roll, 5, 6, 7, 93, 325, 340,
    410n58, 411n62
Mosby, Curtis, 11, 13, 33, 36, 37–38, 40,
    61, 108, 332, 356, 358, 410n58
Mosby, Esvan, 227, 358
Mosley, Walter, xvii
Motion picture industry, 12, 19, 69–70;
    employment of blacks in, 13, 35–36,
    51, 67, 69–70, 113, 203, 321, 324, 333,
    412n74
Motown Records, 51, 375
Moulder, John, 171
Movie stars, 38, 98, 108, 109, 125, 177,
    180, 182, 225, 243, 299–300, 352, 365
Mozart, Wolfgang, 325
Mulligan, Gerry, 261, 267
Mullins, Herb, 172
Mundy, Jimmy, 63
Murray's, 5
Musicians' Club of Los Angeles, 395
Music Performance Trust Fund, 387
Musso, Vido, 227
Myart, Jerome, 141, 213
Myers, Bumps, 39, 58, 62, 63, 103, 104,
    110, 127, 227, 240, 241, 331, 363, 379
"My Old Flame," 37
"My Silent Love," 297

NAACP, 9, 251, 399
Narcotics, 27, 176, 177–78, 180, 211, 269,
    272, 273, 277–78, 296–97, 352, 353,
    357, 379, 384
National Academy of Recording Arts and
    Sciences (NARAS), 51, 341
National Endowment for the Arts, 324,
    342
Nat King Cole Trio, 235, 244, 314
Navy, 284, 300, 331, 332
NBC, 71, 72, 159

Nelson, James, 171, 172, 212
Nelsons (Dunbar owners), 328
Nevins Avenue Elementary School, 24,
   206, 207
Newman, George, 406
New Orleans jazz, 5, 6–7, 93, 325, 358,
   366, 401; revival, 224–26, 308
New Otani Hotel, 333
Newton, James, 135
New York City, 10, 12, 19, 82, 87, 114,
   124, 139–40, 258, 271, 272, 301, 311–12,
   313, 366, 367, 393, 401
New York Philharmonic, 324
Nicholas Brothers, 56
Nickel Spot, 350
Nickodell Restaurant, 159–60
Nightcap, 183, 189
Nimbus Records, 282
Noel, Cliff, 228
Nolan, Lloyd, 330
Noone, Jimmy, 308
Norman, Gene, 351
Normandie Hall, 152
Norris, Charles, 361
Norvo, Red, 160, 233
"Nothing But Soul," 186

Oak Leaf Jazz Band, 11
Oasis, 70, 71, 132, 279, 310, 339, 362, 366,
   384
Oklahoma Blue Devils, 54
"Old Man River," 71
Oliver, Joe "King," 7, 93, 325
Oliver, Sy, 326
Olympia Theatre, 276
118th Army Services Band, 246
125th Street (Harlem), 125, 133, 328, 340,
   366, 367
Onyx Club (Pasadena), 361
Orendorff, George, 40, 61
Original Creole Band, 5
Orpheum Theatre, 155, 167, 208, 314,
   330, 334, 336
Ortega, Anthony, 181, 358, 402, 403
Ory, Kid, 6, 11, 13, 18, 29, 203, 224, 225–
   26, 227, 308; Ory's Creole Orchestra,
   409 n39; Ory's Sunshinne Orchestra, 11

"Ory's Creole Trombone," 11, 409 n39
Otis, Johnny, xvii, 85, 148, 164, 179, 180,
   182, 186, 190, 203, 267, 271, 273, 308,
   342, 357, 358, 375, 403
Overture (union magazine), 391, 392
Oxley, Harold, 182

"Pacific Coast Line," 5
Paderewski, Ignace Jan, 325
Pal Joey, 114
Palmer, Earl, 134
Pan-Afrikan Peoples Arkestra, 164, 282,
   293, 300, 301, 406
Papki (club owner), 83
Paramount Studios, 65, 67
Paramount Theatre, 167, 208, 326, 329
Parker, Charlie, xv, xvi, 47, 145, 146, 148,
   149, 150, 175–76, 184, 185, 222, 263, 268–
   71, 273, 274, 299–300, 307, 342, 353, 357
Parker, William H., Chief, 101, 309
Pashley, Frank, 58
Pass, Joe, 311
Paul, Les, 63
Paul, Maury, 392
Paul Howard's Quality Serenaders, 11, 40,
   57, 226, 238
Pearl Harbor, 201
Peer Gynt suite, 291
Penny Dance, 13
People's World, 171, 393
Pepper, Art, xvi, xvii, 61, 277, 311, 315, 402
Perkins, Bob, 325
Perkins, Carl, 188, 318, 320
Perry, Mr., 111
Perry, Ray, 329–30
Pershing Square, 222, 223
Peterson, Oscar, 51, 65
Petit, Buddy, 6, 93
Petrillo, James C. (Caesar), 158, 251–52,
   278, 385, 393–95
Pettiford, Oscar, 53
Philharmonic Auditorium, 309
Phillips, Esther, 96, 180
Pickford, Jack, 92
Pickford, Lottie, 92
Plantation Club, 81, 82, 92, 109, 183, 201,
   202, 240, 273, 333, 334, 359

Playboy Jazz Festival, 272
Pleasants, Alexander, 283
Point magazine, 188
Police, 56, 83, 101–2, 132, 148, 166, 177, 189, 272–73, 299–300, 309, 313, 365, 404–5
Polytechnic High School, 182, 257
Popkin, Harry L., 213
Porter, Calvin, 338
Porter, Jake, 103, 109, 111, 171, 172, 203, 227
Porter, James, 40
Porter, Roy, xvii, 184, 185, 263, 273, 301, 351, 403
Pot, Pan, and Skillet, 125, 183
Potter, Larry, 225
Powell, Bud, 313
Powell, Seldon, 139
Prairie View Agricultural and Mechanical University (Tex.), 344, 345, 348
Prairie View Coeds, 344, 346, 348
Presley, Elvis, 332
Prestige Records, 154
Price, Arthur, 118
Price, Jesse, 109–10
Prince, Peppy, 56
Prince, Wesley, 60, 244
The Prodigal, 259
Prohibition, 31, 32, 77, 199
Prokofiev, Sergei, 336
Prostitution, 5, 144, 273, 283, 355

Quality Cafe, 11
Quality Serenaders, 11, 40, 57, 226, 238
Queens of Swing, 360, 361
Quick magazine, 188

"Race records," 48, 308
Race relations, 1, 2, 3–4, 48–49, 103, 179, 200–201, 290–91
Rachmaninoff, Sergei, 325
Racism, 1–2, 69, 109–10, 111, 115, 121, 128, 160, 197–98, 201, 220, 242, 253, 286–87, 301, 348, 359, 404–5. *See also* Housing covenants, discriminatory
Radio, 12, 41, 126, 190, 331, 343, 351, 365, 392–93
Radio Room, 244

Raeburn, Boyd, 149
A Raisin in the Sun, 114
Ramey, Gene, 361
Randall's Island (N.Y.), 272
Randolph, A. Philip, 200
Randolph, John, 172
Rape, 259–60
Ratler, Nat, 373, 374
Ray, Floyd, 19, 82, 86, 125, 126, 212, 267, 359
Ray, Johnnie, 189
RCA Victor Records, 37, 343
Recording industry, 190–91; early recordings, 11, 12; sessions, 49; studios, 255, 298, 365, 369
Red car rail system, 180
Redd, Alton, 30, 41, 47, 247, 256, 364
Redd, Vi, 181, 202, 247, 257, 364, 403
Reddy, Helen, 203
Red Feather Tavern, 5
Redman, Don, 37, 325
Reed, Blanche, 92
Reed, George, 119, 140
Reed, Leonard, 334
Reed, Tom, xvii
Reese, Lloyd, 18, 39, 42, 61, 104, 142–43, 146, 150, 171, 172, 236, 237, 238, 242, 245, 248, 294, 315, 329, 358, 364, 377, 402
Reform measures, 198–99
The Regal, 327
René, Leon, 41
René, Otis, 41, 335
Rex (gambling ship), 32, 39
Reyes, Jesus "Chuey," 208–9
Rheinshagen, Herman, 138, 175
Rhumboogie (Chicago), 382, 383
Rhumboogie (Los Angeles), 144
Rhythm and blues, 48, 107, 179, 186, 203, 228, 275–76, 287, 307, 308, 320, 358, 401
Rhythm Club, 395, 396
Ricardi, Rex, 394
Rice, Willie, 373
Richardson, Jerome, 139, 145, 221
Richmond, Dannie, 124
Riddle, Nelson, 114, 203
Rigney, Bill, 46
Rio Brothers, 330

Risatto Brothers, 35
Ritz (club), 108, 199, 240
Riverside Rancho, 338
Riviera (St. Louis), 335–36
RKO Studios, 186
RKO Theater, 156
Roach, Max, 314, 361, 366, 401, 406
Roadhouses, 76
Roark, Todd, 313
Roberts, Caughey, 58, 204, 209, 219, 226, 228, 377–78
Robertson, Lester, 357, 358
Robeson, Paul, 133, 162–63, 399
Robinson, Gail, 386, 387, 391
Robinson, Jackie, 159
Robinson, James "Sweet Pea," 153, 163, 266, 380
Robinson, Minor, 136
Robinson, Miss (teacher), 165
Robinson, Sugar Ray, 99
Rock and roll, 188, 203, 287, 320
Rodia, Simon, 136, 166, 179
Rogers, Timmie, 314
Romero, Caesar, 352
Rooney, Joe, 122
Rooney, Mickey, 65, 66, 122, 141
Roosevelt, Franklin D., 200, 359
Rooster (performer), 34
Rose, Atwell, 30
Rose, Herb, 242
Ross, Annie, 311
Ross, Arnold, 318
Roth, Esther, 386, 387
Roth, Henry, 386, 387
Rowles, Jimmy, 62
Royal, Ernest, 24, 26, 27, 28, 104
Royal, Ernestine Walton, 21, 22, 26, 27
Royal, Ernie, 25, 37, 44, 45, 46, 58, 105, 117, 119, 120, 127, 139, 141, 145, 181, 210, 221, 235, 329, 403
Royal, Evelyn, 35, 48, 50, 362
Royal, Marshal, 18, 20, 22–50, 53, 58, 61, 68, 70, 105, 117, 124, 127, 201, 209, 210, 211 218–19, 221, 234, 329, 362
Royal, Marshal, Sr., 22, 24, 26–27, 28, 29, 37, 42, 145, 234
Royal Room, 243

Royal Theatre (Baltimore), 345
Ruben's (New York), 312, 319
Rubinstein, Artur, 313
Rucker, T. C., 97
Rumsey, Howard, 94
Run for Your Life, 164
Rushing, Jimmy, 262
Russell, Ross, xv
"The Russian Rag," 6

Sabu the Elephant Boy, 313
Sailes, Jessie, 97, 105, 119, 140
St. Antoine Street (Detroit), 328
St. Cyr, Lili, 141
St. Louis, Mo., 334, 336
St. Mary's College Pre-flight School (Moraga, Calif.), 46, 145, 220, 221, 245
Sampson, Bill, 351
Sanderson, Stutz, 325
Santa Fe (club), 5
Sapp, Hosea, 229
Satchell McVea's Howdy Entertainers, 219
Savoy (club), 174
Savoy Hotel, 77
Savoy Records, 187, 191, 274, 307
Sawdust Inn, 47
Schildkret, Nathaniel, 333
Schwartz, Willie, 53
Scott, Bud, 225
Scott's (Kansas City club), 373
Sears Roebuck, 111
Sebastian, Frank, 11, 18, 38, 39, 42, 60
Segregation, 2, 4, 45, 47, 101, 115–16, 197, 198, 264, 289
Selig Zoo (ballroom), 212
Senator Hotel (Sacramento), 42
Send Me No Flowers, 311
Sendry, Al, 156
Sepia magazine, 299
Severinsen, Doc, 22
Shackleford, Johnny, 171
Shades of L.A.: Pictures from Ethnic Family Albums, xvii
Shank, Bud, 174
Shaw, Artie, 261–62
Sheklow, Seymour, 159, 386, 387
Shelton, Lois, xvi, xviii

Shepp's Playhouse, 85, 182, 185, 333, 334, 351
"The Shimmy," 92
Shirley's Ritz Club, 315
Shostakovich, Dimitri, 336
Shrine Auditorium, 9, 188, 212, 326, 329
Shubert Theatre, 22
Silver, Horace, 261
Simmons, John, 61, 70
Simpkins, Andy, 311
Sims, Zoot, 311
Sinatra, Frank, 157, 369
Singer, Hal, 190
Singleton, Zutty, 308
"Sing, Sing, Sing," 234
Skirts Ahoy, 51, 71
The Sky's the Limit, 51
Slack, Freddy, 383
Slater, Vernon, 136
Slim and Slam, 62, 241
Small's Paradise, 271
Smith, Ada "Bricktop," 5, 92
Smith, Bessie, 166
Smith, Fletcher, xxiii, 21, 74–87, 124, 199
Smith, Gertrude, 207
Smith, Jimmy 114
Smith, John, 373, 374
Smith, Noodles, 34
Smith, O. C., 295
Smith, Stuff, 167
Smith, Willie, 36, 63, 326, 331
Smock, Emma "Ginger," 202, 211, 247, 350, 362, 364, 375
Snow, Valaida, 257
"Society Blues," 11
Solomon, Clifford, 181
Solomon, Eisler, 156
Solomon's Penny Dance, 40
"Someday Sweetheart," 10, 410n58
Somerville, John, 9, 10
Somerville Hotel, 9, 32, 34
"Something on Your Mind," 179
Sophisticated Ladies, 22, 114
"Sophisticated Lady," 78, 105
The Sound of Music, 114
Sousa, John Philip, 118

South, Eddie, 30n
Southard, Harry, 6, 10, 289, 292
South Central Los Angeles, xv, 358
Southern Pacific Railroad, 3, 204
South Gate, Calif., 242
South Gate Junior High School, 135
South Park, 359, 378
South Park Street (Chicago), 328, 340
Specialty Records, 229
Spikes, Benjamin "Reb," 10, 11, 40, 92, 408n27, 409n39, 410n58, 411n62, 411n67, 413n11
Spikes, Johnny, 10, 40, 410n58
Spikes brothers, 11, 409n39, 411n62
Spikes' Seven Pods of Pepper, 11
Spirits of Our Ancestors, 155
Spirits of Rhythm, 241
Spirituals, 287
Spivak, Charlie, 343
Standard Oil broadcasts, 308
Stanley, Harold "Hal," 149, 335
Stanley Theatre (Pittsburgh), 345
Starks, Willie, 24
Starr, Jean, 345
Starr, Kay, 89, 233, 311, 321, 335, 336
Stars of Swing, 129–30, 148, 149–50
Steffens, Lincoln, 9
Stepin Fetchit, 125, 217, 313
Stern, Mr., 111
Stewart, Robert W., 1
Stewart, Slam, 241
Still, William Grant, 209
Stokowski, Leopold, 243
Stoll, Georgie, 65, 68, 70
Stoller, Mike, 315
Stone, April, 357
Stone, Charles, 360
Stone, Joseph (Joe), 355, 358
Storm, Tempest, 141
Storyville (New Orleans), 5, 6
Stravinsky, Igor, 336
Strayhorn, Billy, 64, 78, 337
Streetser, William, 184
Streets of Paris (Hollywood), 84, 85
Strike Up the Band, 51, 65, 68
Strip City, 322

Sturdevant, John, 34
Sturdevant, Mrs., 34
Sturdevant, Wilbert, 212
Subway (Kansas City club), 87
Sugar Hill cases, 309–10
Sturgis, Ida Herrington, 164
"Suite for Harp and Flute," 134
Sunnyland Jazz Orchestra, 10
Sunset Records, 51
Sunshine Record Company, 11
Supreme Court, 309, 310; decision of
    1954, 230, 231, 309, 310, 399, 404
Supremes, 311
Susie Q (club), 84, 85
Swanee Inn, 60
Sweethearts of Rhythm, 257–58, 345,
    346, 359
Sweet Man, 18
Swing Club, 62, 199, 201, 241, 279, 314
Swing era, 272, 358, 401
Switcher, Mr., 167

Taft High School, 295
"Take the A Train," 64
T and D Theatre, 82
Tanjah, 255
Tap dancing, 52, 56, 66, 83
Tapscott, Cecilia, 292, 301
Tapscott, Horace, 164, 173, 176, 197,
    282–303, 406
Tapscott, Mary Lou, 282, 285, 286, 287,
    288, 289, 293, 294
Tapscott, Robert, 282, 285
Tate, Buddy, 344
Tatum, Art, xvi, 42, 47, 65, 108, 171–72,
    233, 236, 242–44, 292, 312–13, 318–20,
    323, 329, 335, 358
Taxi dances, 29–30
Teddy Buckner Dixieland Band, 104,
    226
te Groen, John, 393, 394, 395, 396
Television shows, 361–62, 363, 369
The Ten Commandments, 259
Terrell, Willie Lee, 361
Terry, Clark, 139, 140, 145, 311, 331
Texas Playgirls, 346

Texas-style jazz, 229
"That Sweet Something Dear," 11
Theater Owners Booking Association
    (TOBA), 34, 52
Thigpen, Ed, 265
This Is the Army, 331
Thomas, Elizabeth, 344
Thomas, Joe, 326
Thompson, Chuck, 154
Thompson, Lucky, 47, 48, 67, 68, 85,
    129, 130, 146, 149, 175, 184, 223, 376,
    378, 379
Three Blazers, 358
Three Deuces, 323
Three Rockets, 144, 217
Three Spirits of Rhythm, 62
331 Club, 86, 319
Tiffany Club, 319
Tijuana Brass, 297
Title House, 101
Tjader, Cal, 233
Tomkins, Eddie, 326
Tonight Show band, 22, 164
Top Hatters, 217
Toshiko Akiyoshi–Lew Tabackin Big
    Band, 114
Towel, Nat, 84
Town Hall Concert (New York), 139
Trainor, Jack, 171, 331, 334
Trammel, Charles, 351
Traylor, Stella, 382
Treadville, Betty, 80
Treleven, Dale, xviii, xx
The Treniers, 81, 334
Triangle (club), 5
Trianon Ballroom, 64, 201, 226
Trice, Amos, 175
Trouville Club, 62, 63, 241, 329
Truman, Harry, 291
Tucker, Ben, 253
Tufts, Sonny, 352
Turban Room, 242, 314, 350, 358
Turner, Big Joe, 164, 218, 241, 280, 311
Turner, Lana, 159, 299
Turnham, Edythe, 19, 57, 81; and Dixie
    Aces, 19

Turnham, Floyd, 57, 124, 127, 131, 167, 234, 332
"Tuxedo Junction," 345
Twine, Arthur, 62

UCLA, 324, 346, 348, 365, 385, 386
Unemployment, 17–18
Union of God's Musicians and Artists Ascension (UGMAA), 282
Union Station, 5, 289, 328, 347
University of Southern California, 8, 9, 198, 348
Uptown House, 313
Urban League, 197

Vaché, Warren, 22
Valentino, Rudolph, 92
Vaughan, Sarah, 70, 175
Vee Jay Records, 51, 53
Venable (club owner), 82
Victoria Theatre (San Jose), 80
Victor Records, 37, 337
Villa-Lobos, Hector, 336
Villapeg, Paul, 175
Villa Venice, 93
Vine Street (Kansas City), 373
Vine Street (Los Angeles), 61
Vinnegar, Leroy, 315
Viola, Al, 134
Vogue Ballroom, 212
Volcano Blues, 255

Wadsworth school, 25
Waikiki (club), 132
Waldorf Cellar, 351, 361
Waldorf Club, 5
Walker, Dr., 156
Walker, Loyal, 241
Walker, T-Bone, 82, 116, 142, 148, 167, 182, 218, 233, 280, 315, 343, 358
Walker, Thelma, 160
"Walkin' and Singin,'" 202
Waller, Fats, 343
Walters, Tiny, 395
Walton, David, 23
Walton, Mary Alice, 23
Warner, Jack, 27

Warner Brothers Studios, 67, 68, 326, 330; orchestra, 331
Warwick, Dionne, 369
Washington, Booker T., 144
Washington, D.C., 200
Washington, Dinah, 311, 321
Washington, Leon, 197
Washington Boulevard (Los Angeles), 366
Waters, Ethel, 59, 65
Watson, Leo, 241
Watson, Mattie, 361
Watts, 91–93, 179–80; annexation by Los Angeles, 92; black community in, 91, 92; ethnic diversity of, 103, 104, 115–16, 135, 165, 179, 180; "Mudtown," 91; musicians in, 81–83, 92–93, 96–97, 104–5, 140–41, 166–69, 180–81, 213; music scene in, 81–82, 92, 93, 106–7, 116, 167, 180, 240, 334–35; police in, 101; rural origins of, 91, 93, 95, 115, 165, 166, 179–80; "shimmy," 92; uprising of 1965, xv, 141, 405, 406
Watts Country Club, 92, 410 n58
Watts Happening Coffee House, 406
Watts Prophets, 406
Watts Towers, 136, 141, 166, 179
Wayne, John, 119
Wayside Park, 93, 413 n11
Wayside Park Cafe, 409 n39
Webb, Chick, 40
Webster, Ben, 52, 53, 63, 64, 108, 142, 147, 171, 233, 241, 242
Webster, Paul, 326
Wein, George, 139
Welles, Orson, 224, 308
West, Mae, 36, 124
West Coast, 270, 295, 307
West Coast Jazz, xviii, 316, 401, 402
Western Avenue, 132, 231, 279, 310, 339, 366, 367, 402
Western School of Music, 209
Westlake College of Music, 117, 131, 174
West Oakland House Rockers, 308
Weston, Randy, 255
Westside, 310, 322, 375, 401; migration to, 279–80
Westside Jazz Band, 409 n35

Whaley, Wade, 6, 93
"What Will I Tell My Heart?" 42
"When the Swallows Come Back to
  Capistrano," 41
"When You're Alone," 11
Where the Boys Are, 333
White, Leroy "Snake," 78, 124, 240
White, Slappy, 357
"White flight," 48
Whiteman, Paul, 65, 127
White Men Can't Jump, 311
Whiting, Napoleon, 56
Whittier College, 39
Whitworth, Louis, 371
Whorf, Richard, 330
Wiggins, Eleanor Foster, 311
Wiggins, Gerald "Wig," 61, 65, 70, 71,
  99, 161, 164, 233, 236, 242, 243, 307,
  311–23, 358
Wiggins, Jack, 52
Wilburn, Anna Mae, 202
Wilde, Oscar, 209
Wilkerson, Donald, 357
Wilkins, Professor, 25, 209–10
Williams, Alfred, 6
Williams, Billy, 342
Williams, David, Judge, 309, 310, 414n7
Williams, Dootsie, 80, 105, 124, 136, 191
Williams, Esther, 71
Williams, Frances, 162
Williams, Joe, 311, 335
Williams, John, 369
Williams, Mary Lou, 202
Williams, Walter, 331
Will Mastin Trio, 82–83, 109, 148
Wilshire Boulevard, 330, 404
Wilshire Bowl, 330
Wilson, Gerald, 134, 164, 236, 255, 258,
  259, 278, 279, 293, 294, 300, 307, 308,
  311, 324–41, 351, 357, 358
Wilson, Lillian, 324–25
Wilson, Mildred, 325
Wilson, Nancy, 369
Wilson, Shelby James, 325
Wilson, Teddy, 248, 312
Wilson, Wood, 412n71
Wiltern Theatre, 348

Witchard, Al "Cake," 350, 352
Witherspoon, Jimmy, 310, 311, 315, 358,
  383
"With Plenty of Money and You," 42
The Wiz, 114
"Wolverine Blues," 410n58
Women instrumentalists, 20, 34, 111, 202,
  247, 257, 334, 255–60, 342–68
Woodman, Britt, 12, 20, 94, 103, 104,
  105, 106, 107, 114–33, 140, 149, 155,
  167, 169, 174, 292, 294
Woodman, Coney, 12, 94–102, 103, 104,
  105, 114, 116, 117, 119, 120, 127, 140,
  167, 169, 201, 405
Woodman, Emily Riley, 100
Woodman, George, 94, 103, 140, 167
Woodman, William, Jr. "Brother," xxi,
  12, 82, 83, 94, 103–13, 114, 117, 119, 131,
  140, 169, 241, 332–33, 379
Woodman, William, Sr., 12, 82, 94, 95–
  96, 97, 103–4, 105, 106, 114, 115, 116,
  117, 118, 119, 120, 120–21, 125, 140
Woodman Brothers, 45, 82, 93, 97, 107,
  120, 130, 141, 175, 176, 180, 181, 187,
  201; studio, 96, 106, 107, 120, 167
Woodman Brothers Biggest Little Band
  in the World, 94, 96–98, 103, 105–6,
  140, 205
Woods, Phil, 139
Woodson, Buddy, 148, 184
Wood Wilson's Syncopators, 13
Works Progress Administration (WPA),
  165, 170, 359, 370, 371; WPA band, 171,
  370–71
World War I, 6; post–World War I, 8
World War II, 230, 284
Wright, Lamar, 142, 211–12, 235
Wrigley Field, 133, 188

"Yard Dog Mazurka," 327
Yates, Sammy, 352
You Bet Your Life, 135, 159
Young, Alice, 257
Young, Henry, 344
Young, Irma, 20, 51, 52, 55, 56, 257
Young, Lee, 19, 20 48, 51–73, 80, 108, 170,
  199, 238–39, 241, 311, 329, 332, 402

Young, Lester, xvi, 20, 48, 51, 52, 54, 55, 62, 63, 64, 67, 68, 108, 147, 170, 171, 199, 238, 241, 257, 261, 326, 329, 379
Young, Lizette Jackson, 51, 52, 53, 55, 67
Young, Louise Franklin, 59
Young, Marl, xix, xx, 112, 157, 247, 249, 250, 251, 253, 307, 335, 339, 357, 381–99, 403
Young, Snooky, 22, 139, 201, 326, 328, 330, 331, 334, 337
Young, Trummy, 181
Young, Willis "Billy," 51, 52, 53, 54, 56, 57, 59, 64

"You're Just an Old Antidisestablishmentarianismist," 337
"You Stepped Out of a Dream," 379
"You've Got to Crawl Before You Walk," 337
Yule, Joe, 122, 141

Zale, Tony, 99
Zardi's, 243
Zoot Suit riots, 2
Zucca's Terrace, 331